FROM REVIEWS OF THE UNABRIDGED THREE-VOLUME EDITION

"The completion of this monumental new edition, a landmark in the history of the Holocaust, is a tribute to its author's determination, investigatory skill, and ability to make sense of it all. . . . The lasting achievement of Hilberg's volumes is his portrayal of the perpetrators, acting both individually and as part of a horrifyingly effective destructive apparatus. No other work gives such a complete and awesome sense of the Nazis' Final Solution, linking the most banal administrative tasks to mass murder on a scale that defies belief. No other work is so steeped in the details of German policy, carried out over a decade and eventually embracing an entire continent. . . . No single book has contributed more . . . to an understanding of Nazi genocide. **In its originality, scope and seriousness of theme, this is one of the great historical works of our time.**"

—Michael Marrus
in *The Times Literary Supplement*

"**The standard text in its field . . . by the pre-eminent scholar of the Holocaust.** . . . The book marshals a vast array of sources. . . . It is superbly organized. The scholarship is thorough and careful. All information in it is clearly footnoted. The writing is clear, readable, often graceful. . . . The cumulative impact of the sheer numbers—far from turning into a tedious recitation of figures—stuns one into a realization of the vastness of the horror. . . . It is a fortunate circumstance that Mr. Hilberg's outstanding study appears at this time. May it illuminate the field and press others to keep the facts straight and the perspectives reasonable and honest."

—David S. Wyman
in *The New York Times Book Review*

AXIS EUROPE IN MID-1942

Key to Jurisdictions

- ■ Incorporated Areas
- ▤ Reichskommissariate
- ▧ Generalgouvernement
- ⦀ Bialystok district
- ⣿ Military areas
- ▦ Italian domain

NORWAY

SWEDEN

FINLAND

DENMARK

OSTLAND

GREAT BRITAIN

NETHERLANDS

REICH

UKRAINE

SLOVAKIA

HUNGARY

VICHY-FRANCE

ITALY

CROATIA

ROMANIA

SPAIN

SERBIA

BULGARIA

ALBANIA

CORFU GREECE

SALONIKA

TURKEY

Mediterranean Sea

RHODES

CRETE

0   100   200   300   400   500
Miles

THE DESTRUCTION OF THE EUROPEAN JEWS

STUDENT EDITION

RAUL HILBERG

HOLMES & MEIER   NEW YORK   LONDON

First published in the United States of America 1985 by
Holmes & Meier Publishers, Inc.
30 Irving Place
New York, N.Y. 10003

Great Britain:
Hillview House
One Hallswelle Parade
London NW11 ODL, England

Book design by Stephanie Barton

Cover photo: Inmates arriving at Auschwitz. From *The Auschwitz Album,* copyright © 1981 by Peter Hellman, Lili Meier and Beate Klarsfeld. Published by Random House.

Library of Congress Cataloging-in-Publication Data
Hilberg, Raul, 1926–
　The destruction of the European Jews.

　Bibliography: p.
　Includes index.
　1. Holocaust, Jewish (1939–1945)　2. Germany—
Politics and government—1933–1945.　I. Title.
D810.J4H5　1985　　940.53'15'03924　　85-17541
ISBN 0-8419-0910-5 (pbk.)

Manufactured in the United States of America

CONTENTS

CHAPTER ONE 5
PRECEDENTS

CHAPTER TWO 27
DEFINITION BY DECREE

CHAPTER THREE 41
CONCENTRATION
The Reich-Protektorat Area 41
Poland 64
Ghetto Formation 74
Ghetto Maintenance 89
Sickness and Death in the Ghettos 94

CHAPTER FOUR 99
MOBILE KILLING OPERATIONS
Preparations 100
The First Sweep 107
Strategy 107
Cooperation with the Mobile Killing Units 111
The Killing Operations and Their Repercussions 125
The Second Sweep 138

CHAPTER FIVE   157
DEPORTATIONS
Central Agencies of Deportation   168
The Reich-Protektorat Area   174
   Seizure and Transport   175
Poland   187
   Preparations   188
   The Conduct of the Deportations   192

CHAPTER SIX   221
KILLING CENTER OPERATIONS
Origins of the Killing Centers   221
Killing Operations   238
   Concealment   240
   The "Conveyer Belt"   243
   Erasure   249
Liquidation of the Killing Centers and the End of the
Destruction Process   251

CHAPTER SEVEN   263
THE NATURE OF THE PROCESS
The Perpetrators   263
   The Destructive Expansion   264
   The Obstacles   270
      Administrative Problems   270
      Psychological Problems   274
The Victims   293

CHAPTER EIGHT   309
RESCUE

APPENDIX A   334
GERMAN RANKS

APPENDIX B   338
STATISTICAL RECAPITULATION

SELECT BIBLIOGRAPHY   341

INDEX   351

Forty years have passed since the end of the Holocaust, and today the event is more prominent in public consciousness than it was in 1945. College courses are devoted to the topic and research has been intensified. Clearly, a new generation is asking questions that have been avoided in the past, and the demand for answers has not yet been filled.

The following pages contain a brief description of the destruction of the European Jews, with an emphasis on the core of this history. The volume is designed for those who are not familiar with any details, but it is not an outline. All the contents have been taken from the second edition of a larger work, newly published in three volumes under the same title. These, then, are excerpts, pure and simple, tied together to form a smaller coherent whole.

The passages in this volume were chosen on the basis of some experience, inasmuch as several sections and chapters in the first edition of the longer work had already been selected over the years by specialists in various fields for inclusion in readers or for use in classes. The same materials, revised and expanded for the new edition, may now be found between the covers of this book. Those who wish to read also the footnotes and all or some of the omitted portions may consult the three-volume work, which is unabridged.

PREFACE

CHAPTER ONE

PRECEDENTS

The German destruction of the European Jews was a tour de force; the Jewish collapse under the German assault was a manifestation of failure. Both of these phenomena were the final product of an earlier age.

Anti-Jewish policies and actions did not have their beginning in 1933. For many centuries, and in many countries, the Jews had been victims of destructive action. What was the object of these activities? What were the aims of those who persisted in anti-Jewish deeds? Throughout Western history, three consecutive policies have been applied against Jewry in its dispersion.

The first anti-Jewish policy started in the fourth century after Christ in Rome. Early in the fourth century, during the reign of Constantine, the Christian Church gained power in Rome, and Christianity became the state religion. From this period, the state carried out Church policy. For the next twelve centuries, the Catholic Church prescribed the measures that were to be taken with respect to the Jews. Unlike the pre-Christian Romans, who claimed no monopoly on religion and faith, the Christian Church insisted on acceptance of Christian doctrine.

For an understanding of Christian policy toward Jewry, it is essential to realize that the Church pursued conversion not so much for the sake of aggrandizing its power (the Jews have always been few in number), but because of the conviction that it was the duty of true believers to save unbelievers from the doom of eternal hellfire. Zealousness in the pursuit of conversion was an indication of the depth of faith. The Christian religion was not one of many religions, but the true religion, the only one. Those who were not in its fold were either ignorant or in error. The Jews could not accept Christianity.

In the very early stages of the Christian faith, many Jews regarded Christians as members of a Jewish sect. The first Christians, after all, still observed the Jewish law. They had merely added a few nonessential practices, such as baptism, to their religious life. But their view was changed abruptly when Christ was elevated to Godhood. The Jews have only one God. This God is indivisible. He is a jealous God and admits of no other gods. He is not Christ, and Christ is not He. Christianity and Judaism have since been irreconcilable. An acceptance of Christianity has since signified an abandonment of Judaism.

In antiquity and in the Middle Ages, Jews did not abandon Judaism lightly. With patience and persistence the Church attempted to convert obstinate Jewry, and for twelve hundred years the theological argument was fought without interruption. The Jews were not convinced. Gradually the Church began to back its words with force. The Papacy did not permit pressure to be put on individual Jews; Rome prohibited forceful conversions. However, the clergy did use pressure on the whole. Step by step, but with ever widening effect, the Church adopted "defensive" measures against its passive victims. Christians were "protected" from the "harmful" consequences of intercourse with Jews by rigid laws against intermarriage, by prohibitions of discussions about religious issues, by laws against domicile in common abodes. The Church "protected" its Christians from the "harmful" Jewish teachings by burning the Talmud and by barring Jews from public office.

These measures were precedent-making destructive activities. How little success the Church had in accomplishing its aim is revealed by the treatment of the few Jews who succumbed to the Christian religion. The clergy was not sure of its success—hence the widespread practice, in the Middle Ages, of identifying proselytes as former Jews; hence the inquisition of new Christians suspected of heresy; hence the issuance in Spain of certificates of "purity," signifying purely Christian ancestry, and the specification of "half-new Christians," "quarter-new Christians," "one-eighth-new Christians," and so on.

The failure of conversion had far-reaching consequences. The unsuccessful Church began to look on the Jews as a special group of people, different from Christians, deaf to Christianity, and dangerous to the Christian faith. In 1542 Martin Luther, the founder of Protestantism, wrote the following lines:

> And if there were a spark of common sense and understanding in them, they would truly have to think like this: O my God, it does not stand and go well with us; our misery is too great, too long, too hard; God has forgotten us, etc. I am no Jew, but I do not like to think in earnest about such brutal wrath of God against this people, for I am terrified at the thought that cuts through my body and soul: What is going to happen with the eternal wrath in hell against all false Christians and unbelievers?

In short, if *he* were a Jew, he would have accepted Christianity long ago.

A people cannot suffer for fifteen hundred years and still think of itself as the chosen people. But this people was blind. It had been stricken by the wrath of God. He had struck them "with frenzy, blindness, and raging heart, with the eternal fire, of which the Prophets say: The wrath of God will hurl itself outward like a fire that no one can smother."

The Lutheran manuscript was published at a time of increasing hatred for the Jew. Too much had been invested in twelve hundred years of conversion policy. Too little had been gained. From the thirteenth to the sixteenth century, the Jews of England, France, Germany, Spain, Bohemia, and Italy were presented with ultimatums that gave them no choice but one: conversion or explusion.

Expulsion is the second anti-Jewish policy in history. In its origin, this policy presented itself only as an alternative—moreover, as an alternative that was left to the Jews. But long after the separation of church and state, long after the state had ceased to carry out church policy, expulsion and exclusion remained the goal of anti-Jewish activity.

The anti-Semites of the nineteenth century, who divorced themselves from religious aims, espoused the emigration of the Jews. The anti-Semites hated the Jews with a feeling of righteousness and reason, as though they had acquired the antagonism of the church like speculators buying the rights of a bankrupt corporation. With this hatred, the post-ecclesiastic enemies of Jewry also took the idea that the Jews could not be changed, that they could not be converted, that they could not be assimilated, that they were a finished product, inflexible in their ways, set in their notions, fixed in their beliefs.

The expulsion and exclusion policy was adopted by the Nazis and remained the goal of all anti-Jewish activity until 1941. That year marks a turning point in anti-Jewish history. In 1941 the Nazis found themselves in the midst of a total war. Several million Jews were incarcerated in ghettos. Emigration was impossible. A last-minute project to ship the Jews to the African island of Madagascar had fallen through. The "Jewish problem" had to be "solved" in some other way. At this crucial time, the idea of a "territorial solution" emerged in Nazi minds. The "territorial solution," or "the final solution of the Jewish question in Europe," as it became known, envisaged the death of European Jewry. The European Jews were to be killed. This was the third anti-Jewish policy in history.

To summarize: Since the fourth century after Christ there have been three anti-Jewish policies: conversion, expulsion, and annihilation. The second appeared as an alternative to the first, and the third emerged as an alternative to the second.

The destruction of the European Jews between 1933 and 1945 appears to us now as an unprecedented event in history. Indeed, in its dimensions and total configuration, nothing like it had ever happened before. As a result of an organized undertaking, five million people were killed in the short space of a few years. The operation was over before anyone could grasp its enormity, let alone its implications for the future.

Yet, if we analyze this singularly massive upheaval, we discover that most of what happened in those twelve years had already happened before. The Nazi destruction process did not come out of a void; it was the culmination of a cyclical trend. We have observed the trend in the three successive goals of anti-Jewish administrators. The missionaries of Christianity had said in effect: You have no right to live among us as Jews. The secular rulers who followed had proclaimed: You have no right to live among us. The Nazis at last decreed: You have no right to live.

These progressively more drastic goals brought in their wake a slow and steady growth of anti-Jewish action and anti-Jewish thinking. The process began with the attempt to drive the Jews into Christianity. The development was continued in order to force the victims into exile. It was finished when the Jews were driven to their deaths. The German Nazis, then, did not discard the past; they built upon it. They did not begin a development; they completed it. In the deep recesses of anti-Jewish history we shall find many of the administrative and psychological tools with which the Nazis implemented their destruction process. In the hollows of the past we shall also discover the roots of the characteristic Jewish response to an outside attack.

The significance of the historical precedents will most easily be understood in the administrative sphere. The destruction of the Jews was an administrative process, and the annihilation of Jewry required the implementation of systematic administrative measures in successive steps. There are not many ways in which a modern society can, in short order, kill a large number of people living in its midst. This is an efficiency problem of the greatest dimensions, one which poses uncounted difficulties and innumerable obstacles. Yet, in reviewing the documentary record of the destruction of the Jews, one is almost immediately impressed with the fact that the German administration knew what it was doing. With an unfailing sense of direction and with an uncanny pathfinding ability, the German bureaucracy found the shortest road to the final goal.

We know, of course, that the very nature of a task determines the form of its fulfillment. Where there is the will, there is also the way, and if the will is only strong enough, the way will be found. But what if there is no time to experiment? What if the task must be solved quickly and efficiently? A rat in a maze that has only one path to the goal learns to choose that path after many trials. Bureaucrats, too, are sometimes caught in a maze, but they cannot afford a trial run. There may be no time for hesitations and stoppages. This is why past performance is so important; this is why past experience is so essential. Necessity is said to be the mother of invention, but it precedents have already been formed, if a guide has already been constructed, invention is no longer a necessity. The German bureaucracy could draw upon such precedents and follow such a guide, for the German bureaucrats could dip into a vast reservoir of administrative experience, a reservoir that church and state had filled in fifteen hundred years of destructive activity.

In the course of its attempt to convert the Jews, the Catholic church had taken many measures against the Jewish population. These measures were designed to "protect" the Christian community from Jewish teachings and, not incidentally, to weaken the Jews in their "obstinacy." It is characteristic that as soon as Christianity became the state religion of Rome, in the fourth century A.D., Jewish equality of citizenship was ended. The Church and the Christian state, concilium decisions and imperial laws, henceforth worked hand in hand to persecute the Jews. Table 1 compares the basic anti-Jewish measures of the Catholic Church and the modern counterparts enacted by the Nazi regime.

No summation of the canonical law can be as revealing as a description of the Rome ghetto, maintained by the Papal State until the occupation of the city by the Royal Italian Army in 1870. A German journalist who visited the ghetto in its closing days published such a description in the *Neue Freie Presse*. The ghetto consisted of a few damp, dark, and dirty streets, into which 4,700 human creatures had been packed tightly.

To rent any house or business establishment outside of the ghetto boundaries, the Jews needed the permission of the Cardinal Vicar. Acquisition of real estate outside the ghetto was prohibited. Trade in industrial products or books was prohibited. Higher schooling was prohibited. The professions of lawyer, druggist, notary, painter, and architect were prohibited. A Jew could be a doctor, provided that he confined his practice to Jewish patients. No Jew could hold office. Jews were required to pay taxes like everyone else and, in addition, the following: (1) a yearly stipend for the upkeep of the Catholic officials who supervised the Ghetto Finance Administration and the Jewish community organization; (2) a yearly sum of 5,250 lire to the Casa Pia for missionary work among Jews; (3) a yearly sum of 5,250 lire to the Cloister of the Converted for the same purpose. In turn, the Papal State expended a yearly sum of 1,500 lire for welfare work. But no state money was paid for education or the care of the sick.

The papal regime in the Rome ghetto gives us an idea of the cumulative effect of the canonical law. *This* was its total result. More-

T A B L E 1
CANONICAL AND NAZI ANTI-JEWISH MEASURES

Canonical Law	*Nazi Measure*
Prohibition of intermarriage and of sexual intercourse between Christians and Jews, Synod of Elvira, 306	Law for the Protection of German Blood and Honor, September 15, 1935
Jews and Christians not permitted to eat together, Synod of Elvira, 306	Jews barred from dining cars (Transport Minister to Interior Minister, December 30, 1939)
Jews not allowed to hold public office, Synod of Clermont, 535	Law for the Reestablishment of the Professional Civil Service, April 7, 1933
Jews not allowed to employ Christian servants or possess Christian slaves, 3d Synod of Orléans, 538	Law for the Protection of German Blood and Honor, September 15, 1935
Jews not permitted to show themselves in the streets during Passion Week, 3d Synod of Orléans, 538	Decree authorizing local authorities to bar Jews from the streets on certain days (i.e., Nazi holidays), December 3, 1938
Burning of the Talmud and other books, 12th Synod of Toledo, 681	Book burnings in Nazi Germany
Christians not permitted to patronize Jewish doctors, Trullan Synod, 692	Decree of July 25, 1938
Christians not permitted to live in Jewish homes, Synod of Narbonne, 1050	Directive by Göring providing for concentration of Jews in houses, December 28, 1938 (Bormann to Rosenberg, January 17, 1939)
Jews obliged to pay taxes for support of the Church to the same extent as Christians, Synod of Gerona, 1078	The "Sozialausgleichsabgabe" which provided that Jews pay a special income tax in lieu of donations for Party purposes imposed on Nazis, December 24, 1940
Jews not permitted to be plaintiffs, or witnesses against Christians in the Courts, 3d Lateran Council, 1179, Canon 26	Proposal by the Party Chancellery that Jews not be permitted to institute civil suits, September 9, 1942 (Bormann to Justice Ministry, September 9, 1942)
Jews not permitted to withhold inheritance from descendants who had accepted Christianity, 3d Lateran Council, 1179, Canon 26	Decree empowering the Justice Ministry to void wills offending the "sound judgment of the people," July 31, 1938
The marking of Jewish clothes with a badge, 4th Lateran Council, 1215, Canon 68 (Copied from the legislation by Caliph Omar II [634–644], who had decreed that Christians	Decree of September 1, 1941

T A B L E 1

CANONICAL AND NAZI ANTI-JEWISH MEASURES (Continued)

wear blue belts and Jews, yellow belts)	
Construction of new synagogues prohibited, Council of Oxford, 1222	Destruction of synagogues in entire Reich, November 10, 1938 (Heydrich to Göring, November 11, 1938)
Christians not permitted to attend Jewish ceremonies, Synod of Vienna, 1267	Friendly relations with Jews prohibited, October 24, 1941 (Gestapo directive)
Jews not permitted to dispute with simple Christian people about the tenets of the Catholic religion, Synod of Vienna, 1267	
Compulsory ghettos, Synod of Breslau, 1267	Order by Heydrich, September 21, 1939
Christians not permitted to sell or rent real estate to Jews, Synod of Ofen, 1279	Decree providing for compulsory sale of Jewish real estate, December 3, 1938
Adoption by a Christian of the Jewish religion or return by a baptized Jew to the Jewish religion defined as a heresy, Synod of Mainz, 1310	Adoption of the Jewish religion by a Christian places him in jeopardy of being treated as a Jew (Decision by Oberlandesgericht Königsberg, 4th Zivilsenat, June 26, 1942)
Jews not permitted to act as agents in the conclusion of contracts, especially marriage contracts, between Christians, Council of Basel, 1434, Sessio XIX	Decree of July 6, 1938, providing for liquidation of Jewish real estate agencies, brokerage agencies, and marriage agencies catering to non-Jews
Jews not permitted to obtain academic degrees, Council of Basel, 1434, Sessio XIX	Law against Overcrowding of German Schools and Universities, April 25, 1933

over, the policy of the Church gave rise not only to ecclesiastical regulations; for more than a thousand years, the will of the Church was also enforced by the state. The decisions of the synods and councils became basic guides for state action. Every medieval state copied the canonical law and elaborated upon it. Thus there arose an "international medieval Jewry law," which continued to develop until the eighteenth century. The governmental refinements and elaborations of the clerical regime may briefly be noted in Table 2, which shows also the Nazi versions.

These are some of the precedents that were handed down to the Nazi bureaucratic machine. To be sure, not all the lessons of the past

T A B L E   2
PRE-NAZI AND NAZI ANTI-JEWISH MEASURES

Pre-Nazi Development	Nazi Measure
The property of Jews slain in a German city considered as public property, "because the Jews with their possessions belong to the Reich chamber," provision in the 14th-century code *Regulae juris "Ad decus"*	13th Ordinance to the Reich Citizenship Law providing that the property of a Jew be confiscated after his death, July 1, 1943
Confiscation of Jewish claims against Christian debtors at the end of the 14 century in Nuremberg	11th Ordinance to the Reich Citizenship Law, November 25, 1941
"Fines": for example, the Regensburg fine for "killing Christian child," 1421	Decree for the "Atonement Payment" by the Jews, November 12, 1938
Marking of documents and personal papers identifying possessor or bearer as a Jew	Decree providing for identification cards, July 23, 1938
Around 1800, the Jewish poet Ludwig Börne had to have his passport marked "Jud von Frankfurt"	Decree providing for marking of passports, October 5, 1938
Marking of houses, special shopping hours, and restrictions of movement, 17th century, Frankfurt	Marking of Jewish apartments, April 17, 1942 Decree providing for movement restrictions, September 1, 1941
Compulsory Jewish names in 19th-century bureaucratic practice	Decree of January 5, 1937 Decree of August 17, 1938

were still remembered in 1933; much had been obscured by the passage of time. This is particularly true of negative principles, such as the avoidance of riots and pogroms. In 1406 the state sought to make profits from mob violence in the Jewish quarter of Vienna. Christians suffered greater losses in this pogrom than Jews, because the Jewish pawnshops, which went up in smoke during the great ghetto fire, contained the possessions of the very people who were rioting in the streets. This experience was all but forgotten when, in November 1938, Nazi mobs surged once more into Jewish shops. The principal losers now were German insurance companies, who had to pay German owners of the damaged buildings for the broken window glass. A historical lesson had to be learned all over again.

If some old discoveries had to be made anew, it must be stressed that many a new discovery had not even been fathomed of old. The administrative precedents created by church and state were in themselves incomplete. The destructive path charted in past centuries was an interrupted path. The anti-Jewish policies of conversion and expulsion could carry destructive operations only up to a point. These policies were not only goals; they were also limits before which the bureaucracy had to stop and beyond which it could not pass. Only the removal of these restraints could bring the development of destructive operations to its fullest potentiality. That is why the Nazi administrators became improvisers and innovators; that is also why the German bureaucracy under Hitler did infinitely more damage in twelve years than the Catholic Church was capable of in twelve centuries.

The administrative precedents, however, are not the only historical determinants with which we are concerned. In a Western society, destructive activity is not just a technocratic phenomenon. The problems arising in a destruction process are not only administrative but also psychological. A Christian is commanded to choose good and to reject evil. The greater his destructive task, therefore, the more potent are the moral obstacles in his way. These obstacles must be removed; the internal conflict must somehow be resolved. One of the principal means through which the perpetrator attempts to clear his conscience is by clothing his victim in a mantle of evil, by portraying the victim as an object that must be destroyed.

In recorded history we find many such portraits. Invariably they are floating effusively like clouds through the centuries and over the continents. Whatever their origins or destinations, the function of these stereotypes is always the same. They are used as justification for destructive thinking; they are employed as excuses for destructive action.

The Nazis needed such a stereotype. They required just such an image of the Jew. It is therefore of no little significance that when Hitler came to power, the image was already there. The model was already fixed. When Hitler spoke about the Jew, he could speak to the Germans in familiar language. When he reviled his victim, he resurrected a medieval conception. When he shouted his fierce anti-Jewish attacks, he awakened his Germans as if from slumber to a long-forgotten challenge. How old, precisely, are these charges? Why did they have such an authoritative ring?

The picture of the Jew we encounter in Nazi propaganda and Nazi correspondence had been drawn several hundred years before. Martin Luther had already sketched the main outlines of that portrait, and the Nazis, in their time, had little to add to it. We shall look here at a few excerpts from Luther's book *About the Jews and Their Lies*. In doing so, let it be stressed that Luther's ideas were shared by others in his century, and that the mode of his expression was the style of his times. His work is cited here only because he was a towering figure in the development of German thought, and the writing of such a man is not to be forgotten in the unearthing of so crucial a conceptualization as this. Luther's treatise about the Jews was addressed to the public directly, and, in that pouring recital, sentences descended upon the audience in a veritable cascade. Thus the passage:

> Herewith you can readily see how they understand and obey the fifth commendment of God, namely, that they are thirsty bloodhounds and murderers of all Christendom, with full intent, now for more than fourteen hundred years, and indeed they were often burned to death upon the accusation that they had poisoned water and wells, stolen children, and torn and hacked them apart, in order to cool their temper secretly with Christian blood.

And:

> Now see what a fine, thick, fat lie that is when they complain that they are held captive by us. It is more than fourteen hundred years since Jerusalem was destroyed, and at this time it is almost three hundred years since we Christians have been tortured and persecuted by the Jews all over the world (as pointed out above), so that we might well complain that they had now captured us and killed us—which is the open truth. Moreover, we do not know to this day which devil has brought them here into our country; we did not look for them in Jerusalem.

Even now no one held them here, Luther continued. They might go whenever they wanted to. For they were a heavy burden, "like a plague, pestilence, pure misfortune in our country." They had been driven from France, "an especially fine nest," and the "dear Emperor Charles" drove them from Spain, "the best nest of all." And this year they were expelled from the entire Bohemian crown, including Prague, "also a very fine nest"—likewise from Regensburg, Magdeburg, and other towns.

> Is this called captivity, if one is not welcome in land or house? Yes, they hold us Christians captive in our country. They let us work in the sweat of our noses, to earn money and property for them, while they sit behind the oven, lazy, let off gas, bake pears, eat, drink, live softly and well from our wealth. They have captured us and our goods through their accursed usury; mock us and spit on us, because we work and permit them to be lazy squires who own us and our realm; they are therefore our lords, we their servants with our own wealth, sweat, and work. Then they curse our Lord, to reward us and to thank us. Should not the devil laugh and dance, if he can have such paradise among the Christians, that he may devour through the Jews—his holy ones—that which is ours, and stuff our mouths and noses as reward, mocking and cursing God and man for good measure.
>
> They could not have had in Jerusalem under David and Solomon such

fine days on their own estate as they have now on ours—which they rob and steal daily. But still they complain that we hold them captive. Yes, we have and hold them in captivity, just as I have captured my calculum, my blood heaviness, and all other maladies.

What have the Christians done, asks Luther, to deserve such a fate? "We do not call their women whores, do not curse them, do not steal and dismember their children, do not poison their water. We do not thirst after their blood." It was not otherwise than Moses had said. God had struck them with frenzy, blindness, and raging heart.

This is Luther's picture of the Jews. First, they want to rule the world. Second, they are archcriminals, killers of Christ and all Christendom. Third, he refers to them as a "plague, pestilence, and pure misfortune." This Lutheran portrait of Jewish world rule, Jewish criminality, and the Jewish plague has often been repudiated. But, in spite of denial and exposure, the charges have survived. In four hundred years the picture has not changed.

In 1895 the Reichstag was discussing a measure, proposed by the anti-Semitic faction, for the exclusion of foreign Jews. The speaker, Ahlwardt, belonged to that faction. We reproduce here a few excerpts from his speech:

> It is quite clear that there is many a Jew among us of whom one cannot say anything bad. If one designates the whole of Jewry as harmful, one does so in the knowledge that the racial qualities of this people are such that in the long run they cannot harmonize with the racial qualities of the Germanic peoples, and that every Jew who at this moment has not done anything bad may nevertheless under the proper conditions do precisely that, because his racial qualities drive him to do it.
>
> Gentlemen, in India there was a certain sect, the Thugs, who elevated the act of assassination to an act of policy. In this sect, no doubt, there were quite a few people who personally never committed a murder, but the English in my opinion have done the right thing when they exterminated this whole sect, without regard to the question whether any particular member of the sect already had committed a murder or not, for in the proper moment every member of the sect would do such a thing.

Ahlwardt pointed out that the anti-Semites were fighting the Jews not because of their religion but because of their race. He then continued:

> The Jews accomplished what no other enemy has accomplished: they have driven the people from Frankfurt into the suburbs. And that's the way it is wherever Jews congregate in large numbers. Gentlemen, the Jews are indeed beasts of prey. . . .
>
> Mr. Rickert [another deputy who had opposed the exclusion of the Jews] started by saying that we already had too many laws, and that's why we should not concern ourselves with a new anti-Jewish code. That is

really the most interesting reason that has ever been advanced against anti-Semitism. We should leave the Jews alone because we have too many laws?! Well, I think, if we would do away with the Jews, we could do away with half the laws that we have now on the books.

Then, Deputy Rickert said that it is really a shame—whether he actually said that I don't know because I could not take notes—but the sense of it was that it was a shame that a nation of 50 million people should be afraid of a few Jews. [Rickert had cited statistics to prove that the number of Jews in the country was not excessive.] Yes, gentlemen, Deputy Rickert would be right, if it were a matter of fighting with honest weapons against an honest enemy; then it would be a matter of course that the Germans would not fear a handful of such people. But the Jews, who operate like parasites, are a different kind of problem. Mr. Rickert, who is not as tall as I am, is afraid of a single cholera germ—and, gentlemen, the Jews are cholera germs.

(Laughter)

Gentlemen, it is the infectiousness and exploitative power of Jewry that is involved.

Ahlwardt then called upon the deputies to wipe out "these beasts of prey," and continued:

If it is now pointed out—and that was undoubtedly the main point of the two previous speakers—that the Jew is human too, then I must reject that totally. The Jew is no German. If you say that the Jew is born in Germany, is raised by German nurses, has obeyed the German laws, has had to become a soldier—and what kind of soldier, we don't want to talk about that—

(Laughter in the right section)

has fulfilled all his duties, has had to pay taxes, too, then all of that is not decisive for nationality, but only the race out of which he was born is decisive. Permit me to use a banal analogy, which I have already brought out in previous speeches: a horse that is born in a cowbarn is still no cow. *(Stormy laughter)* A Jew who is born in Germany, is still no German; he is still a Jew.

Ahlwardt then remarked that this was no laughing matter but deadly serious business.

It is necessary to look at the matter from this angle. We do not even think of going so far as, for instance, the Austrian anti-Semites in the Reichsrath, that we demand an appropriation to reward everybody who shoots a Jew, or that we should decide that whoever kills a Jew, inherits his property. *(Laughter, uneasiness)* That kind of thing we do not intend here; that far we do not want to go. But we do want a quiet and common-sense separation of the Jews from the Germans. And to do that, it is first of all necessary that we close that hatch, so that more of them cannot come in.

It is remarkable that two men, separated by a span of 350 years, can still speak the same language. Ahlwardt's picture of the Jews is in its basic features a replica of the Lutheran portrait. The Jew is still (1) an enemy who has accomplished what no external enemy has accomplished: he has driven the people of Frankfurt into the suburbs; (2) a criminal, a thug, a beast of prey, who commits so many crimes that his elimination would enable the Reichstag to cut the criminal code in half; and (3) a plague or, more precisely, a cholera germ. Under the Nazi regime, these conceptions of the Jew were expounded and repeated in an almost endless flow of speeches, posters, letters, and memoranda. Hitler himself preferred to look upon the Jew as an enemy, a menace, a dangerous cunning foe. This is what he said in a speech delivered in 1940, as he reviewed his "struggle for power":

> It was a battle against a satanical power, which had taken possession of our entire people, which had grasped in its hands all key positions of scientific, intellectual, as well as political and economic life, and which kept watch over the entire nation from the vantage of these key positions. It was a battle against a power which, at the same time, had the influence to combat with the law every man who attempted to take up battle against them and every man who was ready to offer resistance to the spread of this power. At that time, all-powerful Jewry declared war on us.

Gauleiter Julius Streicher emphasized the contention that the Jews were criminal. The following is an excerpt from a typical Streicher speech to the Hitler Youth. It was made in 1935.

> Boys and girls, look back to a little more than ten years ago. A war— the World War—had whirled over the peoples of the earth and had left in the end a heap of ruins. Only one people remained victorious in this dreadful war, a people of whom Christ said its father is the devil. That people had ruined the German nation in body and soul.

But then Hitler arose and the world took courage in the thought that now

> the human race might be free again from this people which has wandered about the world for centuries and millennia, marked with the sign of Cain.
> Boys and girls, even if they say that the Jews were once the chosen people, do not believe it, but believe us when we say that the Jews are not a chosen people. Because it cannot be that a chosen people should act among the peoples as the Jews do today.
> A chosen people does not go into the world to make others work for them, to suck blood. It does not go among the peoples to chase the peasants from the land. It does not go among the peoples to make your fathers poor and drive them to despair. A chosen people does not slay and

torture animals to death. A chosen people does not live by the sweat of others. A chosen people joins the ranks of those who live because they work. Don't you ever forget that.

Boys and girls, for you we went to prison. For you we have always suffered. For you we had to accept mockery and insult, and became fighters among the Jewish people, against that organized body of world criminals, against whom already Christ had fought, the greatest anti-Semite of all times.

A number of Nazis, including the chief of the German SS and Police Himmler, the jurist and Generalgouverneur of Poland Hans Frank, and Justice Minister Thierack, inclined to the view that the Jews were a lower species of life, a kind of vermin, which upon contact infected the German people with deadly diseases. Himmler once cautioned his SS generals not to tolerate the stealing of property that had belonged to dead Jews. "Just because we exterminated a bacterium," he said, "we do not want, in the end, to be infected by that bacterium and die of it." Frank frequently referred to the Jews as "lice." When the Jews in his Polish domain were killed, he announced that now a sick Europe would become healthy again. Justice Minister Thierack once wrote the following letter to a worried Hitler:

> A full Jewess, after the birth of her child, sold her mother's milk to a woman doctor, and concealed the fact that she was a Jewess. With this milk, infants of German blood were fed in a children's clinic. The accused is charged with fraud. The purchasers of the milk have suffered damage, because the mother's milk of a Jewess cannot be considered food for German children. The impudent conduct of the accused is also an insult. However, there has been no formal indictment in order to spare the parents—who do not know the facts—unnecessary worry. I will discuss the race-hygienic aspects of the case with the Reich Health Chief.

The twentieth-century Nazis, like the nineteenth-century anti-Semites and the sixteenth-century clerics, regarded the Jews as hostile, criminal, and parasitic. Ultimately the very word *Jew* was infused with all these meanings. But there is also a difference between the recent writings and the older scripts that requires explanation. In the Nazi and anti-Semitic speeches we discover references to race. This formulation does not appear in the sixteenth-century books. Conversely, in Luther's work there is repeated mention of God's scorn, thunder and lightning worse than Sodom and Gomorrah, frenzy, blindness, and raging heart. Such language disappeared in the nineteenth century.

There is, however, a close functional relationship between Luther's references to divine blows and Ahlwardt's reliance upon race characteristics, for both Luther and Ahlwardt tried to show that the Jew could not be changed, that a Jew remained a Jew. "What God does not improve with such terrible blows, that we shall not change with words and deeds." There was some evil in the Jew that even the fires of God, burning high and hot, could not extinguish. In Ahlwardt's time these evil qualities, fixed and unchangeable, are traced to a definite cause. The Jew "cannot help himself" because his racial qualities drive him to commit antisocial acts. We can see, therefore, that even the race idea fits into a trend of thought.

Anti-Jewish racism had its beginning in the second half of the seventeenth century, when the "Jewish caricature" first appeared in cartoons. These caricatures were the first attempt to discover racial characteristics in the Jew. However, racism acquired a "theoretical" basis only in the 1800s. The racists of the nineteenth century stated explicitly that cultural characteristics, good or bad, were the product of physical characteristics. Physical attributes did not change; hence social behavior patterns also had to be immutable. In the eyes of the anti-Semite, the Jews therefore became a "race."

The destruction of European Jewry was fundamentally the work of German perpetrators, and hence it is to them that we must devote our primary attention. What happened to the Jews cannot be understood without insight into decisions made by German officials in Berlin and in the field. Yet every day German exertions and costs were being affected by the behavior of the victims. To the extent that an agency could marshal only limited resources for a particular task, the very progress of the operation and its ultimate success depended on the mode of the Jewish response.

The Jewish posture in the face of destruction was not shaped on the spur of the moment. The Jews of Europe had been confronted by force many times in their history, and during these encounters they had evolved a set of reactions that were to remain remarkably constant over the centuries. This pattern may be portrayed by the following diagram:

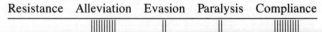

Resistance   Alleviation   Evasion   Paralysis   Compliance

Preventive attack, armed resistance, and revenge were almost completely absent in Jewish exilic history. The last, and only, major revolt took place in the Roman Empire at the beginning of the second century, when the Jews were still living in compact settlements in the eastern Mediterranean region and when they were still envisaging an independent Judea. During the Middle Ages the Jewish communities no longer contemplated battle. The medieval Hebrew poets did not celebrate the martial arts. The Jews of Europe were placing themselves under the protection of constituted authority. This reliance was legal, physical, and psychological.

The psychological dependence of European Jews is illustrated by the following incident. In 1096, when the Jewish communities of Germany were warned by letters and emissaries from France that the crusaders were coming to kill them, the Jewish leadership of Mainz replied: "We are greatly concerned with your well-being. As for ourselves, there is no great cause for fear. We have not heard a word of such matters, nor has it been hinted that our lives are threatened by the sword." Soon the crusaders came, "battalion after battalion," and struck at the Jews of Speyer, Worms, Mainz, and other German cities. More than eight hundred years later, a president of the Jewish council in Holland was to say: "The fact that the Germans had perpetrated atrocities against Polish Jews was no reason for thinking that they behave [sic] in the same way toward Dutch Jews, firstly because the Germans had always held Polish Jews in disrepute, and secondly because in the Netherlands, unlike Poland, they had to sit up and take notice of public opinion." In the Netherlands, as in Poland to the east, Jewry was subjected to annihilation.

For the Diaspora Jews, acts of armed opposition had become isolated and episodic. Force was not to be a Jewish strategy again until Jewish life was reconstituted in a Jewish state. During the catastrophe of 1933–45 the instances of opposition were small and few. Above all, they were, whenever and wherever they occurred, actions of last (never first) resort.*

On the other hand, alleviation attempts were typical and instanteous responses by the Jewish community. Under the heading of alleviation are included petitions, protection payments, ransom arrangements, anticipatory compliance, relief, rescue, salvage, reconstruction—in short, all those activities designed to avert danger or, in the event that force has already been used, to diminish its effects. Let us give a few illustrations.

The ancient city of Alexandria, Egypt, was divided into five districts: α, β, δ, γ, and ε. The Jews were heavily concentrated in the Delta (waterfront section), but they had residences also in other parts of town.

---

*From 1789 Jews had gained military experience in the armies of continental Europe. In 1794 and 1831 they had fought in their own detachments on the side of Polish forces in Warsaw. During 1903–1904 Jewish self-defense units, armed with clubs, confronted drunken mobs invading the Jewish quarters of several Russian cities. Yet these experiences, often cited in literature, were limited precedents. The Jewish soldiers of the German or Austrian armies did not wear a Jewish uniform. The Jewish detachments in Warsaw fought as residents of Poland for a Polish cause. The self-defense units in Russia did not challenge the Russian state. Even so, it is noteworthy that the death camp revolts in Treblinka and Sobibór were planned by Jewish inmates who had been officers, that the principal ghetto rising took place in Warsaw, and that Jewish partisan activity was concentrated in parts of the occupied USSR.

In A.D. 38, Emperor Caligula wanted to be worshipped as a half-god. The Jews refused to pay him the desired respect. Thereupon, riots broke out in Alexandria. The Jews were driven into the Delta, and the mob took over abandoned apartments. Equality of rights was temporarily abolished, the food supply to the Delta was cut off, and all exits were sealed. From time to time, a centurion of Roman cavalry would enter Jewish homes on the pretext of searching for arms. Under these conditions, which have a peculiarly modern flavor, the Jews sent a delegation to Rome to petition Emperor Caligula for relief. The delegation included the famous philosopher Philo, who disputed about the matter in Rome with the anti-Jewish public figure Apion. This is one of the earliest examples of Jewish petition diplomacy. More than nineteen hundred years later, in 1942, a delegation of Bulgarian Jews petitioned for a similar purpose: the Jews were attempting to ward off ejection from their homes.

Sometimes the Jews attempted to buy protection with money. In 1384, when much Jewish blood was flowing in Franken, the Jews sought to ransom themselves. Arrangements for payment were made with speed. The city of Nuremberg collected the enormous sum of 80,000 guilders. King Wenzel got his share of 15,000 guilders from that amount. The representatives of the king, who participated in negotiations with other cities, received 4,000 guilders. Net profit to the city: over 60,000 guilders, or 190,000 thaler. The Jews in Nazi-occupied Europe, from the Netherlands to the Caucasus, made identical attempts to buy safety from death with money and valuables.

One of the most sagacious alleviation reactions in the Jewish arsenal was anticipatory compliance. The victim, sensing danger, combatted it by initiating a conciliatory response *before* being confronted by open threats. He therefore gave in to a demand on his own terms. An example of such a maneuver was the effort of European Jewish communities before 1933 to bring about a significant shift in the Jewish occupational structure from commerce and law to engineering, skilled labor, and agricultural work. This movement, which in Germany was known as occupational redistribution, was prompted by a hope that in their new economic role the Jews were going to be less conspicuous, less vulnerable, and less subject to the criticism of unproductiveness. Another illustration of anticipation is the self-restraint by Jewish firms of pre-1933 Germany in the hiring of Jewish personnel. Jewish enterprises had already become the employers of most Jewish wage earners, but now some companies instituted quotas to avoid an even greater manifestation of such Jewishness. Several years later, in Nazi-dominated Europe, Jewish councils spent many hours trying to anticipate German requirements and orders. The Germans, they reasoned, would not be concerned about the impact of a particular economic measure on those Jews who were least capable of shouldering another burden, whereas the councils might at least try to protect the weakest and neediest Jews from harmful effects. In this vein, the Jewish Council of Warsaw considered confiscating Jewish belongings wanted by the Germans, and for the same reason the council devised a system for drafting Jewish labor, with provisions exempting well-to-do Jews for a fee in order that the money might be used to make payments to families of poorer Jews who were working without wages for German agencies.

The alleviations that followed disaster were developed to a very high degree in the Jewish community. Relief, rescue, and salvage were old Jewish institutions. The relief committees and subcommittees formed by "prominent" Jews, which are so typical of the United Jewish Appeal machinery today, were commonplace in the nineteenth century. Already during the 1860s, collections for Russian Jews were conducted in Germany on a fairly large scale. Reconstruction—that is to say, the rebuilding of Jewish life, whether in new surroundings or, after abatement of persecution, in the old home—has been a matter of automatic adjustment for hundreds of years. Reconstruction is identical with the continuity of Jewish life. The bulk of any general Jewish history book is devoted to the story of the constant shifts, the recurring readjustments, the endless rebuilding of the Jewish community. The years after 1945 were marked by one of the largest of these reconstructive efforts.

Next in our scale is the reaction of evasion, of flight. In the diagram the evasive reaction is not marked as strongly as the alleviation attempts. By this we do not mean the absence of flight, concealment, and hiding in the Jewish response pattern. We mean, rather, that the Jews have placed less hope, less expectation, and less reliance on these devices. It is true that the Jews have always wandered from country to country, but they have rarely done so because the restrictions of a regime became too burdensome. Jews have migrated chiefly for two reasons: expulsion and economic depression. Jews have rarely run from a pogrom. They have lived through it. The Jewish tendency has been not to run from but to survive with anti-Jewish regimes. It is a fact, now confirmed by many documents, that the Jews made an attempt to live with Hitler. In many cases they failed to escape while there was still time and, more often still, they failed to step out of the way when the killers were already upon them.

There are moments of impending disaster when almost any conceivable action will only make suffering worse or bring final agonies closer. In such situations the victims may lapse into paralysis. The reaction is barely overt, but in 1941 a German observer noted the symptomatic fidgeting of the Jewish community in Galicia as it awaited death, between shocks of killing operations, in "nervous despair." Among Jews outside the destruction arena, a passive stance manifested itself as well. In 1941 and 1942, just when mass killings began, Jews all over the world looked on helplessly as Jewish populations of cities and entire countries vanished.

The last reaction on the scale is compliance. To the Jews compliance with anti-Jewish laws or orders has always been equivalent to survival. The restrictions were petitioned against and sometimes evaded, but when these attempts were unsuccessful, automatic compliance was the normal course of action. Compliance was carried to the greatest lengths and in the most drastic situations. In Frankfurt, on September 1, 1614, a mob under the leadership of a certain Vincenz Fettmilch attacked the Jewish quarter in order to kill and plunder. Many Jews fled to the cemetery. There they huddled together and prayed, dressed in the ritual shrouds of the dead and waiting for the killers. This example is particularly pertinent, because the voluntary assembly at graves was repeated many times during the Nazi killing operations of 1941.

The Jewish reactions to force have always been alleviation and compliance. We shall note the reemergence of this pattern time and again. However, before we pass on, it should be emphasized again that the term "Jewish reactions" refers only to ghetto Jews. This reaction pattern was born in the ghetto and it will die there. It is part and parcel of ghetto life. It applies to *all* ghetto Jews—assimilationists and Zionists, the capitalists and the socialists, the unorthodox and the religious.

One other point has to be understood. The alleviation-compliance response dates, as we have seen, to pre-Christian times. It has its beginnings with the Jewish philosophers and historians Philo and Josephus, who bargained with the Romans on behalf of Jewry and who cautioned the Jews not to attack, in word or deed, any other people. The Jewish reaction pattern assured the survival of Jewry during the Church's massive conversion drive. The Jewish policy once more assured to the embattled community a foothold and a chance for survival during the periods of expulsion and exclusion.

If, therefore, the Jews have always played along with an attacker, they have done so with deliberation and calculation, in the knowledge that their policy would result in least damage and least injury. The Jews knew that measures of destruction were self-financing or even profitable up to a certain point but that beyond that limit they could be costly. As one historian put it: "One does not kill the cow one wants to milk." In the Middle Ages the Jews carried out vital economic functions. Precisely in the usury so much complained of by Luther and his contemporaries, there was an important catalyst for the development of a more complex economic system. In modern times, too, Jews have pioneered in trade, in the professions, and in the arts. Among some Jews the conviction grew that Jewry was "indispensable."

In the early 1920s Hugo Bettauer wrote a fantasy novel entitled *Die Stadt ohne Juden* (The City without Jews). This highly significant novel, published only eleven years before Hitler came to power, depicts an expulsion of the Jews from Vienna. The author shows how Vienna cannot get along without its Jews. Ultimately, the Jews are recalled. That was the mentality of Jewry, and of Jewish leadership, on the eve of the destruction process. When the Nazis took over in 1933, the old Jewish reaction pattern set in again, but this time the results were catastrophic. The German bureaucracy was not slowed by Jewish pleading; it was not stopped by Jewish indispensability. Without regard to cost, the bureaucratic machine, operating with accelerating speed and ever-widening destructive effect, proceeded to annihilate the European Jews. The Jewish community, unable to switch to resistance, increased its cooperation with the tempo of the German measures, thus hastening its own destruction.

We see, therefore, that both perpetrators and victims drew upon their age-old experience in dealing with each other. The Germans did it with success. The Jews did it with disaster.

CHAPTER TWO

DEFINITION BY DECREE

A destruction process is a series of administrative measures that must be aimed at a definite group. The German bureaucracy knew with whom it had to deal: the target of its measures was Jewry. But what, precisely, was Jewry? Who was a member of that group? The answer to this question had to be worked out by an agency that dealt with general problems of administration—the Interior Ministry. In the course of the definition-making, several other offices from the civil service and the party became interested in the problem.

The problem of defining the Jews was by no means simple; in fact, it was a stumbling block for an earlier generation of anti-Semites. Hellmut von Gerlach, one of the anti-Semitic deputies in the Reichstag during the 1890s, explained in his memoirs why the sixteen anti-Semitic members of the legislature had never proposed an anti-Jewish law: they could not find a workable definition of the concept *Jew*. All had agreed upon the jingle:

> Never mind to whom he prays,
> The rotten mess is in the race.

But how to define race in a law? The anti-Semites had never been able to come to an agreement about that question. That is why "everybody continued to curse the Jews, but nobody introduced a law against them." The people who wrote the Nazi Party program in 1920 did not supply a definition either. They simply pointed out that a member of the community could only be a person of "German blood, without regard to confession."

When the Interior Ministry drafted its first anti-Jewish decree for the dismissal of Jewish civil servants, it was confronted by the same problem that had troubled the anti-Semites and the early Nazis. But the bureaucrats of the Interior Ministry attacked the problem systematically, and soon they found the answer.

The decree of April 7, 1933, provided that officials of "non-Aryan descent" were to be retired. The term *non-Aryan descent* was defined in the regulation of April 11, 1933, as a designation for any person who had a Jewish parent or grandparent; the parent or grandparent was presumed to be Jewish if he (or she) belonged to the Jewish religion.

The phraseology of this definition is such that it could not be said to have run counter to the stipulations of the party program. The ministry had divided the population into two categories: "Aryans," who were people with no Jewish ancestors (i.e., pure "German blood"), and "non-Aryans," who were all persons, Jewish or Christian, who had at least one Jewish parent or grandparent. It should be noted that this definition is in no sense based on racial criteria, such as blood type, curvature of the nose, or other physical characteristics. Nazi commentators, for propagandistic reasons, called the decrees "racial laws," and non-German writers, adopting this language, have also referred to these definitions as "racial." But it is important to understand that the sole criterion for categorization into the "Aryan" or "non-Aryan" group was religion, not the religion of the person involved but the religion of his ancestors. After all, the Nazis were not interested in the "Jewish nose." They were concerned with the "Jewish influence."

The 1933 definition (known as the *Arierparagraph*) did give rise to difficulties. One problem arose from the use of the terms *Aryan* and *non-Aryan,* which had been chosen in order to lend to the decrees a racial flavor. Foreign nations, notably Japan, were offended by the general implication that non-Aryans were inferior to Aryans. On November 15, 1934, representatives of the Interior Ministry and the Foreign Office, together with the chief of the party's Race-Political Office, Dr. Gross, discussed the adverse effect of the Arierparagraph on Far Eastern policy. The conferees had no solution. The Foreign Office reported that its missions abroad had explained the German policy of distinguishing between the *types* of races, rather than the *qualities* of the races. According to this view, each race produced its own social characteristics, but the characteristics of one race were not necessarily inferior to those of other races. In short, racial "type" comprised physical and spiritual qualities, and German policy attempted no more than the promotion of conditions that would permit each race to develop in its own way. However, this explanation did not quite satisfy the Far Eastern states, who still felt that the catchall term *non-Aryan* placed them in the same category as Jews.

There was another difficulty that reached into the substance of the measure. The term *non-Aryan* had been defined in such a way as to include not only full Jews—that is to say, persons with four Jewish grandparents—but also three-quarter Jews, half Jews, and one-quarter Jews. Such a definition was considered necessary in order to eliminate from official positions all persons who might have been carriers of the "Jewish influence" even in the slightest degree. Nevertheless, it was recognized that the term *non-Aryan,* aside from embracing the full Jews, included also a number of persons whose inclusion in subsequent more drastic measures would result in difficulties. In order to narrow the application of subsequent decrees to exclude such persons, a definition of what was actually meant by the term *Jew* became necessary.

At the beginning of 1935 the problem received some attention in party circles. One of the meetings was attended by Dr. Wagner, then chief medical officer of the party; Dr. Gross, head of the Race-Political Office; and Dr. Blome, at that time secretary of the medical association. Dr. Blome spoke out against a special status for part-Jews. He did not want a "third race." Consequently, he proposed that all quarter-Jews be considered Germans and that all half-Jews be considered Jews. Reason: "Among half-Jews, the Jewish genes are notoriously dominant." This view later became party policy, but the party never succeeded in imposing that policy on the Interior Ministry, where the decisive decrees were written.

On the occasion of the Nuremberg party rally, Hitler ordered, on September 13, 1935, that a decree be written—in two days—under the title "Law for the Protection of German Blood and Honor." Two experts of the Interior Ministry, *Ministerialrat* Medicus and Ministerialrat Lösener, were thereupon summoned to Nuremberg by plane. When they arrived they found *Staatssekretäre* Pfundtner and Stuckart, Ministerialrat Seel (civil service expert of the Interior Ministry), Ministerialrat Sommer (a representative of the Führer's Deputy Hess), and several other gentlemen in the police headquarters, drafting a law. Interior Minister Frick and Chief Medical Officer Wagner shuttled between Hitler's quarters and the police station with drafts. In the midst of the commotion, to the accompaniment of music and marching feet and in a setting of flags, the new decree was hammered out. The law no longer dealt with "non-Aryans" but with "Jews." It prohibited marriages and extramarital intercourse between Jews and citizens of "German or related blood," the employment in Jewish households of female citizens of "German or related blood" under the age of forty-five, and the raising by Jews of the Reich flag. None of the terms used were defined in the decree.

On the evening of September 14, Frick returned to his villa from a visit to Hitler and told the exhausted experts to get busy with a draft of a Reich citizenship law. The Staatssekretäre and Ministerialräte now went to work in the music room of Frick's villa to write a citizenship law. Soon they ran out of paper and requisitioned old menu cards. By 2:30 A.M. the citizenship law was finished. It provided that only persons of "German or related blood" could be citizens. Since "citizenship" in Nazi Germany implied nothing, no interest attaches to the drafting of this decree, except for a provision to the effect that "full Jews" could not be citizens. This implied a new categorization differentiating between Germans and part-Jews, on the one hand, and such persons regardless of religion who had four Jewish grandparents, on the other. Hitler saw this implication immediately and crossed out the provision.

The attitudes of the party and of the civil service toward part-Jews had not emerged quite clearly. The party "combatted" the part-Jew as a carrier of the Jewish influence," whereas the civil service wanted to protect in the part-Jew "that part which is German." The final definition was written in the Interior Ministry, and so it is not surprising that the party view did not prevail.

The authors of the definition were Staatssekretär Dr. Stuckart and his expert in Jewish affairs, Dr. Lösener. Stuckart was then a young man of thirty-three. He was a Nazi, a believer in Hitler and Germany's destiny. He was also regarded as a party man. There is a difference between these two concepts. Everyone was presumed to be, and was accepted as, a Nazi unless by his own conduct he insisted otherwise. But not everyone was regarded as a party man. Only those people were party men who held positions in the party, who owed their positions to the party, or who represented the party's interests in disagreements between the party and other hierarchies. Stuckart was in the party (he had even joined the SS in an honorary capacity), he had risen to power more quickly than other people, and he knew what the party wanted. But Stuckart refused to go along with the party in the definition business.

Stuckart's expert on Jewish affairs, Dr. Bernhard Lösener, had been transferred to the Interior Ministry after long service in the customs administration. Definitions and Jewish affairs were an entirely new experience to him. Yet he became an efficient "expert" in his new assignment. Ultimately he drafted, or helped draft, twenty-seven Jewish decrees. He is the prototype of other "experts" in Jewish matters in the Finance Ministry, the Labor Ministry, the Foreign Office, and many other agencies.

The two men had an urgent task to perform. The terms *Jew* and *German* had already been used in a decree that contained criminal sanctions. There was no time to be lost. The final text of the definition corresponds in substance to a memorandum written by Lösener and dated November 1, 1935. Lösener dealt in his memorandum with the critical problem of the half-Jews. He rejected the party's proposal to equate half-Jews with full Jews. In the first place, Lösener argued, such a categorization would strengthen the Jewish side. "In principle, the half-Jew should be regarded as a more serious enemy than the full Jew because, in addition to Jewish characteristics, he possesses so many Germanic ones which the full Jew lacks." Second, the equation would result in an injustice. Half-Jews could not emigrate and could not compete with full Jews for jobs with Jewish employers. Third, there was the need of the armed forces, which would be deprived of a potential 45,000 men. Fourth, a boycott against half-Jews was impractical (the German people would not go along). Fifth, half-Jews had performed meritorious services (recital of names). Sixth, there were many marriages between Germans and half-Jews. Suppose, for example, that Mr. Schmidt finds out, after ten years of marriage, that his wife is half-Jewish—a fact that, presumably, all half-Jewish wives kept secret.

In view of all these difficulties, Lösener proposed that the half-Jews be sorted into two groups. There was no practical way of sorting half-Jews individually, according to their political convictions. But there was an automatic way of dealing with that problem. Lösener proposed that only those half-Jews be counted as Jews who belonged to the Jewish religion or who were married to a Jewish person.

The Lösener proposal was incorporated into the First Regulation to the Reich Citizenship Law, dated November 14, 1935. In its final form the automatic sorting method separated the "non-Aryans" into the following categories: Everyone was defined as a Jew who (1) descended from at least three Jewish grandparents (full Jews and three-quarter Jews) or (2) descended from two Jewish grandparents (half-Jews) and (a) belonged to the Jewish religious community on September 15, 1935, or joined the community on a subsequent date, or (b) was married to a Jewish person on September 15, 1935, or married one on a subsequent date, or (c) was the offspring of a marriage contracted with a three-quarter or full Jew after the Law for the Protection of German Blood and Honor had come into force (September 15, 1935), or (d) was the offspring of an extramarital relationship with a three-quarter or full Jew and was born out of wedlock after July 31, 1936. For the determination of the status of the grandparents, the presumption remained that the grandparent was Jewish if he or she belonged to the Jewish religious community.

Defined *not* as a Jew but as an individual of "mixed Jewish blood" was (1) any person who descended from two Jewish grandparents (half-Jewish), but who (a) did not adhere (or adhered no longer) to the Jewish religion on September 15, 1935, and who did not join it an any subsequent time, *and (b)* was not married (or was married no longer) to a Jewish person on September 15, 1935, and who did not marry such a person at any subsequent time (such half-Jews were called *Mischlinge* of the first degree), and (2) any person descended from one Jewish grandparent (Mischling of the second degree). The designations "Mischling of the first degree" and "Mischling of the second degree" were not contained in the decree of November 14, 1935, but were added in a later ruling by the Interior Ministry.

In practice, therefore, Lösener had split the non-Aryans into two groups: Mischlinge and Jews. The Mischlinge were no longer subjected to the destruction process. They remained non-Aryans under the earlier decrees and continued to be affected by them, but subsequent measures were, on the whole, taken only against "Jews." Henceforth the Mischlinge were left out.

The administration of the Lösener decree, and of the Arier-paragraph that preceded it, was a complicated procedure, which is interesting because it affords a great deal of insight into the Nazi mentality. In the first place, both decrees were based on descent: the religious status of the grandparents. For that reason, it was necessary to *prove* descent. In this respect the decrees affected not only "non-Aryans"; any applicant for a position in the government or the party could be requested to search for the records of his ancestors. For such proof of ancestry seven documents were required: a birth or baptismal certificate, the certificates of the parents, and the certificates of the grandparents.

Prior to 1875–76, births were registered only by churches. Thus the churches were drawn into an administrative role in the implementation of the first measure of the destruction process, a task they performed as a matter of course. Not so simple was the attempt to obtain the cooperation of officeholders. Although civil servants had to fill out a form only if it could be presumed that the information disclosed therein would result in their dismissal, the disquiet, not to speak of the paper work, was still considerable. At one point the Interior Ministry proposed that proof of descent be supplied by all civil servants and their wives, and the Justice Ministry demanded this evidence of notaries. At least some universities (counting their non-Aryan students) contented themselves with the honor system, but the party insisted on procedures, even if not always with complete success. As late as 1940 the chief of the party's foreign organization had to remind his personnel to submit the documents. Most employees in the office had simply ignored an earlier directive for submission of records, without even giving an excuse or explanation for failure to comply.

Even in the early 1930s a whole new profession of licensed "family researchers" had appeared on the scene to assist applicants and officeholders in finding documents. The researchers compiled ancestor charts, which listed parents and grandparents. Sometimes it was necessary to do research on great-grandparents also. Such procedures, however, were limited to two types of cases: (1) applications for service in such party formations as the SS, which, in the case of officers, required proof of non-Jewish descent from 1750, and (2) attempts to show that a Jewish grandparent was actually the offspring of Christian parents. The latter procedure was possible because a grandparent was only *presumed* to be Jewish if he (or she) belonged to the Jewish religion. In the same way, inquiry into the status of the great-grandparents could be used to the detriment of an applicant. For if it was shown that a Christian grandparent had actually been the child of Jews, the grandparent would be considered a Jew, and a "downward" classification would result.

The final decision about the correctness of the facts was made by the agency that had to pass on the applicant, but in doubtful cases a party office on family research rendered expert opinions for the guidance of agency heads. There was a very interesting category of doubtful cases: the offspring of extramarital relationships. The status of these individuals raised a peculiar problem. How was one to classify someone whose descent could not be determined? This problem was divided into two parts: individuals with Jewish mothers and individuals with German mothers.

In cases of offspring of unmarried Jewish mothers, the Family Research Office presumed that any child born *before* 1918 had a Jewish father and that any child born *after* 1918 had a Christian father. The reason for this presumption was a Nazi hypothesis known as the "emancipation theory," according to which Jews did not mix with Germans before 1918. However, after 1918 the Jews had the opportunity to pursue the systematic disintegration of the German people. This activity included the fostering of extramarital relationships.

In commenting on this theory, Judge Klemm of the party's Legal Office pointed out that it was quite true that Jews were guilty of this practice but that, after all, the practice was intended only to violate German *women*. It could hardly be assumed that a Jewish woman undertook pregnancy in order to harm the German *man*. According to the criteria used by the research office, complained Klemm, a Jewish mother could simply refuse to tell the office who the father was, and her child would automatically become a Mischling of the first degree. Klemm's comments were probably quite correct. This was perhaps the only Nazi theory that worked to the complete advantage of a number of full Jews.

The "emancipation theory" does not seem to have been applied to the offspring of unwed German mothers. The reason was simple: the party's research office rarely, if ever, got such cases. If it had gotten them, just about all of Germany's illegitimate children born after 1918 would have been classified as Mischlinge of the first degree. But since the party did not get the cases, the illegitimate offspring of a German mother remained a German, with all the rights and obligations of a German in Nazi Germany. However, there were a few instances when a Jew or Mischling had acknowledged paternity of a German mother's child. In some of the cases, persons who had been classified as Mischlinge went to court, pointing out that the legal father was not the actual father and that, therefore, there was ground for reclassification. For such cases the Justice Ministry laid down the rule that the courts were not to inquire into the motives of the person who had acknowledged fatherhood and that they were to reject any testimony by the mother, "who is only interested in protecting her child from the disadvantages of Jewish descent."

The cumbersome task of proving descent was not the only problem that complicated the administration of the decrees. Although the definition appeared to be airtight in the sense that, given the facts, it should have been possible at once to determine whether an individual was a German, a Mischling, or a Jew, there were in fact several problems of interpretation. Consequently, we find a whole number of administrative and judicial decisions that were designed to make the definition more precise.

The principal problem of interpretation hinged on the provision in the Lösener decree according to which half-Jews were classified as Mischlinge of the first degree if they did not belong to the Jewish religion and were not married to a Jewish person on or after September 15, 1935. There was no legal difficulty in determining whether a person was married; marriage is a clearly defined legal concept. But the determination of criteria for adherence to the Jewish religion was not so simple. Whether a half-Jew was to be classified as a Jew or a Mischling of the first degree ultimately depended on the answer to the question: Did the man regard himself as a Jew?

In 1941 the Reich Administrative Court received a petition from a half-Jew who had not been raised as a Jew and who had never been affiliated with any synagogue. Nevertheless, the court classified the petitioner as a Jew because there was evidence that on various occasions since 1914 he had designated *himself* as a Jew in filling out forms and official documents, and he had failed to correct the impression of the authorities that he was a Jew. Toleration of a presumption was sufficient conduct for the purpose of classification as a Jewish person.

In a later decision the highest court in Germany ruled that conduct was not enough; the attitude disclosed by the conduct was decisive. The particular case concerned a young woman, half-Jewish, who had married a half-Jew (Mischling of the first degree). The marriage consequently did not place her into the Jewish category. Now, however, there was the matter of her religion. The evidence showed that in 1923 and 1924 she had had Jewish religious instruction upon the insistence of her Jewish father. In subsequent years she accompanied her father to the synagogue, once a year, on Jewish high holy days. After her father died in 1934, she discontinued visits to the synagogue, but, in asking for a job in a Jewish community organization, she listed her religion as Jewish. Until 1938, moreover, she was entered as a member of a synagogue. The court decided that she was *not* Jewish. The evidence showed that she had resisted her father's attempt to have her formally accepted with prayer and blessing into the Jewish religion. She had visited the synagogue not for religious reasons but only in order to please her father. In asking for a position with the Jewish community organization, she was motivated not by a feeling of Jewishness but solely by economic considerations. As soon as she discovered her entry in the Jewish community list, she requested that her name be struck out.

The attitude and intention of the individual was decisive in another case, which is very interesting from a psychological point of view. A half-Jew who had married a German woman in 1928 had thereupon ceased to be a member of his synagogue. In 1941 the Jewish community organization in Berlin, which was then performing important functions in the destruction process, suddenly demanded information about the man's personal finances, and when this information was refused, the Jewish community went to court, claiming that the defendant had quit his synagogue but not his religion. The court rejected the Jewish organization's argument, pointing out that the Jewish religious community had no legal personality and no public law status. Consequently, any man who had quit his synagogue had quit his religion at the same time, unless there was evidence that he still regarded himself as a Jew. There was no such evidence in this case. To the contrary, the defendant had provided proof of his membership in party organizations, and in every other respect the court was satisfied that this man had intended to sever his connections with Jewry when he left the synagogue.

This decision was one of the few that were assailed by the party's Race-Political office. A lawyer of that office, Dr. Schmidt-Klevenow, referring to the fact that the Jewish community itself had claimed the defendant to be a member, asked whether the court had to be "more pontifical than the pontiff."

From all these decisions the judiciary's concern with half-Jews is quite evident. This concern was the product of a desire to balance the protection of the German community against the destruction of the Jews. When a person was both German and Jewish by parental descent, the judges had to determine which element was dominant. To do this, they only had to be a little more precise than Lösener had been in asking the question of how the individual had classified himself.

The court interpretations of the Lösener decree illustrate once more that there is nothing "racial" in the basic design of the definition. In fact, there are a few very curious cases in which a person with *four* German grandparents was classified as a Jew because he belonged to the Jewish religion. In its decision one court pointed out that Aryan treatment was to be accorded to persons who had the "racial" requirements, "but that in cases when the individual involved feels bound to Jewry in spite of his Aryan blood, and shows this fact externally, his attitude is decisive." In another decision, by the Reich Finance Court, it was held that an Aryan who adhered to the Jewish religion was to be treated as a Jew for the duration of his adherence to the Jewish faith. According to the court, an individual "who is racially a non-Jew but who openly claims membership in the Jewish community, belongs to the community and therefore has placed himself in the ranks of the Jews."

While the judiciary closed the loopholes of the Lösener definition by making it more precise, it became necessary in an increasing number of cases to make exceptions on behalf of individuals whose categorization into a particular group was considered unjust. In creating the Mischlinge, Lösener had constructed a so-called third race, that is, a group of people who for administrative purposes were neither Jews nor Germans. Mischlinge of the first degree, in particular, were to suffer from a series of increasingly burdensome discriminations, including dismissals from the civil service, the requirement of special consent for marriages with Germans, exclusion from active service in the armed forces, nonadmission to secondary schools and colleges, and (by the fall of 1944) forced labor to build fortifications.

Because of these discriminations, pressure for exceptional treatment was applied by colleagues, superiors, friends, and relatives. Consequently, in 1935, a procedure was instituted for the reclassification of a Mischling into a higher category, i.e., Mischling of the first degree to Mischling of the second degree, or Mischling of the second degree to German, or Mischling of the first degree to German. This procedure was known as liberation. There were two kinds: "pseudoliberations" and "genuine liberations." The pseudoliberation was a reclassification based on a clarification of the facts or of the law. It was achieved by showing, for example, that an allegedly Jewish grandfather was not really Jewish or that a presumed adherence to the Jewish religion had not existed. The "real liberation," however, was granted on showing the applicant's "merit." Applications for real liberations were routed through the Interior Ministry and the Reich Chancellery to Hitler if the petitioner was a civilian, and through the Army High Command and the Führer Chancellery if the petitioner was a soldier.

The recipients of this favor sometimes were high officials. Ministerialrat Killy of the Reich Chancellery, a man who performed significant functions in the destruction of the Jews, was a Mischling of the second degree. His wife was a Mischling of the first degree. He had joined the party and had entered the Reich Chancellery without telling anyone about his origin. When the decree of April 7, 1933 *(Arierparagraph)*, was issued, Killy informed Lammers about the state of affairs and offered to resign. Lammers thought the situation quite grave because of Killy's wife but advised Killy not to resign. Thereupon Lammers spoke to Hitler, who agreed to Killy's continuing service. Then, on Christmas Eve in 1936, while the Killy family was sitting around the tree and opening gifts, a courier brought a special present: a liberation for Killy and his children.

The "liberations" increased in volume to such an extent that on July 20, 1942, Lammers informed the Highest Reich Authorities of Hitler's desire to cut down on their number. The applications had been handled too "softly." Hitler did not think that the blameless conduct of a Mischling was sufficient ground for his "liberation." The Mischling had to show "positive merit," which might be proved if, for example, without awareness of his ancestry, he had fought for the party uninterruptedly and for many years prior to 1933.

Lest we leave the impression that the tendency to equate Mischlinge with Germans was unopposed, we should point out that there was another tendency to eliminate the "third race" by reclassifying Mischlinge of the second degree as Germans and transforming all Mischlinge of the first degree into Jews. This pressure, which came from party circles and the police, reached its zenith in 1942. However, it never succeeded.

Thus we find that the Lösener definition remained the basis of categorization throughout the destruction process. Even though different definitions were later adopted in some occupied countries and Axis states, the basic concept of these early decrees remained unchanged.

In summary, here is a recapitulation of the terms and their meanings:

DEFINITION BY DECREE

Non-Aryans
{
Mischlinge of the second degree:
Persons descended from one Jewish grandparent

Mischlinge of the first degree:
Persons descended from two Jewish grandparents but not belonging to the Jewish religion and not married to a Jewish person on September 15, 1935

Jews:
Persons descended from two Jewish grandparents belonging to the Jewish religion or married to a Jewish person on September 15, 1935, and persons descended from three or four Jewish grandparents.

CHAPTER THREE

CONCENTRATION

THE REICH—PROTEKTORAT AREA

A major step of the destruction process was the concentration of the Jewish community. In Germany concentration comprised two developments: the crowding of the Jews into large cities and the separation of the Jews from the German population. The urbanization process was a consequence of anti-Jewish economic constrictions between 1933 and 1939. The ghettoization process was deliberately planned, measure for measure.

Even before the Nazis came to power, the Jewish community in Germany had already been highly urbanized, but after 1933 a further crowding into the cities became noticeable. Isolated Jewish families departed from villages to towns. From there the stream continued to Berlin, Vienna, Frankfurt, and other large population centers. Taking the area of the Old Reich and Austria as a whole, the percentage of Jews living in cities with populations of more than 100,000 rose from 74.2 in 1933 to 82.3 in 1939. The census of May 17, 1939, revealed a Jewish population of 330,892. More than two-thirds of this number lived in ten cities. More than half lived in Vienna and Berlin.

To repeat: the Germans did not plan this movement. The migration was caused mainly by the gradual impoverishment of the Jewish community, which gave rise to increasing intra-Jewish dependence, particularly the dependence of poor Jews on Jewish relief organizations. At least one mayor, the Oberbürgermeister of Frankfurt, made inquiries of his police chief whether the influx of country Jews into his city could not somehow be stopped. The police chief replied that "unfortunately" he had no legal means of doing so.

Unlike the uncontrolled movement of the Jews into the cities, the ghettoization of the Jewish community (i.e., its isolation from the surrounding German population) was directed, step by step, by the bureaucracy. Ghettoization does not mean that Jewish districts, complete with walls, were set up in cities of the Reich and the Bohemian-Moravian Protektorat. Such districts were later established in Poland and Russia to the east, but the Jewish community in Germany was subjected to conditions that had many characteristics of the ghetto. These characteristics are reflected in five steps of the ghettoization process: (1) the severance of social contacts between Jews and Germans, (2) housing restrictions, (3) movement regulations, (4) identification measures, and (5) the institution of Jewish administrative machinery.

The severance of social contacts was the first step toward Jewish isolation. In a country where members of a minority group enjoy close personal relations with the dominant group, drastic segregation measures cannot be successful until these relations are dissolved and until a certain distance is established between the two groups. The dissolution of social relations began with the dismissals of Jews from the civil service and industry, and with the acquisition or liquidation of Jewish business establishments. These measures, however, were primarily economic. Their social consequences were incidental.

There were also calculated measures against Jewish-German mingling. These decrees fell into two categories, one based on the assumption that the Germans were too friendly with the Jews and that therefore such expressions of friendship had to be prohibited in the interest of German purity and National Socialist ideals, the other founded on the opposite premise, that the Germans were so hostile to the Jews that segregation was required for the maintenance of public order. The apparent contradiction in this reasoning has a simple explanation. In the first case, measures were involved that, for their administrative effectiveness, had to be enforced against Germans, whereas in the second type of ordinance the aim of separations could be achieved with restrictions applied only to the Jews.

The earliest decree against mixing was the Law for the Protection of German Blood and Honor. In one of its provisions, the employment in Jewish households of German women under the age of forty-five years was prohibited. The era of domestic servants had not passed by 1935, and the forced departure of German women by the thousands from middle-class Jewish homes brought forth a flood of calls for replacements from the ranks of needy Jewish women. The household stipulation was instituted by analogy in hotels and guest houses at health resorts. Insofar as German female personnel under forty-five were employed there, Jewish guests were to be barred.

More complicated effects of the Blood and Honor Law were to flow from its prohibition of marriages and extramarital relationships between Jews and citizens of German or kindred blood. These ramifications became manifest in the interpretations and enforcement of the law. If an intermarriage was contracted after the decree's entry into force, it was considered null and void, and the parties to such a marriage were automatically guilty of extramarital intercourse as well. Under the penalty provisions, both man and woman could be punished by penitentiary sentences for entering into an intermarriage, but only the *man* (whether he was Jew or German) could be sent to jail for extramarital intercourse. It was Hitler's wish that the *woman* (Jewish or German) be immune from prosecution.

We do not know the reason for Hitler's insistence upon this exemption. It may have been a sense of chivalry or, more likely, the belief that women (even German women) were very weak individuals without wills of their own. At any rate, neither the judiciary nor the Security Police were happy with the exemption. During a judicial conference, it was therefore decided to heed Hitler's wish in the literal sense only. No German woman would be punished for intercourse with a Jew (or for *Rassenschande* [race defilement], as that crime became known), but if she was trapped into telling a lie during the proceedings against the man, she could be sent to jail for perjury. *Gruppenführer* Heydrich of the Security Police on his part decided that a Jewish woman could not remain free if her German partner went to jail. Such an arrangement went against his grain, Hitler order or no Hitler order. Accordingly, he issued secret instructions to his State Police and Criminal Police offices to follow up the lawful conviction of a German man for Rassenschande with the immediate arrest of his Jewish woman partner, who was to be spirited away to a concentration camp.

Other modifications in the direction of more severity were proposed in connection with the Mischlinge. Just what was the status of Mischlinge under the Law for the Protection of German Blood and Honor? The law obviously mentioned only Jews and Germans. To the creators of this "third race" it was evident that the Mischlinge—as persons who were neither Jews nor citizens of "German or related blood"—were actually a bridge between the Jewish and German communities. Without an additional concurrent regulation, a Mischling would have been in a position to marry anyone or to have extramarital relations with anyone. The prospect of such a situation was awkward enough to require some action. So far as marriages were concerned, several prohibitions were therefore put into effect immediately. (The rules are listed in Table 3. To understand the regulation of Mischling marriages, it may be useful to recall that a Mischling of the first degree was a person with *two* Jewish grandparents, who did not belong to the Jewish religion, and who was not married to a Jewish person on the target date of September 15, 1935. A Mischling of the second degree had only *one* Jewish grandparent.)

These regulatory impediments tended to isolate the Mischling of the first degree. Except by official permission, such an individual was not allowed to marry anyone but another Mischling of the first degree or a Jew. The choice of a Jewish partner resulted in the extinction of

---

T A B L E   3
REGULATION OF MISCHLING MARRIAGES

Permitted Marriages

German–German
Mischling of the second degree–German
Mischling of the first degree–Mischling of the first degree
Mischling of the first degree–Jew
Jew–Jew

Prohibited Except by Special Consent

Mischling of the first degree–German
Mischling of the first degree–Mischling of the second degree

Prohibited

German–Jew
Mischling of the second degree–Jew
Mischling of the second degree–Mischling of the second degree

---

Mischling status and an automatic reclassification as a member of the Jewish community. Curiously enough, however, the Mischlinge of the first degree were unhampered in their extramarital relations. They could not commit Rassenschande, whether they chose a Jewish or a German partner. Needless to say, attempts were made to close this loophole. In 1941 Hitler himself requested an amendment to the Blood and Honor Law which would have prohibited the extramarital relations of a Mischling of the first degree with a German. But, after a conference and much discussion, the matter was dropped with Hitler's consent. Apparently the bureaucracy was not confident that it could enforce such a prohibition.

This brings us to a consideration of the enforcement of the Rassenschande decree in general. Just how successful was it? If the repetition of an illegal act is a criterion of the enforceability of a law, the bureaucracy had tough going. In 1942 no fewer than sixty-one Jews were convicted of Rassenschande in the Old Reich. (This figure naturally includes only Jewish men, not women.) It compares with fifty-seven convictions for passport fraud and fifty-six convictions for currency violations. Why, then, this continuing need for associations between Jews and Germans? We must understand that the Blood and Honor Law caught a great many mixed couples, who had intended to be married, before they had an opportunity to carry out their plans. Such a couple had three choices. It could separate—that was the aim of the decree. Alternatively, the couple could emigrate. Third, it could "live in sin."

The alternative of emigration was, incidentally, considered an offense. There is at least one case of a German who became a Jew in 1932 in order to marry a Jewish woman, and who subsequently emigrated to Czechoslovakia, where he married her. He was caught after the occupation of Czechoslovakia and convicted of Rassenschande. The defendant argued that he was a Jew, but the court rejected his argument. He also argued the general legal principle that a law subjects people to its provisions only within the territorial jurisdiction. The law had no language indicating its applicability to German citizens living abroad. But the court held that the defendant had violated the law by leaving the country for the purpose of doing something contrary to its stipulations. His emigration was part of the total offense. He had therefore violated the law when he was still within German frontiers.

One reason, then, for the large number of convictions was the unwillingness of mixed couples to separate in the face of a blanket marriage prohibition. There was, however, still another reason why the statistics were a little high. Rassenschande cases were almost always treated harshly by the courts. There were no mitigating circumstances, and there was no need for elaborate proof. The burden was entirely on the defense. An accused could not claim, for example, that he was unaware of the status of his woman partner; in fact, the highest court held that any German man wishing to have extramarital intercourse with *any* woman had the legal duty of inspecting her papers to make sure that she was not Jewish under the law. He had to be especially careful with half-Jewish women, who might either be Jewish (prohibited relationship) or Mischlinge of the first degree (permitted relationship), depending on complex legal questions relating to religious adherence. The accused was helpless also against the assertion of unproved allegations. Needless to say, extramarital intercourse is not easily proved, but in the German courts the barest indications of a friendly relationship could suffice for a strong presumption. The most flagrant example of such a case, "which kicked up a lot of dust in the judiciary," was the accusation against Lehmann Katzenberger, chief of the Jewish Community in Nuremberg.

The facts of this case were as follows: In 1932, Katzenberger owned a wholesale shoe establishment in Nuremberg. He was then a prosperous man, fifty-nine years old, the father of grown-up children. During that year, a young unmarried German woman, twenty-two years of age, arrived in Nuremberg to manage a photography business in Katzenberger's building. Her father asked Katzenberger to look after her. In the course of the years, Katzenberger helped the young woman with her problems, occasionally lending her some money and giving her little presents. This friendship continued after the girl was married and after the war had broken out. One day the woman, Mrs. Irene Seiler, was summoned by the District Party Office and warned to discontinue the acquaintance. She promised to do so, but shortly thereafter Katzenberger was arrested, to be tried for Rassenschande in the criminal chamber of an ordinary court. Katzenberger was then in his late sixties; Mrs. Seiler was over thirty.

The prosecutor who had charge of the case, Hermann Markl, considered the matter quite routine. He looked forward to a "moderate" sentence. (Under the Blood and Honor Law, a man convicted of Rassenschande could be sentenced to any term in prison.) However, the presiding justice of the local special court heard of the proceeding and immediately became interested in it. According to prosecutor Markl, this justice, *Landgerichtsdirektor* Dr. Rothaug, had a "choleric" disposition. He was an obstinate and tough fanatic who inspired fear even in his prosecutors. When the Katzenberger case came to his attention, he ordered the transfer of the proceedings to his court. In the words of another prosecutor, Dr. Georg Engert, Justice Rothaug "drew" the case into his court, for he was determined not to miss this opportunity to sentence a Jew to death.

The proceedings in Rothaug's special court turned out to be a show trial. He goaded witnesses. When the defense attorney proved testimony to be false, he was dismissed with the ruling that the witness had simply made a mistake. Rothaug frequently broke in with insulting remarks about the Jews. When Katzenberger wanted to speak, the judge cut him off. In his final plea, Katzenberger tried to reiterate his innocence and reproached Rothaug for harping on the Jews and forgetting that he, Katzenberger, was a human being. Then Katzenberger brought up the name of Frederick the Great. Rothaug broke in immediately to object to the "besmirching" of the name of the great Prussian king, especially by a Jew.

On March 13, 1942, Landgerichtsdirektor Dr. Rothaug, joined by *Landgerichtsräte* Dr. Ferber and Dr. Hoffmann, gave his decision. He summarized the "evidence" as follows:

> So it is said that the two had approached each other sexually in various ways, including also intercourse. They are alleged to have kissed each other, sometimes in the apartment of Mrs. Seiler, at other times in Katzenberger's business premises. Seiler is alleged to have sat on Katzenberger's lap and Katzenberger, with intent to have sexual satisfaction, is said to have stroked her thigh over [not under] her clothes. On such occasions Katzenberger is alleged to have pressed Seiler close and to have placed his head on her bosom.

Seiler admitted that she had kissed Katzenberger, but playfully. Rothaug dismissed the playful motive by pointing out that she had accepted money from Katzenberger. She was therefore "accessible." Pronouncing sentence, Rothaug condemned Katzenberger to death and sent Mrs. Seiler to prison for perjury.

After pronouncement of judgment, there was one more incident in the case. Though the time was March 1942 and in Russia a great spring offensive was being prepared, the commander of the German armed forces and Führer of the German Reich, Adolf Hitler, had heard of the decision and protested that his injunction against sentencing the woman had not been heeded. No woman, said Hitler, could be sentenced for Rassenschande. He was quickly informed that Mrs. Seiler had been imprisoned not for Rassenschande but for lying on oath. This explanation mollified Hitler. In June, Katzenberger was put to death, but a short time thereafter Mrs. Seiler, having served six months of her sentence, was released.

The Katzenberger case was symptomatic of an attempt to break friendly relations between Jews and Germans. We must keep in mind that Lehmann Katzenberger was president of the Jewish Community in Nuremberg (tenth largest in the Reich), that before Rothaug had a chance to rule on the case, Katzenberger had been accused before an ordinary court, and that before Katzenberger was accused, Mrs. Seiler had been warned by the party to discontinue her acquaintance with the Jewish leader. The Katzenberger case is thus not without administrative significance; it was part of an attempt to isolate the Jewish community. We find confirmation of this fact in an order issued by the Security Police headquarters on October 24, 1941, to all Gestapo offices:

> Lately it has repeatedly become known that, now as before, Aryans are maintaining friendly relations with Jews and that they show themselves with them conspicuously in public. In view of the fact that these Aryans still do not seem to understand the elementary basic principles of National Socialism, and because their behavior has to be regarded as disrespect toward measures of the state, I order that in such cases the Aryan party is to be taken into protective custody temporarily for educational purposes, and that in serious cases they be put into a concentration camp, grade I, for a period of up to three months. The Jewish party is in any case to be taken into protective custody until further notice and to be sent to a concentration camp.

Needless to say, Security Police proceedings were entirely extrajudicial. They involved no confrontation in a court, ordinary or extraordinary. The order was designed to deter relationships that could not always be classified as Rassenschande (namely friendly relations between Jews and Germans, particularly manifest, open friendliness as shown by conversation in the streets or visits to homes). There was, perhaps, some apprehension that the toleration of such friendliness might encourage some Germans to offer Jews sanctuary in the deportation roundups. But that fear was unfounded, for, when the hour of decision came, few Germans made any move to protect their Jewish friends.

The Blood and Honor Law and the order by Security Police Chief Heydrich were intended to sever close personal relations, whether intimate or platonic, between Jews and Germans. Because these measures had to be directed not only at the Jewish party but also at the German, they were reminiscent of medieval strictures against heresy, which they resembled in content and form. The German who left the country in order to marry his Jewish girl friend was guilty of heresy. He could not claim that he was a Jew. Similarly, the German who stopped in the street to talk to an old Jewish acquaintance was also guilty of a lack of understanding of and respect for Nazi "principles."

Of course, ghettoization went a little further than that. An attempt was made to keep Germans and Jews apart as long as possible and as much as possible. These measures could be taken only by barring Jews at certain times from certain places. The rationalization for these decrees was that the Germans did not like the Jews, that Aryans were "inconvenienced" by the presence of Jews, and that therefore the Jews had to be kept out or kept away.

The most important of these antimixing ordinances was the Law against Overcrowding of German Schools of April 25, 1933, which reduced the admission of non-Aryans to each school or college to the proportion of all non-Aryans in the entire German population. The acceptance quota was accordingly fixed at 1.5 percent, while enrollment ceilings were devised with a view to the progressive reduction of the Jewish student body as a whole. By 1936 more than half of the Jewish children in the age group of six to fourteen years were being accommodated in schools operated by the Jewish community. There were, however, no Jewish technical colleges or universities, and the position of Jews enrolled in German institutions of higher learning was becoming more and more tenuous. As of November 1938, the remaining Jewish students in the German school system were expelled. From that date, Jews were permitted to attend only Jewish schools.

Although the school segregation measures created a very serious problem for the Jewish community, they provoked less discussion and less controversy in the upper levels of the German bureaucracy than the orders pertaining to Jewish traveling on trains. Propaganda Minister Goebbels came to a conference of November 12, 1938, well prepared with proposals for travel regulations. Here is an excerpt from the discussion:

GOEBBELS: It is still possible today for a Jew to share a compartment in a sleeping car with a German. Therefore, we need a decree by the Reich Ministry for Transport stating that separate compartments shall be available for Jews; in cases where compartments are filled up, Jews cannot claim a seat. They will be given a separate compartment only after all Germans have secured seats. They will not mix with Germans, and if there is no room, they will have to stand in the corridor.

GÖRING: In that case, I think it would make more sense to give them separate compartments.

GOEBELLS: Not if the train is overcrowded!

GÖRING: Just a moment. There'll be only one Jewish coach.

GOEBBELS: Suppose, though, there aren't many Jews going on the express train to Munich, suppose there are two Jews on the train and the other compartments are overcrowded. These two Jews would then have a compartment all for themselves. Therefore, I say, Jews may claim a seat only after all Germans have secured a seat.

GÖRING: I'd give the Jews one coach or one compartment. And should a case like you mention arise and the train be overcrowded, believe me, we won't need a law. We'll kick him out and he'll have to sit all alone in the toilet all the way!

GOEBBELS: I don't agree; I don't believe in this. There ought to be a law. . . .

More than a year passed before the Transport Minister issued a directive on Jewish travel. "In the interest of the maintenance of order in the passenger trains," Jews of German nationality and stateless Jews were barred from the use of all sleepers and dining cars on all railway lines within "Greater Germany." However, the directive did not introduce separate compartments, an arrangement that the Transport Minister considered impractical. Not until July 1942 were Jews barred from waiting rooms and restaurants in railway stations. This measure, however, was ordered not by the Transport Ministry but by the Security Police. The Transport Ministry did not concern itself with the compartment problem anymore.

The school and railway ordinances were accompanied by many other measures designed to alleviate "overcrowding," to promote the "convenience" of the German population, and to maintain the "public order." Special shopping hours were introduced by the Food and Agriculture Ministry. At the insistence of Propaganda Minister Goebbels and Security Police Chief Heydrich, Jews were barred from resorts and beaches. Hospitalized Jews were transferred to Jewish institutions, and the services of Aryan barbershops were no longer extended to Jews.

The anti-mixing decrees constituted the first phase of the ghettoization process. Most were drafted in the 1930s, and their aim was limited to social separation of Jews and Germans. In the second phase, the bureaucracy attempted a physical concentration by setting aside special Jewish housing accommodations. This type of ghettoization measure is always a very difficult administration problem, because people have to change apartments.

Before any serious move was made in the housing field, Göring brought up a very fundamental question in the conference of November 12, 1938: Should Jews be crowded into ghettos or only into houses? Turning to Security Police Chief Heydrich, who was proposing all sorts of movement restrictions and insignia for Jews, Göring said:

> But my dear Heydrich, you won't be able to avoid the creation of ghettos on a very large scale, in all cities. They will have to be created.

Heydrich replied very emphatically:

> As for the question of ghettos, I would like to make my position clear right away. From the point of view of the police, I don't think a ghetto, in the form of a completely segregated district where only Jews would live, can be put up. We could not control a ghetto where Jews congregate amid the whole Jewish people. It would remain a hideout for criminals and also for epidemics and the like. We don't want to let the Jews live in the same house with the German population; but today the German population, their blocks or houses, force the Jew to behave himself. The control of the Jew through the watchful eye of the whole population is better than having him by the thousands in a district where I cannot properly establish a control over his daily life through uniformed agents.

The "police point of view" is most interesting in two respects. Heydrich looked upon the whole German population as a kind of auxiliary police force. They were to make sure that the Jew "behaved" himself. They were to watch all Jewish movements and to report anything that might be suspicious. Interesting also is Heydrich's prediction of epidemics. Of course, epidemics are not necessary concomitants of ghetto walls; but they do occur when housing deteriorates, when medical services are inadequate, and, above all, when the food supply is shut off. In the Polish ghettos Heydrich's predictions came true and epidemics *did* break out. Göring heeded Heydrich's advice and, on December 28, 1939, he issued a directive that Jews be concentrated in houses rather than in districts.

Now that the moving was to start, one other question had to be resolved: the problem of mixed marriages. In the Blood and Honor Law the bureaucracy had prohibited the formation of *new* intermarriages, but that law did not affect *existing* intermarriages. Under the marriage law, intermarriages were subject to the same regulations as other marriages: no divorce could be granted unless one of the parties had done something wrong or unless the parties had been separated for at least three years.

Only one provision affecting intermarriages had been written into the marriage law of 1938. Under that provision the Aryan party to a mixed marriage could obtain a divorce if he (or she) could convince the court that after the introduction of the Nuremberg laws he had obtained such enlightenment about the Jewish question that he was now convinced that if he had only had such enlightenment before the intermarriage had occurred, he would never have entered into it. This conviction, of course, had to be proven to the satisfaction of the court. Moreover, the Aryan party was given only until the end of 1939 to institute a divorce proceeding on such a ground. Apparently, only a few Germans took advantage of this cumbersome and potentially embarrassing procedure. In 1939 there were still about 30,000 intermarried couples in the Reich-Protektorat area: that is, almost one out of every ten Jews was married to a non-Jewish partner. The problem now facing the bureaucracy was what to do with these 30,000 couples. Should they too be moved into special Jewish houses?

The Göring directive of December 28, 1938, solved this problem by dividing the intermarried couples into two categories: "privileged" and "not privileged." The classification criteria are indicated in Table 4.

It should be noted that the decisive factor for the classification of all intermarried couples with children was the religious status of the child. If the offspring was not raised in the Jewish religion, he was a Mischling of the first degree. As such, he was liable for induction into the armed forces or into the Labor Service. Göring did not want such Mischlinge to be "exposed to Jewish agitation" in houses occupied by Jews; hence he exempted all couples with such children. In the case of childless couples, the Jewish wife of a German husband was considered priv-

T A B L E 4
CLASSIFICATION OF INTERMARRIAGES

	Children Not Raised as Jews (Mischlinge of the First Degree)	*Children Raised as Jews*	*Childless*
Jewish wife–German husband	Privileged	Not privileged	Privileged
Jewish husband–German wife	Privileged	Not privileged	Not privileged

ileged, possibly because the household belonged to the German spouse. On the other hand, the German wife of a Jewish husband was liable to be moved into a Jewish house. Göring hoped that these German wives would divorce their husbands and "return" to the German community. Judging from partial statistics, the privileged couples outnumbered the unprivileged ones nearly three to one. The reason for this ratio is not hard to find: the large majority of mixed couples did not raise their children in the Jewish religion.

It may be noted that the housing exemption granted to couples in privileged mixed marriages was extended with few modifications to wage and food regulations. Moreover, in 1941–44 the Jews in mixed marriages, including those in *unprivileged* mixed marriages, were *not* subjected to deportation. This phenomenon was characteristic of the step-by-step destruction process. Once a group was taken out of the circle of victims for the purpose of one measure, it was immune to subsequent measures as well. To put it another way, if the privilege was upheld in the matter of changing apartments, it was also upheld in the application of more drastic measures. For just as the party was dissatisfied with the exemption of Mischlinge of the first degree, so the party men challenged the privilege of mixed marriage which was in large measure an outgrowth of the Mischling concept.

The actual implementation of the housing restrictions was a very slow process. A great many Jewish families had to be evicted, but eviction was no solution so long as these Jewish families had no place to go. It was practicable only if the homeless family could be quartered in another Jewish household or if there was a vacancy in a house designated for Jewish occupancy. The first eviction regulation against Jews is to be found in the decree of July 25, 1938, which allowed German landlords to terminate leases for Jewish doctors' apartments. The year 1938 was a period of very loose court interpretation of tenancy regulations and leases. During that year many Jews emigrated, and consequently there were vacancies. In a decision dated September 16, 1938, a Berlin court went so far as to rule that the tenancy laws did not apply to Jews at all. Inasmuch as Jews were not members of the people's community, they could not be members of the housing community. This decision anticipated matters a bit, but in effect it was put into a decree dated April 30, 1939, and signed by Hitler and several ministers. The decree provided that Jews could be evicted by a German landlord if the landlord furnished a certificate showing that the tenant could live somewhere else. At the same time, the decree stipulated that homeless Jewish families had to be accepted as tenants by other Jews still in possession of their apartments.

Now the crowding of Jews into Jewish houses could begin. Selecting the houses and steering the Jews into them was the job of the local housing authorities. In larger cities the housing offices had special divisions for the movement of Jews. By 1941 the movement had evidently progressed far enough to entrust the remaining apartment allocations to the Jewish community organization, which kept a close watch on vacancies or space in the Jewish houses. The Jewish bureaucrats worked under the close supervision of the State Police (Gestapo).

The housing restrictions were not intended to be the only constraint on the Jews. Almost contemporaneously with the housing regulations, the bureaucracy tightened Jewish movements and communications. Many of these regulations were issued by organs of the police. On December 5, 1938, the newspapers published a provisional ordinance of the Reichsführer-SS Himmler depriving Jews of their drivers' licenses. Although extremely few people were affected by this announcement, it has considerable significance because of the manner in which it was brought out. Himmler had not previously submitted his order through normal channels to a legal gazette, and he could cite no law or decree that authorized his measure. Yet he was to be upheld by the high court itself. From the sheer publication of the ordinance and the subsequent silence of the Highest Reich Authorities, the court assumed their consent. Hence it was valid and effective from the day that it appeared.

In September 1939, shortly after the outbreak of war, the local police offices ordered the Jews off the streets after 8 P.M. The Reich press chief instructed the newspapers to justify this restriction with the explanation that "Jews had often taken advantage of the blackout to molest Aryan women." On November 28, 1939, Security Police Chief Heydrich signed a decree in which he authorized the *Regierungspräsidenten* in Prussia, Bavaria, and the Sudeten area, the Mayor of Vienna, the *Reichskommissar* in the Saar, and the competent authorities in other areas to impose movement restrictions on Jews, whereby Jewish residents could be barred not only from appearing in public at certain times but also from entering specified areas at any time. The police president of Berlin thereupon declared certain areas to be forbidden zones. The police president of Prague (Charvat) forbade Jews to change their address or to leave the city limits, except for purposes of emigration. On July 17, 1941, Charvat also forbade the Jews to enter the woods at Prague. By a decree of September 1, 1941, Jews were forbidden to leave the boundary of their residential districts without carrying written permission of the local police authority. (Jews in mixed marriages were exempted from this restriction.) The ghetto began to take shape.

Movement *within* the cities was regulated still more by orders concerning the use of city transporation by Jews. In Prague the police president forbade to Jews the use of trolleys and buses in his decree of December 12, 1941. In the Reich area, including Austria, the Transport Ministry ruled on September 18, 1941, that Jews could no longer use city transportation during rush hours, and that at other times they were to take seats only when no Germans were standing.

On March 24, 1942, Security Police Chief Heydrich, in agreement with the Transport Ministry and the Postal Ministry, issued an order that sharply restricted the right of Jews to use public transportation, including subways, street cars, and buses. Henceforth the Jews required police permits (issued by the local Order Police) for use of any such transportation. Permits were to be granted to workers if they could prove that the distance from home to their place of work was seven kilometers (a little over four miles) or one hour. Sick persons or disabled workers could obtain permits for relatively shorter distances. School children were to be given a permit provided that their distance was at least five kilometers (over three miles) or one hour each way. Lawyers and doctors could obtain a permit for any distance.

Communications were cut still more by withdrawal of the right to use telephones. In 1941 private telephones were ripped out of Jewish apartments. This measure was followed by a prohibition to use public telephones except for conversations with Aryans. Finally, this permission was withdrawn, and all telephone booths were marked with signs reading "Use by Jews prohibited."

These elaborate restrictions were reinforced by an elaborate system of identifications. The first element in this system concerned personal documents. Identification papers are an important ingredient of any police state system. In the case of Jews, the document requirements were especially stringent. Files at the University of Freiburg reveal that as early as 1933, non-Aryan students had to exchange their regular brown identification cards for yellow ones. Five years later, on July 23, 1938, a decree prepared by the Interior and Justice ministries required all Jews of German nationality to apply (stating that they were Jews) for identification cards. The cards had to be asked for by December 31, 1938. Jews over fifteen years of age had to carry their cards with them at all times. In dealings with party or ministerial offices, Jews were to indicate that they were Jews and were to show their cards without being asked to do so.

Jews who were about to emigrate also had to obtain passports. At first, nothing in a passport indicated whether the bearer was a Jew. Apparently, no one thought of making any changes in passports issued to Jews or held by Jews until action was initiated by officials of a foreign country. That country was Switzerland. After the Austrian Anschluss, many Jews had taken advantage of a German-Swiss agreement for the abolition of the visa requirement to cross into Switzerland. On June 24, 1938, the chief of the Federal Swiss Police, Heinrich Rothmund, protested to the German legation in Bern against what he called the "inundation" of Switzerland by Viennese Jews, for whom, he said, the Swiss had no more use than Germany did.

On August 10 the Swiss Minister in Berlin looked up the chief of the Political Division of the German Foreign Office to tell him that the flow of Jews to Switzerland had reached "extraordinary proportions." In one day forty-seven Jews had arrived in Basel alone. The Swiss government was decidedly against the "Judaification" of the country, which is something the Germans could understand. Under the circumstances, the Swiss were now considering the reimposition of visa controls. On August 31, Bern denounced the visa agreement. Three days later, however, the Swiss police chief (Rothmund) informed the German Minister in Bern that he was ready to compromise. The Swiss government would be willing to restrict its visa requirement to German *Jews* if the passports would indicate clearly that their holders were Jews. This condition was accepted after some haggling about "reciprocity" (i.e., visa requirements for Swiss Jews, which the Swiss were reluctant to accept). On September 26, Rothmund went to Berlin. On September 29 a treaty was signed providing that the Reich would undertake to mark *all* passports of its Jews (whether traveling to Switzerland or not) with a sign identifying the bearers as Jews. A few days after this agreement had been negotiated, a passport decree was drafted.

The decree, dated October 5, 1938, and signed by the head of the administrative office of the Security Police, Ministerialdirigent Best, provided that all German passports held by Jews be stamped with a large, red *J.* In a letter to *Vortrangender Legationsrat* Rödiger of the Legal Division of the Foreign Office, dated October 5, 1938, Best requested that passports of Jews residing abroad be stamped whenever the documents were presented to consulates or missions for renewal or some other purpose, and that lists be made of Jews abroad who did not respond to invitations to have their passports stamped.

On October 11, Rödiger wrote to the German diplomatic and consular representatives abroad, repeating and elaborating on these requests. Specifically, invitations were to be issued to holders of passports valid for over six months, other Jews were to have their passports stamped only when they presented them, no charge was to be made for the entry, and so on. These instructions have significance because they extended the identification system to tens of thousands of emigrated Jews in countries later occupied by the Germans.

The document stamping did not stop with passports. On March 11, 1940, the Food and Agriculture Ministry directed that ration cards belonging to Jews be marked with a *J* for identification, and on September 18, 1942, Staatssekretär Riecke of the Food and Agriculture Ministry ordered that ration cards issued to Jews be marked obliquely and throughout with the word *Jude*.

The second part of the identification system consisted of the assignment of Jewish names. The process was already begun in 1932, when restrictions were placed on name changes. To be sure, that internal directive was limited in scope, and for the next few years a number of proposals came to the Interior Ministry from party members who were interested in the subject of names. In March 1933, Staatssekretär Bang of the Economy Ministry suggested to Lammers a revocation of name changes granted since November 1918. In June 1936, Himmler informed Pfundtner that the Führer did not want Jews to carry the names Siegfried and Thusnelda. On January 5, 1938, one measure was put into effect. The decree to that date provided that name changes granted before January 30, 1933, could be revoked.

The revocation was followed by the decree of August 17, 1938, drafted by Ministerialrat Globke, name expert of the Interior Ministry, and signed by Staatssekretär Stuckart and Justice Minister Gürtner. This decree stipulated that Jewish men had to add to their regular first name the middle name Israel, and Jewish women the name Sara, unless they already had a first name included in an approved list of the Interior Ministry. The approved list—which, incidentally, had to be used for the naming of newly born children—was also drawn up by the expert Globke.

In compiling the list, Globke necessarily had to omit Hebrew names that in the popular mind were no longer regarded as alien first names, because they had been completely Germanized. Hence he omitted such names as Adam, Daniel, David, Michael, and Raphael for men, and Anna, Debora, Esther, Eva, and Ruth for women. Instead, he supplied (for boys) Faleg, Feibisch, Feisel, Feitel, Feiwel, and Feleg, plus (for girls) Scharne, Scheindel, Scheine, Schewa, Schlämche, Semche, Simche, Slowe, and Sprinzi, as well as many other distortions and figments of the imagination. The name changes and new names had to be recorded in birth and marriage certificates by the local Order Police. The new designations henceforth appeared not only in personal documents of Jews but also in court records and all official correspondence dealing with individually named Jews.

The third component of the identification system was the outward marking of persons and apartments. Outward marking was designed to set off visually the Jews from the rest of the population. An indirect marking process had already started in the mid-1930s. It was customary in Germany, especially in big cities, to hoist the red-white-black flag from the windows on holidays (more ardent Nazis put color pictures of Hitler in their windows), to wear Nazi insignia and swastika armbands, and to give the "German salute": the outstretched arm and "Heil Hitler." All these manifestations of membership in the German community were successively denied to Jews. The Blood and Honor Law prohibited Jews from displaying the Reich colors and expressly permitted them to display the Zionist blue-white-blue flag. The decree of November 14, 1935, regulated the use of insignia, medals, titles, and so on. Finally, a ruling of the Justice Ministry, dated November 4, 1937, deprived those Jews who were prone to give the "German salute" of a chance to hide their identity.

Direct marking was first proposed by Heydrich in the conference of November 12, 1938. As Heydrich outlined his proposal, chairman Göring, who was not only Germany's first industrialist but also its first designer of uniforms, suggested hopefully: "A uniform?" Not to be deterred, Heydrich answered: "An insignia." However, Hitler opposed the marking of the Jews at that time, and Göring disclosed the decision at the Gauleiter conference of December 6, 1938.

The marking of the Jews was first applied in Poland, where, it was felt, the Hitler prohibition was not in force. It is characteristic of the development of the destruction process that in spite of the veto by the highest authority of the Reich, recurrent suggestions for introducing the measure in Greater Germany were circulated in the ministerial offices of the bureaucracy. On July 30, 1941, Staatssekretär and SS-Gruppenführer Karl Hermann Frank of the Protektorat administration in Prague urgently requested in a letter to Lammers that he be permitted to mark the Jews in Bohemia-Moravia. Lammers forwarded the request to the Interior Ministry. Stuckart replied on August 14, 1941, raising the question whether the decree could be applied to the entire Reich-Protektorat area. However, he wanted first to have the opinion of the Foreign Office and of the Labor Ministry.

On August 20, 1941, the Propaganda Ministry seized the initiative and requested Hitler to change his mind. Hitler agreed. Having scored this success, the Propaganda Ministry circulated the news and invited the interested ministries to a conference, which was held under the chairmanship of Staatssekretär Gutterer of the Propaganda Ministry. The Interior Ministry's expert on Jewish affairs (Ministerialrat Lösener), who attended this meeting, said after the war: "I had assumed that, as usual, it would be a small conference of the participating experts." Instead, there were speeches. "Then there was applause, not like in a conference—but as if it were an election campaign." However, in the end, the drafting of the decree was entrusted to Lösener.

In its final form the decree, dated September 1, 1941, provided that

Jews six years or over were to appear in public only when wearing the Jewish star. The star had to be as large as the palm of a hand. Its color had to be black, the background color yellow, and for the center of the star the decree prescribed the black inscription *Jude*. The victims were to sew the star tightly on the left front of their clothing. Jews in privileged mixed marriages were exempt.

The stars were manufactured by the Berliner Fahnenfabrik Geitel & Co. and distributed immediately. There were no major repercussions. Some Jews attempted to hide the emblem with a briefcase or a book, a practice the Berlin Gestapo considered inadmissible. The factory management of Siemens, Kabelwerk Gartenfeld, did not want its Jewish work force to wear the star on the premises, claiming that the Jews were already segregated there. The question of whether a plant was a public place within the meaning of the decree consequently had to be pondered by the Reich Security Main Office. The party, apprehensive about the possibility that the display of the star in the streets would result in new disturbances, issued circulars warning party members not to molest Jews. Children especially were to be cautioned. But there is no record of violence. In fact, there is a story of a little girl who went out of her way to greet politely a Jewish community worker. She said, "Heil Hitler, Mr. Jew."

An awkward situation was created for the churches when baptized Jews with stars turned up for services. In Breslau, the elderly Cardinal Bertram, head of the Catholic Church in eastern Germany, issued instructions that "the conduct of special services" for star wearers was to be "weighed" only in the event of "major difficulties," such as the staying away or ostentatious departure from services by civil servants or party members. The representatives of the Evangelical-Lutheran church in seven provinces invoked the teachings of Martin Luther to declare that racially Jewish Christians had no place and no rights in a German Evangelical church.

The Security Police, in the meantime, extended the marking to apartments. In 1942 the Jews were ordered to paste the star on their doors, in black print on white paper.

The whole identification system, with its personal documents, specially assigned names, and conspicuous tagging in public, was a powerful weapon in the hands of the police. First, the system was an auxiliary device that facilitated the enforcement of residence and movement restrictions. Second, it was an independent control measure in that it enabled the police to pick up any Jew, anywhere, anytime. Third, and perhaps most important, identification had a paralyzing effect on its victims. The system induced the Jews to be even more docile, more responsive to command that before. The wearer of the star was exposed; he thought that all eyes were fixed upon him. It was as though the whole population had become a police force, watching him and guarding his actions. No Jew, under those conditions, could resist, escape, or hide without first ridding himself of the conspicuous tag, the revealing middle name, the telltale ration card, passport, and identification papers. Yet the riddance of these burdens was dangerous, for the victim could be recognized and denounced. Few Jews took the chance. The vast majority wore the star and, wearing it, were lost.

We have now seen how, in consecutive steps, the Jewish community was isolated socially, crowded into special houses, restricted in its movements, and exposed by a system of identification. This process, which we have called ghettoization, was completed with the institution of a Jewish administrative apparatus through which the Germans exercised a stranglehold on the Jewish population. For our understanding of how the Jews were ultimately destroyed, it is essential to know the origins of the Jewish bureaucratic machine. The Jews had created that machine themselves.

Before 1933 the Jewish community organization was still decentralized. Each city with a Jewish population had a *Gemeinde* (Community Organization) with a *Vorstand* (Board) responsible for the operation of Jewish schools, the synagogues, hospitals, orphanages, and welfare activities. By law, the Gemeinden could levy a tax from all those who had been born into the Jewish faith and who were living in the locality, so long as they did not formally resign from membership. There were also regional organizations *(Landesverbände),* which in the southern German states (Baden, Württemberg, and Bavaria) had statutory powers to control budgets and appointments in the Gemeinden, but which were only confederations of local community delegates in Saxony and Prussia. The Prussian Landesverband covered 72 percent of Germany's Jews, including the important cities of Berlin, Frankfurt am Main, Breslau, and Cologne. Its chairman, Rabbi Leo Baeck, was working on a "concordat" with Prussia in 1932, on the eve of Hitler's rise to power.

At that time, the Jewish communities, mirroring the post-1918 political trend in Germany as a whole, were on the verge of centralization. Various drafts of a central Jewish organization had been prepared during the days of the Weimar Republic. In 1928, pending an establishment of a *"Reichsorganisation,"* delegates of the Landesverbände meeting in conference, constituted themselves into a working group, deputized the Prussian Landesverband to keep the books of the group, and created a committee that would represent Jewish interests before official agencies in the German Reich.

In the spring of 1933, a rudimentary central Jewish organization was formed. During the following years, it was to evolve in several steps into a Jewish apparatus with increasingly significant functions. The stages of its evolution, two of them in 1933 alone, are indicated in the following changes of title:

1933   *Reichsvertretung der jüdischen Landesverbände*
      (Reich Representation of Jewish Land Federations)
        Leo Baeck and Kammergerichtsrat Leo Wolff, cochairmen
      Reichsvertretung der deutschen Juden
      (Reich Representation of German Jews)
        Leo Baeck, president
        Ministerialrat Otto Hirsch, deputy
1935   *Reichsvertretung der Juden in Deutschland*
      (Reich Representation of Jews in Germany)
        Leo Baeck
        Otto Hirsch, deputy
1938   *Reichsverband der Juden in Deutschland*
      (Reich Federation of Jews in Germany)
        Leo Baeck
        Otto Hirsch, deputy
1939   *Reichsvereinigung der Juden in Deutschland*
      (Reich Association of Jews in Germany)
        Leo Baeck
        Heinrich Stahl, deputy

When the Jewish leadership was confronted by the Nazi takeover in 1933, it sought first of all an "open debate," a "dignified controversy" with the Nazis on the subject of anti-Semitism and the Jewish future in Germany. In March 1933, Baeck himself and the Vorstand of the Berlin community at the time, Kleemann, dispatched a letter to Hitler in which they enclosed a public statement expressing consternation about the Nazi boycott, calling attention to the 12,000 Jewish dead of the First World War, and refusing responsibility for the "misdeeds of a few." Again and again the heads of various Jewish interest groups—among them the Central-Verein, war veterans, and Zionists—sought interviews with Hitler and other high-ranking Nazi officials. One delegation was received by Göring on March 25, 1933, but this meeting was to be the last of its kind. In later years the Jewish leaders, not only in the Reich but also in occupied territory, were forced to deal with German officials of lower and lower rank, until they were appealing to SS captains. In 1933 they did not foresee this future, and they strove to create an overall representation as a matter of the highest priority. The *Reichsvertretung der jüdischen Landesverbände* was the initial manifestation of this aim, but it was little more than an enlargement of the Berlin community and the Prussian Landesverband. Rabbi Baeck recognized the limitations of this powerless agency and resigned from it after a few months.

During the late summer of 1933, a group of Jewish leaders in Essen led a campaign to revamp the Reichsvertretung. They wanted much heavier representation from communities outside Berlin and the inclusion of national organizations. Their strategy was to "isolate" Berlin and to offer the leadership of the new Reichsvertretung to the man who, in their eyes, stood above factional politics: Leo Baeck. On August 28, 1933, a meeting was held in the Essen synagogue to hammer out a plan. The participants formed a working committee under the direction of Dr. Georg Hirschland (Essen) and authorized him to recruit the Zionists—heretofore a small minority but now growing in influence—into their fold. Ministerialrat Dr. Otto Hirsch of Stuttgart was asked to work out the guidelines. Hirsch drafted a proclamation addressed "To the German Jews," informing them in the original wording that "with the consent of all Jewish Landesverbände and all major organizations, we have taken over the leadership of the Reichsvertretung of German Jews."

On September 3, 1933, Hirschland's working committee met in Berlin. The conferees spoke of a leadership of personalities which was to supplant the existing establishment. The list from which the future leaders were to be drawn included Martin Buber, the philosopher, and Richard Willstätter, the Nobel laureate in chemistry. The committee then chose Baeck as president and Hirsch as executive chairman.

Two weeks after the September 3 meeting, the new Reichsvertretung came into being. It did not include some of the Orthodox Jews (Agudah), who looked askance at the liberal Rabbi Leo Baeck and his scholarly studies of Christian doctrines, nor was it supported by assimilationist Jews espousing German nationalism, who believed that their special sacrifices for Germany entitled them to rights greater than those of other Jews, nor—at the opposite end of the spectrum—by Zionist Revisionists, who believed in the necessity of total emigration. Still, the group had a broad enough base to require care in the allocation of positions to its presidium. Spaces had to be reserved for the newly recruited Zionists, the other major Jewish organizations, and the larger communities, including that of Berlin, which numbered a third of all the Jews in Germany. In the end, there was no room for Buber or Willstätter. All the men at the helm of the Reichsvertretung were experienced in the political arena, and almost immediately they were called on to use their expertise, not merely in dealing with each other but with the German state and Jewry's mounting problems.

The initial policy of the Reichsvertretung was founded on the concept that the Jews had to hold out in the hope that Nazi Germany would moderate its anti-Jewish course and would grant the Jewish community sufficient "Lebensraum" for continued existence. As yet, emigration was viewed not as the way, but as a way out. By the end of 1935 this principle was no longer tenable. Symbolically, the Reichsvertretung was required to change its name from a representation of *German Jews* to one of *Jews in Germany*. Substantively, its activities were concentrated on such problems as vocational training and emigration, as well as the continuing tasks of welfare. The Reichsvertretung had to increase its budget accordingly. Although still dependent on funds from communities and Landesverbände, it received increasing amounts from foreign Jewish welfare organizations, thus strengthening its central character.

Further changes occurred in 1938, when many Jews were losing their foothold in the economy. In some smaller communities, shrunk by emigration, questions arose about the administration of communal real property or the proceeds from its sale. The Reichsvertretung all but abandoned its "representational" function and became a *Reichsverband* (federation) for administrative purposes. On July 27, 1938, the Jewish leadership decided that all those in the Old Reich who were Jews by religion should have to belong to the Reichsverband. By February 1939 this new, all-inclusive organization was engaged in correspondence under as yet another name: the *Reichsvereinigung*. It is at this point that the last, critical change occurred. On July 4, 1939, the Reichsvereinigung was taken over, lock, stock, and barrel, by the Security Police.

The decree of July 4, 1939, was drafted by Ministerialrat Lösener and a fellow expert, Rolf Schiedermair. It was signed by Interior Minister Frick, Deputy of the Führer Hess, Minister of Education Rust, and Minister of Church Affairs Kerrl. Part of the decree affirmed the existing state of affairs. The territorial jurisdiction of the Reichsvereinigung was defined as the Old Reich, including the Sudeten area but excluding Austria and the Protektorat. All the local Gemeinden were placed under the Reichsvereinigung in a straight hierarchical relationship. The Reichsvereinigung was charged with the upkeep of Jewish schools and financial support of indigent Jews.

The decree, however, was also a Nazi measure. It specified that the subjects of the Reichsvereinigung were "Jews," not only those who belonged to the Jewish religion but all persons classified as Jews by the definition decree. The framers of the decree inserted another provision, one that was to have profound importance in a few short years. The Interior Ministry (by which was meant the Security Police) was empowered to assign additional tasks to the Reichsvereinigung. These assignments were going to turn the Jewish administrative apparatus into a tool for the destruction of the Jewish community. The Reichsvereinigung, with its Gemeinden and territorial branches, would become an arm of the German deportation machinery.

Significantly, this transformation was being accomplished without any change of personnel or designation. The Germans had not created the Reichsvereinigung and they had not appointed its leaders. Rabbi Leo Baeck, Dr. Otto Hirsch, Direktor Heinrich Stahl, and all the others *were* the Jewish leaders. Because these men were not puppets, they retained their status and identity in the Jewish community throughout their participation in the process of destruction, and because they did not lessen their diligence, they contributed the same ability that they had once marshaled for Jewish well-being to assist their German supervisors in operations that had become lethal. They began the pattern of compliance by reporting deaths, births, and other demographic data to the Reich Security Main Office and by transmitting German regulations in the publication *Jüdisches Nachrichtenblatt* to the Jewish population. They went on to establish special bank accounts accessible to the Gestapo and to concentrate Jews in designated apartment houses. Toward the end, they prepared charts, maps, and lists and provided space, supplies, and personnel in preparations for deportation. The Reichsvereinigung and its counterparts in Vienna and Prague were the prototype of an institution—the Jewish Council—that was to appear in Poland and other occupied territories and that was to be employed in activities resulting in disaster. It was a system that enabled the Germans to save their manpower and funds while increasing their stranglehold on the victims. Once they dominated the Jewish leadership, they were in a position to control the entire community.

The concentration of the Jews marks the close of the preliminary phase of the destruction process in the Reich-Protektorat area. The fatal effects of this preliminary phase were manifested in two phenomena. One was the relationship of perpetrators and victims. When the bureaucracy stood at the threshold of most drastic action, the Jewish community was reduced to utter compliance with orders and directives. The other manifestation of the strangulation regime was the widening gap between births and deaths in the Jewish community. Its birth rate was plunging toward zero; the death rate was climbing to unheard-of heights (see Table 5). The Jewish community was a dying organism.

T A B L E 5
**BIRTHS AND DEATHS OF JEWS IN OLD REICH
(NOT INCLUDING AUSTRIA AND PROTEKTORAT)**

Year	Births	Deaths	Population at End of Year
1940	396	6,199	ca. 175,000
1941	351	6,249	ca. 140,000
1942	239	7,657	[after deportations] 51,327
1940–42	986	20,105	

POLAND

When the German army moved into Poland in September 1939, the destruction process was already well within its concentration stage. Polish Jewry was therefore immediately threatened. The concentration was carried out with much more drastic dispatch then had been dared in the Reich-Protektorat region. The newly occupied Polish territory was, in fact, an area of experimentation. Within a short time the machinery of destruction in Poland overtook and outdid the bureaucracy in Berlin.

There were three reasons for this development. One is to be found in the personnel composition of the German administration in Poland. As we shall see, that administration had a large number of party men in its ranks. It was less careful, less thorough, less "bureaucratic" than the administration in the Reich.

Another, more important reason for the unhesitating action in Eastern Europe was the German conception of the Pole and of the Polish Jew. In German eyes a Pole naturally was lower than a German, and a Polish Jew lower (if such a thing was possible) than a German Jew. The Polish Jew was on the bottom of the German scale—the Germans referred to Eastern Jewry as "subhumanity." In dealing with East Europeans, both Poles and Jews, the bureaucracy could be less considerate and more drastic. In Germany the bureaucracy was concerned with the rights and privileges of Germans. It was careful to deflect destructive measures from the German population. Much thought was given to such problems as couples in mixed marriages, the disruption of German-Jewish business relationships, and so on. In Poland such problems had little importance, for it did not matter that a Pole was hurt in consequence of a measure aimed at the Jews. Similarly, the bureaucracy in Germany made some concessions to Jews who had fought in World War I, who had served for many years in the civil service, or who had done something else for Germany. In Poland such considerations did not apply.

The third and most important reason for the special treatment of the Polish Jews was the weight of their numbers. Ten percent of the Polish population was Jewish; out of 33,000,000 people, 3,300,000 were Jews. When Germany and the USSR divided Poland in September 1939, two million of these Jews were suddenly placed under German domination. Warsaw alone had about 400,000 Jews, that is to say, almost as many as had lived in Germany in 1933 and more than remained in the entire Reich-Protektorat area at the end of 1939. The uprooting and segregation of so many Jews posed altogether different problems and gave rise to altogether different solutions. Thus the concentration in Poland was not confined to a system of composite restrictions such as those discussed in the first section of this chapter. Instead, the bureaucracy in Poland resurrected the medieval ghetto, shut off entirely from the rest of the world.

On September 19, 1939, Security Police Chief Heydrich met with Generalquartiermeister Wagner of the Army High Command to discuss some Polish problems. The two officials agreed upon a "cleanup once and for all," of "Jews, intelligentsia, clergy, nobility." On the next day word came from the Commander-in-Chief of the Army that "the ghetto idea exists in broad outline; details are not yet clear." They were developed twenty-four hours later in a meeting of office chiefs from the Reich Security Main Office (RSHA) and commanders recalled from Security Police units *(Einsatzgruppen)* already in Poland. The decision was to clear German-speaking areas of Jews, to remove the Jewish population from the Polish countryside, and to concentrate Jewry in ghettos within major cities. These conclusions, which were incorporated on the same day in an order directed to the Einsatzgruppen, constituted an ambitious concentration plan.

The introduction of the order makes a brief reference to an ultimate goal, an emigration of the Jews that was to be completed later, but that was not spelled out at the moment. Part I provided that the Jews were to be ejected from the territories of Danzig, West Prussia, Poznań, and Eastern Upper Silesia. These areas later became incorporated territory, that is, territory integrated into the administration of the Reich. The Jews from these areas were to be shoved into the interior of Poland, a territory later known as the "General Government" *(Generalgouvernement)*. The Jews in the General Government were to be concentrated in cities. Only cities that were located at railroad junctions, or at least along a railroad, were to be chosen as concentration points. All Jewish communities of less than five hundred were to be dissolved and transferred to the nearest concentration center.

In part II of the order Heydrich directed that a council of Jewish elders *(Ältestenrat,* also *Judenrat)* composed of influential persons and rabbis was to be set up in each Jewish community. The councils were to be made fully responsible (in the literal sense of the word) for the exact execution of all instructions. They were to take an improvised census of the Jews in their area, and they were to be made personally responsible for the evacuation of the Jews from the countryside to the concentration points, for the maintenance of the Jews during transport, and for housing upon arrival. There was no objection against Jews taking with them their movable possessions. The reason to be given for the concentration was that the Jews had participated decisively in sniper attacks and plundering.

It is interesting to note that the army wanted no part in the execution of this plan. During the Heydrich-Wagner discussion of September 19, 1939, the army quartermaster general had insisted that the military authorities be notified of all activities by the SS and Police but that the "cleanup" take place after the withdrawal of the army and the transfer of power to the civilian administration, that is, not before early December. In view of the army's early abdication of power in Poland, this demand could easily be fulfilled. This time the army did not have to dirty its hands with such business. In 1941, as we shall see, the military could no longer extricate itself from its assigned role in the destruction of the European Jews, but in Poland the concentration process was placed squarely into the laps of the newly formed civil administration.

The Einsatzgruppen, on their part, were not able to accomplish much. Ghettoization was a procedure far too complex for a handful of battalion-sized units that were to be disbanded and transformed into a regular Security Police administration upon the cessation of military rule. They did establish several Jewish councils, simply by calling on an identified Jewish leader to form a "Judenrat." In Warsaw on October 4, 1939, a small Security Police detachment raided the Jewish community headquarters, showing an interest in the safe and asking who the chairman was. The janitor told them it was Adam Czerniaków. On the same day, Czerniaków was driven to the building occupied by the staff of the Einsatzgruppe and told to co-opt twenty-four men to serve on the council and to assume its leadership. For the next few days, Czerniaków made lists and drafted organization charts. The Einsatzgruppe reported back that it had "secured the Jewish community together with president and secretary, just like the museum."

The era of civil administration began at the end of October. There were two kinds of administrative structures, one in territories incorporated into the Reich, the other in the so-called Generalgouvernement. In the incorporated areas, administrative offices were modeled on those of the Reich itself. Two new *Reichsgaue* had been carved out of the conquered incorporated territory: Danzig–West Prussia and the Wartheland. A *Reichsgau* was a territorial unit that combined the features of a Prussian province (or non-Prussian *Land*) and a party district *(Gau)*. The chief of this territorial unit was a regional Reich official *(Reichsstatthalter)*, who was at the same time a regional party official *(Gauleiter)*.

The Reichsstatthalter and Gauleiter of Danzig–West Prussia was a man called Forster. Inasmuch as Forster had already been the Gauleiter of the "Free City" of Danzig, the appointment resulted in a widening of his functions. The Reichsstatthalter and Gauleiter of the Wartheland, Greiser, had previously been the president of the Danzig senate. In that office he had distinguished himself by introducing the whole gamut of anti-Jewish legislation long before the arrival of German troops. The "Free City" had enacted a Law for Blood and Honor, decrees for the removal of Jewish doctors and lawyers, and a systematic Aryanization program. All but a remnant of Danzig's 10,000 Jews had emigrated before the war. After Danzig had been overrun, Senatspräsident Greiser, who was out of a job, was shifted south to become the chief executive of the Wartheland. Unlike his colleague Forster, who had only some tens of thousands of Jews, Greiser had several hundred thousand. His role in the concentration, the deportations, and even the killing operations therefore became crucial.

In addition to the two Reichsgaue, the incorporated territory contained also two smaller units that were parceled out to neighboring Reich provinces. The province of East Prussia annexed some territory in this process, and Silesia became Great Silesia. However, Great Silesia was a cumbersome administrative unit. Thus in January 1941 the Grossgau was divided into two Gaue: Lower Silesia (seat, Breslau), which contained only old German territory and was governed by Oberpräsident and Gauleiter Karl Hanke, and Upper Silesia (seat, Katowice), which consisted mostly of incorporated territory and which was placed under Oberpräsident and Gauleiter Fritz Bracht.

Counterclockwise, the new administrative units, with their chief executives and the number of Polish Jews under their jurisdiction, were therefore as follows:

Danzig–West Prussia (Forster)	Expulsions (no ghettos)
East Prussia (Koch)	30,000 to 40,000
Wartheland (Greiser)	ca. 400,000
Upper Silesia (Bracht)	100,000

East and south of the incorporated territories, the Germans created a new type of territorial administration, first known as the "General Government in Poland" and later referred to simply as the "General Government" (Generalgouvernement). This region held approximately 1,400,000 Jews. The principal difference between the incorporated areas and the Generalgouvernement was the degree of centralization in the bureaucratic machinery. The Reichsstatthalter was primarily a coordinator. Thus the regional offices of the various ministries took all their functional instructions from Berlin and were subject only to territorial orders from the Reichsstatthalter or Oberpräsident.

Generalgouverneur Hans Frank did not have ministerial offices. He

MAP 1
POLAND UNDER GERMAN OCCUPATION

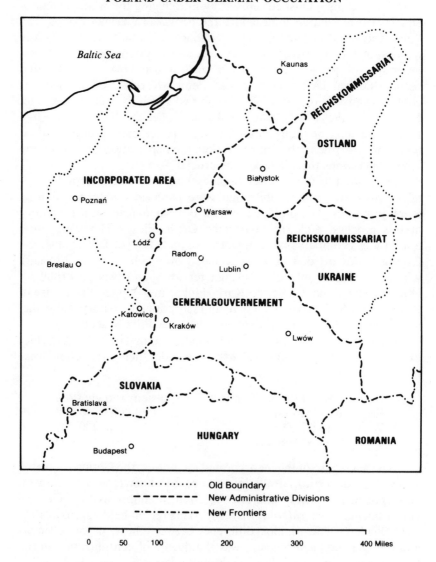

Baltic Sea

Kaunas

REICHSKOMMISSARIAT

OSTLAND

INCORPORATED AREA

Poznań

Białystok

Warsaw

Łódź

REICHSKOMMISSARIAT

Radom

Breslau

Lublin

UKRAINE

GENERALGOUVERNEMENT

Katowice

Kraków

Lwów

SLOVAKIA

Bratislava

HUNGARY

ROMANIA

Budapest

··············· Old Boundary
— — — — — New Administrative Divisions
—··—··—··— New Frontiers

| 0 | 50 | 100 | 200 | 300 | 400 Miles |

had main divisions which were responsible only to him. Frank as Generalgouverneur had more authority than a Reichsstatthalter or an Oberpräsident. He also had more prestige, for he was a Reichsminister without portfolio, a Reichsleiter of the party, the president of the German Academy of Law—in short, a top Nazi in every respect. When Frank came to Poland, he brought with him a retinue of party dignitaries who occupied some of his main divisions.

The regional network of the Generalgouvernement administration closely paralleled the regional machinery in the Reich, but the titles varied somewhat. The Gouverneur was originally called *Distriktchef,* but the new title was conferred as a boost to morale. There were four Gouverneure in Poland in 1939. After the outbreak of war with Russia, the German army overran Galicia, and this area became the fifth district of the Generalgouvernement (in August 1941). It may be noted that, as a rule, the Gouverneur was a party man, but his administrative deputy was a civil servant. The Generalgouvernement administration combined party initiative on the top with bureaucratic thoroughness on the bottom.

Generalgouverneur Hans Frank was a moody autocrat who displayed sentimentality and brutality. He was a jurist who often used the eloquent and precise language of the law, but he was also a party man who could address the mob in the language of the street. In his castle in Kraków, Frank behaved like a cultured ruler who entertained the guests by playing Chopin's piano music. In the conference room, however, he was one of the principal architects of the destruction process in Poland. He was powerful but vain. The party treasurer, Schwarz, once referred to him as "*König* Frank," which means "King Frank" or "the royal Frank."

The Generalgouverneur was an uneasy king. He did not fear the Poles and much less the Jews, but he fought a desperate battle with certain personalities in Berlin who wanted to rob him of his authority and his power. Frank never tired of pointing out that he was an absolute dictator responsible only to Hitler, that the Generalgouvernment was his private preserve, and that no one was permitted to do anything in this preserve unless he took orders from the castle in Kraków. "As you know," he said, "I am a fanatic of the unity of administration." "Unity of administration" meant that no one holding an office in the Generalgouvernement was supposed to take orders from anyone but Frank. The attempt by Berlin agencies to give instructions to offices in the Generalgouvernement Frank called *hineinregieren* (to "reign into" his domain). He did not tolerate that. But the unity of administration was actually a fiction, at least so far as three agencies were concerned.

The first exception was the army. Frank had no authority over the troops. The authority was held exclusively by a general who was called, successively, *Oberbefehlshaber Ost* (Generaloberst Blaskowitz), *Militärbefehlshaber im Generalgouvernement* (General der Kavalleri Kurt Freiherr von Gienanth), and, ultimately, *Wehrkreisbefehlshaber im Generalgouvernement* (Gienanth and General der Infanterie Haenicke). The army controlled not only troops but also war production, which was in the hands of the *Rüstungsinspektion,* or Armament Inspectorate (Generalleutnant Schindler). Gienanth and Schindler had subordinate but not unimportant functions in the destruction process.

The second exception to Frank's unity of administration was the railway system. Although Frank had a Main Division Railway under the direction of Präsident Gerteis, that official was also the Generaldirektor of the *Ostbahn,* which in turn was run by the *Reichsbahn.* The Ostbahn operated the confiscated Polish State Railways in the Generalgouvernement, and its key personnel consisted of 9,000 Germans. However, the railway had taken over, in addition to the Polish equipment, about 40,000 railway employees. By the end of 1943 the Ostbahn was still run by 9,000 Germans, but by that time it employed 145,000 Poles plus a few thousand Ukrainians. These statistics are not without significance, because the railway administration was to play a crucial role in the concentrations, and a decisive one in the deportations.

The third and most important exception to Frank's absolute authority was the SS and Police, the apparatus of Heinrich Himmler. What was the Himmler apparatus and how did it assert its authority in the Generalgouvernement?

Himmler, the son of a professor and rector of a *Gymnasium,* had barely missed combat in World War I and had turned briefly to agronomy thereafter. His diary, which he kept as an adolescent and as a young man, reveals a normal bourgeois childhood, an early concern with what was proper, and habits of meticulousness with a hint of pedantry. Conservative, conventional, and patriotic, he read fairly widely and kept a list of the books he read. Comparatively little in this literature was anti-Semitic, and from the diary it would seem that Himmler developed any anti-Jewish notions very slowly. Hungry for power, he joined the Nazi movement while still in his early twenties and took over its formation of bodyguards: the *Schutzstaffel,* or SS. The attributes of his youth were still evident in his wartime leadership of the SS and Police. He was forever on the lookout for corruption, especially in the ranks of his rivals. As he expanded his power base in various directions, he became involved in all manner of things. His interests encompassed foreign affairs, internal administration, armament production, the resettlement of populations, the conduct of the war, and, of course, the destruction of the Jews. He could talk about these subjects at great length, and he often held his audience for three hours at a stretch. (It may be added that the audience consisted of his own SS generals.) Above all, Himmler's power rested on his independence. This is a fact of utmost importance. Himmler was not part of any hierarchy, but he had his foothold everywhere. In the machinery of destruction he is, perforce, placed between two hierarchies: the ministerial bureaucracy and the party. Himmler received most of his funds from the Finance Ministry and recruited most of his men from the party. Both fiscally and in its personnel structure, the SS and Police was consequently a civil service–party amalgamation.

The SS and Police operated centrally through main offices, the chiefs of which were directly responsible to Himmler, and regionally through Higher SS and Police Leaders *(Höhere SS- und Polizeiführer),* who also were answerable to him directly.

The central organization consisted of twelve main offices. The police components of this machinery are to be found in the *RSHA* and in the *Hauptamt Ordnungspolizei,* the one a relatively small organization in which the Gestapo was the predominant element, the other an old institution on the German scene.

RSHA

Sicherheitspolizei (Security Police)	
Gestapo	ca. 40,000 to 45,000
Kripo (Criminal Police)	ca. 15,000
Sicherheitsdienst (Security Service, originally the party's intelligence arm)	A few thousand

Ordnungspolizei

Einzeldienst (stationary)	ca. 250,000 (including reservists)
Urban: *Schutzpolizei* Rural: *Gendarmerie*	
Truppenverbände (units)	ca. 50,000 (including reservists)

The regional network of the main offices was topped by more than thirty Higher SS and Police Leaders. (The number varied from time to time.) The five with jurisdiction in Poland were:

Generalgouvernement, Krüger (Koppe)
Danzig–West Prussia, Hildebrandt
Wartheland, Koppe
East Prussia, Rediess (Sporrenberg)
Silesia, Schmauser

The regional machinery of the main offices was coordinated by the Higher SS and Police Leaders.

We shall be concerned primarily with the regional machinery of two main offices: the Main Office Order Police and the Reich Security Main Office (RSHA). These two main offices had three types of regional machinery: one in the Reich, another in occupied territories, the third in areas undergoing invasion (see Table 6).

It should be noted that the mobile units of the Order Police were permanent formations that could be shifted from one country to another. The Generalgouvernement was in fact garrisoned by such units, numbering more than 10,000, under a BdO. As a matter of functional jurisdiction, the Order Police asserted control over regular indigenous police left or reorganized in occupied territories. In the Generalgouvernement, Polish police (and after the attack on the USSR, also Ukrainian police in the Galician area) totaled over 16,000. The Security Police was stretched thin in occupied Europe. Its mobile units *(Einsatzgruppen),* formed anew for every deployment in an invaded area, were basically improvised and temporary, while its stationary personnel always remained sparse. In the Generalgouvernement, there were barely 2,000 men. Any special indigenous police organs under Security Police supervision, such as native Criminal Police offices, were comparatively small.

In the Generalgouvernement, the key police officials (in succession) were:

BdO: Becker, Riege, Winkler, Becker, Grünwald, Höring
BdS: Streckenbach, Schöngarth, Bierkamp

The SS and Police organization was centralized not only at the

T A B L E 6
REGIONAL MACHINERY OF THE ORDER POLICE AND RSHA

	Reich	*Occupied Territory*	*Invaded Areas*
Order Police	*Inspekteur der Ordnungspolizei* (IdO) (Inspector of Order Police)	*Befehlshaber der Ordnungspolizei* (BdO) (Commander of Order Police)	*Truppenverbände* (troop units) organized in police regiments and police battalions
RSHA	*Inspekteur der Sicherheitspolizei und des Sicherheitsdienstes* (IdS) (Inspector of Security Police and Security Service)	*Befehlshaber der Sicherheitspolizei und des Sicherheitsdienstes* (BdS) (Commander of Security Police and Security Service)	Mobile units organized in Einsatzgruppen (battalion size) and Einsatzkommandos (company size)

Generalgouverneur level but also under the Gouverneure. The five SS and Police Leaders (in succession) were:

Kraków: Zech, Schedler, Scherner, Their
Lublin: Globocnik, Sporrenberg
Radom: Katzmann, Oberg, Böttcher
Warsaw: Moder, Wigand, von Sammern, Stroop, Kutschera, Geibel
Galicia: Oberg, Katzmann, Diehm

Each SS and Police Leader disposed over a *Kommandeur der Ordnungspolizei* (KdO) and a *Kommandeur der Sicherheitspolizei und des Sicherheitsdienstes* (KdS).

Frank imagined himself in front of Krüger as a kind of supreme territorial chief. To make sure of such a relationship, Frank had in fact appointed Krüger as his Staatssekretär for Security. The new title was intended not as an honor but as a device to ensure that Krüger would take orders from Frank. Himmler, of course, regarded such a relationship as an absurdity. Just as Frank was a "fanatic" of territorial centralization, Himmler was a fanatic of functional centralization. From *his* men Himmler demanded 100 percent accountability to himself.

Thus from the very beginning Frank and Himmler were enemies. It is not accidental that this friction should find its first target in the Jews, for the Himmler apparatus claimed primary authority in Jewish matters throughout Poland, and that was a big claim. We can understand the basis for this assertion of jurisdiction if we examine the closing stages of the concentration process in the Reich-Protektorat area. In the enforcement of movement restrictions and identification measures, and particularly in the direction of Jewish administrative machinery, the SS and Police emerged gradually as the most important control mechanism. As the destruction process proceeded to its more drastic phases, it began to take on more and more the characteristics of a police operation. Movement control, roundups, concentration camps—all these are police functions.

In the Reich-Protektorat area the rise of the SS and Police was imperceptible. The increasing importance of the Himmler apparatus in the home area grew out of the natural development of the destruction process. In Poland, however, the destruction process was introduced in its concentration stage. The immediate entry of the SS and Police on a very high level of policy formation was therefore conspicuous, and troublesome. In fact, we have noted that Security Police Chief Heydrich issued his ghettoization order on September 21, 1939, *before* the civil administration had a chance to organize itself. This means that in Jewish matters Himmler was not only independent of but ahead of Frank. The destruction process in Poland was thus to be carried out by these two men. It is characteristic that, as enemies and rivals, Himmler and Frank competed only in ruthlessness. The competition did not benefit the Jews; it helped to destroy them.

GHETTO FORMATION

From the fall of 1939 to the fall of 1941, three expulsion movements had taken place from west to east: (1) Jews (and Poles) from the incorporated territories of the Generalgouvernement; (2) Jews (and Gypsies) from the Reich-Protektorat area to the Generalgouvernement; (3) Jews (and Gypsies) from the Reich-Protektorat area to the incorporated territories. These movements are significant not so much for their numerical extent as for their psychological mainsprings. They are evidence of the tensions that then convulsed the entire bureaucracy. The period 1939–41 was a time of transition from the forced emigration program to the "Final Solution" policy. At the height of this transition phase, transports were pushed from west to east in efforts to arrive at "intermediary" solutions. In the Generalgouvernement the nervousness was greatest because 1,500,000 Jews were already in the area and there was no possibility of pushing them farther east.

If the expulsions were regarded as temporary measures toward intermediary goals, the second part of the Heydrich program, which provided for the concentration of the Jews in closed ghettos, was intended to be no more than a makeshift device in preparation for the ultimate mass emigration of the victims. In the incorporated territories the administration looked forward only to the expulsion of its Jews to the Generalgouvernement, and the Generalgouverneur was waiting only for a "victory" that would make possible the forced relocation of all his Jews to the African colony of Madagascar. We can understand, therefore, in what spirit this ghettoization was approached. During the first six months there was little planning and much confusion. The administrative preliminaries were finished quickly enough, but the actual formation of the ghettos was tardy and slow. Thus the walls around the giant ghetto of Warsaw were not closed until the autumn of 1940. The Lublin ghetto was not established until April 1941.

The preliminary steps of the ghettoization process consisted of marking, movement restrictions, and the creation of Jewish control organs. Inasmuch as these measures were being aimed at "Jews," the term had to be defined. Characteristically, not much initial thought was being given in the Generalgouvernement to the feelings or interests of the Polish community in matters of categorization. In December 1939, Stadtkommissar Drechsel of Petrikau (Piotrków Trybunalski) decided that all persons with a Jewish parent were Jews. During the following spring the newly appointed specialist in Jewish affairs in the Generalgouvernement's Interior Division, Gottong, proposed a definition that would have included not only all the half-Jews but also the non-Jewish partners in undissolved mixed marriages. Finally, in July 1940 the Nuremberg principle was introduced into the Generalgouvernement by decree. By then, the process of concentration was already well under way.

As early as the beginning of November 1939, Frank issued instructions that all "Jews and Jewesses" who had reached the age of twelve be forced to wear a white armband with a blue Jewish star. His order was carried out by the decree of November 23, 1939. In the incorporated territories a few Regierungspräsidenten imposed markings of their own. For the sake of uniformity, Reichsstatthalter Greiser of the Wartheland ordered that all Jews in his Reichsgau wear a four-inch yellow star sewed on the front and back of their clothes. The Jews took to the stars immediately. In Warsaw, for example, the sale of armbands became a regular business. There were ordinary armbands of cloth and fancy plastic armbands that were washable.

In conjunction with the marking decrees, the Jews were forbidden to move freely. Under the Generalgouvernement decree of December 11, 1939, signed by the Higher SS and Police Leader Krüger, Jews were forbidden to change residence, except within the locality, and they were forbidden to enter the streets between 9 P.M. and 5 A.M. Under the decree of January 26, 1940, the Jews were prohibited also from using the railways, except for authorized trips.

The most important concentration measure prior to the formation of the ghettos was the establishment of Jewish councils *(Judenräte)*. According to the Generalgouvernement decree of November 28, 1939, every Jewish community with a population of up to 10,000 had to elect a Judenrat of twelve members, and every community with more than 10,000 people had to choose twenty-four. The decree was published after many of the councils had already been established, but its issuance signified an assertion of civil jurisdiction over the councils and a confirmation of their character as public institutions.

In Poland, as in the Reich, the Judenräte were filled with prewar Jewish leaders, that is to say, men who were holdovers from Jewish community councils that had existed in the Polish republic, or who had served on municipal councils as representatives of Jewish political parties, or who had held posts in Jewish religious and philanthropic organizations. As a rule, the prewar council chairman (or, in the event of his unavailability, his deputy or some other willing council member) would be summoned by an Einsatzgruppen officer or a functionary of the new civil administration and told to form a Judenrat. Often the rapid selection of the membership resulted in many retentions and few additions. In Warsaw and Lublin, for example, most of the remaining old members were renamed, and new appointments were made primarily in order to assemble the required twenty-four men. If there was a subtle shift in the traditional alignment of leaders, it manifested itself in the greater presence of men who could speak German and in fewer inclusions of Orthodox rabbis, whose garb or speech might have been provocative to the Germans, or of socialists, whose past activities might have proved dangerous.

Radically different from the old days were the circumstances surrounding the newly installed Judenräte. However eager some of the Judenrat members might have been for public recognition before the occupation, now they felt anxieties as they thought about the unknowns. One veteran Jewish politician chosen to serve in the Warsaw Judenrat recalls the day when Adam Czerniaków (a chemical engineer by training) met with several of the new appointees in his office and showed them where he was keeping a key to a drawer of his desk, in which he had placed a bottle contining twenty-four cyanide pills.

Before the war, these Jewish leaders had been concerned with synagogues, religious schools, cemeteries, orphanages, and hospitals. From now on, their activities were going to be supplemented by another, quite different function: the transmission of German directives and orders to the Jewish population, the use of Jewish police to enforce German will, the deliverance of Jewish property, Jewish labor, and Jewish lives to the German enemy. The Jewish councils, in the exercise of their historic function, continued until the end to make desperate attempts to alleviate the suffering and to stop the mass dying in the ghettos. But, at the same time, the councils responded to German demands with automatic compliance and invoked German authority to compel the community's obedience. Thus the Jewish leadership both saved and destroyed its people, saving some Jews and destroying others, saving the Jews at one moment and destroying them in the next. Some leaders refused to keep this power, others became intoxicated with it.

As time passed, the Jewish councils became increasingly impotent in their efforts to cope with the welfare portion of their task, but they made themselves felt all the more in their implementation of Nazi decrees. With the growth of the destructive function of the Judenräte, many Jewish leaders felt an almost irresistible urge to look like their German masters. In March 1940 a Nazi observer in Kraków was struck by the contrast between poverty and filth in the Jewish quarter and the businesslike luxury of the Jewish community headquarters, which was filled with beautiful charts, comfortable leather chairs, and heavy carpets. In Warsaw the Jewish oligarchy took to wearing boots. In Łódź the ghetto "dictator," Rumkowski, printed postage stamps bearing his likeness and made speeches that contained expressions such as "my children," "my factories," and "my Jews." From the inside, then, it seemed already quite clear that the Jewish leaders had become rulers, reigning and disposing over the ghetto community with a finality that was absolute. On the outside, however, it was not yet clear to whom these absolute rulers actually belonged.

Under the Generalgouvernement decree of November 28, 1939, the Judenräte were placed under the *Stadthauptmänner* (in the cities) and the *Kreishauptmänner* (in the country districts). Similarly, in the incorporated territories the Judenräte were responsible to the Bürgermeister in the cities and to the Landräte in the country (see Table 7).

Under the decree of November 28, the authority of the regional offices over the Judenräte was unlimited. The members of a Judenrat were held personally responsible for the execution of all instructions. In fact, the Jewish leaders were so fearful and tremulous in the presence of their German overlords that the Nazi officers merely had to signal their desire. As Frank pointed out in a moment of satisfaction and complacency: "The Jews step forward and receive orders." But this arrangement did not remain unchallenged.

On May 30, 1940, at a meeting in Kraków, the SS and Police made a bid for power over the Judenräte. Opening the attack, the commander of the Security Police and Security Service units in the Generalgouvernement, Brigadeführer Streckenbach, informed his civilian colleagues

T A B L E 7
GERMAN CONTROLS OVER JEWISH COUNCILS

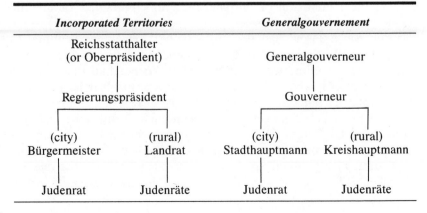

Incorporated Territories		Generalgouvernement	
Reichsstatthalter (or Oberpräsident)		Generalgouverneur	
Regierungspräsident		Gouverneur	
(city) Bürgermeister	(rural) Landrat	(city) Stadthauptmann	(rural) Kreishauptmann
Judenrat	Judenräte	Judenrat	Judenräte

that the Security Police were "very interested" in the Jewish question. That was why, he said, the Jewish councils had been created. Now, he had to admit that local authorities, by close supervision of the councils' activities, had gained something of an insight into Jewish methods. But, as a result of this arrangement, the Security Police had been partly edged out, while all sorts of agencies had stepped into the picture. For example, in the matter of labor procurement everyone was planlessly approaching the Judenräte: the Kreishauptmann, the Gouverneur, the Stadthauptmann, or possibly even the Sicherheitspolizei (the Security Police). If Streckenbach recommended his Security Police, he did so for "functional reasons." Sooner or later, he said, all questions pertaining to Jewish matters would have to be referred to the Security Police, especially if the contemplated action required "executive enforcement." Experience had shown, furthermore, that only the Security Police had a long-range view of conditions affecting Jewry. All this did not mean in the least that the Security Police desired to skim off the cream, so to speak. The Security Police were not interested in Jewish property; they were receiving all their money from Germany and did not desire to enrich themselves. Streckenbach would therefore propose that the Jewish councils "and thereby Jewry as a whole" be placed under the supervision of the Security Police and that all demands upon Jewry be handled by the Security Police. If the Jewish communities were to be further exploited as much as they already had been, then one day the Generalgouvernement would have to support millions of Jews. After all, the Jews were very poor; there were no rich Jews in the Generalgouvernement, only a "Jew proletariat." He would therefore welcome the transfer of power to the Security Police. To be sure, the Security Police were by no means eager to shoulder this additional burden, but experience had shown that the present arrangement was not "functional."

At the conclusion of the speech, Frank remained silent. The Gouverneur of Lublin, Zörner, gave an account of conditions in his district. Since Frank had not spoken, the Gouverneur ventured to suggest that the Security Police could not handle the Judenräte because of insufficient numerical strength. After Zörner had finished, the Gouverneur of Kraków, Wächter, made a speech in which he alluded to Streckenbach's remarks by pointing out that in Jewish matters the civil administration could not get along without the Security Police and that, conversely, the Security Police could not act without the civil apparatus. Cautiously Wächter suggested that perhaps the two bodies could cooperate. Finally, Frank spoke up. In terse legal language he rejected Streckenbach's suggestions. "The police," he said, "are the armed force of the Reich government for the maintenance of order in the interior. . . . The police have no purpose in themselves."

The opening move by the police had failed. Yet the challenge had been made, and for the next few years the struggle over the Jews was to continue unabated. Ultimately the police emerged victorious, but their prize was a heap of corpses.

The three preliminary steps—marking, movement restrictions, and the establishment of Jewish control machinery—were taken in the very first few months of civil rule. But then a full year passed before the actual formation of the ghettos began in earnest. Ghetto formation, that is to say, the creation of closed Jewish districts, was a decentralized process. The initiative in each city and town was taken by the competent Kreishauptmann or Stadthauptmann and, in the case of major ghettos only, by a Gouverneur or by Frank himself.

Military headquarters (the *Oberfeldkommandantur,* or OFK) in the Warsaw district complained that, because each Kreishauptmann had been allowed to decide the manner of gathering up his Jews, the migration, rather than presenting a uniform picture, created an impression of constant movements this way and that. One might add that in cities, uniform planning was completely out of the question, if only because of complex population distributions, intertwined economic activities, and intricate traffic problems.

The earliest ghettos appeared in the incorporated territories during the winter of 1939–40, and the first major ghetto was established in the city of Łódź in April 1940. During the following spring the ghetto-formation process spread slowly to the Generalgouvernement. The Warsaw ghetto was created in October 1940; the smaller ghettos in the Warsaw district were formed in the beginning of 1941. For the Jews remaining in the city of Kraków, a ghetto was established in March 1941. The Lublin ghetto was formed in April 1941. The double ghetto of Radom, shaped into two separate districts, was finished that same month. The ghettos of Częstochowa and Kielce in the Radom district also came into existence at that time. In August 1941 the Generalgouvernement acquired its fifth district, Galicia, an area that the German army had wrested from Soviet occupation. The Galician capital, Lwów (Lemberg), became the site of Poland's third-largest ghetto in December 1941. The ghetto-formation process in the Generalgouvernement was, on the whole, completed by the end of that year. Only a few ghettos remained to be set up in 1942.

Although the creation of the closed districts did not proceed from any order or basic plan, the procedure was remarkably similar in all cities. This should hardly be surprising, for the problems of ghetto formation were largely the same everywhere. Let us look at the first major ghetto-forming operation, which was the prototype of all subsequent operations: the establishment of the Łódź ghetto.

On December 10, 1939, the Regierungspräsident in Kalisz, Uebelhoer, appointed a "working staff" to make preparations for the formation of the ghetto. Uebelhoer himself took over the chairmanship. He appointed his representative in Łódź, Oberregierungsrat Dr. Moser, as deputy. The working staff also included members of the party, the offices of the city, the Order Police, the Security Police, the Death's-Head Formation of the SS, the Łódź Chamber of Industry and Commerce, and the Financial Office in Łódź. The preparations were to be made in secret; the moving was to be sudden and precise. This secrecy was needed in order to assure the hurried abandonment of a lot of Jewish property, which could then be conveniently confiscated.

Uebelhoer did not look upon the ghetto as a permanent institution. "The creation of the ghetto," he said in his order, "is, of course, only a transition measure. I shall determine at what time and with what means the ghetto—and thereby also the city of Łódź—will be cleansed of Jews. In the end, at any rate, we must burn out this bubonic plague."

The working staff selected a slum quarter, the Bałuty area, as the ghetto site. The district already contained 62,000 Jews, but more than 100,000 Jews who lived in other parts of the city and its suburbs had to be moved in. On February 8, 1940, the Polizeipräsident of Łódź, Brigadeführer Schäfer, issued his sudden and precise orders. Poles and ethnic Germans had to leave the ghetto site by February 29. The Jews had to move into the ghetto in batches. Every few days the Polizeipräsident published a moving schedule affecting a certain quarter of the city. All Jews living in that quarter had to move into the ghetto within the time allotted. The first batch had to vacate its apartments between February 12 and February 17, the last moved in on April 30. Ten days later, on May 10, Polizeipräsident Schäfer issued the order that closed off the ghetto population from the rest of the world. "Jews," he ordered, "must not leave the ghetto, as a matter of principle. This prohibition applies also to the Eldest of the Jews [Rumkowski] and to the chiefs of the Jewish police. . . . Germans and Poles," he continued, "must not enter the ghetto as a matter of principle." Entry permits could be issued only by the Polizeipräsident. Even within the ghetto, Jews were not allowed freedom of movement; from 7 P.M. to 7 A.M. they were not permitted to be on the streets.

After the movements had been completed, the Germans threw a fence around the ghetto. The fence was manned by a detachment of the Order Police. The more intriguing job of secret police work was entrusted to the Security Police. This organization consisted of two branches: State Police (Gestapo) and Criminal Police (Kripo). The State Police, as its title implies, concerned itself with enemies of the state. Since the Jews were enemies par excellence, the State Police established an office within the ghetto. The Criminal Police was competent in the handling of common crimes. A Criminal Police detachment of twenty men was consequently attached to the Order Police that guarded the ghetto. The function of the detachment was to prevent smuggling, but the arrangement irked the Criminal Police. Like their colleagues of the Gestapo, the Criminal Police men wanted to be *inside* the ghetto. Accordingly, Kriminalinspektor Bracken drafted a memorandum in which he set forth the reason for the urgent necessity of moving his detachment across the fence. "In the ghetto," he said "live, at any rate, about 250,000 Jews, all of whom have more or less criminal tendencies." Hence the necessity for "constant supervision" by officials of the Criminal Police. The detachment moved in.

As Regierungspräsident Uebelhoer had predicted, the ghetto was a transitional measure, but the transition did not lead to emigration. It led to annihilation. The inmates of the Łódź ghetto either died there or were deported to a killing center. The liquidation of the ghetto took a very long time. When it was finally broken up in August 1944, it had existed for four years and four months. This record was unequaled by any ghetto in Nazi Europe.

Across the border from the incorporated territories, in the General-gouvernement, three specific arguments were made for the formation of ghettos. One was put forth by German physicians, who were convinced that the Jewish population was spreading typhus. Another was the allegation that Jews, as urban residents and as holders of ration cards that—in the words of the Food and Agriculture chief of the Warsaw district—entitled them for practical purposes only to bread, were bidding for unrationed foods and creating a black market in rationed items. The third was the claim that suitable apartment space was unavailable to German officials and members of the armed forces. The answer each time appeared to be ghettoization. To be sure, when the ghettos were in place, spotted fever was rising in the congested Jewish houses, smuggling by Jews was increasing to stave off starvation, and apartments were still needed by Germans. In fact, the three principal explanations for creating the ghettos were going to be revived at a later time as reasons for dissolving them and for removing their Jewish inhabitants altogether.

Ghetto formation was not an easy undertaking from the start. In the case of Warsaw, where the process took a year, the first step was taken early in November 1939, when the military commander established a "quarantine" in an area within the old part of the city, inhabited largely by Jews, from which German soldiers were to be barred. On November 7, Gouverneur Fischer of the Warsaw district proposed that the Warsaw Jews (whose number he estimated at 300,000) be incarcerated in a ghetto, and Frank gave his immediate consent to the proposal. During the winter, Fischer created a Resettlement Division under Waldemar Schön, who was going to have a major role in ghetto planning and who was subsequently deputized to carry out the plan. The first idea, in February, to locate the ghetto on the eastern bank of the Vistula River, was turned down in a meeting on March 8, 1940, on the ground that 80 percent of Warsaw's artisans were Jews and that, since they were indispensable, one could not very well "encircle" them. Doubts were also expressed about supplying a closed ghetto with food. On March 18, 1940, Czerniaków noted cryptically: "A demand that the Community ring the 'ghetto' with wire, put in fenceposts, etc., and later guard it all." The quotation marks around the word *ghetto* refer to the previously established quarantine. By March 29, Czerniaków noted that the ghetto was to be "walled in," and the next day he argued with Stadtkommandant Leist about the "virtual impossibility of building a wall (damaging the water installations, electric and telephone cables, etc.)." Wall building was actually suspended in April, while the Germans were considering a short-lived idea of dumping the Jews in the Lublin district. Schön's Resettlement Division then examined the feasibility of setting up two ghettos, one in a western section (Koło and Wola) and another in the east (Grochów) to minimize any disturbance in the city's economy and traffic flow, but this plan was abandoned after word of the Madagascar project had reached Warsaw. Czerniaków on July 16, noted a report to the effect that the ghetto was not going to be formed after all. In August 1940, however, Subdivision Health of the Generalgouvernement's Interior Division, pointing to increased troop concentrations in the area, demanded the formation of ghettos in the district. The nonmedical officials of the Interior Division, acquiescing, argued only against sealing the ghettos heremetically, lest they could not survive economically. On September 6, 1940, Obermedizinalrat Dr. Walbaum, citing statistics of typhus among Jews, insisted in a *ceterum censeo* speech on their incarceration in a closed ghetto as a health-political measure. Six days later Frank announced during a conference of main division chiefs that 500,000 Jews in the city were posing a threat to the whole population and that they could no longer be allowed to "roam around." Czerniaków, who had still harbored hopes for an "open" ghetto that would have combined compulsory residence with freedom of movement, knew of this decision by September 25. On that day he wrote "ghetto" without any doubt about its character.

The "Jewish district" of Warsaw was established over a period of six weeks during October and November 1940, in an area covering about two-thirds of the old quarantine. In the course of the move, 113,000 Poles left the ghetto site and 138,000 Jews took their place. T-shaped, the ghetto was narrowest at a point where an "Aryan" wedge separated the larger, northern portion from the smaller southern one. The borders, drawn with a view to utilizing existing fire walls and minimizing the security problem, were not final. During September 1941, in a spirit of creeping annexationism, some German officials considered severing the southern part of the ghetto. At this point, an unusual man in the German administration made an unusual move. He was the chief physician of the German city apparatus, Dr. Wilhelm Hagen. In a blunt letter to the Stadthauptmann, he predicted a worsening of the typhus epidemic and called the proposed plan "insanity." The southern ghetto remained, but more blocks were chopped off, more wall building was ordered, and, as the only link between the two ghetto sections, there was now a foot bridge over what had become an "Aryan" corridor.

The Warsaw ghetto was never open to unhindered traffic, but at the beginning there were twenty-eight points for exit and entry, used by about 53,000 persons with passes. The Warsaw district health chief, Dr. Lambrecht, objected to the number of permits, arguing that they defeated the entire purpose of the ghetto. The gates were then reduced to fifteen. The Warsaw police regiment (Lt. Col. Jarke) was responsible for guarding the ghetto. This duty was carried out by a company of the 304th Battalion (from the second half of 1941, the 60th), augmented by Polish police and the Jewish police (*Ordnungsdienst,* or Order Service). At each gate, one man from each of these services might have been seen, but inside there were 2,000 men of the Order Service.

After the Warsaw ghetto had been closed, Stadthauptmänner and Kreishauptmänner in all parts of the Generalgouvernement followed suit. In town after town, local officials followed the same three-stage process. They selected the location of the ghetto, issued the sudden movement orders, and sealed off the finished ghetto. There were some variations. A number of small Jewish communities were incarcerated in ghetto towns; that is, whole towns became ghettos. The larger communities were crowded into closed-off city districts, each of which became a city within a city.

As may be seen from the statistics in Table 8, a ghetto was usually a tightly packed slum area without parks, empty lots, or open spaces. In spite of its small size, a ghetto, placed in the middle of a metropolis, invariably created traffic problems. In Warsaw, trolley lines had to be rerouted, In Łódź the city administration had to install a new bus line that skirted the ghetto, while in Lublin, Stadthauptmann Saurmann had

TABLE 8
DENSITIES IN THE GHETTOS OF WARSAW AND ŁÓDŹ

	City of Warsaw, March 1941	"Aryan" Warsaw	Ghetto of Warsaw	Ghetto of Łódź, September 1941
Population	1,365,000	920,000	445,000	144,000
Area (square miles)	54.6	53.3	1.3	1.6
Rooms	284,912	223,617	61,295	25,000
Persons per room	4.8	4.1	7.2	5.8

to build a detour road around the Jewish quarter. Traffic problems also determined to a large extent the method of sealing a ghetto. Only a few cities, such as Warsaw, Kraków, Radom, and Nowy Sącz surrounded their ghettos with massive, medieval-like walls and built-in gates. Some ghettos, such as Łódź, were fenced in only with barbed wire. Still others, including Lublin, could not be sealed at all.

While not every ghetto could be closed completely, no Jew was permitted to remain outside its boundaries. In Łódź, Jews in mixed marriage with their Polish spouses, and Mischlinge of all degrees were pushed into the ghetto. On February 26, 1941, the First Secretary of the Soviet Embassy, Bogdanov, inquired why certain nationals of the Soviet Union were forced to live in certain places. Unterstaatssekretär Wörmann of the Foreign Office replied that the nationals involved were Jews and that Jews of Soviet nationality were receiving the same treatment as Jews of other nationalities.

By the end of 1941 almost all Jews in the incorporated territories and the Generalgouvernement were living in the ghettos. Their incarceration was accompanied by changes in German control machinery and enlargements of the Jewish bureaucracy. In Łódź and Warsaw, new German offices for ghetto supervision came into being.

The Łódź Jewish Council was placed under a "Food and Economic Office Ghetto." Originally this office regulated only economic questions affecting the ghetto. Soon, however, its title was changed to *Gettoverwaltung Litzmannstadt* (Ghetto Administration, Łódź), and with the change of title there was also a change of function. The office took charge of all ghetto affairs. The place of Gettoverwaultung in the local governmental structure is indicated in Table 9.

In Warsaw the administrative changes also took place in stages. Initially the Judenrat was answerable to Einsatzgruppe IV and thereafter it received instructions from the Stadthauptmann. During the process of ghetto formation, control over the council passed into the hands of the Resettlement Division (Schön) of the district administration. Schön formed a Transferstelle (under Palfinger) to regulate the flow of goods to and from the ghetto. By May 1, 1941, a Kommissar for the Jewish district was appointed by Gouverneur Fischer. The office was occupied by a young attorney, Heinz Auerswald, who had previously served as a section chief in the Interior Division for Population and Welfare. Adam Czerniaków was almost twice his age. The Transferstelle was placed under an experienced banker (formerly employed by the Länderbank, Vienna), Max Bischof, who held the position under a contract. The Auerswald-Bischof administration is depicted in Table 10.

Ghettoization generated a far-reaching metamorphosis in the Jewish councils. In their original form, the Judenräte had been fashioned into a link between German agencies and the Jewish population, and their early activities were concentrated on labor recruitment and welfare. In the ghetto each chairman of a Judenrat became, *de facto,* a mayor (Czerniaków received the title as well), and each council had to perform the functions of a city administration. The incipient Jewish bureaucracy, heretofore consisting of small staffs engaged in registration or finance, was now being expanded and diversified to address such urgent problems as housing, health, and public order. The apparatus was swelled with a multitude of functionaries, paid and unpaid, capable and incompetent, honest, and self-serving. Patronage, favoritism, and

TABLE 9
GERMAN CONTROLS OVER THE ŁÓDŹ GHETTO

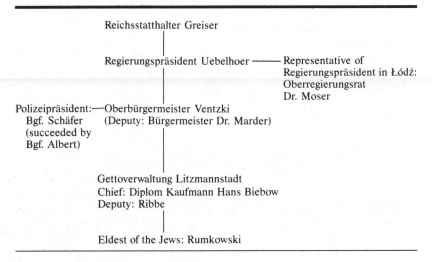

Reichsstatthalter Greiser

Regierungspräsident Uebelhoer ———— Representative of Regierungspräsident in Łódź: Oberregierungsrat Dr. Moser

Polizeipräsident:—Oberbürgermeister Ventzki
Bgf. Schäfer   (Deputy: Bürgermeister Dr. Marder)
(succeeded by
Bgf. Albert)

Gettoverwaltung Litzmannstadt
Chief: Diplom Kaufmann Hans Biebow
Deputy: Ribbe

Eldest of the Jews: Rumkowski

T A B L E   10

GERMAN CONTROLS OVER THE WARSAW GHETTO

Gouverneur Fischer

Kommissar für den jüdischen Wohnbezirk ──────── Transferstelle
Auerswald   Bischof
Deputy: Grassler   Deputy: Rathje

Chairman of the Jewish Council
Czerniaków
Deputy: Lichtenbaum

---

outright corruption became inviting possibilities and soon enough were commonplace.

There were some differences between ghettos, both in the extent of council operations and in the mode of council government. Some ghettos, notably Łódź, maintained shops and industries, whereas others, such as Warsaw, featured private enterprise. Some functioned in a dictatorial manner, and in others responsibilities were shared or divided in various ways.

Measured in its powers to regulate and interfere with the life of the inhabitants, the Jewish bureaucracy of the Łódź ghetto was probably the most totalitarian of all ghetto bureaucracies. The following is a list of the offices operated under the Łódź Judenrat in 1940:

The Eldest of the Jews
Council of Elders with the Eldest of the Jews
Central Bureau *(Zentrale)*
   Central Negotiations Office *(Zentral-Verhandlungsstelle)*
   Correspondence Division *(Präsidialabteilung)*
   Personnel Bureau
   Main Treasury and Bookkeeping
   Information Office
   Cemetery Division
   Rabbinical Office
   Bureau of the Eldest of the Jews for the Children's Colony
Registration and Records
   Registration Office
   Records Office
   Statistical Division
Police Headquarters *(Ordnungsdienst Kommando)*
   Law Division

4 Precincts
2 Reserves (Mobile)
Auxiliary Police (*Hilfsordnungsdienst* or "Hido")
Sanitation Control
Price Enforcement
Special Commando *(Sonderkommando)*
Fire-fighting Division
Main Post Office and Post Office Branch
Control Commission for German and Polish Property in the Ghetto
Housing Division
Finance Division
   Rent Office
   Tax Office
   Executor's Office *(Vollstreckungsstelle)*
   Bank (Main Building and Branch)
   Purchasing Office for Valuables and Clothes
Economy Division
   Real Estate Administration
   Janitor Division
   Chimney Sweeps
   Technical Renovation
   Garbage and Sewage Disposal *(Müll- und Fäkalienabfuhr)*
   Warehouses
   Sales Office for Household Items
Agricultural Division (Main Office and Branch)
School Division
Central Bureau for Labor
   4 Tailors' Divisions
   2 Carpenters' Divisions
   1 Shoemakers' Division
   1 Textile Workers' Division
Public Works Division
   Works Assignment Office
   Construction Office
Supply Division
   Receiving Station
   Central Bureau
   Auditing Office
   Main Depot
      Vegetable Depot
      Coal Depot
      Dairy Depot
      Meat Depot
      Meat Cold Storage Depot
      Cigarette and Tobacco Depot
   Community Bakery
   36 Food Distribution Points

17 Stores for Sale of Milk, Butter, and Foods Purchasable upon
   Doctor's Prescription
14 Butcher Shops
Welfare Division
   Relief Division (Money and Products)
   Nursery
   2 Orphanages
   Home for the Aged
   Invalids' Home
   Collecting Point for Homeless People
   Public Kitchens
   Children's Colony
   Children's Sanatorium
Health Division
   Central Bureau
   4 Hospitals
   4 Dispensaries
   Dental Clinic
   Central Drug Store and 6 Branch Drug Stores
   2 Ambulance Units
   Laboratory
   Laboratory for Bacteriological Examination
   Disinfection Division

The Jewish machinery in Łódź reflected in its very organization the peculiar double role of the ghetto in the destruction process. The survival function of the ghetto is illustrated primarily by the three divisions on the bottom of the list: health, welfare, and supply. The destructive function is recognized most clearly in the Central Bureau, the Registration and Records Office, and, above all, in the police. It is characteristic that the office that was most openly destructive in its function, the police, followed the German model even in its organization. A close look at the structure of the ghetto police reveals that it was divided into a kind of Order Police (complete with precincts, reserves, auxiliaries, and sanitation control) and a kind of Security Police: a price-control force that had criminal functions, and a Sonderkommando that had Gestapo functions. In one respect the Łódź ghetto machine was even more advanced than its Nazi prototype: the Judenrat had no separate justice department: the only legal office in the ghetto was incorporated into its police.

The Warsaw council was organized in a more complex manner. Council deliberations mattered in the Warsaw ghetto, and the regular agendas of council meetings were prepared by commissions, initially composed of council members but eventually including experts who wanted to exercise influence. The administrative departments, whose heads were not necessarily council members, included Order Service, Hospitals, Health, Housing, Labor, Economy, Law, Finance, Social Welfare, Cemeteries, Appeals, Education, Real Property, Vital Statistics, Audit, Contributions, Postal Service, and even Archives. Four important divisions were actually transformed into independent bodies. The Provisioning Division, which dispensed food and coal, became the Provisioning Authority, the Production Division was incorporated as the Jüdische Produktion GmbH, the Trade Division was reorganized as a sales firm for deliveries outside the ghetto (Lieferungsgesellschaft), and the Bank Division was renamed the Genossenschaftsbank für den jüdischen Wohnbezirk.

Police was a special problem. The Order Service of the Warsaw ghetto was the largest Jewish police force in occupied Poland. (At its peak it numbered about two thousand.) Czerniaków, insisting on professionalism especially in this component of the ghetto administration, appointed to some of the top positions people with police experience. Such individuals, especially the chief, former Lieutenant Colonel of Polish Police Szeryński, were converts to Christianity. Given the special role of these people in the operation of the ghetto, Czerniaków did not hear the end of discontent and protest about their employment. Complicating Czerniaków's life was the existence of another Jewish police, similar to the one in the Łódź Ghetto, which was suspected by the Jewish inhabitants of serving under German Security Police auspices. Its official name was "The Control Office for Combatting the Black Market and Profiteering in the Jewish District," but the popular designation, based on the address of its headquarters on 13 Leszno Street, was "The Thirteen." In addition to "The Thirteen," which had about five hundred men, there was a smaller but equally suspect "Ambulance Service." In August 1941, Czerniaków succeeded, with the help of Kommissar Auerswald, in dissolving the troublesome Control Office, which had interfered with the principle of undivided jurisdiction in the offices of Czerniaków and Auerswald alike. In this respect, at least, the struggle of a ghetto leader and that of his German supervisor could be waged on a parallel plane.

GHETTO MAINTENANCE

The ghetto was a captive city-state in which territorial confinement was combined with absolute subjugation to German authority. With the creation of the ghettos, the Jewish community of Poland was no longer an integrated whole. Each ghetto was on its own, thrown into sudden isolation, with a multiplicity of internal problems and a reliance on the outside world for basic sustenance.

Fundamental to the very idea of the ghetto was the sheer segregation of its residents. Personal contacts across the boundary were sharply curtailed or severed altogether, leaving in the main only mechanical channels of communication: some telephone lines, banking connections, and post offices for the dispatch and receipt of letters and parcels. Physically the ghetto inhabitant was henceforth incarcerated. Even in a large ghetto he stood never more than a few minutes' walk from a wall or fence. He still had to wear the star, and at night, during curfew hours, he was forced to remain in his apartment house.

Having brought the ghetto into existence, the Germans took immediate advantage of its machinery and institutions to rid themselves of an administrative burden that had tied up personnel and that could now be transferred to the Jewish community. They could not, however, evade the question of how the ghetto was going to be maintained, how people bereft of enterprises and jobs that had sustained them in the past were going to fend for themselves behind walls in the future.

When Gauleiter Greiser of the Wartheland visited Frank in July 1940, he asserted that his recent establishment of the Łódź ghetto was solely a provisional measure. He could not even conceive of retaining the Jews he had stuffed into the ghetto beyond the winter. It is this experience in Łódź that Generalgouvernement specialists were studying for months before they went ahead with their own ghettoization in the city of Warsaw. Yet, having established the ghetto in November 1940, they debated in two meetings during April 1941 how it was going to be able to pay for food, coal, water, electricity, gas, rent, removals of human waste, and taxes, and how it was going to discharge debts owed to public agencies or Polish creditors.

Gouverneur Fischer of the Warsaw district felt that, whereas in Łódź a mistake had been made when machines and raw materials had been removed from the ghetto site, developments in Warsaw were better than expected. The Jews in the ghetto had supplies, they were working for Polish firms, they were paying their rent, and they had enough food. *Bankdirigent* Paersch disagreed. The Łódź ghetto, he said, was requiring a subsidy of a million reichsmark a month, and the Warsaw ghetto would have to be supported as well. For *Finanzpräsident* Spindler an annual outlay of 70 or 100 million zloty for the Warsaw ghetto was simply "unbearable." The Generalgouvernement's economic chief, Dr. Emmerich, saw the basic issue in the ghetto's balance of payments. The problem would not be solved, he said, by pointing to current stocks of ghetto supplies, because the ghetto had not been created for just one year. One would have to think about a larger time frame and about the relationship over that period between the ghetto and the Polish economy with regard to such questions as payments by Jews of debts to Poles and competition between the ghetto and Polish enterprises for raw materials.

Ministerialdirigent Walter Emmerich then introduced an economist, Dr. Gate, who had studied the Warsaw ghetto as a specialist in the rationalization and planning of production. Dr. Gate offered the following scenario: If 60,000 or 65,000 Jews could be employed in the ghetto under the assumption that daily productivity would be averaging 5 zloty per worker (in terms of an implied formula whereby "productivity" + raw materials + other costs + profits = value of finished product at controlled prices) and if the present contingent of Jews laboring in projects outside the ghetto for seven or eight months a year would continue to work in this manner for prevailing wages, enough money could be earned for about a half-million-zloty-worth of supplies per day, or 93 groszy per person. This figure, he emphasized, was not an estimate of minimum need for survival but an amount based on the projected balance of payments. Moreover, the achievement of even this goal would require an investment by major German firms, and they in turn would need credits in the amount of 30 to 40 million zloty annually. For *Reichsamtsleiter* Schön these ideas were "too theoretical," and when later that month Bischof was being recruited by Fischer for the position of director of the Transferstelle, the question raised by Bischof was whether the aspired economic independence of the Jewish quarter, now that it was closed, could be attained at all.

The pessimists had ample grounds for their doubts. The ghetto population was out of work. The creation of the ghettos was the last and insurmountable act of economic dismemberment that befell a community already weakened in the 1930s by depression and in 1939 by war. Jewish enterprises still functioning after 1939 had rapidly been liquidated. Markets of the remaining factories and artisan shops in the ghetto were severed by the wall. Middlemen, such as the ragpickers in Warsaw, were cut off from suppliers and customers alike. Jobs that had still been held outside the ghetto boundaries were lost. The ghetto economy had to be built from the bottom up.

The hypothetical production discussed by Generalgouvernement economists in conferences was not within reach overnight, and hardly any ghetto had any immediate prospect of supporting itself, even theoretically, by means of exports alone. This was going to be the case regardless of whether all shipments would have to be sent out through official channels or whether some could be directed, for higher prices, to the black market. At the outset the ghetto inhabitants were therefore forced to use their private assets (in the main, leftover past earnings consisting of cash, valuables, furnishings, or clothes) for essential purchases. These resources were finite—once used up or sold, they were gone. Thus the survival of the ghetto was predicated in the first instance on the ability of the organizers of production to replace diminishing personal reserves in time, a precarious proposition for sustaining an export-import balance.

The ghetto was facing not only the necessity of external payments; it had internal problems as well. There were people with a few possessions and there were those without means, some with work and many more who were unemployed. Unredressed, this imbalance had ominous implications for a large part of the ghetto population, but any method of redistribution or equalization was going to be difficult. The charitable effort was inherently limited, and the raising of taxes was confounded, particularly in Warsaw, by the many black-market transactions that, in their very nature, were unrecorded. In general, taxes could be levied only at that point at which money was surfacing in nonillicit payments. Revenue was consequently made up of a mix that typically included most of the following:

Payroll taxes
Head taxes
Taxes on rationed bread
Payments by persons exempted from forced labor
Rental taxes
Cemetery taxes
Postal surcharges
Fees for drugs
Registration fees

In Warsaw, where the bread tax was important, the revenue structure had the appearance of exactions from the poor to keep alive the destitute. For this reason, Czerniaków also attempted to obtain contributions from Jewish entrepreneurs, by strong-arm methods if need be. In the business sector of the ghetto, his tactic gave rise to the complaint that he was ruining the capital market.

The chronic deficiency of funds in ghetto treasuries resulted in such "borrowing" as nonpayment of employees' wages. Given the sheer number of ghetto employees who did not have much to do and whose main reason for clinging to their positions was eligibility for greater food rations and other privileges, much of this free labor was not really labor and not really free. Even so, Czerniaków was concerned that his Order Service was not being paid, for he wanted it to be a professional force.

The Germans on their part understood the limited capacity of the ghetto economy, and they were aware of the role of the councils as stabilizers in a situation of massive, abject poverty. To the extent that German agencies had to maintain a ghetto, they had to reinforce the power of its council to deal with elementary needs, lest it become incapable of carrying out German demands and directives altogether. From time to time, German officials would therefore make "concessions" to the councils, allowing them to borrow sums from sequestered Jewish funds, or considering a rebate to a Jewish charitable organization of social welfare taxes paid by Jews to Polish municipalities that no longer helped the Jewish poor, or supporting requests by the councils to raise new revenues from the Jewish population. When Czerniaków asked for permission to levy a variety of such taxes and fees, the deputy chief of the Resettlement Division, Mohns, backing Czerniaków's proposal, stated that "it lies in the interest of the difficult administration of the Jewish district that the authority of the Jewish Council be upheld and strengthened under all circumstances." This line of reasoning was enunciated even more explicitly by the Warsaw ghetto Kommissar, Auerswald, a few months later. "When deficiencies occur," he wrote, "the Jews direct their resentment against the Jewish administration and not against the German supervision."

Even though these Germans supervisors had a vital interest in assuring a basic orderly life behind the walls, they did not refrain from implementing measures against the Jewish population that seriously weakened the ghetto's viability. The three principal means by which German agencies added to deprivation were (1) confiscatory acts eroding the ghetto's ability to export products through legal or illegal channels, (2) labor exploitation, whereby outside employers could increase their profits at the expense of Jewish wages, and (3) food embargoes, which made it impossible for the ghettos to convert the proceeds of exports into effective purchasing power for the acquisition of bread, thereby forcing many individual Jews to buy black-market food at much higher prices.

The Jewish councils on their part attempted to surmount every reversal, but they were playing a determined game in that the German agencies, which had originally created the problem, were ultimately in control of the solutions. The councils were thus enmeshed in a dilemma from which they could no longer extricate themselves: they could not serve the Jewish people without automatically enforcing the German will. Jewry, without weapons, clung only to hope. "The Jews, said

Auerswald, "are waiting for the end of the war and in the meantime conduct themselves quietly. There has been no sign of any resistance spirit to date."

SICKNESS AND DEATH IN THE GHETTOS

The incarceration of the Jews was an act of total spoliation. The enfeebled ghetto Jews, without significant capital or valuables, had been rendered helpless. The German agencies continued to take what they could—furs, bed sheets, musical instruments—and they encouraged the creation of a Jewish work force that might produce new values for German enrichment. They had to make some shipments of their own, however, if only to maintain the ghetto system and to keep alive its laborers. In the main, they regarded their deliveries of food, coal, or soap as a sacrifice, and they thought about these supplies often enough to conjure up an image of themselves not as willing spoliators of the Jewish community but as unwilling contributors to its welfare. They did not hesitate to reduce the contribution to levels clearly below the bare essentials, and they made these decisions without inquiring into the consequences. Soon enough the effects were clearly visible.

Disease was one manifestation of the constrictions. On October 18, 1941, the director of Subdivision Health in the Radom district, Dr. Waisenegger, noted that typhus was virtually confined to the Jews. The reasons, he said, were insufficient coal and soap, excessive room density resulting in the multiplication of lice, and lack of food lowering resistance to disease *in toto*. In the Warthegau the summer epidemics of 1941 took on such proportions that Bürgermeister and Landräte clamored for the dissolution of the ghettos and the transfer of 100,000 inmates to the overcrowded Łódź ghetto. The chief of the Gettoverwaltung in Łódź, Biebow, vigorously opposed this suggestion and warned that the "frivolous" transfer of such masses of people into his ghetto would be devastating. On July 24, 1941, Regierungspräsident Uebelhoer prohibited the transfer of any sick Jews from the small Warthegau ghettos into Łódź. On August 16, 1941, Uebelhoer ordered drastic measures in the stricken Warthegau ghettos: the victims of the epidemic were to be completely isolated; entire houses were to be evacuated and filled with sick Jews.

The situation in the Warsaw ghetto also deteriorated. The Warsaw epidemics started in the synagogues and other institutional buildings, which housed thousands of homeless people. During the winter of 1941–42, the sewage pipes froze. The toilets could no longer be used, and human excrement was dumped with garbage into the streets. To combat the typhus epidemic the Warsaw Judenrat organized disinfection brigades, subjected people to "steaming action"; set up quarantine stations, hospitalized serious cases, and as a last resort instituted "house blockades," imprisoning in their homes the sick and the healthy alike. The one useful article, serum, was almost unavailable. A single tube of antityphus medicine cost several thousand zloty.

Although typhus was the ghetto disease par excellence, it was not the only one. A Łódź ghetto chronicler, writing early in 1944, saw disease as unending: intestinal typhus in the summer, tuberculosis in the fall, influenza in the winter. His "superficial statistic": about forty percent of the ghetto was ill.

The second rising curve in the ghettos was that of mortality. As ghetto hunger raged unchecked, a primitive struggle for survival began. On March 21, 1942, the Propaganda Division of the Warsaw district reported laconically:

> The death figure in the ghetto still hovers around 5,000 per month. A few days ago, the first case of hunger cannibalism was recorded. In a Jewish family the man and his three children died within a few days. From the flesh of the child who died last—a twelve-year-old boy—the mother ate a piece. To be sure, this could not save her either, and she herself died two days later.

The ghetto Jews were fighting for life with their last ounce of strength. Hungry beggars snatched food from the hands of shoppers. yet, after persistent undernourishment, the victim was no longer able to digest his bread normally. His heart, kidneys, liver, and spleen shrank in size, his weight dropped, and his skin withered. "Active, busy, energetic people," wrote a ghetto physician, "are changed into apathetic, sleepy beings, always in bed, hardly able to get up to eat or go to the toilet. Passage from life to death is slow and gradual, like death from physiological old age. There is nothing violent, no dyspnea, no pain, no obvious changes in breathing or circulation. Vital functions subside simultaneously. Pulse rate and respiratory rate get slower and it becomes more and more difficult to reach the patient's awareness, until life is gone. People fall asleep in bed or on the street and are dead in the morning. They die during physical effort, such as searching for food, and sometimes even with a piece of bread in their hands." Indeed, a common sight in the ghetto was the corpses lying on the sidewalk, covered with newspapers, pending the arrival of cemetery carts. The bodies, said Gouverneur Fischer to Czerniaków, were creating a bad impression.

The Jewish community of Poland was dying. In the last prewar year, 1938, the monthly average death rate of Łódź was 0.09 percent. In 1941, the rate jumped to 0.63 percent, and during the first six months of 1942 it was 1.49. The same pattern, compressed into a single year, may be noted for the Warsaw ghetto, where the monthly death rate during the first half of 1941 was 0.63, and in the second half 1.47. In their rise to this plateau, the two cities were almost alike, even though Łódź was a hermetically closed ghetto, which had its own currency and in which the black market was essentially the product of internal barter, whereas Warsaw was engaged in extensive smuggling "quietly tolerated" by the Germans. The birthrates in both cities were extremely low: Łódź had one birth for every twenty deaths, while in Warsaw at the beginning of 1942 the ratio was 1:45. The implication of these figures is quite clear. A population with a net loss of one percent a month shrinks to less than five percent of its original size in just twenty-four years.

In absolute figures the long lasting Łódź ghetto, with a cumulative population (including new arrivals and births) of about 200,000, had more than 45,000 dead. The Warsaw Ghetto, with around 470,000 inhabitants over the period from the end of 1940 to the end of the mass deportations in September 1942, buried 83,000 people. The two ghettos contained less than a fourth of the Polish Jews, and although there were communities with attrition rates lower than those of Łódź and Warsaw, the impact of ghettoization in any locality was but a matter of time. For the German decision makers, the pace was not fast enough. They could not wait two or three decades, or entrust the task of "solving the Jewish problem" to a future generation. They had to "solve" this problem, one way or another, right then and there.

CHAPTER FOUR

MOBILE KILLING OPERATIONS

W hen the bureaucracy had completed all those measures that comprised the definition of the Jews, the expropriation of their property, and their concentration in ghettos, it had reached a dividing line. Any further step would put an end to Jewish existence in Nazi Europe. In German correspondence the crossing of this threshold was referred to as "the final solution of the Jewish question." The word *final* harbored two connotations. In a narrow sense it signified that the aim of the destruction process had now been clarified. If the concentration stage had been a transition to an unspecified goal, the new "solution" removed all uncertainties and answered all questions. The aim was finalized—it was to be death. But the phrase "Final Solution" also had a deeper, more significant meaning. In Himmler's words, the Jewish problem would never have to be solved again. Definitions, expropriations, and concentrations can be undone. Killings are irreversible. Hence they gave to the destruction process its quality of historical finality.

The annihilation phase consisted of two major operations. The first was launched on June 22, 1941, with the invasion of the USSR. Small units of the SS and Police were dispatched to Soviet territory, where they were to kill all Jewish inhabitants on the spot. Shortly after these mobile killings had begun, a second operation was instituted, in the course of which the Jewish population of central, western, and south-eastern Europe were transported to camps equipped with gassing installations. In essence, the killers in the occupied USSR moved to the victims, whereas outside of this arena the victims were brought to the killers. The two operations constitute an evolution not only chronologically but also in complexity. In the areas wrested from the Soviet Union, the mobile units could fan out with maximum freedom to the farthest points reached by German arms. The deportations, by contrast, were the work of a much larger apparatus that had to deal with a host of constraints and requirements. The effort, as we shall see, was deemed necessary to accomplish the "Final Solution" on a European-wide scale.

PREPARATIONS

The invasion of the Soviet Union and the mobile killings carried out in its wake mark a break with history. This was not an ordinary war for ordinary gain. The battle plans were discussed in the Army High Command as early as July 22, 1940, eleven months before the armies crossed the Soviet border. No ultimatum was to alert the Soviet government to any danger. No peace treaty was envisaged to bring the war to its conclusion. The objectives of the campaign were not limited, and the means with which it was to be fought were not restricted. In unprecedented numbers, a ground force was assembled that was to be engaged in what was soon to be called "total war."

The invading army groups were accompanied by small mechanized killing units of the SS and Police that were tactically subordinated to the field commanders but otherwise free to go about their special business. The mobile killing units operated in the front-line areas under a special arrangement and in a unique partnership with the German army. To understand what made this partnership work, it is necessary to have a closer look at the two participants: the German *Wehrmacht* (Armed Forces) and the Reich Security Main Office of the SS and Police.

The Wehrmacht was one of the four independent hierarchies in the machinery of destruction. Unlike the party, the civil service agencies, and the business enterprises, the armed forces had no major role to play in the preliminary phase of the destruction process. But in the inexorable development of the process, every segment of organized German society was drawn into the destructive work. We may recall that even in 1933 the Wehrmacht was interested in the definition of "Jews." Later the army was affected by the appropriation of Jewish enterprises producing war materials. In Poland the generals narrowly escaped from an entanglement in the concentration process. Now, with the onset of the mobile killing operations, the armed forces found themselves suddenly in the very center of the holocaust.

Broadly speaking, the military authority over civilians increased with the increased distance of the territory from the Reich. In Germany proper, that authority was virtually nonexistent; in the newly invaded areas it was nearly absolute. The forward region, from army group rear areas to the front line, was considered an operational zone. There an administrative body, not part of the armed forces, could operate only under a special arrangement with the Wehrmacht.

The only agency admitted to the forward areas during the Russian campaign was the Reich Security Main Office (the RSHA). It was the agency that, for the first time in modern history, was to conduct a massive killing operation. What sort of an organization was the RSHA?

The RSHA was a creation of Reinhard Heydrich. We have already seen Heydrich in the concentration process within the German and Polish spheres. However, the Heydrich organization did not assume a preeminent place in the machinery of destruction until 1941. That year was crucial for the development of the entire destruction process, for it was during that period that Reinhard Heydrich laid the administrative foundations for the mobile killing operations and for the deportations to the killing centers.

The Heydrich organization reflected in its personnel composition a characteristic of German government as a whole. The RSHA and its regional machinery was an organization of party men and civil servants. The fusion of these two elements in the RSHA was so complete that almost every man could be sent into the field to carry out the most drastic Nazi plans with bureaucratic meticulousness and Prussian discipline. This personnel amalgamation in the RSHA was accomplished over a period of years, in which Heydrich put his organization together piece by piece.

The building process began in the early days of the Nazi regime, when Himmler and his loyal follower Heydrich raided the Prussian Interior Ministry and took over its newly organized Secret State Police (*Geheime Staatspolizei,* or Gestapo). Göring was then Interior Minister and Daluege the chief of police.

Next, Heydrich (as Himmler's deputy) took over a special division in the office of the police president of Berlin: the *Landeskriminalpolizeiamt,* or Criminal Police (Kripo). The Gestapo and the Criminal Police were subsequently detached from their parent organizations and joined together into the *Hauptamt Sicherheitspolizei* (Main Office Security Police). Heydrich had all key positions in this office.

The creation of the Security Police as an agency of the state was accompanied by the parallel formation of a party intelligence system, the so-called Security Service (*Sicherheitsdienst,* or SD). Heydrich now had *two* main offices: the Hauptamt Sicherheitspolizei, which was a state organization, and the Sicherheitshauptamt, which was a party organization. On September 27, 1939, Himmler issued an order in pursuance of which the two main offices were amalgamated into the Reich Security Main Office (*Reichssicherheitshauptamt,* or RSHA).

The RSHA revealed in its structure the history of its organization. Thus the Security Police comprised Offices IV and V (Gestapo and Kripo), while the Security Service functioned in Offices III (Inland) and VI (Foreign). Heydrich himself henceforth carried the title *Chef der Sicherheitspolizei und des SD,* abbreviated *Chef SP und SD.*

The RSHA had a vast regional network, including three types of organization: one in the Reich and incorporated areas, another in occupied territories, a third in countries undergoing invasion. Outside the Reich the Security Police and SD were completely centralized, down to the local (or unit) level. For the moment, however, we shall be concerned only with the machinery in the newly invaded areas: the so-called *Einsatzgruppen*. These groups were the first mobile killing units.

The context for deploying the Einsatzgruppen was operation "Barbarossa"—the invasion of the USSR. A written notation of the mission appeared in the war diary of the OKW's (High Command of the Armed Forces) Wehrmachtführungsstab (WFSt—Operations) on March 3, 1941, at a time when invasion plans were already far advanced. The topic of the entry was a draft directive to troop commanders, which had been prepared by General Warlimont's office (defense) in the WFSt, and which had been submitted by WFSt Chief Jodl to Hitler for approval. The war diary contains Jodl's enclosure of Hitler's comments, including a philosophical point defining the coming battle as a confrontation of two world views, and several specific statements, in one of which Hitler declared that the "Jewish-Bolshevik intelligentsia" would have to be "eliminated." According to Hitler, these tasks were so difficult that they could not be entrusted to the army. The war diary went on with Jodl's instructions to Warlimont for revising the draft in conformity with Hitler's "guidelines." One question to be explored with the Reichsführer-SS, said Jodl, was the introduction of SS and Police organs into the army's operational area. Jodl felt that such a move was needed to assure that Bolshevik chieftains and commissars be "rendered harmless" without delay. In conclusion, Warlimont was told that he could contact the OKH (High Command of the Army) about the revisions, and that he was told to submit a new draft for signature by OKW Chief Keitel on March 13, 1941.

On the specified date, the revised directive was signed by Keitel. The decisive paragraph was a statement informing the troop commanders that the Führer had charged the Reichsführer-SS with carrying out special tasks in the operational area of the army. Within the framework of these tasks, which were the product of a battle to the finish between two opposing political systems, the Reichsführer-SS would act independently and on his own responsibility. He was going to make sure that military operations would not be disturbed by the implementation of his task. Details would be worked out directly between the OKH and the Reichsführer-SS. At the start of operations, the border of the USSR would be closed to all nonmilitary traffic, except for police organs dispatched by the Reichsführer-SS pursuant to directive of the Führer. Quarters and supplies for these organs were to be regulated by OKH/

GenQu (High Command of the Army/General Quartermaster—Wagner).

Halder, Chief of the OKH, had been informed of Himmler's "special task" as early as March 5, and when the OKW directive was issued eight days later, he made a cryptic notation of a "Discussion Wagner-Heydrich: police questions, border customs."

The circuitous Hitler-Jodl-Warlimont-Halder-Wagner-Heydrich chain of communications was certainly not the only one. Shorter and more direct was the route from Hitler to Himmler and from Himmler to Heydrich, but there is no record of instructions or "guidelines" passed through this channel during the first two weeks of March.

The army's correspondence goes on. It includes a draft of an agreement resulting from the Wagner-Heydrich negotiations. Dated March 26, 1941, the Army-RSHA accord outlined the terms under which the Einsatzgruppen could operate in the occupied USSR. The crucial sentence in the draft provided that "within the framework of their instructions and upon their own responsibility, the Sonderkommandos are entitled to carry out executive measures against the civilian population." The two agencies also agreed that the mobile units could move in army group rear areas and in army rear areas. It was made clear that the Einsatzgruppen were to be administratively subordinated to the military command but that the RSHA was to retain functional control over them. The armies were to control the movements of the mobile units. The military was to furnish the Einsatzgruppen with quarters, gasoline, good rations, and, insofar as necessary, radio communications. On the other hand, the killing units were to receive "functional directives" from the Chief of the Security Police and SD (Heydrich).

The relations of the Einsatzgruppen with the army's Secret Field Police (*Geheime Feldpolizei,* or GFP) were to be based on a strict separation of jurisdictions. Any matter affecting the security of the troops was to be handled exclusively by the Secret Field Police, but the two services were to cooperate by prompt exchange of information, the Einsatzgruppen to report to the GFP on all matters of concern to it, and, conversely, the GFP to turn over to the Einsatzgruppen all information pertaining to their sphere of competence.

The final discussions between the army and the RSHA were carried out in May 1941. At first the negotiators were Generalquartiermeister Wagner and Gestapo chief Müller. The two could come to no final agreement. At the request of Wagner, Müller was therefore replaced by a subordinate, SS-Sturmbannführer Regierungsrat Schellenberg, then chief of IV E. Schellenberg, who was chosen because of his experience in matters of protocol, drew up the final terms. They differed from the earlier draft in only one important respect. The Einsatzgruppen were to be permitted to operate not only in army group rear areas and army rear areas but also in the corps areas right on the front line. This concession was of great importance to the Einsatzgruppen, for the victims were to be caught as quickly as possible. They were to be given no warning and no chance to escape. The final version of the agreement was signed at the end of May by Heydrich for the RSHA and by Wagner for the OKH. The partnership was established.

The next step, so far as the RSHA was concerned, was the formation of the Einsatzgruppen. Mobile units were not kept on hand; they had to be formed anew for each new invasion. Accordingly, orders were sent out to Security Police and SD men in the main office and regional branches to proceed to the Security Police training center at Pretzsch and from there to the assembly point at Düben.

Altogether, four Einsatzgruppen were set up, each of battalion size. The operational units of the Einsatzgruppen were Einsatzkommandos and Sonderkommandos, of company size. Einsatzgruppen as well as Kommandos had large staffs with sections representing the Security Service, Gestapo, and Criminal Police. The number of officers was much larger than in a military combat unit of comparable size, and their ranks were higher.

Who were these men? Where did they come from? Two of the initial Einsatzgruppen commanders were taken straight from the RSHA: Criminal Police Chief Nebe and Chief of SD-Inland Otto Ohlendorf. The story of Ohlendorf's assignment sheds a great deal of light on the attitude of the killers and, in a larger sense, on the whole destruction process.

In 1941 Ohlendorf was a young man of thirty-four. He had studied at three universities (Leipzig, Göttingen, and Pavia) and held a doctor's degree in jurisprudence. As a career man he had successfully worked himself up to a research directorship at the Institute for World Economy and Maritime Transport in Kiel. By 1938 he was also *Hauptgeschäftsführer* in the Reichsgruppe Handel, the German trade organization. Although Ohlendorf had joined the party in 1925, the SS in 1926, and the SD in 1936, he regarded his party activities, and even his position as chief of SD-Inland, as a sideline of his career. Actually, he devoted only four years (1939–43) to full-time activity in the RSHA, for in 1943 he became a Ministerialdirektor and deputy to the Staatssekretär in the Economy Ministry.

Heydrich was a man who did not like subordinates with divided loyalties. Ohlendorf was too independent. Heydrich wanted no one who functioned in an honorary capacity. The "executive measures" to be taken in Russia required complete and undivided attention. Thus it came about that the intellectual Otto Ohlendorf found himself in command of Einsatzgruppe D.

A similar story can be told about Ernst Biberstein, who took over Einsatzkommando 6 in Einsatzgruppe C in the summer of 1942. Biberstein was a somewhat older man, born in 1899. He had been a private in the First World War, and after his release from the army he devoted himself to theology. In 1924 he became a Protestant pastor and in 1933 he rose to *Kirchenprobst*. After eleven years as a minister, Biberstein entered the Church Ministry. In 1940 he was transferred to the RSHA. This transfer should not be too surprising, for the Church Ministry was an agency of the state. Besides, Biberstein had joined the party in 1926 and the SS in 1936.

But Biberstein was still a man of the church. When he was shown around the offices of the RSHA, he developed some misgivings about his new surroundings. Heydrich thereupon sent him to Oppeln to take over the local Gestapo office. In this position Biberstein was already drawn into the destruction process, because he had to concern himself with the deportation of the Jews from the city of Oppeln to the killing centers in the East. In the spring of 1942, Heydrich was assassinated and Biberstein, no longer protected by his personal understanding with the RSHA chief, was suddenly transferred to the field to conduct killings.

Like Ohlendorf and Biberstein, the great majority of the officers of the Einsatzgruppen were professional men. They included a physician (Weinmann), a professional opera singer (Klingelhöfer), and a large number of lawyers. These men were in no sense hoodlums, delinquents, common criminals, or sex maniacs. Most were intellectuals. By and large, they were in their thirties, and undoubtedly they wanted a certain measure of power, fame, and success. However, there is no indication that any of them sought an assignment to a Kommando. All we know is that they brought to their new task all the skills and training that they were capable of contributing. These men, in short, became efficient killers.

The total strength of the Einsatzgruppen was about 3,000 men. Not all the personnel were drawn from the Security Police and SD. In fact, most of the enlisted personnel had to be borrowed. A whole battalion of Order Police was dispatched to the Einsatzgruppen from Berlin because the Security Police could not put so many people into the field. In addition, the Einsatzgruppen received Waffen-SS men. Finally, they rounded out their strength in the field by adding indigenous units of Lithuanians, Estonians, Latvians, and Ukranians as auxiliary police. The resulting personnel composition is indicated in the following table showing a distribution of the members of Einsatzgruppe A:

Waffen-SS	340
Motorcycle riders	172
Administration	18
Security Service (SD)	35
Criminal Police (Kripo)	41
State Police (Stapo)	89
Auxiliary Police	87
Order Police	133
Female employees	13
Interpreters	51
Teletype operators	3
Radio operators	8
Total	990

Einsatzgruppe A, incidentally, was the largest group. The smallest was Einsatzgruppe D, which had 400 to 500 men.

While the Einsatzgruppen were being assembled, a plenary meeting took place in June, in the OKW building in Berlin. It was attended by OKW Intelligence Chief Canaris, Wagner, Heydrich, Schellenberg, and a large number of Ic (intelligence) officers. This was the last opportunity to plan for the close coordination of the Einsatzgruppen.

According to Ohlendorf, the commanders of the Einsatzgruppen were briefed by Himmler personally. They were informed that an important part of their task was elimination of Jews—women, men, and children—and of Communist functionaries. Standartenführer Jäger of Einsatzkommando 3 recalls a meeting of about fifty SS leaders in Berlin, where Heydrich declared that in the event of war with Russia the Jews in the east would have to be shot. One of the Gestapo men asked: "We should shoot the Jews?" Heydrich then answered: "Of course." In the training center of Pretzsch, the RSHA personnel chief Streckenbach addressed the Einsatzgruppen members in more general terms. He told them where they were going and instructed them to proceed ruthlessly.

At the beginning of June the four Einsatzgruppen assembled at Düben. After speeches by Heydrich and Streckenbach, the mobile killing units moved into position. Einsatzgruppe A was assigned to Army Group North; Einsatzgruppe B was detailed to Army Group Center; Einsatzgruppe C moved into the sector of Army Group South; and Einsatzgruppe D was attached to the Eleventh Army, operating in the extreme south. As the armies pushed over the first Soviet outposts, the Einsatzgruppen followed, ready to strike.

T H E   F I R S T   S W E E P

When the Einsatzgruppen crossed the border into the USSR, five million Jews were living under the Soviet flag. The majority of the Soviet Jews were concentrated in in the western parts of the country. Four million were living in territories later overrun by the German army:

Buffer Territories:
(Soviet since 1939–40)

Baltic area.	260,000
Polish territory	1,350,000
Bukovina and	
Bessarabia	up to 300,000
	up to 1,910,000

Old Territories:

Ukraine (pre-1939	
borders)	1,533,000
White Russia (pre-1939	
borders)	375,000
RSFSR	
Crimea	50,000
Other areas seized by	
Germans	200,000
	ca. 2,160,000

About one and a half million Jews living in the affected territories fled before the Germans arrived.

Not only were the Jews concentrated in an area within reach of the German army, but they lived in the cities. Jewish urbanization in the old USSR was 87 percent; in the buffer territories it was over 90 percent.

STRATEGY

The geographic distribution of Soviet Jewry determined to a large extent the basic strategy of the mobile killing units. To reach as many cities as fast as possible, the Einsatzgruppen moved closely on the heels of the advancing armies, trapping the large Jewish population centers before the victims had a chance to discover their fate. (It was for this reason that the RSHA had insisted on the right to send its mobile units to the front lines.) In accordance with the agreement, units of Einsatzgruppe A entered the cities of Kaunas, Liepāja, Jelgava, Riga,

Tartu, Tallinn, and the larger suburbs of Leningrad with advance units of the army. Three cars of Einsatzgruppe C followed the first tanks into Zhitomir. Kommando 4a of the same Einsatzgruppe was in Kiev on September 19, the day that city fell. Members of Einsatzgruppe D moved into Hotin while the Russians were still defending the town.

Such front-line movements did entail some difficulties. Occasionally the Einsatzgruppen found themselves in the middle of heavy fighting. Einsatzkommando 12, moving on the coastline east of Odessa to perform mass shootings of Jews, was surprised by a Soviet landing party of 2,500 men and fled hurriedly under fire. Sometimes an army commander took advantage of the mobile killing units to order them to clear out an area infested by partisans or snipers. Only in rare cases, however, did an army order direct the suspension of a killing operation because of the front-line situation. On the whole, the Einsatzgruppen were limited in their operations only by their own size in relation to the ground they had to cover.

The Einsatzgruppen did *not* move as compact units. The Kommandos generally detached themselves from the group staffs and operated independently. Often the Kommandos themselves split up into advance detachments *(Vorkommandos),* keeping pace with the troops and platoon-size working parties *(Teilkommandos)* that penetrated into remote districts off the main roads.

The relative thoroughness of the killings was a function of the density of Jewish settlement and the speed of the German advance. Several districts, such as Białystok, Galicia, and Bessarabia, were covered rather rapidly and sporadically. In those areas many Jews were subsequently deported to camps. In the Baltic region, on the other hand, detachments of Einsatzgruppe A stayed behind to move back and forth for more extensive killing operations. A summary report of Einsatzkommando 3 in Lithuania reveals a series of such repetitive movements. The Kommando covered a large part of the Lithuanian area, with salients in Dvinsk (Daugavpils), Latvia, and near Minsk in White Russia. Its report, dated December 1, 1941, contains 112 entries of shootings. One or another entry refers to several adjacent localities or several consecutive days. The number of place names is seventy-one, and in fourteen of these communities the Kommando struck more than once. Thus the towns of Babtai, Kedainiai, Jonava, and Rokiškis were raided twice; Vandžiogala, Utena, Alytus, and Dvinsk, at least three times; Rašeiniai and Ukmerge, four; Marijampole, five; Panevėžys, six; Kovno (Kaunas), thirteen; and Vilna (Vilnius), fifteen times. The interval between raids in these cities ranged from a fraction of a day to forty-two days, and the median pause was a week. Some of the major massacres occurred after the third, fourth, or fifth round.

The Einsatzkommandos that moved with the armies farther to the east encountered fewer and fewer Jews. The victims were thinning out for two reasons. The first was geographic distribution. By October--November 1941, the largest concentrations of Jews had already been left behind. In the eastern Ukraine and beyond the White Russian areas around Smolensk, the Jewish communities were smaller and more widely dispersed. The second reason was the decreasing percentage of Jews who stayed behind. With increasing distance from the starting line, the Soviet evacuation of factory and agricultural workers gained momentum. Many Jews were evacuated, and many others fled on their own. On September 12, 1941, Einsatzgruppe C reported that "across the lines, rumors appear to have circulated among the Jews about the fate which they can expect from us." The Einsatzgruppe which operated in the central and eastern Ukrainian territories found that many Jewish communities were reduced by 70 to 90 percent and some by 100 percent.

Such reports began to multiply in the fall. In Melitopol an original Jewish population of 11,000 had dwindled to 2,000 before Einsatzgruppe D arrived. Dnepropetrovsk had a prewar Jewish community of 100,000; about 30,000 remained. In Chernigov, with a prewar Jewish population of 10,000, Sonderkommando 4a found only 309 Jews. In Mariupol and Taganrog, Einsatzgruppe D encountered no Jews at all. On the road from Smolensk to Moscow, Einsatzgruppe B reported that in many towns the Soviets had evacuated the entire Jewish population, while in the frozen areas near Leningrad, Einsatzgruppe A caught only a few strayed Jewish victims. These figures are not an accurate indication of the number of Jews who succeeded in getting away, for many of the victims fled only a short distance and—overtaken by the German army—drifted back into the towns. Nevertheless, a comparison of the original number of Jewish inhabitants with the total number of dead will show that upwards of 1,500,000 Jews did succeed in eluding the grasp of the mobile killing units. Most Jews, however, were trapped.

The Einsatzgruppen had moved with such speed behind the advancing army that several hundred thousand Jews could be killed like sleeping flies. Einsatzgruppe A reported on October 15, 1941, that it had killed 125,000 Jews. Einsatzgruppe B reported on November 14, 1941, an incomplete total of 45,000 victims. Einsatzgruppe C reported on November 3, 1941, that it had shot 75,000 Jews. Einsatzgruppe D reported on December 12, 1941, the killing of 55,000 people.

Although over a million Jews had fled and additional hundreds of thousands had been killed, it became apparent that many Jewish communities had hardly been touched. They had been bypassed in the hurried advance. To strike at these Jews while they were still stunned and helpless, a second wave of mobile killing units moved up quickly behind the Einsatzgruppen.

From Tilsit, in East Prussia, the local Gestapo sent a Kommando into Lithuania. These Gestapo men shot thousands of Jews on the other side of the Memel River. In Kraków the *Befehlshaber der Sicherheitspolizei und des SD* (BdS) of the Generalgouvernement, SS-Oberführer Schöngarth, organized three small Kommandos. In the middle of July these Kommandos moved into the eastern Polish areas and, with headquarters in Lwów, Brest-Litovsk, and Białystok, respectively, killed tens of thousands of Jews. In addition to the Tilsit Gestapo and the Generalgouvernement Kommandos, improvised killing units were thrown into action by the Higher SS and Police Leaders. In the newly occupied Soviet territories, Himmler had installed three of these regional commanders:

HSSPf Nord (North):
    OGruf. Prützmann (Jeckeln)
HSSPf Mitte (Center):
    OGruf. von dem Bach-Zelewski
HSSPf Süd (South):
    OGruf. Jeckeln (Prützmann)

Each Higher SS and Police Leader was in charge of a regiment of Order Police and some Waffen-SS units. These forces helped out considerably.

In the northern sector the Higher SS and Police Leader (Prützmann), assisted by twenty-one men of Einsatzkommando 2 (Einsatzgruppe A), killed 10,600 people in Riga. In the center the Order Police of Higher SS and Police Leader von dem Bach helped kill 2,278 Jews in Minsk and 3,726 in Mogilev. (The beneficiary of this cooperation was Einsatzgruppe B.) In the south Higher SS and Police Leader Jeckeln was especially active. When Einsatzkommando 4a (Einsatzgruppe C) moved into Kiev, two detachments of Order Police Regiment South helped kill over 33,000 Jews. The role of the regiment in the Kiev massacre was so conspicuous that Einsatzkommando 4a felt obliged to report that, apart from the Kiev action, it had killed 14,000 Jews "without any outside help."

But Jeckeln did not confine himself to helping the Einsatzgruppen. His mobile killing units were responsible for some of the greatest massacres in the Ukraine. Thus when Feldmarschall Reichenau, commander of the Sixth Army, ordered the 1st SS Brigade to destroy remnants of the Soviet 124th Division, partisans, and "supporters of the Bolshevik system" in his rear, Jeckeln led the brigade on a three-day rampage, killing 73 Red Army men, 165 Communist party functionaries, and 1,658 Jews. A few weeks later, the same brigade shot 300 Jewish men and 139 Jewish women in Starokonstantinov "as a reprisal measure for the uncooperative attitude of the Jews working for the Wehrmacht."

Next Jeckeln struck at Kamenets-Podolsky, shooting there a total of 23,600 Jews. Another action followed in Berdichev, where Jeckeln killed 1,303 Jews, "among them 875 Jewesses over twelve years of age." In Dnepropetrovsk, where Jeckeln slaughtered 15,000 Jews, the local army command reported that to its regret it had not received prior notification of the action, with the result that its preparations to create a ghetto in the city, and its regulation (already issued) to exact a "contribution" from the Jews for the benefit of the municipality, had come to naught. Yet another massacre took place in Rovno, where the toll was also 15,000. In its report about Rovno, Einsatzgruppe C stated that, whereas the action had been organized by the Higher SS and Police Leader and had been carried out by the Order Police, a detachment of Einsatzkommando 5 had participated to a significant extent in the shooting.

Although the total number of Jews shot by the Higher SS and Police Leaders cannot be stated exactly, we know that the figure is high. Thus in the single month of August the Higher SS and Police Leader South alone killed 44,125 persons, "mostly Jews."

The mobile killing strategy was an attempt to trap the Jews in a wave of Einsatzgruppen, immediately followed up by a support wave of Gestapo men from Tilsit, Einsatzkommandos from the Generalgouvernement, and formations of the Higher SS and Police Leaders. Together, these units killed about five hundred thousand Jews in five months. (The locations of the mobile killing units in July and November 1941 are shown on Maps 2 & 3.)

COOPERATION WITH THE MOBILE KILLING UNITS

Movement was the basic problem of the mobile killing units during the first sweep. Once the killing units had arrived at a desired spot, however, they had to deal with a host of problems. The success of the operation from that point on depended on the attitudes of the military authorities, the native population, and the victims themselves.

The army cooperated with the Einsatzgruppen to an extent that far exceeded the minimum support functions guaranteed in the OKH-RSHA agreement. This cooperation was all the more remarkable because the Security Police had expected little more than grudging acquiescence in the killing operations. On July 6, 1941, Einsatzkommando 4b (Einsatzgruppe C) reported from Tarnopol: "Armed forces surprisingly welcome hostility against Jews." On September 8, Ein-

MAP 2
POSITIONS OF THE MOBILE KILLING UNITS
JULY 1941

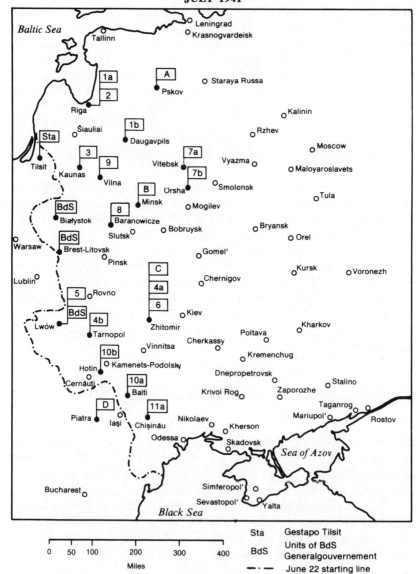

Sta	Gestapo Tilsit
BdS	Units of BdS Generalgouvernement
—·—	June 22 starting line

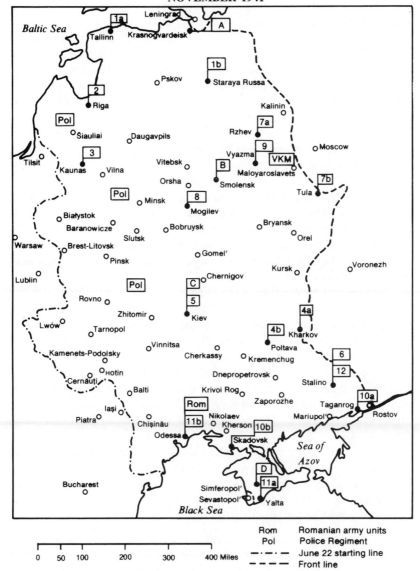

MAP 3
POSITIONS OF THE MOBILE KILLING UNITS
NOVEMBER 1941

Baltic Sea

1a
Leningrad
Tallinn
Krasnogvardeisk
A

1b
Pskov
Staraya Russa

2
Riga

Pol
Siauliai
Daugavpils
Kalinin

7a
Rzhev
9
Moscow

3
Vilna
Vitebsk
Vyazma
VKM

Tilsit
Kaunas
B
Maloyaroslavets
7b

Orsha
Smolensk
Tula

Pol
Minsk
8
Mogilev

Białystok
Baranowicze
Bobruysk
Bryansk

Slutsk
Orel

Warsaw
Brest-Litovsk
Gomel'

Pinsk
Kursk
Voronezh

Lublin
Pol
C
Chernigov

Rovno
5

Lwów
Zhitomir
Kiev
4a

Tarnopol
4b
Kharkov

Kamenets-Podolsky
Vinnitsa
Poltava

Cherkassy
Kremenchug
6

Hotin
Dnepropetrovsk
Stalino
12

Cernăuţi
Balti
Krivoi Rog
10a

Rom
Zaporozhe
Taganrog

Iaşi
Nikolaev
Mariupol'
Rostov

Piatra
Chişinău
11b
Kherson
10b

Odessa
Skadovsk
Sea of Azov

D

Bucharest
11a
Simferopol'

Sevastopol'
Yalta

Black Sea

	Rom	Romanian army units
	Pol	Police Regiment
—·—·—		June 22 starting line
——————		Front line

0   50   100   200   300   400 Miles

113

satzgruppe D reported that relations with military authorities were "excellent." The commander of Einsatzgruppe A (Brigadeführer Dr. Stahlecker) wrote that his experiences with Army Group North were very good and that his relations with the Fourth Panzer Army under Generaloberst Hoepner were "very close, yes, almost cordial."

These testimonials were given to the army because it went out of its way to turn over Jews to the Einsatzgruppen, to request actions against Jews, to participate in killing operations, and to shoot Jewish hostages in "reprisal" for attacks on occupation forces. The generals had eased themselves into this pose of cooperation through the pretense that the Jewish population was a group of Bolshevist diehards who instigated, encouraged, and abetted the partisan war behind the German lines. The army thus had to protect itself against the partisan menace by striking at its presumable source—the Jews.

The first consequence of army "security" policy was the practice of handing over Jews to the Einsatzgruppen for shooting. In Minsk the army commander established a civilian internment camp for almost all the men in the city. Secret Field Police units and Einsatzgruppe B personnel together "combed out" the camp. Thousands of "Jews, criminals, functionaries, and Asiatics" were caught in the roundup. In Zhitomir, General Reinhardt assisted Einsatzgruppe C in a "comb-out" of the town. Outside the cities several military units turned in stray Jews fleeing on the roads or in the woods.

The second application of the theory that Jews were the instigators of the partisan war was army initiation of action against the Jews. In Kremenchug the Seventeenth Army requested Kommando 4b to wipe out the Jews of the city because three cases of cable sabotage had occurred there. In other towns army commanders did not even wait for sabotage occurrences, but requested anti-Jewish action as a "precautionary" measure. Thus in the town of Kodyma an illiterate Ukranian woman who claimed to understand Yiddish was brought before Hauptmann (Captain) Krämer of Secret Field Police Group 647 with the XXX Corps. She revealed that she had overheard a Jewish plot to attack the army in the city. That same afternoon, Einsatzkommando 10a in Olshanka was asked to send a detachment to Kodyma. The detachment, assisted by Secret Field Police men, then carried out the killings. At Armyansk in the Crimea, the local military commander sent the following report to his superior:

> For protection against the partisan nuisance and for the security of the troops in this area, it became absolutely necessary to render the fourteen local Jews and Jewesses harmless. Carried out on November 26, 1941.

The third effect of the German theory of a "Jewish-Bolshevist" conspiracy was a policy of taking Jewish hostages and suspects in the occupied territories. The Seventeenth Army ordered that whenever sabotage or an attack on personnel could not be traced to the Ukrainian population, Jews and Communists (especially Jewish Komsomol members) were to be shot in reprisal. The commander of the Southern Army Group Rear Area explained a similar order in the following terms:

> We must convey the impression that we are just. Whenever the perpetrator of an act of sabotage cannot be found, Ukrainians are not to be blamed. In such cases reprisals are therefore to be carried out only against Jews and Russians.

Perhaps the most interesting order was issued by the Sixth Army Ia/OQu at Kharkov. The order provided that Jews and other hostages be placed in big buildings. It was suspected that some of these buildings were mined. Now that the supposed perpetrators were in the buildings, the military expected that reports of the location of the mines would soon be made to army engineers. At least one unit carried its suspicion of the Jews so far as to order, in one breath, that all Red Army men in uniform or civilian clothes caught "loafing around," Jews, commissars, persons who carried a weapon, and those suspected of partisan activities were to be shot at once.

It is difficult to estimate how many Jewish hostages or suspects fell victim to the German army. Einsatzgruppe A reported that in White Russia alone, Army Group Center had shot 19,000 "partisans and criminals, that is, in the majority Jews," up to December 1941. The Jewish victims of army action were thus no insignificant group of people. The army was pitching in very seriously to help the Heydrich forces reduce the Jewish population of the east.

In all the examples cited so far, partisan activity was the explicit or implicit justification for the army's actions. Interestingly enough, however, there were instances after the start of operations when the military went out of its way to help the mobile killings units for no apparent reason save the desire to get things over with. The growth of this callousness in the face of mass death is illustrated by the following two stories.

In Dzhankoy on the Crimean peninsula, the local mayor had established a concentration camp for Jews without notifying anyone. After a while, famine raged in the camp and epidemics threatened to break out. The military commander approached Einsatzgruppe D with a request to kill the Jews, but the Security Police turned down the request because it did not have enough personnel. After some haggling, the army agreed to furnish its Feldgendarmerie for blocking the area off so that a Kommando of the Einsatzgruppe could perform the killings.

In Simferopol, the Crimean capital, the Eleventh Army decided that it wanted the shooting to be completed before Christmas. Accordingly, Einsatzgruppe D, with the assistance of army personnel and with army trucks and gasoline, completed the shootings in time to permit the army to celebrate Christmas in a city without Jews.

From an initial reluctance to participate in the destruction process, the generals had developed such an impatience for action that they were virtually pushing the Einsatzgruppen into killing operations. The German army could hardly wait to see the Jews of Russia dead—no wonder that the commanders of the Einsatzgruppen were pleasantly surprised.

While most of the mobile killing units were operating in the territorial domain of the German army, Einsatzkommandos of Groups C and D also moved into sectors of the Hungarian and Romanian armies. A novel situation faced the Security Police in these sectors. The RSHA had made no agreements with the satellite commands. The German government had not even informed its allies of the special mission of the Reichsführer-SS. New experiences were therefore in store for Himmler's men as they moved into areas held by alien authority.

References to the relations with the Hungarians are scarce, and whenever we find them they do not show the Hungarians in a cooperative attitude. In Zhitomir, for instance, the Hungarian army stopped an action by native police against the Jews. Again, farther to the south, Einsatzgruppe D reported at the end of August that it had "cleared of Jews" a territory bordering on the Dniester from Hotin to Yampol, *except* for a small area occupied by Hungarian forces. The Romanian attitude, on the other hand, was quite different. Repeatedly, Romanian forces on the march invaded Jewish quarters and killed Jews, and their actions took the form of atrocities rather than well-planned or well-reasoned killing operations. The German witnesses of that Romanian fury were slightly disturbed by what they saw and at times attempted to introduce discipline into the ranks of their ally.

Early in July, Sonderkommando 10a of Einsatzgruppe D moved into the city of Bălți. The Sonderkommando sent search parties into the Jewish quarter of the Romanian-occupied city. "In one room," reported Obersturmbannführer Seetzen, "a patrol last evening discovered fifteen Jews, of different ages and both sexes, who had been shot by Romanian soldiers. Some of the Jews were still alive; the patrol shot them to death for mercy's sake." Another incident in the same town occurred on the evening of July 10. Romanian army authorities drove together four hundred Jews of all ages and both sexes in order to shoot them in retaliation for attacks on Romanian soldiers. The commander of the 170th Division in the area was taken aback by the spectacle. He requested that the shooting be limited to fifteen Jewish men. By July 29 another report from Bălți indicated that the Romanians were shooting Jews en masse. "Romanian police in Bălți and surrounding area pro-

ceeding sharply against Jewish population. Number of shootings cannot be determined exactly." Kommando 10a pitched in by shooting the
Jewish community leaders in the town.

The Einsatzgruppe also had trouble with the Romanians in Cernăuţi. In that city the Romanians were busily shooting Ukranian intellectuals "in order to settle the Ukranian problem in the North
Bukovina once and for all." Among the victims the Security Police
found many Ukrainian nationalists who had been potential collaborators in German service. Kommando 10b consequently had a dual
reason for interfering. It requested the release of the pro-German nationalists (OUN men) in exchange for Communists and Jews. The
arrangement was successful. Two weeks later, Einsatzgruppe D and
Romanian police were jointly shooting thousands of Jews.

The occurrences at Bălţi and Cernăuţi were destined to be dwarfed
by a bloodbath that followed in the fall. The city with the largest Jewish
population in the USSR, Odessa, was captured by the Fourth Romanian Army after a long siege, on October 16, 1941. During the first days
of the occupation, fires broke out night after night, but—in the eyes of a
German observer—the Romanians were proceeding against the Jewish
"elements" with "relative loyalty." There were no "special excesses."
In the late afternoon of October 22, however, partisans blew up the
Romanian headquarters on Engel Street, killing the commander of the
10th Division, General Glogojanu, and his entire staff. The number of
identified dead was forty-six, of whom twenty-one were officers, including some Germans. Others were believed buried in the debris. That
evening, the deputy commander of the 13th Division, General Trestioreanu, reported that he was taking measures to hang Jews and Communists in public. During the night, Odessa was the scene of numerous
hangings and shootings. These killings had hardly ceased when, on
October 23, Romanian gendarmerie began a major roundup. According
to an Abwehr liaison officer with Romanian intelligence, who was in
Odessa at the time, about 19,000 Jews were shot that morning in a
square surrounded by a wooden fence in the harbor area. Their bodies
were covered with gasoline and burned. At 12:30 P.M. of the same day,
the Romanian dictator, Marshal Ion Antonescu, issued instructions that
200 Communists be executed for every officer—Romanian or German—killed in the explosion, and that 100 Communists be executed for
every dead enlisted man. All Communists in Odessa, as well as one
member of every Jewish family, were to be held as hostages. The
Odessa prisons were now filling rapidly with more victims. On October
24, masses of Jews were moved some ten miles west of the city to the
collective farm of Dalnik, where they were to be shot in antitank
ditches. The shootings, which took place in batches of forty to fifty

along a two-mile stretch, were too slow for the Romanian officers in charge of the operation. The remaining Jews were thereupon crowded into four sizable warehouses and sprayed with bullets fired through holes in the walls. One warehouse after another was then set on fire. A Romanian indictment presented in a postwar trial contains an estimate of 25–30,000 dead at Dalnik. The Abwehr officer in Odessa was told by the Romanian director of telephone "surveillance" that 40,000 Odessa Jews had been "conveyed to Dalnik." Some tens of thousands of Jews remained in Odessa after the October massacres. They were to be swept up in a second wave during the following months.

The mobile killings had thus become an operation of SS, police, and military units, Romanian as well as German. Much, however, depended also on the attitude of the civilian population. How were the Slavs going to react to the sudden annihilation of an entire people living in their midst? Would they hide the Jews or hand them over to German occupation authorities? Would they shoot at the killers or help in the killings? These were vital questions for Einsatzgruppen commanders and their subordinates.

In fact, the behavior of the population during the killing operations was characterized by a tendency toward passivity. This inertness was the product of conflicting emotions and opposing restraints. The Slavs had no particular liking for their Jewish neighbors, and they felt no overpowering urge to help the Jews in their hour of need. Insofar as there were such inclinations, they were effectively curbed by fear of reprisals from the Germans. At the same time, however, the Slavic population stood estranged and even aghast before the unfolding spectacle of the "Final Solution." There was on the whole no impelling desire to cooperate in a process of such utter ruthlessness. The fact that the Soviet regime, fighting off the Germans a few hundred miles to the east, was still threatening to return undoubtedly acted as a powerful restraint on many a potential collaborator. The ultimate effect of this psychological constellation was an escape into neutrality. The population did not want to take sides in the destruction process. If few were on the side of the Germans, fewer still were on the side of the Jews.

In all the Einsatzgruppen reports, we discover only one indication of the pro-Jewish act in the occupied lands. Sonderkommando 4b reported that it had shot the mayor of Kremenchug, Senitsa Vershovsky, because he had "tried to protect the Jews." This incident appears to have been the only case of its kind. The counterpressure was evidently too great. Whoever attempted to aid the Jews acted alone and exposed himself as well as his family to the possibility of a death sentence from a German Kommando. There was no encouragement for a man with an awakened conscience. In Lithuania, Bishop Brizgys set an example for the entire population by forbidding the clergy to aid or intercede for the Jews in any way.

Across the whole occupied territory Jews were turning to the Christian population for assistance—in vain. Einsatzgruppe C reported that many Jews who had fled from their homes were turning back from the countryside. "The population does not house them and does not feed them. They live in holes in the earth or pressed together in old huts."

Sometimes the failure to help the Jews appears to have weighed on the conscience of the population. Thus in the northern sector, south of Leningrad, Einsatzgrupe A reported a subtle attempt by the local residents to justify their inactivity. The following anecdote was circulating in that sector: A group of Soviet prisoners of war was requested by its German captors to bury alive a number of Jewish fellow prisoners. The Russians refused. The German soldiers thereupon told the Jews to bury the Russians. The Jews, according to the anecdote, immediately grabbed the shovels.

The refusal to help the Jews was only a little more tenacious than the reluctance to help the Germans. On July 19, Einsatzgruppe B in White Russia had already noted that the population was remarkably "apathetic" to the killing operations and that it would have to be asked to cooperate in the seizure of Communist functionaries and the Jewish intelligentsia. From the Ukraine, Einsatzkommando 6 of Einsatzgruppe C reported as follows:

> Almost nowhere can the population be persuaded to take active steps against the Jews. This may be explained by the fear of many people that the Red Army may return. Again and again this anxiety has been pointed out to us. Older people have remarked that they had already experienced in 1918 the sudden retreat of the Germans. In order to meet the fear psychosis, and in order to destroy the myth which, in the eyes of many Ukrainians, places the Jew in the position of the wielder of political power, Einsatzkommando 6 on several occasions marched Jews before their execution through the city. Also, care was taken to have Ukrainian militiamen watch the shooting of Jews.

This "deflation" of the Jews in the public eye did not have the desired effects. After a few weeks, Einsatzgruppe C complained once more that the inhabitants did not betray the movement of hidden Jews. The Ukrainians were passive, benumbered by the "Bolshevist terror." Only the ethnic Germans in the area were busily working for the Einsatzgruppe.

Neutrality is a zero quantity that helps the stronger party in an unequal struggle. The Jews needed native help more than the Germans did. The Einsatzgruppen, however, not only had the advantage of a generally neutral population; they also managed to obtain—at least from certain segments of the local citizenry—two important forms of cooperation in the killing opeations: pogroms and the help of auxiliary police in seizures and shootings.

What are pogroms? They are short, violent outbursts by a community against its Jewish population. Why did the Einsatzgruppen endeavor to start pogroms in the occupied areas? The reasons that prompted the killing units to activate anti-Jewish outbursts were partly administrative, partly psychological. The administrative principle was very simple: every Jew killed in a pogrom was one less burden for the Einsatzgruppen. A pogrom brought them, as they expressed it, that much closer to the "cleanup goal." The psychological consideration was more interesting. The Einsatzgruppen wanted the population to take part—and a major part at that—of the responsibility for the killing operations. "It was not less important, for future purposes," wrote Brigadeführer Dr. Stahlecker of Einsatzgruppe A, "to establish as an unquestionable fact that the liberated population had resorted to the most severe measures against the Bolshevist and Jewish enemy, on its own initiative and without instructions from German authorities." In short, the pogroms were to become a defensive weapon with which to confront an accuser, or an element of blackmail that could be used against the local population.

It may be noted in passing that Einsatzgruppen and military interests diverged on the matter of pogroms. The military government experts, like the civilian bureaucrats at home, dreaded any kind of uncontrollable violence. One rear (security) division, issuing a long directive for anti-Jewish measures, included also this sharply worded paragraph in its order: "Lynch justice against Jews and other terror measures are to be prevented by all means. The armed forces do not tolerate that one terror [the Soviet one] be relieved by another." Most of the pogroms, therefore, took place in those areas that had not yet been placed in the firm grip of military government experts.

The Einsatzgruppen were most successful with "spontaneous" outbursts in the Baltic area, particularly in Lithuania. Yet even there Dr. Stahlecker observed: "To our surprise, it was not easy at first to set in motion an extensive pogrom against the Jews." The Lithuanian pogroms grew out of a situation of violence in the capital city of Kaunas. As soon as war had broken out, anti-Communist fighting groups had gone into action against the Soviet rear guard. When an advance detachment of Einsatzkommando 1b (Einsatzgruppe A) moved into Kaunas, the Lithuanian partisans were shooting it out with retreating Red Army men. The newly arrived Security Police approached the chief of the Lithuanian insurgents, Klimaitis, and secretly persuaded him to turn his forces on the Jews. After several days of intensive pogroms, Klimaitis had accounted for 5,000 dead: 3,800 in Kaunas, 1,200 in other towns. Moving farther north, Einsatzgruppe A organized a pogrom in Riga, Latvia. The Einsatzgruppe set up two pogrom units and let them loose in the city; 400 Jews were killed. Both in Kaunas and in Riga, the Einsatzgruppe took photographs and made films of the "self-cleansing actions" as evidence "for later times" of the severity of native treatment of the Jews. With the disbanding of the anti-Communist partisans, the northern pogroms ended. No other outbursts took place in the Baltic states.

In addition to Stahlecker's Einsatzgruppe in the north, Einsatzgruppe C had some success with pogroms in the south. The southern pogrom area was largely confined to Galicia, an area that was formerly Polish territory and that had a large Ukrainian population. The Galician capital of Lwów was the scene of a mass seizure by local inhabitants. In "reprisal" for the deportation of Ukrainians by the Soviets, 1,000 members of the Jewish intelligentsia were driven together and handed over to the Security Police. On July 5, 1941, about seventy Jews in Tarnopol were rounded up by Ukrainians when three mutilated German corpses were found in the local prison. The Jews were killed with dynamite. Another twenty Jews were killed by Ukrainians and German troops.

In Krzemieniec (Kremenets), 100 to 150 Ukrainians had been killed by the Soviets. When some of the exhumed corpses were found without skin, rumors circulated that the Ukrainians had been thrown into kettles full of boiling water. The Ukrainian population retaliated by seizing 130 Jews and beating them to death with clubs. Although the Galician pogroms spread still further, to such places as Sambor and Czortków, the Ukrainian violence as a whole did not come up to expectations. Only Tarnopol and Czortków were scored as major successes.

Three observations about the pogroms may be noted. First, truly spontaneous pogroms, free from Einsatzgruppen influence, did not take place. All outbreaks were either organized or inspired by the Einsatzgruppen. Second, all pogroms were implemented within a short time after the arrival of the killing units. They were not self-perpetuating, nor could new ones be started after things had settled down. Third, most of the reported pogroms occurred in buffer territory, areas in which submerged hostility toward the Jews was apparently greatest and in which the Soviet threat of a return could most easily be discounted, for the Communist government had been in power there for less than two years.

We come now to a second and somewhat more efficient form of local cooperation, namely the help extended to the Einsatzgruppen by auxiliary police. The importance of the auxiliaries should not be under-estimated. Roundups by local inhabitants who spoke the local language resulted in higher percentages of Jewish dead. This fact is clearly indicated by the statistics of Kommandos that made use of local help. As in the case of the pogroms, the recruitment of auxiliaries was most successful in the Baltic and Ukrainian areas.

In the Baltic states the auxiliary police were organized very rapidly. The Lithuanian anti-Soviet partisans, who had been engaged in the pogroms, became the first manpower reservoir. Before disarming and disbanding the partisans, Einsatzgruppe A picked out "reliable" men and organized them into five police companies. The men were put to work immediately in Kaunas. The ensuing "actions" in that city were, in Standartenführer Jäger's words, "like shooting at a parade." In July 1941, 150 Lithuanians were assigned to participate in the "liquidation" of the Jewish community in Vilna, where every morning and afternoon they seized and concentrated about five hundred people, who were "subjected to special treatment on the very same day." By mid-September 1941, a detachment of Einsatzkommando 3 had swept through the districts of Rašeiniai, Rokiškis, Sarasai, Persai, and Prienai and, with the help of local Lithuanians, rendered them "free of Jews." The operations assisted by the Lithuanians accounted for more than half of the Einsatzkommando's killings by that date.

In Latvia auxiliaries were similarly used by Einsatzkommandos 1b and 2. Like the Lithuanians, the Latvians were able helpers. There was at least one case of trouble. A Latvian Kommando was caught in Karsava by German army men while stuffing its pockets with the belongings of dead Jews. The Latvian detachment in question had to be disbanded. In the northernmost country, Estonia, the army had set up an indigenous auxiliary (Selbstschutz) which was taken over by Son-derkommando 1 of Einsatzgruppe A to do its entire dirty work of shooting a handful of Jews left behind after the Soviet retreat.

In addition to the Baltic Selbstschutz used by Einsatzgruppe A, a Ukrainian militia was operating in the areas of Einsatzgruppen C and D. The Ukrainian auxiliaries appeared on the scene in August 1941, and Einsatzgruppe C found itself compelled to make use of them because it was repeatedly diverted from its main task to fight the "partisan nui-sance." The network of local Ukrainian militias was paid by the munici-palities, sometimes with funds confiscated from Jews. The Ukrainians were used principally for dirty work. Thus Einsatzkommando 4a went so far as to confine itself to the shooting of adults while commanding its Ukrainian helpers to shoot children.

In the south the SS drew upon a sizable population of resident ethnic Germans to organize a Selbstschutz of several thousand men. Einsatzgruppe D discovered that the local Germans were eager volunteers during shootings. In that connection, a former chief of Einsatzkommando 6 (Biberstein) commented after the war: "We were actually frightened by the bloodthirstiness of these people."

The Einsatzgruppen profited from the assistance of the military, and they made what use they could of local help. More important than the cooperation of the army and the attitude of the civilian population, however, was the role of the Jews in their own destruction. For when all was said and done, the members of the Einsatzgruppen were thousands. The Jews were millions.

When we consider that the Jews were not prepared to do battle with the Germans, we might well ask why they did not flee for their lives. We have mentioned repeatedly that many Jews had been evacuated and that many others fled on their own, but this fact must not obscure another, no less significant phenomenon: most Jews did not leave. They stayed. What prompted such a decision? What chained the victims to cities and towns that were already within marching reach of the approaching Germany army? People do not voluntarily leave their homes for uncertain havens unless they are driven by an acute awareness of coming disaster. In the Jewish community that awareness was blunted and blocked by psychological obstacles.

The first obstacle to an apprehension of the situation was a conviction that bad things came from Russia and good things from Germany. The Jews were historically oriented away from Russia and toward Germany. Not Russia but Germany had been their traditional place of refuge. Such thinking was not entirely extinguished in October and November 1939, when thousands of Jews moved from Russian-occupied to German-occupied Poland. The stream was not stopped until the Germans closed the border. Similarly, one year later, at the time of Soviet mass deportations in the newly occupied territories, the Attaché Division of the OKH and Amt Ausland-Abwehr of the OKW received reports of widespread unrest in these areas. "Even Poles and Jews," read the reports, "are waiting for the arrival of a German army." When the army finally arrived in the summer of 1941, old Jews in particular remembered that in World War I the Germans had come as quasi-liberators. These Jews did not expect that now the Germans would come as persecutors and killers.

The following note was handed by a Jewish delegation of the little town of Kamenka in the Ukraine to a visiting German dignitary, Friedrich Theodor Prince zu Sayn und Wittgenstein, in the late summer of 1941:

> We, the old, established residents of the town of Kamenka, in the name of the Jewish population, welcome your arrival, Serene Highness and heir to your ancestors, in whose shadow the Jews, our ancestors and we, had

lived in the greatest welfare. We wish you, too, long life and happiness. We hope that also in the future the Jewish population shall live on your estate in peace and quiet under your protection, considering the sympathy which the Jewish population has always extended to your most distinguished family.

The prince was unmoved. The Jews, he said, were a "great evil" in Kamenka. Although he had no authority to impose any solutions (final or interim) upon his greeters, he instructed the local mayor to mark the Jews with a star and to employ them without pay in hard labor.

Another factor that blunted Jewish alertness was the haze with which the Soviet press and radio had shrouded events across the border. The Jews of Russia were ignorant of the fate that had overtaken the Jews in Nazi Europe. Soviet information media, in pursuance of a policy of appeasement, had made it their business to keep silent about Nazi measures of destruction. The consequences of that silence were disastrous. A German intelligence official reported from White Russia on July 12, 1941:

> The Jews are remarkably ill-informed about our attitude toward them. They do not know how Jews are treated in Germany, or for that matter in Warsaw, which after all is not so far away. Otherwise, their questions as to whether we in Germany make any distinctions between Jews and other citizens would be superfluous. Even if they do not think that under German administration they will have equal rights with the Russians, they believe, nevertheless, that we shall leave them in peace if they mind their own business and work diligently.

We see therefore that a large number of Jews had stayed behind not merely because of the physical difficulties of flight but also, and perhaps primarily, because they had failed to grasp the danger of remaining in their homes. This means, of course, that precisely those Jews who did *not* flee were less aware of the disaster and less capable of dealing with it than those who did. The Jews who fell into German captivity were the vulnerable element of the Jewish community. They were the old people, the women, and the children. They were the people who at the decisive moment had failed to listen to Russian warnings and who were now ready to listen to German reassurances. The remaining Jews were, in short, physically and psychologically immobilized.

The mobile killing units soon grasped the Jewish weakness. They discovered quickly that one of their greatest problems, the seizure of the victims, had an easy solution. We have noted that in several places the Einsatzgruppen had enlisted the army's support in combing out prospective victims, and, as far as possible, Einsatzgruppen commanders had relied also upon the local population to discover Jewish residences and hideouts. Now, however, the Kommandos had found their most efficient helpers: the Jews themselves. In order to draw together and assemble large numbers of Jews, the killers had only to "fool" the victims by means of simple ruses.

The first experiment with ruses was made in Vinnitsa, where a search for members of the Jewish intelligentsia had produced meager results. The commander of Einsatzkommando 4b called for "the most prominent rabbi in town" and told him to collect within twenty-four hours the most intelligent Jews for "registration work." When the result still did not satisfy the Einsatzkommando, the commander sent the group back to town with instructions to bring more Jews. he repeated this stunt once more before deciding that he had a sufficient number of Jews to shoot. In Kiev, Einsatzkommando 4a followed the much simpler expedient of using wall posters to assemble the Jews for "resettlement." Variations of the registration and resettlement legends were used repeatedly throughout the occupied territories.

The psychological traps were effective not only for the seizure of Jews within the cities; the Einsatzgruppen actually managed to draw back large numbers of Jews who had already fled from the cities in anticipation of a disaster. We have seen that the Jews who had taken to the roads, the villages, and the fields had great difficulty in subsisting there because the German army was picking up stray Jews and the population refused to shelter them. The Einsatzgruppen took advantage of this situation by instituting the simplest ruse of all: they did nothing. The inactivity of the Security Police was sufficient to dispel the rumors that had set the exodus in motion. Within a short time the Jews flocked into town. They were caught in the dragnet and killed.

THE KILLING OPERATIONS AND THEIR REPERCUSSIONS

During the first sweep, the mobile killing units reported approximately one hundred thousand victims a month. By now we can understand how it was possible to seize so many people in the course of a mobile operation. A simple strategy—combined with a great deal of army assistance, native collaboration, and Jewish gullibility—had transformed the occupied Soviet cities into a series of natural traps. Now, however, we have to find out what happened after the Jews were caught; for with the seizure of the victims, the administrative problems of the Einsatzgruppen were not entirely solved, while the psychological difficulties were only just beginning.

In their daily operations, the Einsatzgruppen were preoccupied with preparations, logistics, maintenance, and reporting. They had to plan their movements, select the sites for shootings, clean weapons, and count the victims one by one—man, woman, or child, Jew, communist, or Gypsy. Depending on the size of a Jewish community selected for decimation or obliteration, the strength of a killing party ranged from about four men to a full Einsatzkommando, supplemented by units of the Order Police or the army. (The Higher SS and Police Leaders could assign larger formations to an operation.) In almost every major action the victims outnumbered their captors 10 to 1, 20 to 1, or even 50 to 1; but the Jews could never turn their numbers into an advantage. The killers were well armed, they knew what to do, and they worked swiftly. The victims were unarmed, bewildered, and followed orders.

The Germans were able to work quickly and efficiently because the killing operation was standardized. In every city the same procedure was followed with minor variations. The site of the shooting was usually outside of town, at a grave. Some of the graves were deepened antitank ditches or shell craters, others were specially dug. The Jews were taken in batches (men first) from the collecting point to the ditch. The killing site was supposed to be closed off to all outsiders, but this was not always possible, and, as we shall see, a lot of trouble resulted from this fact. Before their death the victims handed their valuables to the leader of the killing party. In the winter they removed their overcoats; in warmer weather they had to take off all outergarments and, in some cases, underwear as well.

From this point on, the procedure varied somewhat. Some Einsatzkommandoes lined up the victims in front of the ditch and shot them with submachine guns or other small arms in the back of the neck. The mortally wounded Jews toppled into their graves. Some commanders disliked this method, which possibly reminded them of the Russian NKVD. Blobel, the commander of Einsatzkommando 4a, stated that he personally declined to use specialists in shooting in the neck. Ohlendorf, too, spurned the technique because he wanted to avoid "personal responsibility." Blobel, Ohlendorf, and Haensch are known to have employed massed fire from a considerably distance. There was, however, still another procedure which combined efficiency with the impersonal element. This system has been referred to as the "sardine method," and was carried out as follows. The first batch had to lie down on the bottom of the grave. They were killed by cross-fire from above. The next batch had to lie down on top of the corpses, heads facing the feet of the dead. After five or six layers, the grave was closed.

It is significant that the Jews allowed themselves to be shot without resistance. In all the reports of the Einsatzgruppen there were few references to "incidents." The killing units never lost a man during a shooting operation. All their casualties were suffered during antipartisan fighting, skirmishes on the front, or as a result of sickness or accident. Einsatzgruppe C remarked:

> Strange is the calmness with which the delinquents allow themselves to be shot, and that goes for non-Jews as well as Jews. Their fear of death appears to have been blunted by a kind of indifference which has been created in the course of twenty years of Soviet rule.

This comment was made in September 1941. It turned out in later years that the non-Jewish "delinquents" could not be shot so easily after all, but the Jews remained paralyzed after their first brush with death and in spite of advance knowledge of their fate.

Although the Jews were being killed smoothly, the Einsatzgruppen commanders were worried about possible repercussions on the population, the army, and their own personnel. Repercussions are problems that arise or continue after the completion of action. Like pebbles thrown into quiet ponds, these aftereffects cause ripples that travel far and wide from the scene of the event.

To minimize the shock of the shootings at its source, the Einsatzgruppen commanders, their deputies, and their adjutants frequently visited the killing sites. Ohlendorf tells us that he inspected shootings in order to be certain that they were military in character and "humane under the circumstances." Ohlendorf's adjutant, Schubert, describes the reasons for the inspections more deliberately. Schubert supervised the killing operation in Simferopol, the capital of the Crimea. He watched the loading on trucks to make sure that the non-Jewish population was not disturbed. Furthermore, he kept an eye on the guards to prevent them from beating the victims. He worried about unauthorized traffic at the killing site and ordered that all outsiders be detoured. During the collection of valuables, he saw to it that the Order Police and Waffen-SS did not pocket anything. Finally, he convinced himself that the victims were shot humanely, "since, in the event of other killing methods, the psychic burden would have been too great for the execution Kommando." A former sergeant tells us of one more reason—an important one—for the inspections. When Ohlendorf arrived at the killing site of Sonderkommando 10b one time, he complained to the commander, Persterer, about the manner of burial. Ohlendorf ordered that the victims be covered a little better.

In spite of the precautions taken by Einsatzgruppen commanders, the emergence of repercussions was inevitable. The inhabitants at first seemed to be unworried and carefree. Commanders reported that the population "understood" the shootings and judged them "positively." In one town, Khemelnik, the inhabitants were reported to have gone to church in order to thank God for their "deliverance" from Jewry. However, the idyllic picture of a population completely at ease and even thankful for the elimination of the Jews soon began to fade away.

In February 1942, Heydrich reported to the defense commissars in the army districts that the shootings were now being carried out in such a manner that the population hardly noticed them. The inhabitants, and even the surviving Jews, had frequently been left with the impression that the victims had only been resettled. The Security Police thought it wise to hide the killings, for it could no longer trust a population that was itself chafing under the increasing harshness of German rule and that was already fearful for its own security and safety.

A German eyewitness (in Borisov, White Russia) who knew Russian spoke to a number of local residents before the mass shooting of the Jews was to start in the town. His Russian landlord told him: "Let them perish, they did us a lot of harm!" But on the following morning the German heard comments like these: "Who ordered such a thing? How is it possible to kill 6,500 Jews at once? Now it is the turn of the Jews; when will it be ours? What have these poor Jews done? All they did was work! The really guilty ones are surely in safety!" During the following year, the Germans observed a wave of mysticism, including dream interpretations, premonitions, and prophecies in Borisov. People were now saying: "The Jews were killed for their sins, as was prophesied them in the holy books. In the Holy Bible one must also be able to find out what kind of fate is awaiting us."

The following report was sent by an army officer stationed in the Crimea to the Economy-Armament Office (OKW/Wi Rü) in Berlin:

> In the present situation of unrest the most nonsensical rumors—the bulk of which are started by partisans and agents—find willing ears. Thus, a few days ago, a rumor circulated that the Germans were intending to do away with all the men and women over fifty. The *Ortskommandantur* [in Simferopol] and other German offices were mobbed with questions about the veracity of the report. In view of the fact that the total "resettlement" of the Jewish population and the liquidation of an insane asylum with about 600 inmates cannot be hidden forever, such rumors are bound to gain in credibility among the inhabitants.

Gradually then, the local non-Jewish witnesses of the destruction process perceived the true nature of the German racial ladder. The lowest rung was already afire, and they were but one step above it.

The killing operations had repercussions not only for the population but also for the military. One of these consequences was an undercurrent of criticism in the army's ranks. On October 10, 1941, Feldmarschall Reichenau, commander of the Sixth Army, sent an order to the troops in which he exhorted them to be a little harsher in their treatment of partisans. He explained that this was not an ordinary war and recited all the dangers of the Jewish-Bolshevist system to German culture. "Therefore," he continued, "the soldier must have full understanding of the necessity for harsh but just countermeasures against Jewish subhumanity." These measures, Reichenau pointed out, had the added purpose of frustrating revolts behind the back of the fighting troops, for it had been proved again and again that the uprisings were always being instigated by Jews. Hitler read this order and found that it was "excellent." Feldmarschall von Rundstedt, commander of the Southern Army Group, sent copies to the Eleventh and Seventeenth armies, as well as to the First Panzer Army, for distribution. Von Manstein, the Eleventh Army commander, elaborated on the order, explaining that the Jew was the liaison man between the Red Army on the front and the enemy in the rear.

A second problem, more serious than lack of "understanding" of the killings, was soon discovered with dismay by unit commanders. Among the troops the shootings had become a sensation. Many years after having become a witness to such an event, a former soldier recalled: "Although we were forbidden to go there, it drew us magically." They watched, took pictures, wrote letters, and talked. With rapidity, the news spread in the occupied territories, and gradually it seeped into Germany.

To the army this was an embarrassing business. In Kiev a group of foreign journalists who had been invited to view the "Bolshevist destruction" of the city quickly looked up the representative of the civil administration with Army Group Center, Hauptmann Koch, and questioned him about the shootings. When Koch denied everything, the journalists told him that they had pretty exact information about these matters anyway. The members of a Swiss army medical mission with the German forces were similarly informed. One of the Swiss officers, Dr. Rudolf Bucher, not only reported his experiences to his superiors but gave numerous lectures about what he had heard and seen to military and professional audiences in Switzerland.

The German army attempted to take various countermeasures. Initially, several officers blamed the Einsatzgruppen for performing the shootings where everybody could see them. One such protest was sent by the deputy commander of Army District IX in Kassel (Schniewindt) to Generaloberst Fromm, the chief of the Replacement Army. In his protest the army district official dealt with the rumors about the "mass executions" in Russia. Schniewindt pointed out that he had considered these rumors to be vast exaggerations until he received a report from a subordinate, Major Rösler, who had been an eyewitness.

Rösler commanded the 528th Infantry Regiment in Zhitomir. One day while he was sitting in his headquarters and minding his own business, he suddenly heard rifle volleys followed by pistol shots. Accompanied by two officers, he decided to find out what was happening. The three were not alone. From all directions, soldiers and civilians were running toward a railroad embankment. Rösler, too, climbed the embankment. What he saw there was "so brutally base that those who approached unprepared were shaken and nauseated."

He was standing over a ditch with a mountain of earth on one side, and the wall of the ditch was splattered with blood. Policemen were standing around with bloodstained uniforms, soldiers were congregating in groups (some of them in bathing shorts), and civilians were watching with wives and children. Rösler stepped closer and peeked into the grave. Among the corpses he saw an old man with a white beard and a cane on his arm. Since the man was still breathing, Rösler approached a policeman and asked him to kill the man "for good." The policeman replied in the manner of someone who does not need advice: "This one has already got something seven times into his——he is going to perish by himself." In conclusion, Rösler stated that he had already seen quite a few unpleasant things in his life but that mass slaughter in public, as if on an open-air stage, was something else again. It was against German customs, upbringing, and so on. Not once in his account did Rösler mention Jews.

Complaints in the field were not lacking either. A local battalion commander at Genicke protested (complete with sketch map) that a killing operation had been carried out near the city limit, that troops and civilians alike had become involuntary witnesses of the shooting, and that they had also heard the "whining" of the doomed. The SS officer in charge replied that he had done the job with only three men, that the nearest house was 500 to 800 yards from the spot, that military personnel had insisted on watching the operation, and that he could not have chased them away.

As late as May 8, 1942, the military government officers of Rear Army Group Area South met in conference and resolved to persuade the killing units in a nice way to conduct their shootings, "whenever possible," not during the day but at night, except of course for those "executions" that were necessary to "frighten" the population.

However, in spite of the occasional attempts to regulate the location or even the time of the shootings, the army soon realized that it could not remove the killing sites from the reach of "involuntary" (let alone "voluntary") witnesses. The only other way to stop the entertainment (and the flow of rumors resulting from it) was to conduct an educational campaign among the soldiers. The army then tried this method also.

Even during the first weeks of the war, soldiers of the Eleventh Army watched Romanian shootings at Bălţi. Since the killers were Romanians, the chief of staff of the Eleventh Army, Wöhler, allowed himself the use of some blunt language. Without making direct references to the incident, he wrote:

> In view of a special case, the following has to be pointed out explicitly.
> Because of the eastern European concept of human life, German soldiers may become witnesses of events (such as mass executions, the murder of civilians, Jews, and others) which they cannot prevent at this time but which violate German feelings of honor most deeply.
> To every normal person it is a matter of course that he does not take photographs of such disgusting excesses or report about them when he writes home. The distribution of photographs and the spreading of reports about such events will be regarded as a subversion of decency and discipline in the army and will be punished strictly. All pictures, negatives, and reports of such excesses are to be collected and are to be sent with a notation listing the name of the owner to the Ic/AO of the army.
> To gaze at such procedures curiously is beneath the dignity of the German soldier.

Sensationalism and rumor spreading did not exhaust the army's troubles. The operations of the mobile killing units had created another problem, even more far reaching and disturbing in its implications. It happened that Jews were killed by military personnel who acted *without* orders or directives. Sometimes soldiers offered their help to the killing parties and joined in the shooting of the victims. Occasionally, troops participated in the pogroms, and once in a while members of the German army staged killing operations of their own. We have pointed out that the army had helped the mobile killing units a great deal. Why, then, was the military leadership concerned with these individual actions?

The army had several administrative reasons for anxiety. As a matter of status, the idea that soldiers were doing police work was not very appealing. Pogroms were the nightmare of military government experts, and unorganized killings on the roads and in occupied towns were dangerous, if only because of the possibility of mistakes or accidents. But in addition to these considerations, there was an overall objection that was rooted in the whole psychology of the destruction process. The killing of the Jews was regarded as historical necessity. The soldier had to "understand" this. If for any reason he was instructed to help the SS and Police in their task, he was expected to obey orders. However, if he killed a Jew spontaneously, voluntarily, or without instruction, merely because he *wanted* to kill, then he committed an abnormal act, worthy perhaps of an "Eastern European" (such as a

Romanian) but dangerous to the discipline and prestige of the German army. Herein lay the crucial difference between the man who "overcame" himself to kill and one who wantonly committed atrocities. The former was regarded as a good soldier and a true Nazi; the latter was a person without self-control, who would be a danger to his community after his return home. This philosophy was reflected in all orders attempting to deal with the problem of "excesses."

On August 2, 1941, the XXX Corps (in the Eleventh Army) distributed an order, down to companies, that read as follows:

Participation by soldiers in actions against Jews and Communists.

The fanatical will of members of the Communist Party and of the Jews, to stem the advance of the German Army at any price, has to be broken under all circumstances. In the interest of security in the Rear Army Area it is therefore necessary to take drastic measures. This is the task of the Sonderkommandos. Unfortunately, however, military personnel have participated in one such action. Therefore, I order for the future:

Only those soldiers may take part in such actions as have specifically been ordered to do so. Furthermore, I forbid any member of this unit to participate as a spectator. Insofar as military personnel are detailed to these actions, they have to be commanded by an officer. The officer has to see to it there there are no unpleasant excesses by the troops.

An order by the commander of Rear Army Group Area South pointed out:

The number of transgressions by military personnel against the civilian population is increasing. . . . It has also happened lately that soldiers and even officers independently undertook shootings of Jews, or that they participated in such shootings.

After an explanation that "executive measures" were in the exclusive province of the SS and Police, the order continued:

The army itself finishes on the spot only those local inhabitants who have committed—or are suspected of having committed—hostile acts, and that is to be done only upon order of an officer. Moreover, collective measures may be taken only if authorized by at least a battalion commander. Any kind of doubt about this question is inadmissible. Every unauthorized shooting of local inhabitants, including Jews, by individual soldiers, as well as every participation in executive measures of the SS and Police, is disobedience and therefore to be punished by disciplinary means, or—if necessary—by court martial.

Clearly, the killing operations seriously affected the local inhabitants and the army. Among the population the operations produced a submerged, deep-seated anxiety, and in the army they brought into the open an uncomfortably large number of soldiers who delighted in death as spectators or as pereptrators.

The third group to be confronted with major psychological problems was the mobile killing personnel themselves. The leaders of the Einsatzgruppen and Einsatzkommandos were bureaucrats—men who were accustomed to desk work. In the east it was their job to supervise and report about the operations. This was not mere desk work. We have already noted that "inspections" took the Einsatzgruppen leaders and their staffs to the killing sites. In Einsatzgruppe C, everybody had to watch shootings. A staff member, Karl Hennicke, tells us that he had no choice about the matter:

> I myself attended executions only as a witness, in order not to lay myself open to charges of cowardice. . . . Dr. Rasch [Einsatzgruppe commander] insisted on principle that all officers and noncommissioned officers of the Kommando participate in the executions. It was impossible to stay away from them, lest one be called to account.

The Einsatzgruppe officer had to "overcome" himself. He had to be in this business completely, not as a reporter but as a participant, not as a possible future accuser but as one who would have to share the fate of those who did this work. One of the officers who one day had been commanded to watch the shootings suffered the most horrible dreams during the following night. Even the Higher SS and Police Leader Central Russia, Obergruppenführer von dem Bach-Zelewski, was brought into a hospital with serious stomach and intestinal ailments. Following surgery, his recovery was slow, and Himmler dispatched the top physician of the SS, Grawitz, to the bedside of his favorite general. Grawitz reported that von dem Bach was suffering especially from reliving the shooting of Jews that he himself had conducted, and other difficult experiences in the East.

The commanders of the mobile killing units attempted to cope systematically with the psychological effects of the killing operations. Even while they directed the shooting, they began to repress as well as to justify their activities. The repressive mechanism is quite noticeable in the choice of language for reports of individual killing actions. The reporters tried to avoid the use of direct expressions such as "to kill" or "murder." Instead the commanders employed terms that ended either to justify the killings or to obscure them altogether. The following is a representative list:

hingerichtet: put to death, executed
exekutiert: executed
ausgemerzt: exterminated

liquidiert: liquidated
Liquidierungszahl: liquidation number
Liquidierung des Judentums: liquidation of Jewry
erledigt: finished (off)
Aktionen: actions
Sonderaktionen: special actions
Sonderbehandlung: special treatment
sonderbehandelt: specially treated
der Sonderbehandlung unterzogen: subjected to special treatment
Säuberung: cleansing
Großsäuberungsaktionen: major cleaning actions
Ausschaltung: elimination
Aussiedlung: resettlement
Vollzugstätigkeit: execution activity
Exekutivmassnahme: executive measure
entsprechend behandelt: treated appropriately
der Sondermassnahme zugeführt: conveyed to special measure
sicherheitspolizeiliche Massnahmen: Security Police measures
sicherheitspolizeilich durchgearbeitet: worked over in Security
  Police manner
Lösung der Judenfrage: solution of the Jewish question
Bereinigung der Judenfrage: cleaning up of the Jewish question
judenfrei gemacht: (area) made free of Jews

Aside from terminology designed to convey the notion that the killing operations were only an ordinary bureaucratic process within the framework of police activity, we find—in logical but not psychological contradiction—that the commanders of the Einsatzgruppen constructed various justifications for the killings. The significance of these rationalizations will be readily apparent once we consider that the Einsatzgruppen did not have to give any reasons to Heydrich; they had to give reasons only to themselves. Generally speaking, we find in the reports one overall justification for the killings: the Jewish danger. The fiction was used again and again, in many variations.

A Kommando of the BdS Generalgouvernement reported that it had killed 4,500 Jews in Pińsk because a member of the local militia had been fired on by Jews and another militia man had been found dead. In Bălţi the Jews were killed on the ground that they were guilty of "attacks" on German troops. In Starokonstantinov the 1st SS Brigade shot 439 Jews because the victims had shown an "uncooperative" attitude toward the Wehrmacht. In Mogilev the Jews were accused of attempting to sabotage their own "resettlement." In Novoukrainka there were Jewish "encroachments." In Kiev the Jews were suspected of having caused the great fire. In Minsk about twenty-five hundred Jews were shot because they were spreading "rumors." In the area of

Einsatzgruppe A, Jewish propaganda was the justification. "Since this Jewish propaganda activity was especially heavy in Lithuania," read the report, "the number of persons liquidated in this area by Einsatzkommando 3 has risen to 75,000." The following reason was giving for a killing operation in Ananiev: "Since the Jews of Ananiev had threatened the ethnic German residents with a bloodbath just as soon as the German Army should withdraw, the Security Police conducted a roundup and, on August 28, 1941, shot about 300 Jews and Jewesses." On one occasion Einsatzgruppe B substituted for rumor spreading, propaganda, and threats the vague but all-inclusive accusation of a "spirit of opposition." At least one Einsatzgruppe invoked the danger theory without citing any Jewish resistance activity at all. When Einsatzgruppe D had killed all Jews in the Crimea, it enclosed in its summary report a learned article about the pervasive influence that Jewry had exercised on the peninsula before the war.

An extreme example of an accusatory posture may be found in an anonymous eyewitness report of a shooting in the area of Mostovoye, between the Dniester and the Bug rivers. An SS detachment had moved into a village and arrested all its Jewish inhabitants. The Jews were lined up along a ditch and told to undress. The SS leader then declared in the presence of the victims that inasmuch as Jewry had unleashed the war, those assembled here had to pay for this act with their lives. Following the speech, the adults were shot and the children were assaulted with rifle butts. Gasoline was poured over their bodies and ignited. Children still breathing were thrown into the flames.

Charges of dangerous Jewish attitudes and activities were sometimes supplemented with references to the hazard that Jews presented as carriers of sickness. The Jewish quarters in Nevel and Yanovichi were doomed because they were full of epidemics. In Vitebsk the threat of an epidemic sufficed. The following explanation was given for the shootings in Radomyshl. Many Jews from surrounding areas had flocked into the city. This led to an overcrowding of Jewish apartments—on the average, fifteen persons lived in one room. Hygienic conditions had become intolerable. Every day several corpses of Jews had to be removed from these houses. Supplying food for Jewish adults as well as children had become "impracticable." Consequently, there was an ever increasing danger of epidemics. To put an end to these conditions, Sonderkommando 4a finally shot 1,700 Jews.

It should be emphasized that psychological justifications were an essential part of the killing operations. If a proposed action could not be justified, it did not take place. Needless to say, the supply of reasons for anti-Jewish measures never ran out. However, just once, explanations did exhaust themselves with respect to the killings of mental patients.

Einsatzgruppe A had killed 748 insane people in Lithuania and northern Russia because these "lunatics" had no guards, nurses, or food. They were a "danger" to security. But when the army requested the Einsatzgruppe to "clean out" other institutions that were needed as billets, the Einsatzgruppe suddenly refused. No interest of the Security Police required such action. Consequently, the army was told to do the dirty job itself.

Like the leaders of the mobile killing units, the enlisted personnel had been recruited on a jurisdictional basis. While they had all had some ideological training, they had not volunteered to shoot Jews. Most of these men had drifted into the killing units simply because they were not fit for front-line duty. They were older men, not teen-agers. Many had already assumed the responsibility of caring for a family; they were not irresponsible adolescents.

It is hard to say what happened to these men as a result of the shootings. For many, undoubtedly, the task became just another job, to be done correctly and mechanically, i.e., the men made some sort of "adjustment" to the situation. However, every once in a while a man did have a nervous breakdown, and in several units the use of alcohol became routine. At the same time, indoctrination was continued, and occasionally commanders made speeches before major operations.

Once, in mid-August, 1941, Himmler himself visited Minsk. He asked Einsatzgruppe B Commander Nebe to shoot a batch of a hundred people, so that he could see what one of these "liquidations" really looked like. Nebe obliged. All except two of the victims were men. Himmler spotted in the group a youth of about twenty who had blue eyes and blond hair. Just before the firing was to begin, Himmler walked up to the doomed man and put a few questions to him.

> Are you a Jew?
> Yes.
> Are both of your parents Jews?
> Yes.
> Do you have any ancestors who were not Jews?
> No.
> Then I can't help you!

As the firing started, Himmler was even more nervous. During every volley he looked to the ground. When the two women could not die, Himmler yelled to the police sergeant not to torture them.

When the shooting was over, Himmler and a fellow spectator engaged in conversation. The other witness was Obergruppenführer von dem Bach-Zelewski, the same man who was later delivered to a hospital. Von dem Bach addressed Himmler:

Reichsführer, those were only a hundred.

What do you mean by that?

Look at the eyes of the men in this Kommando, how deeply shaken they are! These men are finished for the rest of their lives. What kind of followers are we training here? Either neurotics or savages!

Himmler was visibly moved and decided to make a speech to all who were assembled there. He pointed out that the Einsatzgruppen were called upon to fulfill a repulsive duty. He would not like it if Germans did such a thing gladly. But their conscience was in no way impaired, for they were soldiers who had to carry out every order unconditionally. He alone had responsibility before God and Hitler for everything that was happening. They had undoubtedly noticed that he hated this bloody business and that he had been aroused to the depth of his soul. But he too was obeying the highest law by doing his duty, and he was acting from a deep understanding of the necessity for this operation.

Himmler told the men to look at nature. There was combat everywhere, not only among men but also in the world of animals and plants. Whoever was too tired to fight must go under. The most primitive man says that the horse is good and the bedbug is bad, or wheat is good and the thistle is bad. The human being consequently designates what is useful to him as good and what is harmful as bad. Didn't bedbugs and rats have a life purpose also? Yes, but this has never meant that man could not defend himself against vermin.

After the speech Himmler, Nebe, von dem Bach, and the chief of Himmler's Personal Staff, Wolff, inspected an insane asylum. Himmler ordered Nebe to end the suffering of these people as soon as possible. At the same time, Himmler asked Nebe "to turn over in his mind" various other killing methods more humane than shooting. Nebe asked for permission to try out dynamite on the mentally ill people. Von dem Bach and Wolff protested that the sick people were not guinea pigs, but Himmler decided in favor of the attempt. Much later, Nebe confided to von dem Bach that the dynamite had been tried on the inmates with woeful results.

The eventual answer to Himmler's request was the gas van. The RSHA's technical branch (II-D) reconstructed a truck chassis in such a way that the carbon monoxide of the exhaust could be conducted through a hose to the van's interior. This invention lent itself to stationary killings in Poland and Serbia. By early 1942, two or three vans were sent to each of the Einsatzgruppen as well. Throughout the time the vans were being tested for proper operation in the Kriminaltechnisches Institut (RSHA V-D) of Sturmbannführer Oberregierungsrat Dr. Heess and his assistant for biology and chemistry, Obersturmführer Dr. Widmann. The young Obersturmführer had been in Minsk, where he had blown up the mental patients. He had been under the impression that the vans would be used only for the killing of the insane. When he found out about their application in the east, he complained to Heess that one could not, after all, employ this device against normal people. Dr. Heess addressed him in a familiar tone: "But you see, it is done anyway. Do you want to quit by any chance?" Dr. Widmann remained at his post and was promoted to Hauptsturmführer.

There were many technical and psychological problems with the gas vans in the field. Some of the vehicles broke down in rainy weather; after repeated use they were no longer tightly sealed. Members of Kommandos who unloaded the vans suffered from headaches. If a driver stepped too hard on the accelerator, the bodies removed from the van had distorted faces and were covered with excrement.

Clearly, alcohol, speeches, and gas vans did not eliminate the psychological problems generated by the killings. Yet there was no breakdown in the operations as a whole.

THE SECOND SWEEP

The first sweep was completed toward the end of 1941. It had a limited extension in newly occupied territories of the Crimea and the Caucasus during the spring and summer months of 1942. The second sweep began in the Baltic area in the fall of 1941 and spread through the rest of the occupied territory during the following year. Hence, while the first sweep was still proceeding in the south, the second had already started in the north. At the pivotal point, in the center, the turn came around December 1941.

The machinery employed in the second sweep was larger and more elaborate than that of the first. Himmler's forces were joined by army personnel in mobile and local operations designed for the complete annihilation of the remaining Soviet Jews.

In the ensuing operations the Einsatzgruppen played a smaller role than before. Organizationally they were placed under the direction of the Higher SS and Police Leaders. In the north the chief of Einsatzgruppe A (through 1944: Stahlecker, Jost, Achamer-Pifrader, Panziger, and Fuchs) became the *BdS Ostland,* and in the south the chief of Einsatzgruppe C (Rasch, Thomas, Böhme) became the *BdS Ukraine,* with jurisdiction over the Reichskommissariat as well as over the military areas to the east. Despite such attributes of permanence, the Security Police in the occupied USSR did not grow.

The Order Police, on the other hand, was greatly expanded. The police regiments were increased from three at the beginning of the campaign to nine at the end of 1942. Whereas five of these nine regiments were at the front, the remainder, together with six additional battalions, were at the disposal of the Higher SS and Police Leaders in the rear. The police regiments had a stationary counterpart in the *Einzeldienst* (single-man duty), divided into *Schutzpolizei* (in cities) and *Gendarmerie* (in rural areas). At the end of 1942 the Einzeldienst had 14,953 men, of whom 5,860 were in the Schutzpolizei and 9,093 in the Gendarmerie.

Almost from the beginning, the Order Police was augmented by native personnel. On July 25, 1941, Himmler, noting that the Einsatzgruppen had already added local helpers to their detachments, ordered the rapid formation of a force composed primarily of Baltic, White Russian, and Ukrainian nationalities. During the following months the Order Police set up an indigenous *Schutzmannschaft* in the form of units and precincts. By the second half of 1942, this apparatus had reached sizable proportions. As of July 1, 1942, there were seventy-eight Schutzmannschaft (or Schuma) battalions with 33,270 men, and at the end of the year the count was 47,974. For every German battalion, the Schuma had at least five. Moreover, these units were widely used. Although identified as Lithuanian, Latvian, and so on, some were stationed far from their original bases. The nonmobile component of the Schutzmannschaft was even larger. It consisted of three branches: Einzeldienst, firemen, and auxiliaries serving in labor projects or guarding prisoners of war. The native Einzeldienst was a considerable factor in the second sweep. In the small towns and villages of the Ostland and the Ukrainian regions, it outnumbered the German Gendarmerie nearly ten to one (see Table 11).

T A B L E 11
SIZE OF THE EINZELDIENST DURING THE SECOND SWEEP

| | Ostland* | Ukraine† | |
	Schutzpolizei and Gendarmerie	Schutzpolizei	Gendarmerie
Germans	4,428	3,849	5,614
Indigenous personnel	31,804	14,163	54,794

*As of October 1, 1942.
†Comprising the Reichskommissariat, military area to the east, and Crimea as of November 25, 1942.

Assisting the SS and Police was the network of military rear-echelon offices and their specialized personnel who roamed about the countrysides collecting information about hidden partisans and Jews: offices, military police, intelligence, Secret Field Police, and the so-called partisan hunters, or anti-partisan patrols. The military intelligence machinery was formally incorporated into the killing apparatus by an agreement between Heydrich and Admiral Canaris of the High Command of the Armed Forces for exchange of information in the field. The agreement provided specifically that "information and reports that might bring about executive activities are to be transmitted immediately to the competent office of the Security Police and SD."

During the second sweep, mobile killing operations were also carried out by so-called anti-partisan formations. The employment of these formations derived from one of Hitler's orders, issued in the late summer of 1942, for the centralization of anti-partisan fighting. Pursuant to the order, anti-partisan operations *in the civilian areas* were to be organized by Himmler. In the military areas the same responsibility was to be exercised by the chief of the army's General Staff. Himmler appointed as his plenipotentiary von dem Bach, Higher SS and Police Leader Center, and gave him the title Chief of the Anti-Partisan Formations. In his capacity as anti-partisan chief in the civilian areas, von dem Bach could draw upon army personnel (security divisions, units composed of indigenous collaborators, etc.), SS units, police regiments, and Einsatzgruppen, for as long as he needed them for any particular operation. These units became "anti-partisan formations" for the duration of such an assignment. The device is of interest because, in the guise of anti-partisan activity, the units killed thousands of Jews in the woods and in the swamps.

In the military area the second sweep was comparatively brief. As we have noted, the density of the Jewish population decreased as the mobile killing units pushed east. The slowing of the advance enabled the units to work much more thoroughly. Einsatzgruppe A had little to do in the rear area of Army Group North. Accordingly, it shifted some of its Kommandos to the civilian areas of White Russia to work over terrain through which Einsatzgruppe B had passed hurriedly in the early months of the fall. Einsatzgruppe B spent the winter in the Mogilev-Smolensk-Bryansk sector. Recoiling from the Soviet counteroffensive, the advance Kommandos pulled back, and in the course of the contraction the Einsatzgruppe systematically killed the surviving Jews in the rear areas of Army Group Center. In the meantime isolated Jews in the north and center, fleeing alone or in small groups were hunted down relentlessly by the Secret Field Police, Russian collaborators, an Estonian police battalion, and other units.

To the south, Einsatzgruppen C and D were engaged in heavier operations. In Dnepropetrovsk, 30,000 Jews at the time of the city's occupation were whittled down to 702 by February 1942. During March 1942 several large cities east of the Dnieper, including Gorlovka, Makeyevka, Artemovsk, and Stalino, were "cleared of Jews." In this area the army also tracked down escaping Jews. One security division actually encountered a Jewish partisan group (about twenty-five men) in the Novomoskovsk-Pavlograd area.

Einsatzgruppe D in the Crimea reported on February 18, 1942, that almost 10,000 Jews had now been killed in Simferopol—300 more than had originally registered there. This discovery was the signal for a systematic sweeping operation in the entire Crimea. The drive was conducted with the help of local militia, a network of agents, and a continuous flow of denunciations from the population. The army gave the drive every assistance. On December 15, 1941, Major Stephanus, anti-partisan expert of the Eleventh Army, had ordered the Abwehr (army counter-intelligence) and Secret Field Police to hand over escaped Jews to the Einsatzgruppe. The local Kommandanturen and the Gendarmerie also joined in the operation. By spring the Crimea no longer had any Jews, except for two groups in Soviet-held territory. Einsatzgruppe D caught them in July.

In the Romanian-administered territory between the Dniester and the Bug (Transnistria), killings were conducted even more expeditiously than in the German military area. On November 11, 1941, Governor Alexianu of Transnistria issued a decree requiring Jews to live in localities specified by the Inspector General of Gendarmerie. Pursuant to this ordinance, a large number of Jews in southern Transnistria were moved from their homes to the southern districts of Berezovka and Golta.

Berezovka was the arrival point of almost 20,000 Odessa Jews who had survived the Romanian army massacres of October 1941. The railroad station of the town of Berezovka, some sixty miles northeast of Odessa, was situated in the middle of a cluster of Ukrainian and ethnic German settlements. The Jews, brought there by train, were marched to the countryside and shot by ethnic German Selbstschutz stationed in the area. The death toll at Berezovka was swelled by victims from smaller towns and villages. A cumulative figure was indicated by a member of the German Foreign Office in May. About 28,000 Jews had been brought to German villages in Transnistria, he wrote. "Meanwhile they have been liquidated."

In the Golta prefecture the killings were carried out by the Romanians themselves. The district, under the prefect Lt. Col. Modest Isopescu, was located upstream on the Bug River. Three primitive enclosures were organized in the district: Bogdanovca (Bogdanovka), Acmecetca (Akmechet), and Dumanovca (Domanevka). These hastily assembled concentration camps, which consisted of half-destroyed houses, stables, and pigpens, held a total of 70,000 Jews, most of them from towns and hamlets, some from Odessa. Disease, especially typhus, was rampant, and food was scarce.

At Bogdanovca, the largest and most lethal camp, killings began on December 21. At first, 4,000 to 5,000 sick and infirm Jews were placed in several stables, which were covered with straw, sprinkled with gasoline, and torched. While the stables were still burning, about 43,000 Jews were marched through the woods in groups of 300 to 400 to be shot, kneeling completely naked in the icy weather on the rim of a precipice. This operation continued until December 30, with an interruption for the celebration of Christmas. During January and February 1942, about 18,000 Jews were killed in Dumanovca. At Acmecetca, where Isopescu took pleasure in tormenting and photographing his victims, 4,000 were killed.

Although the Berezovka and Golta prefectures accounted for nearly 100,000 Jewish dead, some tens of thousands, particularly in northern Transnistria, were permitted to languish in ghettos and camps, most of them crowded with Jewish expellees from Bessarabia and Bukovina.

In the civilian territories under German administration, some attempts were made to be efficient as well as rational. These efforts, however, were not always successful. The problems and conflicts arising from repeated combings of the two *Reichskommissariate* (Ostland and Ukraine) became manifest in the Ostland (Baltic area and White Russia) as early as the fall.

On September 11, 1941, the *Gebietskommissar* of Šiauliai (northern Lithuania) sent a letter to Reichskommissar Lohse that contained a short preview of what was going to take place in the coming months. In Šiauliai Einsatzkommando 2 had left behind a small detachment under an SS sergeant. One day, the chief of Einsatzkommando 3 (Jäger) dispatched his Obersturmführer Hammann (commander of the mobile unit organized by Jäger), to Šiauliai, where Hammann looked up the sergeant and declared in an "extraordinarily arrogant tone" that the Jewish situation in Šiauliai was a dirty mess and that all Jews in the city had to be "liquidated." Hamann then visited the Gebietskommissar and repeated "in a less arrogant tone" why he had come. When the Gebietskommissar explained that the Jews were needed as skilled laborers, Hamann declared curtly that such matters were none of his business and that the economy did not interest him at all.

On October 30, 1941, Gebietskommissar Carl of Slutsk reported to

Generalkommissar Kube of White Russia that the 11th Lithuanian Police Battalion had arrived in his city suddenly in order to wipe out the Jewish community. He had pleaded with the battalion commander for a postponement, pointing out that the Jews were working as skilled laborers and specialists and that White Russian mechanics were, "so to speak, nonexistent." Certainly the skilled men would have to be sifted out. The battalion commander did not contradict him, and the interview ended upon a note of complete understanding. The police battalion then encircled the Jewish quarter and dragged out everybody. White Russians in the area tried desperately to get out. Factories and workshops stopped functioning. The Gebietskommissar hurried to the scene. He was shocked by what he saw. "There was no question of an action against the Jews anymore. It looked rather like a revolution." Shots were fired. Lithuanian police hit Jews with rifle butts and rubber truncheons. Shops were turned inside out. Peasant carts, which had been ordered by the army to move ammunition, stood abandoned with their horses in the streets. Outside the town the mass shootings were carried out hurriedly. Some of the Jews, wounded but not killed, worked themselves out of the graves. When the police battalion departed, Gebietskommissar Carl had a handful of Jewish workers left. In every shop there were a few survivors, some of them with bloody and bruised faces, their wives and children dead.

When Kube received this report, he was incensed. He sent it on to *Reichskommissar* Lohse of the Ostland, with a duplicate for Reichsminister Rosenberg (Ministry for Eastern Occupied Territories). Adding a comment of his own, Kube pointed out that the burial of seriously wounded people who could work themselves out of their graves was such a disgusting business that it ought to be reported to Göring and to Hitler.

In October 1941 the Reichskommissar forbade the shooting of Jews in Liepāja (Latvia). The RSHA complained to the East Ministry, and Dr. Leibbrandt, chief of the ministry's Political Division, requested a report. In the correspondence that followed, Regierungsrat Trampedach (Political Division, Ostland) explained that the "wild executions of Jews" in Liepāja had been forbidden because of the manner in which they had been carried out. Trampedach then inquired whether the letter from Dr. Leibbrandt was to be regarded as a directive to kill all Jews in the east, without regard to the economy. The ministry's answer was that economic questions should not be considered in the solution of the Jewish problem. Any further disputes were to be settled on the local level. This declaration ended the incipient struggle for the preservation of the Jewish labor force. The Kommissare were now resigned to its loss.

In the Ukraine the Armament Inspectorate looked forward to the massacres with some apprehension, but declined to fight about the issue. On December 2, 1941, the Armament Inspector sent a report by an expert, Oberkriegsverwaltungsrat Professor Serephim, to the chief of the Economy-Armament Office in the OKW (Thomas). The inspector took pains to point out that the report was personal and unofficial. He requested the receiving agency not to distribute it without the express permission of General Thomas.

Seraphim wrote that, obviously, "the kind of solution of the Jewish problem applied in the Ukraine" was based on ideological theories, not on economic considerations. So far, 150,000 to 200,000 Jews had been "executed" in the Reichskommissariat. One result of this operation was that a considerable number of "superfluous eaters" had been eliminated. Undoubtedly, the dead had also been a hostile element "that hated us." On the other hand, the Jews had been "anxious" and "obliging" from the start. They had tried to avoid everything that might have displeased the German administration. They had played no significant part in sabotage, and they had constituted no danger to the armed forces. Although driven only by fear, they had been producing goods in satisfactory quantities.

Moreover, the killing of the Jews could not be looked upon as an isolated phenomenon. The city population and farm laborers were already starving. "It must be realized," concluded Seraphim, "that in the Ukraine only the Ukrainians can produce economic values. If we shoot the Jews, let the prisoners of war perish, condemn considerable part of the urban population to death by starvation, and lose also a part of the farming population by hunger during the next year, the question remains unanswered: Who in the world is then supposed to produce something valuable here?" The answer to this rehetorical question was soon to be provided by Himmler's men.

The sweep through the Ostland in the fall of 1941 was only a warmup, but it settled a decisive issue. The Jews were at the disposal of the civil and military authorities only at the sufferance of the SS and Police. The killers had first claim.

In the meantime, the Jews kept working. During the quiet months of the winter and spring of 1942, they began to adjust themselves to their hazardous existence. They tried to make themselves to their hazardous existence. They tried to make themselves "indispensable." The most important possession of any Jew in this period was a work certificate. None of the penalties threatened by the Jewish ghetto police for infractions of rules were as severe as the confiscation of a certificate, since it was looked upon as a life insurance policy. Whoever lost it stared death in the face. Some certificate holders grew confident during the lull. In the Kamenets-Podolsky district (Ukraine), one Jewish worker approached a Gendarmerie sergeant and pointed out: "You are not going to shoot us to death; we are specialists."

The civil administration utilized the time to brace itself for the coming sweep. The Kommissare prepared lists of irreplaceable Jewish workers and ordered that the vocational training of non-Jewish youths be stepped up. In June, Regierungsrat Trampedach (Political Division, Reichskommissariat Ostland) wrote to Kube that in the opinion of the BdS (Jost) the economic value of the Jewish skilled worker was not great enough to justify the continuation of dangers arising from Jewish support of the partisan movement. Did Kube agree? Kube replied that he agreed. At the same time, he instructed his Gebietskommissare to cooperate with the SS and Police in a review of the essential status of Jewish workers with the aim of eliminating all those skilled laborers who under the "most stringent criteria" were not "absolutely" needed in the economy.

In the summer of 1942, the second sweep was in full force. The entire machinery of the SS and Police was mobilized for the task, and the Ostland and the Ukraine were covered with a wave of massacres. Unlike the first sweep, which caught the Jews by surprise, the second wave was expected by everyone. It was no longer feasible to employ ruses. The ghetto-clearing operations were carried out in the open, with ruthlessness and brutality. The actions were uncompromising in character and final in their effect. No one could remain alive.

In the bureaucracy the feverish pitch of the killers created a strange transformation. The Gebietskommissare, who had previously protested against the destruction of their labor force and against the methods of the SS and Police, now joined Himmler's men and, in some cases, outdid themselves to make their areas free of Jews. By November 1942, the Reichskommissar Ostland was constrained to forbid the participation of members of the civilian administration in "executions of any kind." Lohse was a little late. In town after town, Jewish communities were disappearing in the frenzy of the killings.

The first step in a ghetto-clearing operation was the digging of graves. Usually, a Jewish labor detachment had to perform this work. On the eve of an *Aktion,* an uneasy air pervaded the Jewish quarter. Sometimes Jewish representatives approached German businessmen with requests to intercede. Jewish girls who wanted to save their lives offered themselves to policemen. As a rule, the women were used during the night and killed in the morning.

The actual operation would start with the encirclement of the ghetto by a police cordon. Most often, the operation was timed to begin at dawn, but sometimes it was carried out at night, with searchlights focused on the ghetto and flares illuminating the countryside all around. Small detachments of police, Kommissariat employees, and railroad men armed with crowbars, rifles, hand grenades, axes, and picks then moved into the Jewish quarter.

The bulk of the Jews moved out immediately to the assembly point. Many, however, remained in their homes, doors locked, praying and consoling each other. Often they hid in cellars or lay flat between the earth and the wooden floors. The raiding parties moved through the streets shouting, "Open the door, open the door!" Breaking into the houses, the Germans threw hand grenades into the cellars, and some "especially sadistic persons fired tracer bullets point-blank at the victims. During an operation in Slonim, many houses were set afire, until the entire ghetto was a mass of flames. Some Jews who still survived in cellars and underground passages choked to death or were crushed under the collapsing buildings. Additional raiders then arrived with gasoline cans and burned the dead and wounded in the streets.

Meanwhile, the Jews who had voluntarily left their homes waited at the assembly point. Sometimes they were forced to crouch on the ground to facilitate supervision. Trucks then brought them in batches to the ditch, where they were unloaded with the help of rifles and whips. They had to take off their clothes and submit to searches. Then they were shot either in front of the ditch or by the "sardine" method in the ditch.

The mode of the shooting depended a great deal on the killers' sobriety. Most of them were drunk most of the time; only the "idealists" refrained from the use of alcohol. The Jews submitted without resistance and without protest. "It was amazing," a German witness relates, "how the Jews stepped into the graves, with only mutual condolences in order to strengthen their spirits and in order to ease the work of the execution commandos." When the shooting took place in front of the ditch, the victims sometimes froze in terror. Just in front of them, Jews who had been shot were lying motionless. A few bodies were still twitching, blood running from their necks. The Jews were shot as they recoiled from the edge of the grave, and other Jews quickly dragged them in.

At the shooting site, too, there were some "mean sadists." According to a former participant in these operations, a sadist was the type of man who would hurl his first into the belly of a pregnant woman and throw her alive into the grave. Because of the killers' drunkenness, many of the victims were left for a whole night, breathing and bleeding. During an operation at Slonim, some of these Jews dragged themselves, naked and covered with blood, as far as Baranowicze. When panic threatened to break out among the inhabitants, native auxiliaries were dispatched at once to round up and kill these Jews.

The Gebietskommissar of Slonim, Erren, used to call a meeting after every ghetto-clearing operation. The meeting was the occasion for a celebration, and employees of the Kommissariat who had distinguished themselves were praised. Erren, who was perhaps more eager than most of his colleagues, acquired the title "Bloody Gebietskommissar."

As the massive killing wave moved westward across the two Reichskommissariate and the Bialystok district, it became clear that in the Ukraine the operations would be over before the end of 1942. In the Volhynian-Podolian Generalkommissariat, the armament industry gradually collapsed. Tens of thousands of Jewish workers in the plants of the western Ukraine were "withdrawn." Ghetto after ghetto was wiped out. In one report, armament officials expressed the opinion that no one, not even skilled workers, would be saved; the very nature of these *Grossaktionen* precluded special arrangements. In Janów, for example, the entire ghetto with all its inhabitants had been burned to the ground. On October 27, 1942, Himmler himself ordered the destruction of the last major Ukrainian ghetto, Pińsk.

In the western Ukraine, workshops that once produced *Panjewagen* (wooden carts), soap, candles, lumber, leather, and ropes for the German army stood abandoned at the end of the year. There were no replacements. A report by the armament command in Łuck tabulated the damage: "The leather works in Dubno are closed. . . In Kowel all *Panjewagen* workshops are paralyzed. . . . In the Kobrýn works we have a single Aryan metals worker. . . . In Brest-Litovsk the Jewish workshops now as before are empty." The Jews of the Ukraine had been annihilated.

A journalist traveling through the Ukraine in June 1943 reported that he had seen only four Jews. He had interviewed a high official of Reichskommissariat who had summed up the holocaust in these words: "Jews were exterminated like vermin."

At the end of 1942 the focus of attention shifted from the Ukraine to the Ostland. There, too, most of the Jews were already dead, but a sizable number (close to 100,000) were still alive. The killing of these remnants was a much more difficult process than the climactic waves of the second sweep could have led anyone to expect.

The Ostland remnant was divided into two groups: the forest Jews and the ghetto Jews (including camp inmates). The Jews in the forests and marshes were a special problem because they were no longer under control. They had run away and were now in hiding. Consequently, they were more important than their numbers (in the thousands) would indicate. In the main, we may distinguish among the forest Jews three types of survivors: (1) individual Jews who were hiding out, (2) Jews in the Soviet partisan movement, and (3) Jews banded together in Jewish units. The Jews still under control were living in the Ostland ghettos, as follows:

Latvia	4,000
Lithuania	34,000
White Russia	30,000
	68,000

These ghettos became a problem because they, too, developed into focal points of resistance.

The drive against the forest Jews was launched early in 1942. During February and March of that year, the SS and Police Leader North (Jeckeln) struck against the partisans in a drive that became the precursor of later "anti-partisan" operations by von dem Bach. Each of these operations covered a specific area. As a rule, the smaller ghettos in the area were wiped out, and any fugitives encountered alone or with the partisans were shot. In the prototype *Aktion Sumpffieber* (Action March Fever), carried out by Jeckeln in February–March, 389 "bandits" were killed in combat, 1,274 persons were shot on suspicion, and 8,350 Jews were mowed down on principle.

Following the establishment of the anti-partisan command under von dem Bach, Bandenkampfverbände led by Brigadeführer von Gottberg were thrown into action in White Russia. On November 26, 1942, von Gottberg reported 1,826 dead Jews, "not counting bandits, Jews, etc., burned in houses or dugouts." This was "Operation Nuremberg." On December 21 von Gottberg reported another 2,958 Jewish dead in "Operation Hamburg." On March 8, 1943, he reported 3,300 dead Jews in "Operation Hornung." In general, we may therefore conclude that this type of operation directed against the forest Jews was quite successful, although several thousand Jews in the woods were able to survive until the arrival of the Red Army.

In October 1942, just before the end of the Ukrainian sweep and in conjunction with the anti-partisan operations, the stage was set for the destruction of the remaining Ostland ghettos, which held altogether about 68,000 to 75,000 Jews. On October 23, 1942, Dr. Leibbrandt, the chief of the Political Division in the East Ministry, sent the following letter to Generalkommissar Kube:

> I request a report about the Jewish situation in the Generalbezirk White Russia, especially about the extent to which Jews are still employed by German offices, whether as interpreters, mechanics, etc. I ask for a prompt reply because I intend to bring about a solution of the Jewish question as soon as possible.

After a considerable delay Kube replied that, in cooperation with the Security Police, the possibilities of a further repression of Jewry were undergoing constant exploration and translation into action. But as late as April 1943 von Gottberg complained that Jews were still being employed in key positions, that Jews were sitting in central offices in Minsk, that even the idea of the court Jew was still alive.

As Kube had indicated, the reduction of the Ostland ghettos with their remnants of the Jewish skilled-labor force was a slow, grinding process. In the course of this process, two centers of resistance emerged in the territory, one within the ghettos, the other in the person of Generalkommissar Kube himself.

Within the ghettos Jewish attempts to organize a resistance movement were largely abortive. In Riga and to a lesser extent in Kaunas, the Jewish police *(Ordnungsdienst)* began to practice with firearms. (However, in both places the police were caught before a shot was fired.)

In the Vilna ghetto, where most Jewish inhabitants had been shot in 1941, a United Partisans Organization was formed in January 1942. Its leadership was composed of Communists, the nationalistic Zionist Revisionists, and members of the Zionist movements Hashomer Hatzair and Hanoar Hazioni. The command of this unusual political amalgamation was entrusted to the Communist Yitzhak Witenberg.

The self-imposed mission of Vilna's Jewish partisans was to fight an open battle at the moment when the ghetto faced total dissolution. While they were waiting for the confrontation, they had to cope with a ghetto population that was prone to illusions, and they had to resolve internal contradictions between Jewish and Communist priorities.

The dilemma of the United Partisans Organization was accentuated when non-Jewish Communists in the woods asked for reinforcements from the ghetto, and when some of the Jewish partisans themselves wanted to leave. Such departures were opposed by the official Jewish ghetto chief, Jacob Gens, whose policy of saving the ghetto by maintaining the largest possible work force required the presence of strong young people for the protection of vulnerable dependents not capable of heavy labor. Gens knew about the resistance, but he tolerated it only as a means of last resort and only under the condition that it would not interfere with his strategy.

In July 1943, the Germans captured the Lithuanian and Polish Communist leaders in Vilna, and discovered Witenberg's identity as a Communist. The German police demanded Witenberg's surrender with implied threats of mass reprisals. As Witenberg was hiding in a ghetto building, Gens dispatched his men armed with stones against assembled partisans. The attack was repelled, but the argument was not over. Witenberg wanted his partisans to fight then and there, yet they did not believe that the hour of ghetto had come or that the Germans were aware of their organization. Hence they overruled him, and Witenberg walked out of the ghetto to his death. According to some reports, Gens had given him a cyanide pill; other accounts indicate that his body was found mutilated the next day.

By August and September 1943, the Vilna ghetto was dissolved. Most of its inmates were sent to Estonia and Latvia, where they were subjected to attrition and shootings, and from where the remainder was subsequently routed to the Stutthof concentration camp. Other thousands were transported to the Lublin death camp, and still others were rounded up and shot. During these deportations, which were represented as work relocations, the United Partisans Organization realized that it did not have the Jewish community's support for a battle. It left the ghetto in small groups for the forest, falling prey to ambushes, regrouping, and holding on. Gens himself was called to a meeting by the Germans. A grave had already been dug for him. His death left the ghetto leaderless in its last days. A survivor who reflected about this history after the war remarked: "Today we must confess the error of the staff decision which forced Vitenberg [sic] to offer himself as a sacrifice for the twenty thousand Jews. . . . We should have mobilized and fought."

Generalkommissar Kube's postclimactic resistance was one of the strangest episodes in the history of the Nazi regime. His battle with the SS and Police was unique. Kube was an "old" Nazi who had once been purged (he had been a Gauleiter). As he had pointed out in one of his letters, he was certainly a "hard" man, and he was ready to "help solve the Jewish question." But there were limits to his ruthlessness.

In 1943 Kube had a serious controversy with the commander of the Security Police and SD (KdS) in White Russia, SS-Obersturmbann-führer Strauch. On July 20, Strauch arrested seventy Jews employed by Kube and killed them. Kube called Strauch immediately and accused him of chicanery. If Jews were killed in his office but Jews working for the armed forces were left alone, said Kube, this was a personal insult. Somewhat dumbfounded, Strauch replied that he "could not understand how German men could quarrel because of a few Jews." His record of the conversation went on:

> I was again and again faced with the fact that my men and I were reproached for barbarism and sadism, whereas I did nothing but fulfill my duty. Even the fact that expert physicians had removed in a proper way the gold fillings from the teeth of Jews who had been designated for special treatment was made the topic of conversation. Kube asserted that this method of our procedure was unworthy of a German man and of the Germany of Kant and Goethe. It was our fault that the reputation of Germany was being ruined in the whole world. It was also true, he said, that my men literally satisfied their sexual lust during these executions. I protested energetically against that statement and emphasized that it was

regrettable that we, in addition to having to perform this nasty job, were also made the targets of mudslinging.

Five days later, Strauch sent a letter to Obergruppenführer von dem Bach in which he recommended Kube's dismissal. In a long list of particulars, Strauch pointed out that Kube had for a long time favored the Jews, especially the Reich Jews. So far as the Russian Jews were concerned, Kube could quiet his conscience because most of them were "partisan helpers," but he could not distinguish between Germans and German Jews. He had insisted that the Jews had art. He had expressed his liking for Offenbach and Mendelssohn. When Strauch had disagreed, Kube had claimed that young Nazis did not know anything about such things. Repeatedly Kube had shown his feelings openly. He had called a policeman who had shot a Jew a "swine." Once, when a Jew had dashed into a burning garage to save the Generalkommissar's expensive car, Kube had shaken hands with the man and had thanked him personally. When the Judenrat in Minsk had been ordered to prepare 5,000 Jews for "resettlement," Kube had actually warned the Jews. He had also protested violently that fifteen Jewish men and women who had been shot had been led, covered with blood, through the streets of Minsk. Thus Kube had sought to pin on the SS the label of sadism.

While the recommendation by Strauch (technically a subordinate of the Generalkommissar) that Kube be dismissed was not carried out, Rosenberg decided to dispatch Staatssekretär Meyer to Minsk in order to give Kube a "serious warning." On September 24, 1943, the German press reported that Kube had been murdered "by Bolshevist agents of Moscow" (he was killed by a woman employed in his household). Himmler thought that Kube's death was a "blessing" for Germany. So far as Himmler was concerned, the Generalkommissar had been heading for a concentration camp anyway, for his Jewish policy had "bordered on treason."

A few months before Kube died, Himmler had decided to liquidate the entire ghetto system. The ghettos were to be turned into concentration camps. His decision appears to have been prompted at least in part by reports that Jews were employed in confidential positions and that, in the words of RSHA Chief Kaltenbrunner, the personal relations between Reich Germans and Jewish women had "exceeded those limits which for world-philosophical and race-political reasons should have been observed most stringently." The East Ministry acquiesced in Himmler's decision.

The changeover to concentration camp administration was carried out in Latvia without disturbance. In Lithuania the surrender of jusrisdiction to the SS and Police was accompanied by large-scale killing operations. In Kaunas several thousand Jews were shot and the remainder distributed in ten labor camps. In the Vilna ghetto, where the SS and Police had encountered "certain difficulties," the ghetto, with its 20,000 inmates, cleared "totally." In White Russia two concentrations of Jews remained, at Lida and Minsk. The Minsk Jews were ordered to Poland. Thus, by the end of 1943, Ostland Jewry had shrunk to some tens of thousands, who could look forward to evacuation or death. They were now concentration camp inmates, wholly within the jurisdiction of the SS and Police. But they were still the subject of some controversy.

As late as May 10, 1944, Ministerialdirektor Allwörden of the East Ministry addressed a letter to Obergruppenführer Pohl of the SS Economic-Administrative Main Office (WVHA) in which he said that the Rosenberg Ministry recognized the exclusive jurisdiction of the SS in Jewish matters. He also granted that the administration of the camps and the work activity in the camps would remain in the hands of the SS. But he "insisted" upon the continued payment of wage differentials to the Finance Office of the Reichskommissar. The Rosenberg ministry simply could not "resign" itself to this loss.

This correspondence preceded the breakup of the Baltic camps by only a few months. From August 1944 to January 1945, several thousand Jews were transported to concentration camps in the Reich. Many thousands of Baltic camp inmates were shot on the spot, just before the arrival of the Red Army.

During the final days of the second sweep, the SS and Police were beset by a weighty problem. The SS (and also the civil administration) was worried about the secrecy of the vast operation that was now coming to an end. Although photography control in the German ranks was now complete, Hungarian and Slovak officers had taken pictures of a number of "executions." The photographs were presumed to have reached America. This was considered especially "embarrassing," but nothing could be done about the matter. Even greater fears of discovery were generated as a result of the Red Army's westward advance. The occupied territories were full of mass graves, and Himmler was determined to leave no graves.

In June 1942, Himmler ordered the commander of Sonderkommando 4a, Standartenführer Paul Blobel, "to erase the traces of Einsatzgruppen executions in the East." Blobel formed a special Kommando with the code designation 1005. The Kommando had the task of digging up graves and burning bodies. Blobel traveled all over the occupied territories, looking for graves and conferring with Security Police officials. Once he took a visitor from the RSHA (Hartl) for a ride and, like a guide showing historical places to a tourist, pointed to the mass graves near Kiev where his own men had killed 34,000 Jews.

From the beginning, however, Blobel had to contend with problems. The BdS Ukraine (Thomas) was apathetic about the entire project. There was a shortage of gasoline. The members of the Kommandos found valuables in the graves and neglected to comply with the rules for handing them in. (Some of the men were later tried in Vienna for stealing Reich property.) When the Russians overran the occupied territories, Blobel had fulfilled only part of his task.

The SS and Police thus left behind many mass graves but few living Jews. The total number killed in this gigantic operation can now be tabulated.

Ostland and Army Group Rear Areas North and Center:

An Einsatzgruppe A draft report (winter 1941–42) listed the following figures of Jews killed:

Estonia	2,000
Latvia	70,000
Lithuania	136,421
White Russia	41,000

Einsatzgruppe B reported on September 1, 1942, a toll of 126,195.

Ukraine, Białystok, Army Group Rear Area South, and Rear Area Eleventh Army:

Einsatzgruppe C reported that two of its Kommandos (4a and 5) had killed 95,000 people up to the beginning of December 1941. Einsatzgruppe D reported on April 8, 1942, a total of 91,678 dead. Himmler reported to Hitler on December 29, 1942, the following numbers of Jews shot in the Ukraine, South Russia, and Białystok:

August 1942	31,246
September 1942	165,282
October 1942	95,735
November 1942	70,948
Total	363,211

These partial figures, aggregating more than 900,000, account for only about two thirds of the total number of Jewish victims in mobile operations. The remainder died in additional shootings by Einsatzgruppen, Higher SS and Police Leaders, Bandenkampfverbände, and the German army, as a result of Romanian operations in Odessa-Dalnik and the Golta camp complex, and in the course of privation in ghettos, camps, and the open woods and fields.

CHAPTER FIVE

DEPORTATIONS

The mobile killing operations in the occupied USSR were a prelude to a greater undertaking in the remainder of Axis Europe. A "Final Solution" was going to be launched in every region under German control.

The idea of killing the Jews had its shrouded beginnings in the far-distant past. There is a hint of killing in Martin Luther's long speech against the Jews. Luther likened the Jews to the obstinate Egyptian Pharaoh of the Old Testament: "Moses," said Luther, "could improve Pharaoh neither with plagues nor with miracles, neither with threats nor with prayers; he had to let him drown in the sea." In the nineteenth century the suggestion of total destruction emerged, in more precise and definite form, in a speech which Deputy Ahlwardt made to the Reichstag. Ahlwardt said that the Jews, like Thugs, were a criminal sect that had to be "exterminated." Finally, in 1939, Adolf Hitler uttered a threat of total annihilation in language far more explicit than that of his predecessors. This is what he said in his speech of January 1939:

> And one other thing I wish to say on this day which perhaps is memorable not only for us Germans: In my life I have often been a prophet, and most of the time I have been laughed at. During the period of my struggle for power, it was in the first instance the Jewish people that received with laughter my prophecies that some day I would take over the leadership of the state and thereby of the whole people, and that I would among other things solve also the Jewish problem. I believe that in the meantime that hyenous laughter of the Jews of Germany has been smothered in their throats. Today I want to be a prophet once more: If international-finance Jewry inside and outside of Europe should succeed once more in plunging nations into another world war, the consequence will not be the Bolshevization of the earth and thereby the victory of Jewry, but the annihilation of the Jewish race in Europe.

These remarks by Hitler have much more significance than the suggestions and hints of earlier German writers and speakers. To start with, the idea of "annihilation" was now emerging in the context of a definite expectation: another world war. As yet the image was not a plan, but there was an implication of imminence in the utterance. In the second place, Hitler was not only a propagandist but also the head of a state. He had at his disposal not only words and phrases, but also an administrative apparatus. He had power not only to speak but to act. Third, Hitler was a man who had a tremendous urge—one could almost say a compulsion—to carry out his threats. He "prophesied." With words he committed himself to action.

Only seven months were to pass before the war began. It provided physical and psychological conditions for drastic action against Jewish communities falling into German hands. Yet, even as the anti-Jewish regime was intensified, unusual and extraordinary efforts were made to reduce Europe's Jewish population by mass emigration. The biggest expulsion project, the Madagascar plan, was under consideration just one year before the inauguration of the killing phase. The Jews were not killed before the emigration policy was exhausted.

Let us examine these emigration plans more closely. Characteristically, the first forced emigration schemes were worked out in 1938, after the Germans had acquired Austria. When Hitler came to power, Germany had about 515,000 Jews. After five years, emigration and death had brought that number down to 350,000. However, in March 1938, when the Germans took Austria, 190,000 Jews were added to the 350,000, bringing the total to approximately 540,000, that is, 25,000 more than the original number. Obviously this was not progress. Some extraordinary measures had to be taken.

Thus we find that, especially toward the end of 1938, Schacht, Wohlthat, and a number of other officials were conferring with the Western democracies on ways and means of facilitating Jewish emigration. In October 1938 the Foreign Office took a look at the statistics on the Jewish population and discovered that about 10 percent of all Jews under German jurisdiction were Polish nationals. However, the Polish government was not anxious to recover its citizens. On October 6, Polish authorities issued a decree providing that holders of Polish passports abroad would be denied entry into Poland after October 29 unless such passports were stamped by an examiner.

The German Foreign Office reacted instantly. By the end of October thousands of Polish Jews were arriving in sealed trains at the Polish frontier town of Zbonszyn. The Poles barred the way. The trains were now sitting in "no man's land" between German and Polish cordons. Soon the Germans discovered that they had made a miscalculation. From the other direction, Polish trains filled with Jews of German nationality were moving toward the German frontier.

On October 29 the chief of the Foreign Office's Political Division, Wörmann, wrote a memorandum in which he expressed the view that conditions on the frontier were "untenable." The Foreign office had not calculated on reprisals. "What will happen now?" asked Wörmann. The administrative chief of the Security Police, Best, proposed that the Polish Jews be withdrawn to concentration camps. Wörmann thought that this solution might be too risky. Finally the problem was "solved" by a partial compromise. The Poles admitted about 7,000 Jews, additional thousands remained in Zbonszyn, the Germans had to take in some of their own nationals, and the remainder of the evacuees were allowed to return temporarily to their homes. During the discussions for the settlement of the problem, Staatssekretär Weizsäcker of the Foreign Office tried to prevail upon Polish Ambassador Lipski to take back the 40,000 to 50,000 Polish Jews in the Reich. Lipski contended that the figure was "exaggerated" and then stated that Weizsäcker was demanding of Poland an "enormous sacrifice."

While Poland refused to accept Jews of its own nationality, some of the Western countries were liberally admitting Jews of German nationality. But even in the West the admission of poor Jews, who had no money, was considered a very painful duty. In December 1938 Ribbentrop had a discussion on Jewish emigration with the foreign minister of the country of traditional asylum, France. This is Ribbentrop's record of his talk with the French Foreign Minister, Georges Bonnet:

> 1. The Jewish Question: After I had told M. Bonnet that I could not discuss this question officially with him, he said that he only wanted to tell me privately how great an interest was being taken in France in a solution of the Jewish problem. To my question as to what France's interest might be, M. Bonnet said that in the first place they did not want to receive any more Jews from Germany and whether we could not take some sort of measures to keep them from coming to France, and in the second place France had to ship 10,000 Jews somewhere else. They were actually thinking of Madagascar for this.
>
> I replied to M. Bonnet that we all wanted to get rid of our Jews but that the difficulties lay in the fact that no country wished to receive them.

The attitude displayed by Ambassador Lipski and Foreign Minister Bonnet prompted Hitler to make the following remark in his speech of January 1939: "It is a shameful example to observe today how the entire democratic world dissolves in tears of pity but then, in spite of its obvious duty to help, closes its heart to the poor, tortured Jewish people." This was not an idle accusation; it was an attempt to drag the Allied powers into the destruction process as passive but willing accomplices. It is significant that much later, when the killing phase was already under way and when its extent had become known in England and America, Goebbels remarked in connection with the Western protests: "At bottom, however, I believe both the English and the Americans are happy that we are exterminating the Jewish riffraff."

As if to strengthen its case, the German bureaucracy continued in 1939 to exhaust the emigration policy. This time, however, the primary effort was internal. Many bureaucratic encumbrances had impeded the emigration process: every prospective emigrant had to acquire more than a dozen official papers, certifying his health, good conduct, property, tax payments, emigration opportunities, and so on. Very soon the overburdened offices were jammed, and stagnation set in. The congestion hit Vienna first. To remedy the situation, Reichskommissar Bürckel (the official in charge of the "reunification of Austria with the Reich") set up, on August 26, 1938, the Central Office for Jewish Emigration. Each agency that had some certifying to do sent representatives to the central office in the Vienna Rothschild Palace. The Jews could now be processed on an assembly-line basis.

The Bürckel solution was soon adopted in the rest of the Reich. On January 24, 1939, Göring ordered the creation of the Reich Central Office for Jewish Emigration. The chief of the Reichszentrale was none other than Reinhard Heydrich. The *Geschäftsführer,* or deputy, taking care of the actual administration details was Standartenführer Oberregierungsrat Müller, later chief of the Gestapo. Other members of the Reichszentrale were Ministerialdirektor Wohlthat (Office of the Four-Year Plan) and representatives of the Interior Ministry, the Finance Ministry, and the Foreign Office.

Emigration was still the policy after the war had broken out. In fact, the first reaction to the victories in Poland and in France was to punish these countries for their attitude toward Jewish emigration by sending there some of the Jews who had previously been kept out. In the beginning of 1940, six thousand Jews were sent from Vienna, Prague, Moravska Ostrava, and Stettin to the Generalgouvernement. In October 1940 two Gauleiter in western Germany, Wagner and Bürckel, secured the cooperation of the Gestapo in the deportation of 6,500 Jews to unoccupied France. But by far the most ambitious project of 1940 was the Madagascar plan.

Until 1940, emigration plans had been confined to a consideration of the resettlement of thousands or, as in the case of the Schacht plan, 150,000 Jews. The Madagascar project was designed to take care of millions of Jews. The authors of the plan wanted to empty the Reich-Protektorat area and all of occupied Poland of their Jewish population. The whole idea was thought up in Section III of Abteilung Deutschland of the Foreign Office. (Indeed, Abteilung Deutschland was to concern itself a great deal with Jewish matters.) The plan was transmitted to a friendly neighboring agency: Heydrich's Reich Security Main Office. Heydrich was enthusiastic about the idea.

The reason for Heydrich's enthusiasm becomes quite clear the moment we look at this plan. Briefly, the African island of Madagascar was to be ceded by France to Germany in a peace treaty. The German navy was to have its pick of bases on the island, and the remainder of Madagascar was to be placed under the jurisdiction of a police governor responsible directly to Heinrich Himmler. The area of the police governor was to become a Jewish reservation. The resettlement of the Jews was to be financed through the utilization of Jewish property left behind.

This plan, according to Abteilung Deutschland, was greatly preferable to the establishment of a Jewish community in Palestine. In the first place, Palestine belonged to the Christian and Moslem worlds. Second, if the Jews were kept in Madagascar, they could be held as hostages to ensure the good conduct of their "racial comrades" in America. Heydrich did not need these arguments. For him it was enough that practically the whole island was to be governed by the SS and Police. But the Madagascar plan did not materialize. It hinged on the conclusion of a peace treaty with France, and such a treaty depended on an end of hostilities with England. With no end to the hostilities there was no peace treaty, and with no peace treaty there was no Madagascar.

The Madagascar plan was the last major effort to "solve the Jewish problem" by emigration. Many hopes and expectations had been pinned on this plan by offices of the Security Police, the Foreign Office, and the Generalgouvernement. Even as it faded, the project was to be mentioned one more time, during early February 1941, in Hitler's headquarters. On that occasion, the party's labor chief, Ley, brought up the Jewish question and Hitler, answering at length, pointed out that the war was going to accelerate the solution of this problem but that he was also encountering additional difficulties. Originally, he had been in a position to address himself at most to the Jews of Germany, but now the goal had to be the elimination of Jewish influence in the entire Axis power sphere. In some countries, such as Poland and Slovakia, he could act alone with his own organs. In France, however, the armistice was an obstacle and precisely there the problem was especially important. If only he knew where he could put these few million Jews; it was not as if there were so many. He was going to approach the French about Madagascar. When Bormann asked how the Jews could be transported there in the middle of the war, Hitler replied that one would have to consider that. He would be willing to make available the entire German fleet for this purpose, but he did not wish to expose his crews to the torpedoes of enemy submarines. Now he was thinking about all sorts of things differently, and not with greater friendliness.

While Hitler was thinking, the machinery of destruction was permeated with a feeling of uncertainty. In the Generalgouvernement, where ghettoization was viewed as a transitional measure, the unsightly Jewish quarters with their impoverished crowds were trying the patience of local German officials. These irritations and frustrations were expressed in monthly reports by the late summer of 1940. In the Lublin district the Kreishauptmann of Krasnystaw, surfeited with his administrative tasks, insisted that Jews who had Polonized their names spell them in German—in Madagascar, he said, they could have Madagascarian names. At the same time, the Kreishauptmann of Jasło (in the Kraków district), noting the "invasion" of his Kreis by Jews expelled from the city of Kraków, invoked the opinion of Polish residents who, he asserted, were doubting the German resolve to undertake an eventual total evacuation of the Jews. Several months later, in the Radom district, the Kreishauptmann of Jędrzejów, complaining about the intractability of inflation, suggested that the principal tool for dealing with price rises was the early solution of the Jewish problem. Generalgouverneur Frank evidently shared these sentiments. On March 25, 1941, he revealed to his close associates that Hitler had promised him "that the Generalgouvernement, in recognition of its accomplishments, would become the first territory to be free of Jews."

In the neighboring Wartheland, a grass-roots movement to eliminate the Jews became even more pronounced. There, Sturmbannführer Rolf-Heinz Höppner wrote a letter to Eichmann on July 16, 1941, pointing out that in the course of various discussions in the office of Reichsstatthalter Greiser, solutions had been proposed that "sound in part fantastic," but that in his view were thoroughly feasible. A camp for 300,000 was to be created with barracks for tailor shops, shoe-manufacturing plants, and the like. Such a camp could be guarded more easily than a ghetto, but it was not going to be a complete answer. "This winter," said Höppner, "there is a danger that not all of the Jews can be fed anymore. One should weigh earnestly," he continued, "if the most humane solution might not be to finish off those of the Jews who are not employable by some quick-working device. At any rate, that would be more pleasant than to let them starve to death." According to Höppner, the Reichsstatthalter had not made up his mind about these suggestions, but by the end of the year the Jews of the Wartheland were being killed in a death camp, Kulmhof, in the province.

In the Reich itself the ministerial bureaucracy was cementing the anti-Jewish process with decrees and ordinances. During the spring of 1941 there were deliberations about a complex legal measure: a declaration that all Reich Jews were stateless or, alternatively, "protectees." The Interior Ministry desired the measure in order to remove the "awkward" fact that harsh action was taken against people who were still viewed, at least in the outside world, as Reich nationals. Because of the legal complexities of the issue, it was decided to submit the question to Hitler.

On June 7, 1941, the Chief of the Reich Chancellery, Lammers, addressed two identical letters to the Interior and Justice Ministries, in which he wrote simply that Hitler considered the measure unnecessary. Lammers then addressed a third letter to his counterpart in the party, Bormann. In that letter Lammers repeated the message with a confidential explanation. "The Führer," he wrote, "has not agreed to the regulation proposed by the Reich Minister of the Interior, primarily because he is of the opinion that after the war there would not be any Jews left in Germany anyhow." Hence it was not necessary to issue a decree that would be difficult to enforce, that would tie up personnel, and that would still not bring about a solution in principle.

Toward the end of the spring of 1941, German officials in occupied France were still approached with applications from Jews who were trying to emigrate. On May 20, 1941, a Gestapo official from the RSHA, Walter Schellenberg, informed the military commander in France that the emigration of Jews from his area was to be prevented because transport facilities were limited and because the "Final Solution of the Jewish question" was now in sight.

Heydrich now took the next step. He instructed his expert in Jewish affairs, Adolf Eichmann, to draft an authorization that would allow him to proceed against Jewry on a European-wide basis. In carefully chosen bureaucratic language the draft, not more than three sentences long, was submitted to Göring, ready for his signature. The text, which was signed by Göring on July 31, 1941, is as follows:

> Complementing the task already assigned to you in the directive of January 24, 1939, to undertake, by emigration or evacuation, a solution of the Jewish question as advantageous as possible under the conditions at the time, I hereby charge you with making all necessary organizational, functional, and material preparations for a complete solution of the Jewish question in the German sphere of influence in Europe.
>
> Insofar as the jurisdiction of other central agencies may be touched thereby, they are to be involved.
>
> I charge you furthermore with submitting to me in the near future an overall plan of the organizational, functional, and material measures to be taken in preparing for the implementation of the aspired final solution of the Jewish question.

With the receipt of this letter, Heydrich held the reins of the destruction process in his hands. Soon he would be able to use his mandate.

For years, the administrative machine had taken its initiatives and engaged in its forays one step at a time. In the course of that evolution, a direction had been charted and a pattern had been established. By the middle of 1941, the dividing line had been reached, and beyond it lay a field of unprecedented actions unhindered by the limits of the past. More and more of the participants were on the verge of realizing the nature of what could happen now. Salient in this crystallization was the role of Adolf Hitler himself, his stance before the world, and, more specifically, his wishes or expectations voiced in an inner circle. Already, Frank had cited Hitler's promise to him with respect to the Generalgouvernement, Lammers had quoted Hitler's intentions for the Reich, and Himmler had invoked Hitler's authority for the Einsatzgruppen operations in the invaded Soviet territories. Then, one day toward the end of the summer, Eichmann was called into Heydrich's office, where the RSHA chief told him: "I have just come from the Reichsführer; the Führer has now ordered the physical annihilation of the Jews. Eichmann could not measure the content of the words, and he believed that not even Heydrich had expected this "consequence" When Eichmann reported to Müller shortly thereafter, he realized from the Gestapo chief's silent nod that Müller already knew. He always knows, thought Eichmann, though he never moves from his desk.

Deportations were now in the offing. On September 18, 1941, Himmler wrote to Geiser about Hitler's wish to empty the Reich-Protektorat area, and suggested Łódź as a stopover for about 60,000 of the deportees. Two weeks later he proposed to Hitler the "storage" of Jews in Riga, Tallinn, and Minsk. By October 10, 1941, at a "Final Solution" conference in the RSHA, Heydrich mentioned possible deportations of 50,000 Jews to Riga and Minsk, and of still others to camps prepared for communists by Einsatzgruppen B and C in the military areas of the occupied USSR. Heydrich was in a pivotal position to carry out such plans, inasmuch as his Gestapo was prepared to organize deportations in the West and his Einsatzgruppen were already conducting killing operations in the East.

The obstacles, however, were considerable. Heydrich could not deport all the Reich Jews before dealing with such knotty problems as intermarriage, the Jews in the armament industry, and the foreign Jews. He could not even begin to move in the occupied areas and Axis satellite states. He knew that he had to call upon all the other agencies that had jurisdiction in Jewish matters to act with him. Accordingly, on November 29, 1941, he sent invitations to a number of Staatssekretäre and chiefs of SS main offices for a "Final Solution" conference. In his invitation Heydrich said:

Considering the extraordinary importance which has to be conceded to these questions, and in the interest of achieving the same viewpoint by all central agencies concerned with the remaining work in connection with this final solution, I suggest that these problems be discussed in a conference, especially since the Jews have been evacuated in continuous transports from the Reich territory, including the Protektorat of Bohemia and Moravia, to the East, ever since October 15, 1941.

The reception of the Heydrich invitation was quite interesting. Heydrich had spoken only of a "Final Solution." He had not defined it and he had not mentioned killings. The meaning of the "Final Solution" had to be surmised. The recipients of the letter knew that the Jews were to be deported, but they were not told what was to be done to the deportees; that was something they had to figure out for themselves. The situation created an intense interest.

In the Generalgouvernement the news of the "final solution" conference was the thought, if not the topic, of the day. Frank was so impatient that he sent Staatssekretär Bühler to Berlin to sound out Heydrich. In personal conversation with the RSHA chief, Bühler found out everything there was to know. The Reich Chancellery, too, was the scene of excited expectation. Even before the Heydrich letter was received, Lammers—who was one of the best-informed bureaucrats in the capital—had alerted his chancellery with an order that "if invitations to a meeting were sent out" by the RSHA, one of the chancellery officials was to attend as a "listening post." In the Foreign Office, Abteilung Deutschland received the news of the conference with enthusiastic endorsement. The experts of the division immediately drew up a memorandum entitled "Requests and Ideas of the Foreign Office in Connection with the Intended Final Solution of the Jewish Question in Europe." The memorandum was a kind of priority deportation schedule, indicating which countries were to be cleared of Jews first.

The conference was originally scheduled for December 9, 1941, but it was postponed, at the last minute, until January 20, 1942, at noon, "followed by luncheon." On that day the conference was held in the offices of the RSHA, Am Grossen Wannsee No. 50/58. The following officials were present:

SS-Obergruppenführer Heydrich, chairman (RSHA)
Gauleiter Dr. Meyer (East Ministry)
Reichsamtsleiter Dr. Leibbrandt (East Ministry)
Staatssekretär Dr. Stuckart (Interior Ministry)
Staatssekretär Neumann (Office of the Four-Year Plan)
Staatssekretär Dr. Freisler (Justice Ministry)
Staatssekretär Dr. Bühler (Generalgouvernement)
Unterstaatssekretär Luther (Foreign Office)
SS-Oberführer Klopfer (Party Chancellery)
Ministerialdirektor Kritzinger (Reich Chancellery)

SS-Obergruppenführer Hofmann (RuSHA)
SS-Gruppenführer Müller (RSHA IV)
SS-Obersturmbannführer Eichmann (RSHA IV-B-4)
SS-Oberführer Dr. Schöngarth (BdS Generalgouvernement)
SS-Sturmbannführer Dr. Lange (KdS Latvia, deputizing for BdS Ostland)

Heydrich opened the conference by announcing that he was the plenipotentiary for the preparation of the "Final Solution of the Jewish question" in Europe; his office was responsible for the central direction of the "Final Solution" regardless of boundaries. Heydrich then reviewed the emigration policy and cited statistics on emigrated Jews. Instead of emigration, he continued, the Führer had now given his sanction to the evacuation of the Jews to the East as a further "solution possibility." The RSHA chief then drew out a chart that indicated the Jewish communities to be evacuated. (The list included even the English Jews.)

Next, Heydrich explained what was to happen to the evacuees: they were to be organized into huge labor columns. In the course of this labor utilization, a majority would undoubtedly "fall away through natural decline." The survivors of this "natural selection" process—representing the tenacious hard core of Jewry—would have to be "treated accordingly," since these Jews had been shown in the light of history to be the dangerous Jews, the people who could rebuild Jewish life. Heydrich did not elaborate on the phrase "treated accordingly," although we know from the language of the Einsatzgruppen reports that he meant killing.

Practically, Heydrich continued, the implementation of the "Final Solution" would proceed from west to east. If only because of the apartment shortage and "socio-political" reasons, the Reich-Protektorat areas were to be placed at the head of the line. Next he touched on the subject of differential treatment of special classes of Jews. The old Jews, Heydrich announced, were to be sent to a ghetto for old people at Theresienstadt in the Protektorat. The Jews who had distinguished themselves on the German side in World War I also were to be sent to Theresienstadt. In that manner, he concluded, all interventions on behalf of individuals would be shut out automatically.

Unterstaatssekretär Luther, speaking for the Foreign Office, then made a few comments. Luther felt that the "deeply penetrating treatment of this problem" would create difficulties in some countries, notably Denmark and Norway. He urged that evacuations in such areas be postponed. On the other hand, he foresaw no difficulties in the Balkans and in Western Europe.

Following the Luther remarks, the conferees got into an involved discussion of the treatment of the Mischlinge and of Jews in mixed marriages. Although this problem affected victims only in the Reich, the Staatssekretäre spent about half the conference time in discussion of the issue.

Finally, Staatssekretär Bühler urged that the "Final Solution" be organized immediately in the Generalgouvernement. He explained that in Poland the transport problem was negligible and that not many Jews were working there. The majority, he said, were incapable of work.

At the conclusion of the conference the participants, already quite relaxed while butlers were pouring brandy, talked about "the various types of solution possibilities." In the course of these remarks, Staatssekretäre Meyer and Bühler urged that certain preparatory measures be started immediately in the occupied eastern territories and the Generalgouvernement.

After the meeting was concluded, thirty copies of the conference record were circulated in the ministries and SS main offices. Gradually the news of the "Final Solution" seeped through the ranks of the bureaucracy. The knowledge did not come to all officials at once. How much a man knew depended on his proximity to the destructive operations and on his insight into the nature of the destruction process. Seldom, however, was comprehension recorded on paper. When the bureaucrats had to deal with deportation matters, they kept referring to a Jewish "migration." In official correspondence the Jews were still "wandering." They were "evacuated" and "resettled." They "wandered off" and "disappeared." These terms were not the product of naïveté, but convenient tools of psychological repression.

On the very highest level the full burden of knowledge revealed itself in the written word. Hitler, Göring, Himmler, and Goebbels had a complete view of the destruction process. They knew the details of the mobile killing operations in Russia, and they saw the whole scheme of the deportations in the rest of Europe. For these men it was difficult to resort to pretense. When Goebbels found out that the SS and Police Leader in Lublin, Globocnik, was constructing killing centers, he wrote: "Not much will remain of the Jews. . . . A judgment is being visited upon the Jews [which is] barbaric. . . . The prophecy which the Führer made about them for having brought on a new world war is beginning to come true in a most terrible manner."

Göring spoke of burned bridges and of a position "from which there is no escape." Himmler and also Goebbels explained that the "Final Solution" was a task that could not have been postponed, because in world history there was only one Adolf Hitler and because the war had presented to the German leadership a unique opportunity for "solving the problem." Later generations would have neither the strength nor the opportunity to finish with the Jews.

Hitler himself addressed the German people and the world once more. This is what he said on September 30, 1942:

> In my Reichstag speech of September 1, 1939, I have spoken of two things: first, that now that the war has been forced upon us, no array of weapons and no passage of time will bring us to defeat, and second, that if Jewry should plot another world war in order to exterminate the Aryan peoples of Europe, it would not be the Aryan peoples, which would be exterminated, but Jewry. . . .
>
> At one time, the Jews of Germany laughed about my prophecies. I do not know whether they are still laughing or whether they have already lost all desire to laugh. But right now I can only repeat: they will stop laughing everywhere, and I shall be right also in that prophecy.

CENTRAL AGENCIES OF DEPORTATION

The implementation of Hitler's prophecy was a vast administrative undertaking. To start with, the preliminary process of defining the victims, attaching their property, and restricting their movements had to be extended to all the areas from which deportations were to be conducted. Before the completion of these steps in a particular territory, that area was not "ready." Even a segregated community could still be tied in countless social and economic relationships to its neighbors. The more "essential" a Jew appeared to be in the economy, the more extensive his legal or family connections with non-Jews, the more medals he had to show for service in the First World War, that much greater was the difficulty of uprooting him from his surroundings. Outside the German and Polish frontiers these complications were multiplied. Wherever Germans did not exercise plenary power, they had to employ foreign machinery for the accomplishment of their aims, and they had to deal with foreign conceptions of the ramifications and consequences of the operation. Only then could transports begin to roll. Finally, the very departure of the Jews generated new tasks. Lost production had to be replaced, unpaid Jewish debts had to be regulated, and—after the fate of the Jewish deportees could no longer be hidden—the psychological repercussions on the non-Jewish population had to be smoothed and eliminated.

The machine that carried out the "Final Solution" consisted of a large array of offices, German and non-German, uniformed and civilian, central and municipal. Two agencies were instrumental in carrying out the deportation process in its very center: one, the RSHA's office IV-B-4, was relatively small; the other, the Transport Ministry, was one of the largest. *Referat* IV-B-4, under Adolf Eichmann, covered the entire deportation area outside of Poland (where SS and Police offices dealt with the dissolution of the ghettos). The Transport Ministry, with its subsidiaries and affiliates, was responsible for trains throughout Axis Europe.

Even so small a section as Eichmann's was involved in manifold decisions. Within the Reich-Protektorat area, Eichmann's jurisdiction extended to seizure and transport. For this purpose he availed himself of the regional Gestapo offices and the Central Offices for Jewish Emigration. In the satellite and occupied countries, from Western Europe to the Balkans, he stationed experts on Jewish affairs with German embassies or Higher SS and Police Leaders to work out deportation plans on the spot. There his control was less total than in the Reich, but in these foreign areas the Eichmann machinery concerned itself with the entire uprooting phase of the deportations, including the initiation of anti-Jewish laws, the various definitions and categorizations of the Jewish victims, and the time and procurement of transportation.

In the RSHA hierarchy Eichmann's office, with its subdivisions, was placed as follows:

RSHA: Obergruppenführer Heydrich (Kaltenbrunner)
  IV (Gestapo): Gruppenführer Müller
    IV-B (Sects): Sturmbannführer Hartl (later vacant)
      IV-B-4 (Jews): Obersturmbannführer Eichmann
        IV-B-4-a (Evacuations): Sturmbannführer Günther
        General matters: Wöhrn
        Transport: Novak (deputy: Hartmann, later Martin)
        Single cases: Moes (Kryschak)
        IV-B-4-b (Law): Sturmbannführer Suhr (later Hunsche)
        Deputy: Hunsche
        Finance and property: Gutwasser
        Foreign areas: Bosshammer

There was a direct line between Gruppenführer Müller, the Gestapo chief, and Eichmann. Müller, as Eichmann recalled after the war, was a "sphinx." A criminologist by background, he acted like a bureaucrat, committing everything to paper and holding frequent conferences with large numbers of subordinates. He also reserved power to himself. Whereas Eichmann made arrangements for deportations, only Müller could "take his orange-colored pencil and . . . write on top *5,000*

Jews." Nevertheless, the relationship between the two men, despite disparity of rank and position, was apparently close. Every Thursday, Müller would invite some of his specialists to an evening in his apartment, serving a little cognac, discussing business, and touching upon the personal affairs of his guests. There were chess games, Müller playing frequently with Eichmann. Müller always won.

Eichmann had come to Office IV from the SD and the Vienna Zentralstelle. In 1941 he was thirty-five years old. At his postwar trial in Jerusalem, he emerged as a drinker who on occasion had used abusive language toward Jews but who had paid a rabbi for Hebrew lessons. With his subordinates Eichmann maintained cordial relations. He played chess with them, and a small IV-B-4 ensemble made music. Eichmann's instrument was the second violin.

In office IV-B-4-a the ascetic Sturmbannführer Günther and his assistant, Hauptsturmführer Novak, dealt with the crucial problem of transport. It is they who requisitioned the trains. The procurement of a transport was predicated on Günther's ability to spccify a point of departure and a place of arrival. If departure was the culmination of an uprooting process, the destination was primarily a matter of administrative preparation. Even so, the choice of a ghetto or camp for unloading a particular train could entail considerations of policy, and, especially at the beginning, such questions might have had to be referred to Himmler himself. When the "Final Solution" was under way, routing became more and more a function of logistics—distances to and capacities of individual camps. Once a timetable with origin and destination was obtained from the Transport Ministry, IV-B-4-a could send the information to the appropriate police office for the seizure of the victims and to the intended camp for their reception. The number of deportees was then noted on a chart attached to the back of Günther's desk.

The transports were carried out by the Reichsbahn. This administrative juggernaut, which in 1942 employed almost half a million civil servants and 900,000 workers, was one of the largest organizations of the Third Reich. It was a component of the Transport Ministry, which dealt also with roads and canals and which was headed by Dorpmüller, an older man who held the office from 1937 to the end of the war. The Staatssekretär in charge of the Reichsbahn was at first Kleinmann and later, from May 23, 1942, Ganzenmüller, a capable thirty-seven-year-old technocrat with Nazi credentials. The Reichsbahn was an insulated, self-contained structure, as "nonpolitical" in its appearance as the Security Police, for its part, was the open epitomization of Nazism. Yet it was upon the railroads that Speer's Ministry for War Production depended for the movement of goods, the armed forces for the transport of troops, and the RSHA for the deportation of the Jews. For all these operations the Reichsbahn was indispensable.

The central apparatus of the Reichsbahn consisted of several divisions. The Traffic Division set priorities and rates, the Operations Division was concerned with train formation and schedules, and Group L worked with OKH/Transport (General Gercke) in the dispatch of trains carrying troops and munitions.

Reichsbahn: Ganzenmüller
  E   I   Traffic and Tariffs: Treibe (from 1942, Schelp)
      (15-17: Passenger Traffic)
     17   International Passenger Traffic: Rau
  E II   Operations: Leibbrand (from 1942, Dilli)
    21   Passenger Trains: Schnell
      211   Special Trains: Stange
  L   (Armed Forces): Ebeling

Territorially the railroad structure was composed of three regional *Generalbetriebsleitungen,* a larger number of subregional *Reichsbahndirektionen,* and many local railway stations. Of the three Generalbetriebsleitungen, the eastern *(Ost)* was preeminent. It was from here that the stream of traffic to the eastern front as well as to the death camps was directed.

Generalbetriebsleitung Ost (Berlin): Ernst Emrich
  I   Operations: Eggert (Mangold)
     L: Bebenroth
     P (Passenger Schedules): Fröhlich
     PW (Passenger Cars): Jacobi
  II   Traffic: Simon (Harttmann)
  III   Main Car Allocation Office [freight cars]: Schultz
Generalbetriebsleitung West (Essen): Sarter
Generalbetriebsleitung Süd (Munich): Wilhelm Emrich

Each Reichsbahndirektion had an operations section and a car bureau. In each operations section there was an office "33" that handled passenger trains.

Even though Jews were carried in freight cars, they were booked by the Reichsbahn's financial specialists as passengers. In principle, any group of travelers was accepted for payment. The basic charge was the third-class fare: 4 pfennig per track kilometer. Children under ten were transported for half this amount; those under four went free. Group fare (half of the third-class rate) was available if at least 400 persons were transported. The agency billed for the money was the one that requisitioned the transport. In the case of the Jewish death trains, that agency was the RSHA. For the deportees one-way fare was payable; for the

171

guards a round-trip ticket had to be purchased. Billings were sometimes channeled through the official travel agency, the Mitteleuropäische Reisebüro, and on occasion payment might be delayed.

The maxim that deportees were travelers was applied also in operations. That is to say that passenger train officials rather than freight car experts were engaged in the formation and scheduling of the death transports. For a deportation originating in the Reich itself, the chain of jurisdiction thus led from the RSHA IV-B-4a (Novak) to 21 and 211 in the Transport Ministry, and through Generalbetriebsleitung (GBL) Ost/ P and PW (a transport from the Rhine river city of Düsseldorf would also be processed by GBL West) to all Reichsbahndirektionen (offices "33") along the route.

The passenger concept was used outside the Reich as well. Payment, however, had to be made in foreign currency, and billings could be more complicated. The actual dispatch of the trains was the work of a large organization of railroads, including those under Reichsbahn control, autonomous railways in satellite countries, and networks supervised by the Chief of Military Transport (Gercke) in areas under military rule. Where German railroad offices were established, as in Poland and France, their structure was patterned after the Reich model, down to offices "33" for the scheduling of Jewish trains. The preservation of these time-honored prerogatives was coupled with an adherence to routine decision making. In the daily administration of transport programs, the deportation of the Jews was therefore embedded in the regular procedures for allocations of rolling stock to users and assignments of time on tracks.

In Reich territory proper (including Austria, Polish incorporated areas, and Białystok, but not the Protektorat and the Generalgouvernement), there were approximately 850,000 freight cars, some 130,000 of which were assembled for loading each day. About 60 percent of the equipment was specialized (open cars for coal or ore), and a large portion of the remainder was used for the armed forces or for vital freight. Given the demands of war, every allocation of space became significant, and at some point a shipment might have to be left behind. This problem existed also outside the Reichsbahn network, throughout Axis Europe. Within the Generalgouvernement, for example, the distances from the ghettos to the death camps were comparatively short, but the capacity of the Generalgouvernement's railways (the Ostbahn) to cope with demand was lower than the Reichsbahn's capability at home, and the number of prospective deportees, as a percentage of the Ostbahn's traffic volume, was much higher than in the Reich. In fact, there were times when all available locomotives and cars were preempted by military or industrial claimants or when civilian traffic as a whole was curtailed or eliminated on congested routes for weeks on end. Such emergencies called for special efforts to assure the loading of the Jews at the earliest possible moment. Indeed, on some occasions the impossible was done, and Jewish transports were dispatched as "armed forces trains" to accelerate their movement.

Generally, the decision flow would begin in the office of Hauptsturmführer Novak in Eichmann's office. Novak would take his request to 21 (Schnell) and 211 (Stange). The chief of 211, who was about sixty years of age, was for practical purposes the principal Jewish expert of the Transport Ministry. He acted as an expediter and as a control point. Closeted in his office, choleric by temperament, he would speak loudly into the telephone. Although he was only an *Amtsrat,* he had held that rank for twenty years, and mail was addressed to him directly by name. The Novak–Stange link of the chain affected transportation in all parts of Europe wherever territorial jurisdictional lines were crossed, as between a satellite system and the Reichsbahn, or between two or more Direktionen of the Reichsbahn itself. Within the Generalgouvernement, Security Police officials who were stationed in the area could negotiate with the Ostbahn directly.

When preparations were completed in the Ministry, a directive would be sent by E II to the appropriate Generalbetriebsleitung for further action. GBL Ost, with its control of car allocation, would be involved in any case. Jewish transports were special passenger trains *(Sonderzüge).* Unlike regular passenger trains, which would always leave at a stated time, no Sonderzug would move without specific orders. The Sonderzüge were marked with a simple code: DA was the designation for Jewish deportation trains originating outside of Poland, Pkr or Pj for Jewish Sonderzüge assembled in the Generalgouvernement. The GBL Ost had a *Sonderzuggruppe* that dealt with Jews, forced laborers, children, and others. The two driving personalities in this group were Reichsbahnoberinspektor Fähnrich (in PW under Jacobi) for car assignments and Reichsbahnoberinspektor Bruno Klemm for scheduling. Periodically the Sonderzuggruppe would meet in Frankfurt am Main, Bamberg, or Berlin, to discuss twenty-five or fifty trains, including DA transports. Generalbetriebsleitung Ost/PW (Jacobi) would then issue a circulatory plan fixing the dates of departure and arrival of each transport as well as the return or rerouting of the empty train. As far as possible, the cars were to be assembled by the Direktion responsible for departure from its own supplies, but in cases of heavy demand, the GBL Ost could shift equipment from one Direktion to another.

The next refinement (at the level of Reichsbahndirektion, Haupteisenbahndirektion, etc.) was the scheduling and assembly of the train. Each Direktion operated with a basic traffic plan, the so-called book timetable, divided into two parts: the regular timetable, devoted to ordinary passenger trains whose schedules were posted, and a demand timetable for trains dispatched only when needed. The latter category comprised freight trains and all irregular passenger trains, including Jewish Sonderzüge. Through traffic was assured by means of an interconnected plan under which segments of the demand timetables belonging to adjacent Direktionen were fused. The Sonderzüge carrying Jews had to be entered on the demand timetable, but in the event that all the time slots were in use, an office "33" could prepare a special schedule to permit the transport to move on empty track between other trains. As Eichmann pointed out, the construction of timetables was a science in itself. The scheduling decisions were finally incorporated in a timetable order specifying not only the exact hours and minutes of departure and traversal but also the station that had to supply the locomotives and cars. Because of wartime conditions, the timetables were frequently altered. Telephone calls and telegrams would then be required to deal with disruptions and congestion. In the end the Jews were delivered to their deaths, and the cars were returned to the circulatory flow. The task was being accomplished.

THE REICH—PROTEKTORAT AREA

The deportations were to begin in the Reich. Decisions made for Germany itself were to be a model for occupied territories and an example to satellite countries. Measures against Jews had been taken over a much longer period in Germany than anywhere else, and the machinery of destruction was larger and more finely honed there than in other areas of Europe. On the other hand, the Reich-Protektorat area posed special problems, and uprooting the Jews of Germany was going to require special efforts.

The early movements of Jews from the Reich to neighboring areas in occupied France and Poland were marked by a sense of impatience. Berlin and Vienna, Hamburg and Munich were to be free of the remaining Jews, or at least free of most of them, as soon as possible. Before long, however, the Heydrich machine was intruding upon various jurisdictions. Many prospective deportees were in controversial categories, in that their inclusion in deportation lists would create complications or entail disadvantages. Among these individuals were the Mischlinge and Jews in mixed marriages, prominent Jews, old Jews, war veterans, foreign Jews, and Jews in the armament industry. Other categories posed custody problems and required special arrangements, namely, the Jews in insane asylums, concentration camps, and prisons. In short, the RSHA had to negotiate on the very highest level with many agencies before deporting the Reich-Protektorat Jews.

With the conclusion of these negotiations, a major problem had been solved. What remained was the seizure and transport of the deportable Jews and the wearisome undertaking of confiscating the belongings they left behind.

SEIZURE AND TRANSPORT

Unlike questions involving definitions and deferments, the seizure of the Jews generated few difficulties and little friction in the bureaucracy. The roundups were in the hands of the Gestapo. To the extent that it could not carry out the task alone, it could call upon the Criminal Police, Order Police, SS, or SA in various cities for assistance. More generally, it could avail itself of the machinery of the Jewish Community, the Reichsvereinigung and the Kultusgemeinden, for lists, notification of victims, maps, supplies, clerks, and auxiliaries. The Jewish orderlies, variously called *Transporthelfer, Ordner, Ausheber,* or *Abholer,* would sometimes accompany police to the apartments of those selected for transport and would help supervise the arrested persons at collecting points, usually converted old-age homes or other institutional buildings renamed *Sammelstellen, Durchgangslager,* or *Abwanderungslager,* until there were enough people to fill a train.

Two phases may be noted in the evolution of the roundup procedure. At first, long lists were submitted by the Jewish Communities, from which the Gestapo could make its selection. During this period there were more victims than available transports or prepared destinations. Jewish Community offices could therefore ask for deferments or exemptions of named individuals, and often these requests were granted. In the initial period, moreover, the victims were told where they were going. On November 13, 1941, for example, the Jewish Community of Cologne sent a letter to all Jews in its jurisdiction announcing "another transport of 1,000 persons, specifically to Minsk," for December 8. In this communication everyone was given instructions on how to prepare for transport, pending subsequent notification by the Community of those who would make the trip.

The second phase, beginning with the operation of the death camps, was carried out with multiple master lists, obtained from police precincts and Community tax records, and supplemented by addresses kept by Community housing offices. In various cities police would then proceed against Jewish residents without notification, appearing at apartment doors in the early morning or late in the evening. The extent of the operation was not concealed from the Jewish leadership. On May 30, 1942, Eichmann went so far as to inform Vienna's Jewish Community chief Löwenherz that he anticipated the complete evacuation of the Jews from the Reich, Austria, and the Protektorat, the old ones to Theresienstadt, the others to the "East." Only the camps were not mentioned, and in the housing registers the whereabouts of the deported Jews were to be entered as "unknown" or a notation was to be made that the former Jewish inhabitants had "emigrated."

Each city had its own deportation history, and each history reveals a great deal about the mechanics of the deportations and the psychological environment in which they took place. The Gestapo, more and more peremptory, gave its orders without elaborate reasons or explanations, emphasizing only that evasions would be purposeless and that they would result in harsher measures. The Jews carried out each directive with exactitude until almost no one remained. The nature of this process may be glimpsed from developments in three cities: Frankfurt, Vienna, and Berlin.

In Frankfurt, where about 10,500 Jews were living at the beginning of October 1941, fewer than a thousand were left a year later. The Frankfurt Gestapo had established its hold on the Community organization many months prior to the first transport. A survivor who worked in the Community's statistical division recalls that every day a representative of the *Kultusgemeinde* had to announce himself to the Gestapo by stating in a loud voice: "Here is the Jew Sigmund Israel Rothschild." During the spring of 1941 the statistical division was instructed to make up a roster of all members of the community in triplicate. One day in the fall, Rothschild brought back a list of 1,200 people from the Gestapo, which had to be supplemented with additional information. Rumors that the list was to serve the purpose of deportation were denied by the Gestapo. Two days later, on October 19, 1941, the roundup began. At 5:30 A.M. elements of two regiments of the SA were assembled and given printed forms for the registration of Jewish property. They were to enter the Jewish apartments at 7 A.M. The SA men, drawn from various walks of life, were not prepared for this "juridical activity," and the Gestapo, evidently short-handed, would often arrive late at the scene. After multiple delays, a procession of Jews was moved through the city in broad daylight, as throngs of people stood on each side of the street watching silently.

Subsequent Frankfurt transports were handled with more expertise. The Community itself would draw up lists in accordance with categories specified by the Gestapo, and it would then send out letters to the persons that had been selected, stating that the recipients were to remain in their apartment as of a certain hour on a certain day. When the Gestapo needed the help of Order Police stationed in outlying areas for the seizure of Jews in the Frankfurt vicinity, it prepared detailed instructions covering every contingency, including the handling of dogs, cats, and birds. The participating personnel were expected to carry out the action with necessary toughness, correctness, and care. In the event that a Jew committed suicide because of the evacuation, procedures for filling out papers were to be followed analogously, as though he were being transported away, but a note was to be made of his death. And so on.

Vienna had a Jewish population of about 51,000 when mass deportations began there in October 1941. For the Viennese Jews, however, these transports were not the first experience with "evacuations." More than six thousand Jews had been sent from Vienna to the Generalgouvernement before the onset of the "Final Solution," about fifteen hundred in the fall of 1939, and five thousand in February–March 1941. In the months prior to the October deportations, the concentration of the Jews within the city had been increased, until 90 percent were living in three districts designated for Jewish residency: the II, IX, and XX. After the Jews were forced to wear the star, they were even more salient and vulnerable. Symbolic was the experience of one star wearer, a welfare official of the Jewish Community, who was a disabled veteran of the First World War, with an artificial leg. He fell on an icy sidewalk and asked passers-by for three hours to help him. They all left him and he finally raised himself with difficulty, breaking his wrist. The Community asked for no assistance. On the contrary, it was working with the Gestapo, and Rabbi Murmelstein did his work assiduously.

The principal personalities of the Gestapo in Vienna were the following:

Director, Stapoleitstelle	ORR and KR Franz Josef Huber
IV-B	Dr. Karl Ebner
Director, Zentrale Stelle:	HStuf. Alois Brunner
Deputy	Anton Brunner
Concentration and seizure	UStuf. Ernst Girzick

The concentration of the Jews at collecting points was called *Kommissionierung*. A card file of the Viennese Jews was kept by the Community, and deportation lists were made up by the Gestapo. The Community could "reclaim" certain individuals on specific grounds but apparently had to nominate replacements in order that the required one thousand people could go out. Girzick recalls that "in principle, the Jews were shoved off in families." The most critical challenge to the Jewish leadership was the demand that they deploy an order service *(Ausheberdienst,* or *Jupo)* that would assist the Gestapo in the round-ups. The Jewish Community was now expected to do the ultimate: Jews had to seize Jews. It did so, rationalizing that thereby it would assure a more humane procedure. Murmelstein's Ausheber would swarm into a Jewish apartment, stationing themselves at the door, while an SS man and the chief of the Jewish Kommando would seat themselves at a table to inquire about family members and to make sure of property declarations. The SS man might then depart, leaving the Jewish raiders with the victims, allowing them to help with the packing but admonishing them to prevent escapes. At the collecting points, service by the Jewish guards was to be arranged in such a way that flight by the inmates would be impossible. For each person missing from the premises, Löwenherz was told, two Jewish guards would be deported instead. The houses converted into collection centers were relatively small and, in order to maximize the amount of space in them, there were no tables, chairs, or beds. The waiting in such a house might last weeks, before the deportees, standing in open trucks and hearing jeers in the street, would be taken in daylight to the train station.

By the middle of October 1942 the Vienna deportations were virtually over, and at year's end Löwenherz reported that fewer than 8,000 Jews remained. In January 1943 the Community's staff was thinned out, and several of its functionaries (including Murmelstein) were sent to Theresienstadt. At about this time Löwenherz appeared in Ebner's office with a question. The following is Ebner's account of the meeting:

> The director of the Israelite Community and later of the Jewish Council of Elders was Dr. Josef Löwenherz. I would come into contact with him several times, one could safely say often. He was the one who first brought to me a rumor that Jews in concentration camps were being gassed and annihilated. He came to me one day after 1942, in other words, presumably in 1943, an utterly broken man, and asked for a meeting with Huber. I asked him what he wanted, and he told me that the Jews were allegedly being put to death, and he wanted to be sure that this was in fact the case. I thought that he was going to have a bad time with the chief and that he might conceivably be charged with spreading enemy radio reports. Löwenherz said that was all the same to him, and thereupon we went to Huber. When Huber was put into the picture, he then called the chief of Office IV in the Reich Security Main Office (Müller) on the direct line, while we waited outside. As we went in again, Huber said to us Müller had dismissed these allegations as evil reports. Löwenherz was visibly relieved.

Almost 73,000 Jews lived in Berlin at the beginning of October 1941. This number was more than 40 percent of all the Jews of the Old Reich.

Inevitably, the fact that the community was in the capital was going to have significance for the RSHA as well as the Stapoleitstelle of Berlin, and its fate was going to preoccupy the national Reichsvereinigung as well as the local *Jüdische Kultusvereinigung zu Berlin*. The following abbreviated chart shows the key individuals of the Berlin Gestapo:

Director, Stapoleitstelle	OStubaf. ORR Otto Bovensiepen (from November 1942, Stubaf. RR Wilhelm Bock)
Jewish Affairs	KK Gerhard Stübbs (from November 1942, KK Walter Stock)
Deputy	Kriminaloberinspektor Franz Prüfer (until November 1942)

The principal figures in the Reichsvereinigung were Leo Baeck, chairman of the board *(Vorstand),* and Paul Eppstein, the main deputy on a daily basis. At the Community level, the chairman was Moritz Henschel, and the migration specialist was Philipp Kozower, who was assisted by the Community's director for housing referral, Dr. Martha Mosse. Baeck and Henschel, and Eppstein and Kozower were organizational counterparts. All four had been Vorstand members in the Reichsvereinigung from the very beginning.

The Berlin Jews, like those of Vienna, had been subjected to increased concentration before the deportations. In Berlin the aim was to move all the Jews into Jewish-owned houses. The Gestapo could reach into the Jewish population also through a variety of files: addresses registered with the police, Community tax records, and Dr. Mosse's card file, which was continually being revised. At the beginning of October 1941 Prüfer summoned two of the Community's Vorstand members (including Henschel) and Dr. Mosse and warned them not to speak to anyone about what he had to say now. The resettlement of the Berlin Jews was going to begin, and the Jewish Community would have to participate in the action lest it be carried out by SA and SS, "and one knows how that is going to be." The Community was to hand in several thousand names and present questionnaires to all those on its list. The Gestapo would then select one thousand for a transport to Łódź. The Community was to see to it that the deportees were well equipped for travel. The entire action was to be represented to the Jewish population as a housing relocation. When Henschel asked whether the Reichsvereinigung could be informed, Prüfer said yes. That same evening, according to Dr. Mosse, Vorstand members of the Reichsvereinigung and of the Community decided to accede to the Gestapo's wishes "in order to be able to do as much good as possible in the interest of the victims."

Although secrecy was increasingly important to the Berlin Gestapo, the dates of forthcoming transports were invariably shared with Jewish officials. Thus on July 29, 1942, Stübbs and Prüfer informed Kozower of three Theresienstadt transports anticipated for August 17, September 14, and October 5, and two "eastern" transports envisaged for August 15 and 31. In his memorandum about the conversation, Kozower indicated that he had communicated its contents to several of his colleagues. He also mentioned the transports in the Vorstand of the Reichsvereinigung, adding that every one present had to remain silent about this information. The reason that the Gestapo took the Jewish leaders into its confidence was its continuing reliance upon them for help in the preparations.

Part of the assistance was administrative. The Berlin Kultusvereinigung provided typists, clerks, baggage handlers, nurses, and *Transporthelfer* or *Ordner* for special work. Although Stübbs and Prüfer harnessed only Gestapo men, Order Police, and Criminal Police for roundups of Jews in their homes, they needed Jewish auxiliaries at the collecting points for the processing and care of the victims until the moment of departure. Once the Kultusvereinigung was required also to march elderly deportees before daybreak to a trolley that was to leave promptly at 5 A.M. for the Anhalter railway station. Provisioning the transports, including those originating in Berlin as well as those passing through the capital, was another Jewish responsibility. Kultusvereinigung officials negotiated with food offices to assure prescribed supplies, particularly when, at the end of a ration period, the selected victims could no longer obtain their allotments. An attempt to procure food for infants failed, however, when Direktor Morawski of the Berlin Food Office explained that Aryan children were not receiving special allocations either.

The Jewish leadership contributed not only personnel, space, and supplies, but it was involved also in the more sensitive task of filling the quotas for the projected deportations. At the beginning the Berlin Kultusvereinigung would prepare long lists of 3,000 to 4,000 names before each transport and intervene in behalf of some of those selected in the hope that the deportations would not be continued. So long as there was still a sufficient number of Jews in the city, the Gestapo would grant such requests without much ado. By early summer of 1942, however, the situation changed. Only 54,000 Jews were left in Berlin at the end of June, and those classified as deferred or exempt had become a much larger percentage of the total. On July 29, 1942, Prüfer demanded that Henschel prepare a complete roster of the Berlin Jews with detailed information about each person. On the same day, Prüfer's assistant, Kirminalsekretär Walter Dobberke, remarked to Kozower that on the basis of existing criteria, not more than 300 Jews could be gathered for the two transports leaving for the East on August 15 and 31, and requiring 1,000 each. In the light of the shortage, Dobberke wondered whether laborers and individuals in mixed marriages might not have to be added. Kozower then suggested that the goal might still be reached if inmates of concentration camps and their families could be included. Stübbs thought that this idea had sufficient merit to be raised at a meeting of German offices. By early September, however, Prüfer and Dobberke brought up the basic question with Kozower and Mosse again, pointing out that "material" for old people's as well as eastern transports had now become very "tight."

At the end of October 1942 the Stübbs-Prüfer regime came to an abrupt end. Both had been suspected of having enriched themselves in the course of their official duties. Stübbs committed suicide before his arrest, and Prüfer died in a bombing attack while under detention. At this point Alois Brunner arrived with several Jupo from Vienna. Brunner changed the atmosphere and introduced a new procedure. From now on, every Jew on the Community premises had to rise when a person of "German blood" entered and maintain a distance of at least two steps from the German. The capacity of collecting points was to be enlarged by the removal of all the furniture. From the center at Grosse Hamburger Strasse, the kitchen was to be taken out as well. Clerks were to do duty day and night. Maps of Berlin were to be prepared, including one with circles around blocks indicating densities of Jewish population. Finally, a Jewish Order Service was to be created to assist the Gestapo in the operations to come. Following these directives, Dr. Eppstein explained to the Community's employees that the Ordner would have to accompany the Gestapo raiders to the homes of Jews and help the victims pack. Whoever refused this duty, warned any Jews, or helped them escape would be shot, and his family would be transported to the East. The Ordner, with red armbands, then moved alongside the Gestapo through the city from house to house.

Although the interim Brunner regime was very brief, it left its mark. Sturmbannführer Stock, who took over at the end of November 1942, ordered Henschel to organize a regular *Abholkolonne* of ninety men for roundups, but the next major action, aimed at the Jewish factory workers, required much larger forces. In the course of this operation, trucks of the SS *Leibstandarte Adolf Hitler* moved into the plants themselves, where the Jews were seized in their working clothes. Other trucks halted at Jewish apartment houses, and anyone found at home was taken away. Dr. Mosse states that Gestapo and Community employees, in a joint effort, then looked for the relatives of arrested persons to "bring families together." From the overfull collecting points, covered trucks and furniture vans went at night with their victims to the train station for transport to Auschwitz.

In the wake of the factory action there were widespread problems.

Some "shortsighted" industrialists, complained Goebbels in his diary, had "warned the Jews in time," and "we therefore failed to lay our hands on about 4,000. They are now wandering about Berlin without homes, are not registered with the police and are naturally quite a public danger. I ordered the police, Wehrmacht, and the party to do everything possible to round these Jews up as quickly as possible."

Only a few hundred Jews in the entire Reich actually succeeded in hiding for any length of time. In Jewish parlance, they were known as *U-Boote* (submarines or U-boats). To be a "U-boat" a man had to have money, steady nerves, unusual presence of mind, and extraordinary social ability. Not many persons possess these qualities. The hidden Jews received a little assistance from a few Germans; the Vienna Jews were helped by a Jewish relief committee in Budapest. Most of the time, however, the "immersed" Jews had to rely upon themselves. Hunted by the Gestapo and professional Jewish informers employed by the Gestapo, dodging the entire network of party offices and Nazi vigilantes, living in ruins and passing themselves off as bombed-out people, the "U-boats" scurried to and fro, waiting for their liberation. Slim as their chances might have been, they still faced better odds than the deportees who arrived at the killing centers.

Even fewer were those who considered any form of opposition. The criminality statistics for the year 1942 indicate the conviction of only one Jew for "resistance to the state." An arresting officer in Berlin recalls that the Jews created the impression of being very composed and that without exception they went with him unprotesting. More than a handful, however, had thought of suicide; thus the "perpetual question" among Jewish acquaintances in Berlin was: "Will you take your life or let yourself be evacuated?"

The seizure of the victims was a weighty step in the process, but for the administrators of the deportations more remained to be done. They had to assure the availability of transport, the presence of police personnel to accompany the train to its destination, and the funding of the fare.

The dispatch of a particular transport would be the subject of negotiation between the RSHA and the Reichsbahn several weeks before its departure. In addition, local arrangements would be made for cars and loading. Thus Da 512, Nuremberg-Theresienstadt, September 10, 1942, appears in a list of special trains for resettlers, harvest helpers, and Jews compiled at a conference in Frankfurt of the Generalbetriebsleitung Ost on August 8, 1942. Details relating to the composition and departure of Da 512 were specified in an order by Reichsbahndirektion Nuremberg/33 (Oberreichsbahnrat Schrenk). The cars were to be taken from an empty train labeled Lp 1511. Several cars of

Lp 1511 were to be dispatched to Bamberg and Würzburg, from where 400 Jews were to be brought to the Nuremberg switching yard. The remaining cars of Lp 1511 were to be readied at the Nuremberg stockyards' dung-loading point by 5 P.M. on September 9 for the Nuremberg deportees and their baggage. At 3 P.M. on the following day, the loaded cars in the stockyards were to be moved to the switching yard to be connected with the cars that were to wait there with the Bamberg and Würzburg Jews, and the fully assembled train Da 512 was to leave at 6:14 P.M. Such elaborate preparations signified that once the Transport Ministry had agreed to a special train, the Gestapo had locked itself in and that the scheduled departure was its deadline. As the RSHA guidelines repeatedly made clear, the available trains had to be utilized to the full, and their timetables were unalterable and binding.

The Reich Security Main Office had no personnel to guard the trains. Help came from the Order Police, which undertook to furnish one officer and twelve men for each transport. Although the terms of this agreement were confined to the Reich-Protekorat area, the RSHA ultimately relied on the Order Police for deportations in other regions as well. In fact, the Order Police came to regard the guarding of special trains as one of its regular functions. Orders and reports in the file of the Police President of Vienna reveal something about the assignments (one officer and six men to Theresienstadt, one officer and fifteen men to the East, all drawn from regular personnel in precincts) and the weapons for each train (two machine pistols with 300 rounds of ammunition each, carbines with 60 rounds each, and pistols with 50 rounds each).

The trains moved slowly. A report of Schupo Lieutenant Josef Fischmann who took Da 38 with 1,000 Jews (men, women, and children) from Vienna to the Sobibór death camp, indicates a route through Brno, Neisse, Oppeln, Czestochowa, Kielce, Radom, and Lublin according to the following actual schedule:

June 14, 1941	Noon	Loading in Vienna
	7:08 P.M.	Departure
June 17, 1942	8:15 A.M.	Arrival in Sobibór
	9:15 A.M.	Unloading

Fischmann reported that there were no incidents during the trip. In Lublin, 51 Jews were taken off the train; in Sobibór, 949 were delivered to the camp commander, Oberleutnant Stangl of the Schupo. The guards, however, were not altogether comfortable. Instead of sitting in a second-class coach, they had to travel third class, and in lieu of rations suitable for the summer, they had been given soft sausages that were beginning to spoil.

A train from Vienna to Minsk, in May 1942, had taken even longer.

The transport, which started out with passenger cars and carried 1,000 Jewish men, women, and children, traversed Olmütz, Neisse, Warsaw, Siedlce, and Wołkowysk:

May 6, 1942	Noon to 4 P.M.	Loading
	7 P.M.	Departure
May 8, 1942	11 P.M.	Arrived in Wołkowysk, followed by transfer of deportees to freight cars
May 9, 1942	2:45 A.M.	Continuation of trip
	2:30 P.M.	Arrival in Koydanov. Train halted there upon orders of Security Police in Minsk. Eight dead Jews taken from cars and buried at railway station
May 11, 1942	9 A.M.	Continuation of trip
	10:30 A.M.	Arrival in Minsk

In addition to its manifest need for assistance to seize and guard the Jews, the Gestapo had a subtle financial problem. As procuror of the transports, it had to pay for them, but its ordinary budget could not cover such major expenses. The solution was to utilize funds of the Jewish Community machinery. The RSHA controlled the finances of the Reichsvereinigung and of the Jewish communities in Vienna and Prague. The Jewish organizations deposited taxes and miscellaneous receipts (such as the proceeds from the sale of land on which burned synagogues had stood before November 1938) into various accounts in banks. Following the first transports on November 21, 1941, Paul Eppstein of the Reichsvereinigung, concerned about the increasing costs of equipping the deportees, asked Hauptsturmführer Gutwasser of the RSHA for permission to impose a special levy on those about to be deported for deposit in its special account W. Gutwasser, seeing nothing wrong with the suggestion, asked for a written proposal and added that account W would probably be used to pay also for railway transports. On December 3, 1941, Eppstein and Lilienthal, invoking instructions of "our supervisory agency," directed communities and branches to induce every member of an evacuation transport to pay no less than 25 percent of his liquid assets (excluding securities) as a donation, the necessity for which was to be made clear in a suitable manner. The deportees were to be told in effect that their donation was required for their own needs, and that any surplus would be used by the Reichsvereinigung for welfare. By December 3, two payments in the amount of RM 24,628.40 and RM 33,158.00 had already been made from funds in account W to the Reichsbahndirektion in Cologne for October transports.

Ministerialrat Maedel of the Finance Ministry, who had discovered this strategem, reported it in a lengthy memorandum to Ministerialdirigent Kallenbach on December 14, 1942. Noting in particular the Reichsvereinigung directive of December 3, 1941, Maedel said that, although the Gestapo did not have the power to dispose of the Jewish funds, occasional conversations with representatives of the Security Police indicated extensive Gestapo influence in the utilization of this money for payments of transport costs, etc. Moreover, similar arrangements had been made in Vienna, where the Gestapo's Zentrale Stelle had received special powers of attorney, and in Prague, where those entitled to dispose of Jewish property could empower the Gestapo to be in charge of it. Maedel saw in these measures the financing of a program outside the budgetary process, and raised questions about Himmler's contention that Jewish properties used for the "Final Solution of the Jewish problem" *were* in the final analysis assets already committed to aims of the Third Reich. Should such self-financing, he asked, be given silent acquiescence? In the end (if not quite silently), it was.

At least 250,000 Jews were deported from the Reich-Protektorat area, half of them from the Old Reich, 50,000 from Austria, and the remainder from the Protektorat. Deportation statistics as of December 31, 1942, before the last major roundups in Berlin, were compiled for the SS by a specialist in numbers, Richard Korherr; they are shown in Table 12.

The Jews deported to the Ostland were shot in Kaunas, Riga, and Minsk. Those who were routed to occupied Poland died there in the death camps at Kulmhof, Auschwitz, Bełżec, Sobibór, Treblinka, and Lublin (Majdanek). Most of the Theresienstadt Jews who did not succumb in the ghetto were ultimately gassed in Auschwitz. For all the secrecy of the killing operations, the signs and signals of a drastic perpetration permeated the entire Reich. Often the roundups of the

T A B L E   12
DEPORTATION STATISTICS FOR THE REICH-PROTEKTORAT AREA

Area	*"Evakuiert"* Deported	Remaining on January 1, 1943	Eligible for Deportation	In Mixed Marriage
Old Reich	100,516	51,327	34,567	16,760
Austria	47,555	8,102	3,299	4,803
Protektorat	69,677	15,550	9,339	6,211
Total	217,748	74,979	47,205	27,774

NOTE: The Old Reich statistics include the Sudeten. The 51,327 Jews in the Old Reich dwindled to 31,910 in the first three months of 1943. On June 19, 1944, the Jewish Council of Elders in Prague reported 69,809 Jews deported to Theresienstadt and 7,000 "evacuated," or a total of nearly 77,000.

victims were seen in the streets. If the seizures were unobserved, the apartments remained conspicuously empty. If the disappearance of the tenants was not noticed, there were stories and reports about the mysterious "East" that seeped into every town and social quarter until the Gestapo was surrounded by whispers.

Above the murmur, one man prepared to raise his voice in protest. On the eve of the deportations, a sixty-six-year-old Catholic priest, Dompropst Bernard Lichtenberg of St. Hedwig's Cathedral in Berlin, dared to pray openly for the Jews, including those who were baptized and those who were unbaptized. Following a denunciation, he was arrested. In the course of a search of his apartment, the police found notes for an undelivered sermon in which the priest was going to ask the congregation to disbelieve the official claim that the Jews wanted to kill all Germandom. Held in custody, he insisted that he wanted to join the Jews in the East to pray for them there. He was placed on trial before a special court and given a sentence of two years. Upon his release on October 23, 1943, he was picked up by the Gestapo to be brought to Dachau. Too sick to travel, he died on the way in a hospital at Hof. Thus a solitary figure had made his singular gesture. In the buzz of the rumormongers and sensation seekers, Bernard Lichtenberg fought almost alone.

To be sure, Lichtenberg was not the only one to be arrested. Every once in a while a careless man made a careless remark to the wrong person. The house painter Louis Birk, of Wiesbaden, could not do his work without a great deal of talk with *Hausfrauen* in whose apartments he was working. The charges assert that "from dark wells he scooped rumors about an unfavorable turn of the war" and spread them to his employers. With respect to the Jewish question, he remarked that all the remaining Jews in Germany would soon be poisoned with gas. Furthermore, he assured the housewives that the party leaders were all black-listed and that they would some day be forced to reconstruct the Jewish synagogues. Louis Birk was executed.

By and large, only a handful of rumor-carriers could be caught, and the Party Chancellery therefore decided to combat the rumor wave by issuing an official explanation of the deportations. The Jews, said the party, were being sent "to the East" in order to be employed there in work camps. Some of the Jews were being sent "farther East." The old Jews and decorated Jews were being resettled in Theresienstadt. "It lies in the nature of things," the party circular concluded, "that these partially very difficult problems can be solved in the interest of the permanent security of our people only with ruthless severity." The rumors continued unabated.

P O L A N D

When the Generalgouvernement administration received an invitation to attend the first "Final Solution" conference in Berlin, Frank immediately dispatched his deputy, Bühler, to Heydrich with instructions to find out more details. Bühler returned with the inside information. Shortly afterward (December 16, 1941) Generalgouverneur Frank, Health Präsident Dr. Walbaum, Labor Präsident Dr. Frauendorfer, Security Police and SD Commander Schöngarth, Gouverneur Kundt of Radom, and Amtschef Dr. Hummel of Warsaw met in Kraków in conference. Frank did not speak about the topic weighing on his mind. Instead, he opened the meeting with a minor matter: measures against Jews who were slipping out of ghettos. It was agreed that they had to be put to death. Such Jews were a health hazard, for they carried typhus to the Polish population. Dr. Hummel said that the Warsaw administration was grateful to the Commander of the Order Police (BdO) for having issued an order in pursuance of which all Jews encountered on country roads were to be shot on sight. The special courts, however, were working too slowly. So far, only forty-five Jews had been condemned to death and only eight sentences had been carried out. Something would have to be done to simplify the procedure. The discussion continued in this vein for a while. Then, suddenly, Frank changed the subject.

"I want to say to you quite openly," he began, "that we shall have to finish with the Jews, one way or another. The Führer once spoke these words: 'If united Jewry should succeed once more in releasing another world war, the peoples who have been hounded into this war will not be the only ones to shed their blood, because the Jew of Europe, too, will then have found his end.' I know that many measures now taken in the Reich are criticized. Consciously, repeated attempts are being made to speak about harshness and brutality. Morale reports indicate that quite plainly. Before I continue to speak, let me therefore ask you to agree with me upon the following principle: we want to have mercy only for the German people, otherwise for no one in the whole world. The others had no mercy for us."

Frank then pointed out that if Jewry survived the war, victory would be in vain. He was therefore approaching the problem from only one point of view: the Jews had to disappear. They had to go. For that reason he had begun negotiations in Berlin to shove the Jews east. In January a big conference was to be held in the Reich Security Main Office; Staatssekretär Bühler was to attend for the Generalgouvernement. "Certainly," said Frank, "a major migration is about to start. But

187

what is to happen to the Jews? Do you think they will actually be resettled in Ostland villages? We were told in Berlin: Why all this trouble? We can't use them in the Ostland either; liquidate them yourselves! Gentlemen, I must ask you to arm yourself against all feelings of sympathy. We have to annihilate the Jews wherever we find them and wherever it is at all possible."

This task, said Frank, would have to be carried out with methods quite different from those that Dr. Hummel had just mentioned. Judges and courts could not be made responsible for such an undertaking, and ordinary conceptions could not be applied to such gigantic and singular events. "At any rate, we will have to find a way that will lead to the goal, and I have my thoughts about that." Frank continued, as though he were almost on the defensive: "The Jews are for us also very parsitical eaters. We have in the Generalgouvernement an estimated 2,500,000 [a gross overestimate], maybe—together with Mischlinge and all that hangs on 3,500,000 Jews. We can't shoot these 3,500,000 Jews, we can't poison them, but we will be able to take some kind of action that will lead to an annihilation success, and I am referring to the measures to be discussed in the Reich. The Generalgouvernement will have to become just as *judenfrei* as the Reich. Where and how this is going to happen is a task for the agencies which we will have to create and establish here, and I am going to tell you how they will work when the time comes."

When the conference was adjourned, its participants were aware that a new phase of the destruction process had been inaugurated in Poland. They knew now that the Jews were to be killed. Still, an air of haze and unreality had pervaded the conference room. What precisely was meant by such phrases as "we can't use them in the Ostland," "liquidate them yourselves," "we can't shoot these 3,500,000 Jews," "we can't poison them," "a task for the agencies which we will have to create and establish here"? Obviously, they were only hints. No one knew that at that very moment experts from the Reich Security Main Office, the Führer Chancellery, and the Inspectorate for Concentration Camps were peering at maps and examining the Polish terrain for places to establish killing installations. Poland was to become the headquarters of the killing centers. Poland was the "East."

PREPARATIONS

The administrative officials in Poland found out about these things only by degrees. In the meantime, however, the bureaucrats lost no time in making preparations. All offices were on the alert, and everyone was in a hurry. Everyone, from top to bottom, was eager to clear the ghettos. In Berlin, Staatssekretär Bühler spoke up at the "Final Solution" conference of January 20, 1942, to demand that the deportations in the Generalgouvernement get under way as soon as possible. To the west of the Generalgouvernement, in the neighboring Wartheland, Reichstatthalter Greiser secured Heydrich's agreement for an immediate Aktion encompassing the "special treatment" of 100,000 Jews in the Gau area. For that purpose, Greiser and the SS and Police in the Gau established a killing center at Kulmhof, in the middle of the Wartheland. Kulmhof served a large part of Greiser's needs. (Incidentally, the camp was the first killing center to go into operation.)

Locally, the civil offices, police, and railways planned together the details of the deportations. What concerned the planners most was the sheer magnitude of the operation. Although at least half a million Jews died in the ghettos, about 2,200,000 still remained in the deportation area, including 1,600,000 in the Generalgouvernement, 400,000 in the incorporated territories, and up to 200,000 in the Białystok district. To the civil offices these figures meant that the entire structure of urban population was to be altered. With the disappearance of the ghettos, important changes in housing accommodations, the food supply, and the productive capacity were to be expected. In the Generalgouvernement the office most immediately concerned with these problems was the Population and Welfare Division of the Interior Main Division. A directive by Staatssekretär Bühler, dated December 16, 1941, consequently empowered the Population and Welfare Division to approve or veto every "resettlement" that affected more than fifty persons.

In the main, the deportees were sent to death camps. The destinations of transports from the incorporated areas and the Generalgouvernement are shown in the following table:

Incorporated Areas	Death Camps
Wartheland	
1941–42	Kulmhof
1944	Kulmhof and Auschwitz
Upper Silesia	Auschwitz
East Prussia	Auschwitz
Białystok district	Auschwitz and Treblinka
Generalgouvernement	
Warsaw district	Treblinka
Radom district	Treblinka
Lublin district	Sobibór, Bełżec, and Lublin
Kraków district	Bełżec
Galicia	Bełżec

After 1942 the Jews from remnant ghettos and labor camps were sent also to Auschwitz, while many in Galicia were shot on the spot.

Police forces available for roundups in occupied Poland included a comparatively thin layer of several thousand Security Police and Security Service personnel, and the larger German Order Police (Einzeldienst in the incorporated areas, units in the Generalgouvernement, and both in the Białystok district). In the Generalgouvernement the ORPO was augmented by Polish and (in the Galician district), by Ukrainian stationary police. In Poland, as elsewhere, the numerical weight of the Order Police was important, but by 1942 Order Police personnel were engaged not only in the deportation of Jews but also in two other major operations: the collection of the Polish harvest for German needs and the seizure of Polish workers for labor in the Reich.

Reinforcements were needed and obtained. In July 1942 the 22d and 272d Latvian battalions were imported from Riga for the great roundup in the Warsaw ghetto, and in 1943 a Ukrainian training battalion was deployed in the Warsaw ghetto battle. Waffen-SS units were occasionally pressed into service, for example in the Sosnowiec area of Upper Silesia, where the personnel of an SS cavalry school were employed in a roundup. The Gettoverwaltung of Łódź furnished about sixty of its employees for seizure operations throughout the Wartheland, and the army regularly dispatched units into action against Jewish escapees banded together in the woods or fields of the Generalgouvernement. Jewish police themselves were frequently used to assist in these operations. The Jewish Order Service of Warsaw was conspicuous in the summer deportations of 1942, but there was an Order Service even in small ghettos such as Rawa Ruska (Galicia), where one roundup was conducted by police teams consisting of one German, one Ukrainian, and one Jew.

In the Generalgouvernement, the major organizers of seizure operations were the SS and Police Leaders. One of them, Globocnik of Lublin, created a special staff under Sturmbannführer Höfle that took charge of roundups not only in the Lublin district but also during the summer of 1942 in Warsaw and in the summer of the following year in the Białystok ghetto. In both of these cities, specialization and, perhaps even more important, the impersonality of men coming from a distance were to leave their mark.

Transport to the death camps was almost invariably accomplished by railway, and this meant that Jews in village would be marched to larger towns from where trains departed. The Jewish communities in the incorporated areas were deported in transports dispatched by the following Direktionen:

Reichsbahndirektion Oppeln (covering departures from Upper Silesia)
Reichsbahndirektion Posen (covering the Wartheland)
Reichsbahndirektion Königsberg (covering the Białystok district and
   areas incorporated into East Prussia)
Reichsverkehrsdirektion (RVD) Minsk (covering the Oranczyce station
   in Reichskommissariat Ukraine, where many Białystok district Jews
   were loaded for deportation to Auschwitz)

Generalgouvernement Jews were moved in trains organized by the
Generaldirektion der Ostbahn (Gedob), an important railway system
with major functions in the destruction of the Jews. In the following
abbreviated table of its organization, special attention is paid to the
Operations Division:

Präsident	Adolf Gerteis
Vizepräsident	Rudolf Fatgen
II Tariffs	Sillich
9 Passenger Trains	Peicher (Koch, Verbeck)
III Locomotives	Scharrer
IV (later V) Operations	Köhle (Massute, Gaecks)
31 Operations	Zahn
33 Passenger Trains	Binger (Zabel, Eugen Meyer)
Special Trains	Stier
34 Freight Trains	Massute (Zabel, Zahn)
Hilfsarbeiter (Deputy) for 33 and 34	Erich Richter (Theodor Schmid)

It should be pointed out that the jurisdiction of the Gedob or a Reichsbahndirektion was not confined to the dispatching of trains, but that it
included traversals and arrivals (e.g., Gedob for Theresienstadt–Generalgouvernement–Minsk, Oppeln for all trains to Auschwitz, Reichsbahndirektion Königsberg for Vienna–Białystok district–Minsk). For
trains originating in their territories, moreover, these Direktionen had
to concern themselves with more than the movement of the transports—they had to provide the rolling stock. Even though the Gedob in
particular needed every car and locomotive at its disposal for the war
effort, and even though it was heavily dependent on Polish employees, it
did not fail to make its contribution to the deportations. Erich Richter,
Hilfsarbeiter in the Gedob's Operations Division, recalls Eugen Meyer
(33) saying to him that in accordance with instructions from the Transport Ministry, Jewish "resettlement trains" were to be dispatched as
soon as they were "announced" by the SS.
   The Gedob would load a train with several thousand deportees and
dispatch it to a death camp. Orders were given to count the victims
(sometimes on arrival) for applicable financial charges. Last but not

least, care was taken to have the empty cars cleaned of all filth at the camp itself or to have them moved back for fumigation.

The mantle of routine was thrown around the entire operation. Commingled with transports carrying troops or supplies, the death trains were moved as a matter of course without so much as a secrecy designation. At most, timetable orders were marked "restricted," and Stier, the Gedob's chief of special trains in 33, tells us that in his office revealing papers were lying around quite openly.

THE CONDUCT OF THE DEPORTATIONS

In the Reich-Protektorat area considerable difficulties were caused by privileged or semiprivileged categories of Jews. No such encumbrances hindered the deportations in Poland. There was no Mischling problem, no mixed-marriage problem, no old-Jews problem, no war-veterans problem. There were only a handful of foreign Jews in Poland, some of whom were pulled out of the ghettos at the very last minute and some of whom were shipped to killing centers by mistake. Only one major difficulty arose in connection with any particular group of Jews, and that problem did not become acute until the end of 1942: the labor shortage. Arrangements had to be made to keep a few skilled laborers alive a little longer. These arrangements were concluded at the close rather than at the beginning of the deportations.

As the ghetto-clearing operations began, notice of roundups would sometimes be given to the Polish population in announcements posted a day or so in advance. The Poles were told that any ghetto passes in their possession were canceled, and they were warned against lingering in the streets or opening windows while the evacuation was in progress. Anyone interfering with the operation or giving shelter to Jews was going to be punished by death, and any unauthorized presence in a Jewish apartment was going to be construed as pillage.

Inside the ghettos, the policemen and their helpers had to cope with another problem: filth, sewage, and vermin. In the words of the Gettoverwaltung, the work was "nauseous in the extreme." In the Galician ghettos the police were confronted by vast epidemics. In the ghetto of Rawa Ruska, the Jewish population had concealed its sick in holes in the hope of saving them from deportation. Before the Rawa Ruska Aktion was over, the SS and Police had dragged 3,000 sick and dying Jews out of their hiding places. We have no overall figures for German losses incurred by reason of the epidemics, but in Galicia alone SS and Police Leader Katzmann reported that one of his men had died of spotted fever and that another 120 had fallen ill with the disease.

After a ghetto was cleared of Jews, the police and municipal officials had to reenter the Jewish quarter and clean it up. Although Poles and Jews could be used for some of the dirtiest labor, the job was still far from pleasant. A large ghetto could be emptied in two or three days, but the cleanup operation required weeks or even months. Thus the Lublin ghetto was disbanded and its inhabitants deported April 17–20, 1942, but the cleanup action *(Säuberungsaktion)* was still in progress two months later.

The operation was carried out in stages. First, a demolition Kommando entered the ghetto and blew up all uninhabitable buildings. Next came the salvage crew, which collected all sorts of junk left behind by the deportees. This detachment was followed by a clearing Kommando, which had to do the hardest work: the cleaning of the latrines. In some latrines the feces were piled up to a height of three feet. The clearing Kommando had to use hoses to clean up the mess. The fourth crew consisted of carpenters and glass workers who sealed hermetically all doors and windows in order to enable the gas column to kill all vermin in the apartments. Finally, the cleanup column was called up to remove the dead rats, mice, flies, and bugs, and to tidy up the place.

Still, the dilapidation in the ghettos was a comparatively minor annoyance in the total picture, and the bureaucrats were not much concerned with it. Their primary worry was the progress of the deportations, the rate at which Jewry was disappearing. The top men were interested only in speed. As early as June 18, 1942, Staatssekretär Dr. Bühler asked Higher SS and Police Leader Krüger when he would finish. Krüger replied that in August he would be able to "survey" the situation.

Krüger was a bit cautious because just then he was experiencing his first *Transportsperre,* a complete shutdown of traffic in deportation trains. The *Transportsperre* was instituted for only two weeks, and Krüger managed even then to wangle a few trains from Präsident Gerteis of the Ostbahn. Moreover, after the lifting of the restrictions, Krüger expected to resume the deportations with redoubled effort. Then, in July, another hitch occurred when the railway line to the killing center of Sobibór, on the Bug, broke down and had to be repaired. The SS and Police had hoped to deport several hundred thousand Jews to Sobibór.

On July 16, 1942, Obergruppenführer Wolff, chief of Himmler's Personal Staff, telephoned Staatssekretär Dr. Ganzenmüller of the Transport Ministry for help. Ganzenmüller looked into the situation and found that the matter had already been settled locally. Three hundred thousand Warsaw ghetto Jews had been diverted from Sobibór to Treblinka. Beginning on July 22, 1942, a daily train crammed with not fewer than 5,000 Jews per run was to leave Warsaw for Treblinka, while twice weekly another train carrying 5,000 Jews was to run from Przemyśl to Bełżec. When Wolff received this news, he wrote the following letter of thanks:

> Dear Party Member Ganzenmüller:
> For your letter of July 28, 1942, I thank you—also in the name of the Reichsführer-SS—sincerely. With particular joy I noted your assurance that for two weeks now a train has been carrying, every day, 5,000 members of the chosen people to Treblinka, so that we are now in a position to carry through this population movement at an accelerated tempo. I, for my part, have contacted the participating agencies to assure the implementation of the process without friction. I thank you again for your efforts in this matter and, at the same time, I would be grateful if you would give to these things your continued personal attention.
> With best regards and
>
> > Heil Hitler!
> > Your devoted
> > W.

At the end of 1942, when the deportations were already two-thirds over, the SS and Police offices were confronted by another breakdown. Urgently, Krüger wrote to Himmler:

> SS and Police Leaders today report unanimously that by reason of Transportsperre every possibility of transport for Jewish resettlement is cut off from December 15, 1942, to January 15, 1943. Because of this measure, our master plan for Jewish resettlement is severely jeopardized.
> Obediently request that you negotiate with central offices of Armed Forces High Command and Transport Ministry for allocation of at least three pairs of trains for this urgent task.

Apparently the negotiations were not very successful this time, for on January 20, 1943, Himmler wrote to Ganzenmüller for more trains. The Reichsführer pointed out that he knew under what strain the railway network was operating but that the allocation of the trains was, in the last analysis, in Ganzenmüller's own interest. The Jews, said Himmler, were responsible for all the railway sabotage in the Generalgouvernement, the Białystok district, and the occupied eastern territories. Hence the sooner the Jews were "cleared out," the better for the railways. While writing about the eastern Jews, Himmler also took occasion to remind Ganzenmüller that unless trains were made available for the Jews of the western occupied areas, sabotage would break out there too.

While the shortage of transport was particularly pressing in the planning of the whole operation, a host of complications was to arise after the organizational problems were solved. These ramifications developed like shock waves from a single point of impact: the discovery by outsiders of the true nature of the "resettlements."

If concealment was difficult within the German-Czech area, it was doubly difficult in Poland. The Reich-Protektorat area had no death camps and most Reich transports were moving out to the east. Poland, on the other hand, was the home of all six killing centers and Polish transports were moving in short hauls of not more than 200 miles in all directions. Many eyes were fixed on those transports and followed them to their destinations. The deputy chief of the Polish Home Army London-directed underground force, General Tadeusz Bor-Komorowski, reports that in the spring of 1942 he had complete information about the Kulmhof (Chełmno) killing center in the Warthegau. When the Germans cleared the Lublin ghetto, the Polish underground traced the transports to Bełżec, but, estimating that 130,000 Jews had been shoved into the camp, the Poles concluded that it "was not big enough to accommodate such a large number of people." In July 1942 the Home Army collected reports from railroad workers that several hundred thousand Jews had disappeared in Treblinka without a trace.

Sometimes the information spilling out of the camps was quite specific. In the Lublin district the council chairman of the Zamość ghetto, Mieczysław Garfinkiel, was a recipient of such news. During the early spring of 1942 he heard that the Jews of Lublin were being transported in crowded trains to Bełżec and that the empty cars were being returned after each trip for more victims. He was asked to obtain some additional facts and, after contacting the nearby Jewish communities of Tomaszów and Bełżec, was given to understand that 10,000 to 12,000 Jews were arriving daily in a strongly guarded compound located on a special railroad spur and surrounded by barbed wire. The Jews were being killed there in a "puzzling manner." Garfinkiel, an attorney, did not give credence to these reports. After a few more days, two or three Jewish strangers who had escaped from Bełżec told him about gassings in barracks. Still he did not believe what he heard. On April 11, 1942, however, there was a major roundup in Zamość itself. Counting the remaining population of his ghetto, Garfinkiel calculated a deficit of 3,150 persons. The next day, the thirteen-year-old son of one of the council functionaries (Wolsztayn) came back from the camp. The boy had seen the naked people and had heard an SS man make a speech to them. Hiding, still clothed, in a ditch, the young Wolsztayn had crawled out under the barbed wire with the secret of Bełżec.

What the Home Army had found out through its investigations, and what Garfinkiel had discovered almost unwittingly, ordinary people were suspecting without much proof. The population drew its conclusions quickly and spread them as rumors throughout the occupied

Polish territory. By late summer of 1942 almost every inhabitant of Poland, whether outside or inside a ghetto, had some inkling of what was going on. In the end even children knew the purpose of the deportations. When, during the summer of 1944 in the Łódź ghetto, the children of an orphanage were piled on trucks, they cried, "We don't want to die!"

What was the overall reaction of the Jews in the face of certain death? Did Jewry prepare for armed resistance? The district propaganda divisions in the Generalgouvernement watched the reactions of the Jewish population minutely. Here are three sample reports from the propaganda division in Lublin. On April 18, 1942, the Lublin division reported that Jews in the Hrubieszów area had approached the Catholic Church with requests for baptisms. On September 26, 1942, the division reported:

> Among the Jews of Cholm there is a rumor that henceforth the extermination of Jewry will be carried out by sterilization. Although this method would be more humane than the current one, it would lead to the ultimate extermination of Jewry nevertheless. The Jews think they will just have to accept this fact.

On November 28, 1942, the Lublin division reported the following incident:

> A seventeen-year-old Jewess reported to the director of the harvest-gathering troop, Majdan-Sopocki, in the Zamość area, and requested to be shot, since her parents had already been shot. She referred to an alleged Führer order in accordance with which all Jews have to be done away with before the end of the year. Since the Jewess was an escapee, she was handed over to the competent offices for further treatment.

With a few powerful strokes of the pen, the Lublin propaganda division had charted the trend of the Jewish reaction: a feeble conversion attempt in April, a sterilization rumor in September, and the offer of a seventeen-year-old girl to give up her life in November. Without a doubt, the Jews were not preparing for armed resistance. They were preparing for automatic compliance with German orders.

The Jewish leadership in the Polish ghettos stood at the helm of the compliance movement, and ghetto chiefs were the implementors of the surrender. Always they delivered up some Jews to save the other Jews. Having "stabilized" the situation, the ghetto administration would bisect the remaining community. And so on. Moses Merin, president of the Central Council of Elders for Eastern Upper Silesia, presided over such a shrinking process. On the eve of the first deportations, Merin made his first decision. "I will not be afraid," he said, to "sacrifice 50,000 of our community in order to save the other 50,000." During the summer of 1942 the other 50,000 Jews were lined up in a mass review, from which half were sent to Auschwitz. Merin commented after that deportation: "I feel like a captain whose ship was about to sink and who succeeded in bringing it safe to port by casting overboard a great part of his precious cargo." By 1943 there were only a few survivors. Merin addressed them in the following words: "I stand in a cage before a hungry and angry tiger. I stuff his mouth with meat, the flesh of my brothers and sisters, to keep him in his cage lest he break loose and tear us all to bits."

Throughout Poland the great bulk of the Jews presented themselves voluntarily at the collecting points and boarded the trains for transport to killing centers. Like blood gushing out of an open wound, the exodus from the ghettos quickly drained the Polish Jewish community of its centuries-old life.

However, in an operation of such dimensions not everybody could be deported so smoothly. As the circle of Jewish survivors shrank, the awareness of death increased, and the psychological burden of complying with German "evacuation" orders became heavier and heavier. Toward the end of the operations increasing numbers of Jews hesitated to move out, while others fled from the ghettos or jumped from trains to find refuge in the woods. In the Warsaw ghetto a few of the surviving Jews rallied in a last-minute stand against the Germans.

The Germans reacted to the recalcitrant Jews with utmost brutality. Howling raiders descended upon the ghettos with hatchets and bayonets. In the Warthegau the police were sent into such actions in a half-drunken stupor. Every Gestapo man assigned to ghetto-clearing duty received daily an extra ration of a little over half a pint of brandy. The Gettoverwaltung in Łódź demanded a brandy allocation for its employees, too, on the ground that employment without such brandy was "irresponsible." In Galicia the Jews were particularly aware of their fate because they had already witnessed the mobile killing operations in 1941. In the words of the SS and Police report, they "tried every means in order to dodge evacuation." They concealed themselves "in every imaginable corner, in pipes, chimneys, even in sewers." They "built barricades in passages of catacombs, in cellars enlarged to dugouts, in underground holes, in cunningly contrived hiding places in attics and sheds, within furniture, etc."

In the Galician operations massacres were interspersed with deportations, particularly during the *Transportsperren* in the early summer of 1942 and in December–January 1942–43. Often, the old and infirm Jews were not transported at all, but shot in the course of the roundup. The general mode of procedure in Galicia may be illustrated by events in three towns.

In Stanisławow, about 10,000 Jews had been gathered at a cemetery and shot on October 12, 1941. Another shooting took place in March 1942, followed by a ghetto fire lasting for three weeks. A transport was sent to Bełżec in April, and more shooting operations were launched in the summer, in the course of which Jewish council members and Order Service men were hanged from lampposts. Large transports moved out to Bełżec in September and October, an occasion marked by the bloody clearing of a hospital and (according to reports heard by a German agricultural official) a procession of Jews moving to the train station on their knees.

The Galician town of Rawa Ruska, only about twenty miles from Bełżec, was a railway junction through which deportation trains passed frequently. A survivor, Wolf Sambol, recalling scenes of shootings in the town, quotes a drunken Gendarmerie man shouting at the victims: "You are not Jews anymore, you are the chosen. I am your Moses and I will lead you through the Red Sea." He then opened fire at the victims with an automatic weapon. The same survivor remembers a little girl under the corpses, pushing herself out covered with blood, and looking carefully to the right and left, running away. Transports moved out of Rawa Ruska as soon as the *Sperre* was lifted in July 1942. Although the nature of Bełżec was no longer a secret that summer, the Rawa Ruska Jewish Council pursued a cooperative course, and large numbers of Jews gathered at the collecting point for transport. Their wish, said Sambol, was to live half an hour longer. Several thousand others, however, sought to hide, and many jumped from trains.

One transport pulled out from the southern Galician town of Kołomyja on September 10, 1942. In its fifty cars it carried 8,205 deportees. Some of the victims had been driven to the train on foot from villages in the area, while others had been waiting in the town itself. Neither group had had much to eat for days before departure. The slowness of the train, pulled by an underpowered locomotive that periodically had to stop, contributed to the agony of the Jews inside. They stripped off their clothes in the heat, ripped off the barbed wire at the aperture near the ceiling of the car, and tried to squeeze through and jump out. The Order Police Kommando, consisting of one officer and fifteen men, shot all of its ammunition, obtained more rounds from army personnel along the way, and finally hurled stones at escapees. When the train arrived in Bełżec, 200 of those aboard were dead.

Such scenes aroused people in the entire district. Once a Polish policeman related his experiences freely to an ethnic German woman who then wrote anonymously to Berlin. Her letter reached the *Reichskanzlei*. The Polish policeman, she wrote, had asked her whether she was not finally ashamed of being an ethnic German. He had now become acquainted with German culture. During the dissolution of the ghettos, children had been thrown on the floor and their heads trampled with boots. Many Jews whose bones had been broken by rifle butts were thrown into graves covered with calcium flour. When the calcium began to boil in the blood, one could still hear the crying of the wounded.

During the second half of 1942, reports were also received about Jews who scattered into the woods during the "evacuations." Again the greatest activity seems to have occurred in Galicia. In October 1942 the propaganda division of Lwów reported:

> The resettlement of the Jews, which in part takes on forms that are no longer worthy of a *Kulturvolk,* actually provokes comparison of the Gestapo with the GPU. The transport trains are said to be in such bad condition that it is impossible to prevent breakouts by Jews. As a consequence there is wild shooting, and there are regular manhunts at the transit stations. Furthermore, it is reported that corpses of shot Jews are lying around for days in the streets. Although the German and also the non-German population are convinced of the necessity of a liquidation of all Jews, it would be appropriate to carry out this liquidation in a manner that would create less sensation and less disgust.

The escapes from ghettos and transports also took place in other districts. On December 7, 1942, Gouverneur Zörner of the Lublin district complained in a Generalgouvernement conference that in the past few weeks the Judenaktion had become somewhat disorganized, with the result that a large number of Jews had left the ghettos and had joined the Polish "bandits." On September 21, 1942, the SS and Police Leader of Radom, Standartenführer Böttcher, complained that Jews from small ghettos in the flatlands of the district were being hidden by Poles. Help to Jews was being given by Poles and Ukrainians also in Galicia. Before long, several thousand Jews were hiding in the woods, joining the partisans and sometimes, banded together in units of their own, shooting it out with German Gendarmerie units. There are reports of such clashes in all five districts of the Generalgouvernement. In the district of Galicia the fleeing Jews were able to buy or acquire rifles and pistols from Italian troops who had fought in Russia and who were now going home. As a result the SS and Police in Galicia had eight dead and twelve wounded in its attempts to seize Jews in bunkers and forests. It appears that the Galician Jews also attempted to fight back with a primitive biological warfare weapon, for the police found several vials filled with lice that carried spotted fever (typhus).

The largest single clash between Jews and Germans occurred in the ghetto of Warsaw. For the further development of the destruction process, this armed encounter was without consequence. In Jewish history, however, the battle is literally a revolution, for after two thousand years of a policy of submission the wheel had been turned and once again Jews were using force.

As might be expected, the Jewish resistance movement did not emerge from the Judenrat, because that organization was composed of precisely those elements of the community that had staked everything on a course of complete cooperation with the German administration. To mobilize the Jews of the ghetto against the Germans, it was necessary to create a new hierarchy that was strong enough to challenge the council successfuly in a bid for control over the Jewish community. The nucleus of such an illegal organization was formed from the political parties that had been represented in the prewar Jewish community machinery. These parties, which had managed to survive in the ghetto by looking out after their members, now banded together into a resistance bloc.

Not all parties veered to a resistance policy with the same speed. The movement began in two extreme camps that had no contact with each other: the Moscow-dominated Communists and the self-reliant nationalists. From there the idea spread to the Zionist youth groups, the socialist trade unionists and the Left Labor Zionists. Ultimately the movement embraced all major parties save one: the Orthodox party. By that time, however, 85 percent of the ghetto Jews were already dead.

In April 1942, when the ghetto community was still intact, the oppositionist movement confined itself to verbal action. Clandestine papers were handed out, and the Gestapo, striking back, shot fifty-one people. Several ranking Judenrat members reacted to this development by expressing the view to the chairman, Czerniaków, that the underground papers might bring untold harm to the Jewish population. At that time the idea of physical resistance was the subject only of conversations. One of these exchanges, between Emmanuel Ringelblum (the ghetto's unofficial historian) and a Jewish welfare official, took place in mid-June. It is revealingly summarized by Ringelblum in his notes:

> I had a talk the other day with a friend from Biała-Podlaska, head of the Social Relief organization. He had been assisting with the population "transfer" (it would be more correct to say "transfer to the other world") to Sobibór near Chelm, where Jews are choked to death with gases. My friend asked in anger, up to when . . . how much longer will we go "as sheep to slaughter?" Why do we keep quiet? Why is there no call to escape to the forests? No call to resist? This question torments all of us, but there is no answer to it because everyone knows that resistance, and particularly

if even one single German is killed, its outcome may lead to a slaughter of a whole community, or even of many communities.

Ringelblum, as well as many others, had not yet concluded that all of Europe's Jews were the target of the German drive and so long as there was no certainty in this matter, resistance was considered a provocation of the Germans and an endangerment of Jews too old, too young, or too ill to defend themselves.

Adam Czerniaków himself had a sense of foreboding from the very beginning. In his diary he entered the reports he heard, more and more of them as the months progressed. Already on October 27, 1941, he referred to "alarming rumors about the fate of the Jews in Warsaw next spring." On January 19, 1942, he heard that Auerswald had been summoned to Berlin. "I cannot shake off the fearful suspicion," he wrote, "that the Jews of Warsaw may be threatened by mass resettlement." It was the day before the "Final Solution" conference in Berlin, in which Staatssekretär Bühler of the Generalgouvernement was an important participant. By February 16 Czerniaków noted that disturbing rumors about expulsions and resettlements were multiplying in the population. In March, as mass deportations were beginning in several cities, Czerniaków made note of what was happening. On March 18 he mentioned deportations in Lwów, Mielec, and Lublin, and on April 1 he recorded the news from Lublin that 90 percent of the ghetto's Jews were going to be moved out in the next few days and that the Lublin council members, including chairman Becker, were under arrest.

Later that month, on April 29, the Warsaw ghetto Kommissar, Auerswald, wanted Czerniaków to supply statistics of the population by street and apartment building, and one of Auerswald's assistants added a request for ten maps of the ghetto. In his diary Czerniaków asked himself: "Is a decision in the offing?" On May 3, when the Transferstelle demanded a list of all those who were working, Czerniaków wondered if the deportation of unproductive elements was being planned. In July, the rumors became numerical: on the 1st, that 70,000 would be deported, on the 16th, that 120,000 would be removed, and on the 18th, that the deportations would begin on the following Monday and that they would encompass all. Czerniaków went on with his daily routine, including the sponsorship of concerts and children's festivals. Invoking the image of the captain on the sinking ship, he noted on July 8 that he had ordered the jazz band to play to raise the spirits of the passengers.

On the 20th of July, as panic increased in the ghetto, Czerniaków asked an SS sergeant whether there was truth in the rumors. The SS man had heard nothing. The chairman then approached an SS Untersturmführer in the Gestapo (Brandt of IV-B) with the same question. Brandt said he knew of no such scheme. Czerniaków then inquired of Obersturmführer Boehm (IV-A) what he knew. Boehm answered that this matter was not in his department, but that Hauptsturmführer Höhmann (Chief of IV-A) might have some information. Höhmann assured Czerniaków that if anything were to happen he would know about it. Yet another Gestapo officer told him it was all nonsense. The very next day, council members were arrested, and at 10 A.M. of the 22nd, Sturmbannführer Höfle of Globocnik's Aussiedlungsstab arrived at the council office. The telephone was disconnected, and Czerniaków, with some of the council staff present, was told that all Jews, irrespective of sex or age save for certain categories, would be deported to the "East."

Höfle decreed that 1,000 Order Service men be assigned to the roundups and that 6,000 Jews be assembled by 4 P.M. that day and every day thereafter. Initial contingents of Jews were to be drawn from the population at large, and directives were going to be issued subsequently for seizures by streets and blocks. Exempt would be only those employed by German offices and firms, Jews capable of labor, employees of the council, members of the Order Service, Jewish hospital and disinfection personnel, all with their wives and children, and hospitalized Jews not capable of travel.

On July 23, Czerniaków, worried about the children in the orphanages, proposed additional categories for exemption to Höfle's deputy, Obersturmführer Worthoff. He was informed that students in vocational schools and husbands of working women could stay, but that the status of the orphans was to be decided by Höfle himself. When Czerniaków asked for how many days a week the operation would go on, he was told seven days a week. Czerniaków, observing the great rush to start new workshops, noted: "A sewing machine can save a life." It was afternoon and he was thinking about 4 P.M. That evening, alone in his office, Czerniaków asked for a glass of water and took a cyanide pill that he had kept in his drawer.

The council promptly elected Czerniaków's deputy, Marek Lichtenbaum, as his successor. The "authorities" (Behörden), said Lichtenbaum in his first monthly report, had promised the council normal rations for August and September and in addition 180,000 kilograms of bread and 36,000 kilograms of marmalade for the resettlers. Three times the Jewish police (in the absence of Józef Szeryński, who was under arrest for alleged corruption, led by his deputy Jakub Lejkin) posted announcements—the last one on August 1—promising 3 kilograms of bread and 1 kilogram of marmalade for every person reporting at the *Umschlagplatz* voluntarily.

While the impotent machinery of the Judenrat responded mechanically to German command, feverish activity began in the Jewish party organizations. Committees were established, meetings were held, coordinating bodies were set up. On the afternoon of July 23, the very day of Czerniaków's suicide, about sixteen representatives of all major parties except the Revisionists (who were not invited) met to discuss the crucial question of immediate resistance. From the fragmentary postwar accounts of that conference, it is not altogether clear how the conferees divided on that question. All accounts agree, however, that the advocates of resistance were voted down. The concensus was that the Germans would deport perhaps 60,000 people but not all 380,000 Jews in the ghetto. It was felt that by resistance the ghetto's doom would be hastened and that, for the acts of a few, the multitude would be punished.

The assumptions of those who had argued against resistance were shown to be false by the end of July. Some 60,000 Jews had already been moved out at that point, and the roundups continued unabated. Soon it was the turn of the orphans for whom Czerniaków had made his last plea. Janusz Korczak, in charge of an orphanage in the ghetto, was given an opportunity to escape. On July 27 Korczak wrote in his diary: "Choose: either get out, or work here on the spot. If you stay, you must do whatever may be necessary for the resettlers. The autumn is near. They will need clothes, footwear, underwear, tools." By August 1, this was his entry: "A casino. Monaco. The stake—your head." On August 4 he decided to hand over a "mentally underdeveloped and maliciously undisciplined" boy to the police in order that the entire house not be exposed to danger. It was Korczak's last entry.

Józef Szeryński, released from German captivity to conduct the roundups, resumed command of the Jewish police. According to a contemporary chronicler, he was approached toward the middle of August by a group of Jewish porters and cart drivers who had a "resistance project." Szeryński told them that he had seen postcards from deportees in Treblinka indicating that everyone there was safe. The porters believed him "with the childish naïveté of athletes."

Starting on August 9, streets were cleared systematically, and by the 18th, the large bulk of the eligible deportees had disappeared. Officials of the German city administration were now expressing concern about unpaid utility bills, and proprietors of German armament firms in the ghetto, together with armament officials and representatives of the Transferstelle, moved quickly to save their Jewish labor. The industrialists had no time to lose. After a lapse of ten days or so, in the course of which the raiders emptied the small ghettos of the Warsaw district, the deportations were resumed. Each Jewish policeman was told to bring seven people for deportation each day or face "resettlement" himself. Now every policeman brought whomever he could catch—friends, relatives, even members of his immediate family. By September 5, about 120,000 to 130,000 Jews remained. On that day all Jews were called out to the Umschlagplatz for a giant selection. During these weeks many had tried to hide or run. In its report for August the Judenrat noted 2,305 deaths from bullet wounds, and for September that figure was 3,158.

When the Aktion was over, 300,000 people had been deported. At most 70,000 were still in the ghetto, half of them registered, the other half in hiding. The size of the ghetto had also been reduced, and the principal inhabited section was now confined to the northeast corner. However, factories were still in existence on Leszno, Karmelicka, Twarda, Prosta, and a few outlying streets (see Map 4). The rest of the ghetto was empty.

Many questions were asked in the ghetto upon the conclusion of the operation, as illustrated by the self-interrogation of the historian Emmanuel Ringelblum, recorded in mid-October:

> Why didn't we resist when they began to resettle 300,000 Jews from Warsaw? Why did we allow ourselves to be led like sheep to the slaughter? Why did everything come so easy to the enemy? Why didn't the hangmen suffer a single casualty? Why could 50 SS men (some people say even fewer), with the help of a division of some 200 Ukrainian guards and an equal number of Letts, carry out the operation so smoothly?

And again:

> The resettlement should never have been permitted. We ought to have run out into the street, have set fire to everything in sight, have torn down the walls, and escaped to the Other Side. The Germans would have taken their revenge. It would have cost tens of thousands of lives, but not 300,000.

The Germans had left behind a relatively large number of people who were capable of asking such questions. The remnant ghetto had very few children or elderly individuals. The weak, the sick, the helpless masses had largely disasppeared. In the remaining registered population the majority fell into the age group 20–39. This was the time, in the fall of 1942, when the Jewish political parties finally banded together and decided to resist further deportations with force. To accomplish this aim, the parties built a complex organization to coordinate their activities. This organization was built from the bottom up. First, the

MAP 4
THE BREAKUP OF THE
WARSAW GHETTO

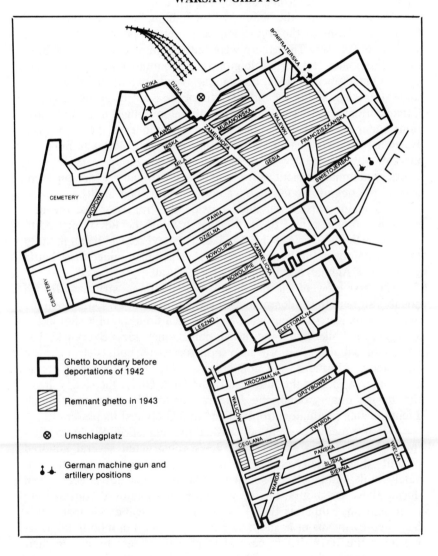

Ghetto boundary before
deportations of 1942

Remnant ghetto in 1943

⊗ Umschlagplatz

German machine gun and
artillery positions

Jewish National Committee (ŻKN) was formed to bring together the Zionist groups and the Communist PPR. A Coordinating Committee (KK) was then established to bring the Bundists an⌐ ˌˌhe merged Zionists and Communists under the same roof. This political amalgamation was accomplished by October 20, 1942.

At the same time, the building of the fighting forces also proceeded from the bottom to the top. Each party set up platoon-size "battle groups" of its own. Thus there were battle groups composed of Bundists, Hashomer Hatzair battle groups, Communist battle groups, and so on. On October 20, 1942, these units, twenty-two in all, were placed under the command of the military arm of the KK: the Jewish Fighting Organization (ŻOB). The ghetto Jews therefore fought in party formations under a centralized command. The commander of the ŻOB was a Hashomer Hatzair leader, Mordechai Anielewicz. What is most remarkable about Anielewicz is that he was twenty-four years old. The doors to command positions in the Jewish community leadership were usually not open to young men who offered only their ability.

Two major parties remained outside the framework of the new resistance organization: the nationalist Jews of the Revisionist party and the Orthodox Jews of the Agudah. The Revisionists had a military force of their own, the *Irgun Zwai Leumi,* which maintained three battle groups. The Agudah had no fighting forces at all.

The first blow of the resistance movement was struck at Jewish collaborators of the Judenrat machinery. On August, 21, 1942, when the deportations were at their peak, Izrael Kanał fired the first shot in the struggle; the bullet felled the Jewish police chief, Józef Szeryński. His successor, Jakub Lejkin, was also shot. Assassins' bullets struck down policemen, informers, and collaborators, including the chief of the economic division of the Judenrat, Izrael First. Under the steady fire of the Jewish underground, the Judenrat, under chairman Ing. Marek Lichtenbaum, gradually atrophied and ultimately lost its power.

Defense measures were now rushed to completion. While pretending to build air-raid shelters, the Jews constructed several hundred dugouts that partially connected with the sewer system. (In the privately built hiding places social stratification was not affected even during these last hours, for the well-to-do Jews enjoyed considerably more luxurious dugouts than the poor.) A propaganda campaign was launched by means of posters, handbills, and word of mouth, impressing upon the Jews that in case of trouble they were to stay in their dugouts, come what might. At the same time negotiations were conducted with General "Rola" Żymierski's Communist People's Guard and with General Rowecki's London-directed Home Army in order to procure arms for the battle groups. According to a postwar Communist account, the People's Guard supplied the Jews with twenty-five rifles, "the last" in its "arsenal." The Home Army described its contribution as "a supply of revolvers, rifles, some machine guns and about a thousand hand-grenades, as well as explosives for the production of mines." In addition, several hundred pistols were acquired by purchase from the Polish population. Thus prepared, the Jews waited for the blow.

In the meantime, the Germans made plans of their own. In January, Himmler visited Warsaw. There he got the information that about 40,000 Jews were still in the ghetto. (The actual number may have been 70,000.) He decided that there were too many and ordered that 8,000 be deported at once; from the remainder he wanted to save about 16,000 for forced labor camps. To Oberst Freter of the Armament Command in Warsaw he remarked that Keitel had agreed to this plan.

The January push came quite suddenly and caught the ghetto defenders by surprise. Sixty-five hundred Jews were deported and 1,171 died of bullet wounds. One German police captain was severely wounded in the abdomen.

After this encounter, Himmler ordered the total dissolution of the ghetto. The emptied Jewish quarter was to be torn down completely. No Poles were to be permitted to settle there, for Himmler did not want Warsaw to grow back to its former size.

The SS and Police Leader in Warsaw, Oberführer von Sammern-Frankenegg, had to anticipate Jewish resistance inside the ghetto and Polish diversionary attacks on its perimeter. He therefore concentrated his own forces and secured some assistance from the army's Ober-feldkommandantur in Warsaw. After making his preparations, on the first day of the Aktion, he was replaced by Brigadeführer Stroop. On the eve of the Warsaw ghetto battle, the opposing sides faced each other in the strength shown in Table 13.

At 3 A.M. on April 19, 1943, the ghetto was surrounded, and three hours later the Waffen-SS entered it at Zamenhof Street (see Map 5). The invaders were met by concentrated fire, and incendiary bottles put the tank out of action. The SS men withdrew with casualties. Later in the morning, raiding parties again entered the ghetto, and this time they proceeded systematically from house to house. By afternoon they encountered machine-gun fire. Since it became apparent that the ghetto could not be cleared in one sweep, the Germans withdrew again at night to resume operations in the morning.

On April 20 and 21, slow progress was made. The Jews held the factories, and it was decided, after some negotiations with the managers and the army, to destroy the buildings with artillery and explosives. By April 22 several sections of the ghetto were afire, and Jews jumped from the upper stories of the burning buildings after having thrown mat-

---

T A B L E   13
COMPARATIVE STRENGTH OF OPPOSING FORCES IN THE WARSAW GHETTO

Jews

Jewish War Organization (*Żydowska Organizacja Bojowa,* or ŻOB)
  Commander: Mordechai Anielewicz
  Manpower: Twenty-two platoon-size "battle groups," composed of men and women between 18 and 25, territorially divided and commanded as follows: Central District (Izrael Kanał), nine battle groups; Többens-Schultz area (Eliezer Geler), eight battle groups; Brushmakers' area (Marek Edelman), five battle groups
Not operating under the ŻOB:
  Irgun Zwai Leumi, under the command of Paul Frenkel, with three battle groups
  A few Poles who were inside the ghetto and Polish partisans (Communists and nationalists) who carried out diversionary attacks outside the ghetto
Total armed strength: about 750
  Total equipment: Two or three light machine guns; about a hundred rifles and carbines (give or take a few dozen); a few hundred revolvers and pistols of all types, including German Lugers and Polish Vis pistols; a few thousand hand grenades (Polish and homemade), homemade incendiary bottles (Molotov cocktails), a few pressure mines and explosive contraptions *(Höllenmaschinen);* gas masks, German steel helmets, and German uniforms

---

tresses and upholstered articles into the street. The raiders attempted to drown Jews moving around in the sewers, but the Jews managed to block off the flooded passages.

After April 22, Jews were caught and killed in increasing numbers. Sewers and dugouts were blown up one by one. Captured Jews reported to the Germans that the inmates of the dugouts "became insane from the heat, the smoke, and the explosions." A few of the Jewish prisoners were forced to reveal hiding places and centers of resistance. The Jewish commander, Mordechai Anielewicz, writing to his deputy on the Aryan side, pointed out that revolvers were useless and that he needed grenades, machine guns, and explosives.

The Jews now tried to slip out of the ghetto through the sewer system. The army engineers countered this move by blowing up the manholes. Smoke candles were lowered into the underground passages, and Jews who mistook the candles for poison gas came up for air. In May the ghetto was a sea of flames. Only a few parties of Jews were still above ground in the burning buildings, and in their dugouts they were buried in debris and suffocated. Corpses were observed floating in the sewers. One desperate Jewish unit, emerging from a sewer, seized a

T A B L E   13 (cont'd.)

Germans

Commander: Oberführer von Sammern-Frankenegg; relieved at 8 A.M. on
     April 19, 1943, by Brigadeführer Stroop
Manpower:
  Waffen-SS men (with three or four weeks of basic training only):
    SS-Armored Grenadier Training and Replacement Battalion No. 3, War-
      saw
    SS-Cavalry Training and Replacement Battalion, Warsaw
  Order Police (including veterans of the eastern front):
    1st and 3d Battalions of the 22d Police Regiment
    Technical Police
    Polish police
    Polish fire brigade
  Security Police (small detachments)
  Army:
    One light anti-aircraft battery
    One howitzer crew
    Two engineer platoons
    A medical unit
  Collaborators (Ukrainians): one battalion from Trawniki camp
  Total strength: ca. 2,000 to 3,000
  Equipment:‡ One captured French tank and two heavy armored cars; three
    light (2-cm) antiaircraft guns; one medium (105-mm) howitzer; flame
    throwers, heavy and light machine guns, submachine guns, rifles, and
    pistols; grenades, smoke candles, and large amounts of explosive
    charges

‡A howitzer is a short-barreled artillery piece designed for close-range destructive
power. Ordinarily, a Panzer-Grenadier battalion was equipped with nine 37-mm antitank
guns, three 75-mm antitank guns, and four 75-mm howitzers. No mention is made of such
weapons in the Stroop report, and it is conceivable that the training unit did not have
them. The Stroop report similarly fails to mention mortars. The absence of mortars is
strange, but it is possible that they were not used.

truck and staged a successful getaway. The Jews were thinning out
rapidly.

On May 8 Anielewicz was killed. The Germans now sent night
patrols into the ghetto, and the remaining Jewish dugouts were systematically destroyed. By May 15 the shooting became sporadic. The Jews
had been overwhelmed. At 8:15 P.M. on May 16, the German commander, Stroop, blew up the great Tlomacki Synagogue in the "Aryan"
section of the city as a signal that the Warsaw ghetto battle was over.

Several thousand Jews had been buried in the debris, and 56,065
had surrendered. Seven thousand of the captured Jews were shot,
another 7,000 were transported to the death camp at Treblinka, 15,000

were shipped to the concentration camp and killing center at Lublin, and the remainder were sent to labor camps. Nine rifles, fifty-nine pistols, several hundred grenades, explosives, and mines were captured. The rest of the Jewish equipment had been destroyed. The losses to the Germans and their collaborators consisted of sixteen dead and eighty-five wounded.

It is possible that in the final tabulation a few casualties were omitted and that additional losses were inflicted upon the Germans after the official end of the fighting. However, there is no doubt that in the main the Stroop report, with all its statistics, is accurate. It must be kept in mind that the Jews did not have enough weapons to equip an infantry company. It must also be remembered that Stroop's report was secret and that he listed the name of every casualty at the beginning of his account, as if to emphasize his losses.

After the armed resistance of the Jews was broken, two tasks had to be completed. In accordance with Himmler's wish, the entire ghetto was to be razed, and every dugout, cellar, and sewer was to be filled in. After the conclusion of this work the whole area was to be covered with earth, and a large park was to be planted in the former ghetto. Thus, in the summer of 1943, Oswald Pohl, the chief of the SS Economic-Administrative Main Office, established a concentration camp in the ruins, and Brigadeführer Dr. Ing. Kammler, chief of the construction division of the Economic-Administrative Main Office, was put in charge of the demolition work. Contracts were let with three construction firms. The Ostbahn laid twelve miles of narrow-gauge railway track to haul away debris. Twenty-five hundred concentration camp inmates and 1,000 Polish workers labored for more than a year in clearing the 445 acres of demolished buildings and breaking down the 3,400,000 cubic yards of wall. The work was interrupted in July 1944, before the park could be planted. For the incomplete job Himmler presented to Finance Minister von Krosigk a bill for 150 million reichsmark. Not all of this money was paid.

More difficult but a little less expensive than the rubble-clearance work was the task of rounding up 5,000 to 6,000 Jews who had escaped from the ghetto before and during the battle and who were now hiding in various parts of the district. The Poles appear to have aided the Germans in this roundup only "in a handful of cases." However, Polish gangs roamed the city, seeking out Jewish hiding places and forcing the victims to pay high sums of money or face denunciation. We have no exact statistics on how many Jews were left when the Red Army arrived in January 1945. In the city itself it seems that only 200 survived.

After the conclusion of the Warsaw ghetto fighting, only a few major ghettos were still in existence, particular Lwów in the Galician district, the Białystok ghetto, and the Warthegau ghetto of Łódź. When Brigadeführer Katzmann, the Galician SS and Police Leader, moved into what was left of the Lwów ghetto in June 1943, he discovered that the 20,000 Jews in the ghetto had begun to build dugouts and bunkers on the Warsaw pattern. "In order to avoid losses on our side," Katzmann reported, "we had to act brutally from the beginning." Blowing up and burning down houses, Katzmann dragged 3,000 corpses out of the hiding places.

The Białystok district was quasi-incorporated territory. Its SS and Police Leader, Hellwig, reported to Sporrenberg, the Higher SS and Police Leader of East Prussia. When a "militant antifascist bloc" was formed in the Białystok ghetto, Eichmann's deputy, Günther, appeared to help uncover the sabotage group. As in the case of Warsaw, the Jews were caught unprepared. The first onslaught, in February 1943, left a thousand dead in the streets and one German casualty. On August 16, 1943, Globocnik arrived on the scene with his Aussiedlungsstab and, superimposing himself on the KdS, Sturmbannführer Zimmerman, entered the ghetto head-on. The Jews defended themselves with pistols, grenades, and two automatic weapons. In the words of Friedel, the local IV-B specialist in the office of the KdS, "there was shooting on both sides and both sides had dead and wounded." Globocnik brought up a tank and broke the ghetto on the same day.

The Łódź ghetto followed the cycle of Warsaw and Lwów; partial reduction of the population, employment in war labor of those able to work, followed by total dissolution. Deportations during the first five months of 1942 resulted in the disappearance of 55,000 Jews, about a third of the ghetto's population. On April 12 official Jewish chroniclers in the ghetto noted the visit of an SS officer who had brought word that the deportees were being housed in a well-equipped camp, previously used for German resettlers, near Warthbrücken and that the Jews were building roads and farming the land. By May 25, however, large shipments of clothes wrapped in blankets and bedsheets began arriving in four ghetto warehouses. The bundles contained prayer shawls, window curtains, skirts, pants, underwear, jackets, and coats with torn seams. During the sorting, letters and identification cards fell out of the garments. To the chroniclers it was clear that these belongings had not been packed by their owners.

In September 1942, two further actions were taken to thin out the Łódź ghetto. This time the ghetto was to become more cost efficient. On September 1–2 the patients in the hospitals were sent off, and the health division was all but dissolved, its employees becoming day laborers. During the week of September 5–12 a total curfew was instituted, and the entire Jewish Order Service was deployed to drag out individuals who were ill at home, the old people, and a large number of children. Following the September reductions, which encompassed almost 16,000 victims, large machines were delivered to the ghetto to modernize the carpentry and metal workshops, and major orders were placed by the army for furs and other clothing. The chief of the Gettoverwaltung, Biebow, sent out the clarion call for work in the following poster:

REOPENING
of all factories and workshops
as of Monday, September 14, 1942
Since the resettlement has been concluded yesterday,
ALL FACTORIES WILL RESUME FULL OPERATION
on Monday, September 14, 1942.

Every foreman, worker, and employee had better report for work as usual, if he desires to protect himself himself against the greatest conceivable unpleasantness. Every recognized [registered] laborer will now be asked to fulfill his task with utmost diligence, and to do his utmost to make up for production lost during the rest period.

I am going to institute the strictest controls for the enforcement of this order.

Gettoverwaltung
BIEBOW

The Jews went on working, even after the disquieting news in October about massive summer deportations in Warsaw. In fact, Łódź had become the largest ghetto by default, its 80,000 people struggling with a prison diet and a twelve-hour day for two more years. Then, in August 1944, announcements were posted in the ghetto under the heading "*Verlagerung des Gettos* [transshipment of the ghetto]." The Jews were ordered to present themselves for Verlagerung on penalty of death.

This time the Jews knew where Biebow wanted to send them, and something like a sitdown strike ensued in workshops I and II. These Jews had held out for so long that now, with the end of the war in sight, they were not willing to go to their deaths voluntarily. The Germans decided to proceed with propaganda warfare. On August 7, 1944, at 4:45 P.M., the Jewish workers were called together for a speech. After a few introductory remarks by the *Präsident of the Ältestenrat,* Chaim Rumkowski, Amtsleiter Biebow of the Gettoverwaltung began to speak. Biebow was not a very fluent speaker, but his words had the desired effect.

"Workers of the ghetto," be began, "I have already spoken to you various times, and I hope that what I have said until now you have always taken to heart. The situation in Litzmannstadt [Łódź] has again changed, and I mean from today noon. There is a total evacuation of women and children on the German side. That means that all ethnic Germans have to leave this place. Whoever thinks that the ghetto is not going to be dissolved totally is making a tremendous mistake. To the last man, everyone has to be out of here and will be out of here. Some will think it is better to be the last to go. In the vicinity of Litzmannstadt bombs have already fallen, and if they had fallen in the ghetto, not one stone would have remained on another."

It would be insanity, Biebow continued, if workshop areas I and II refused to go along. For four and one-half years, they—the Gettoverwaltung and the Jews—had worked together. Biebow had always tried to do his best. He still wanted to do his best—namely, "to save your lives by moving this ghetto." Right now, Germany was fighting with her last ounce of strength. Thousands of German workers were going to the front. These workers would have to be replaced. Siemens and Schuckert needed workers, Union needed workers, the Częstochowa munitions plants needed workers. In Częstochowa everybody was "very satisfied with the Jews, and the Gestapo is very satisfied with their output. After all, you want to live and eat, and that you will have. After all, I am not going to stand here like a silly boy, make speeches, and nobody comes. If you insist upon measures of force, well then, there will be dead and wounded." The trip, said Biebow, was going to take ten to sixteen hours. Food had already been loaded on the trains. Everybody could take along 40 pounds of luggage. Everyone was to hold on to his pots, pans, and utensils, because in Germany such things were given only to bombed-out people. So, common sense. If not, and then force were used, Biebow could not help anymore.

The Jewish workers of workshop areas I and II changed their minds. They surrendered. By the end of August the ghetto was empty except for a small cleanup Kommando. The victims were shipped not to Germany, to work in plants, but to the killing center in Auschwitz, to be gassed to death.

Why did the striking Jewish workers of Łódź surrender to Biebow's appeal? For the Jews of Poland, resistance was not merely a matter of digging fortifications and procuring arms; it required in the first instance a shake-up of the entire institutional structure of the community and a reversal of ancient thought processes. The ghetto inmates of Łódź were not capable of breaking with a historical pattern under which they had survived destruction for two thousand years. That was why the flight into fantasy, the false hopes, and the voice of Biebow were more assuring to them than the new and untried path into violent, desperate self-defense. Only the ghetto of Warsaw had produced the complete turn from compliance to resistance, and that turn was accomplished, after the loss of more than 300,000 Jews, under the leadership of a twenty-four-year-old commander. It came too late to change the fundamental Jewish reaction pattern, and it was too feeble to interfere with German plans.

The Germans did not suffer much from Jewish resistance. However, the breakdown of secrecy resulted in disturbances, not only in the Jewish community but also in the local population and, ultimately, among the Germans themselves. These repercussions were in some respects more serious than the reactions of the Jews. In speaking of the local inhabitants, we must remember that there were essentially *two* populations: the Ukrainians in Galicia and the Poles. The reactions of these two groups were not the same.

The Ukrainians were involved in the fate of Polish Jewry as perpetrators. The SS and Police employed Ukrainian forces in ghetto-clearing operations not only in the Galician district but also in such places as the Warsaw ghetto and the Lublin ghetto. The Ukrainians had never been considered pro-Jewish. The Ukraine had been the scene of intermittent pogroms and oppressions for 300 years. On the other hand, these people had no stomach for the long-range systematic German destruction process. Short violence followed by confession and absolution was one thing, organized killing was quite another.

In September 1943 a French collaborator, going under the name of Dr. Frederic, had a discussion with Monsignor Szepticki, metropolitan of the Greek Catholic Church in Lwów. The metropolitan accused the Germans of inhuman action against the Jews. In Lwów alone they had killed 100,000, and in the Ukraine, millions. He had heard the confession of a young man who had personally slain seventy-five persons in one night at Lwów. Dr. Frederic replied that according to his information the Ukrainians had certainly taken part in these massacres but that, in view of the execution of 18,000 persons in and near Lwów by the Soviets, such participation was only natural. Furthermore, almost all members of the NKVD had been Jews, which should explain the hatred of the population. Moreover, wasn't Jewry a deadly danger to Christendom, and hadn't the Jews avowed the destruction of Christianity? The metropolitan agreed, but repeated that the annihilation of the Jews was an impermissible action.

While the Greek Catholic metropolitan in Lwów was troubled by the fact that the Germans were drawing the Ukrainians into the destruction process as partners, the Poles began to fear that they would soon be joining the Jews as victims. This consideration was expressed in pamphlets circulated in the Warsaw district in August 1942, calling upon the Poles to help the persecuted Jews. The theme of these pamphlets was that only dumb people and idiots, who could not understand that after the Jews the Poles would get the same treatment, would be happy about the Jewish fate.

The Polish leadership (to say nothing of the Polish people) did not know that the Germans actually were toying with the idea of getting rid of the Poles. No one knew, for example, that on May 1, 1942, Gauleiter Greiser had proposed to Himmler the "special treatment" of some 35,000 tubercular Poles in his Gau as a sanitary measure for the protection of the ethnic Germans in the incorporated territory. Even without this knowledge the anxiety was real, not only in informed underground circles but in every workers' section of every Polish city. Their fear came to the surface in October 1942.

The SS and Police (i.e., Himmler) had decided to make Lublin a German city and to make the Lublin district a German district. On October 1, 1942, the police carried out a *razzia* in the northern section of the city of Lublin. All inhabitants of the section were called out and assembled in one place. All work certificates were checked, and all Poles, male or female, who could not prove that they were employed were carted away to a camp, while children under fifteen were sent to an orphanage.

Immediately rumors swept the city like wildfire. Many Poles stopped in the streets and said: "Weren't we right that the resettlement across the Bug was going to come? It has come, earlier than we supposed. Punctually on October 1, 1942, in the morning it has come!" The Poles were convinced that this Aktion was the same as the "resettlement" of the Jews. In Lublin the belief was strong that the Jewish "resettlers" had been killed and that the fat from their corpses had been used in the manufacture of soap. Now pedestrians in Lublin were saying that it was the turn of the Poles to be used, just like the Jews, for soap production.

When the first Polish deportees from Lublin arrived at the labor camp at Lubartów, the rumors were fanned still further, and the belief was formed that all Poles in the Generalgouvernement would be shipped across the Bug. Heaping rumor upon rumor, the Polish residents of Lublin also voiced the opinion that a few privileged Poles would be offered Reich citizenship in preference to "resettlement," and a number of Lublin inhabitants were already discussing the acceptance of such citizenship as an escape from death.

The Polish fears were not altogether irrational. In the German city administration of Warsaw, Dr. Wilhelm Hagen—the man who had pitted himself against a group of planners who had wanted to reduce the size of the Warsaw ghetto in 1941—was himself convinced that an action against Poles was being contemplated. On December 7, 1942, he wrote a letter to Hitler in which he said:

In a tuberculosis meeting, the director of the Population and Welfare Division, Oberverwaltungsrat Weirauch, informed us in secret that of 200,000 Poles who are to be resettled in the east of the Generalgouvernement to make room for German defense farmers, a third—70,000 old people and children under 10—might be dealt with in the same manner as the Jews, that is, it was intended or considered that they might be killed.

Weirauch, incensed, called the charge "nonsense" and attributed to Hagen a desire to give to Poles comprehensive tuberculosis care in contravention to policy established by the Population and Welfare Division. Himmler thought that Hagen should spend the rest of the war in a concentration camp, but Conti dissuaded him from that decision. The killings did not take place, but the Polish population was never completely sure of its safety.

Last but not least, the breakdown of secrecy had repercussions on the Germans themselves. In Poland particularly, the Germans were jittery and afraid. They feared reprisals and retribution. On October 3, 1942, the Propaganda Division in Radom reported a disturbing incident that had resulted from the dispatch of a postcard. The Germans published a paper in Poland, the *Krakauer Zeitung*, for the local German population. The chief of the Radom branch of the paper had received from Lwów a postcard that began (in German): "I don't know German. You can translate everything from the Polish into German." The card then continued in Polish:

You old whore and you old son of a whore, Richard. A child has been born to you. May your child suffer throughout his life, as we Jews have suffered because of you. I wish you that from the bottom of my heart.

This anonymous note actually disturbed its recipient and worried the propaganda experts. The Propaganda Division feared that it was the beginning of a flood of postcards, and the card was transmitted to the Security Police for tracing.

In September 1942 a German army officer in Lublin told a German judge that in the United States reprisals against Germans had started because of the treatment of the Jews in the Generalgouvernement. A large number of Germans, according to this officer, had already been shot in America.

The jittery feeling reached the very top of the German administrative apparatus in Poland. On August 24, 1942, forty-eight officials of the Generalgouvernment met in conference to discuss some problems in connection with anti-Jewish and anti-Polish measures. Generalgouverneur Frank was particularly candid in referring to a "sentence of hunger death" against 1,200,000 Jews. At the end of the meeting Staatssekretär Dr. Boepple pointed out that he had the attendance list and that, if any rumors should reach the public, he would trace them to their source. Again, during the conference of January 25, 1943, after a lot of talk about anti-Jewish measures, Frank remarked:

> We want to remember that we are, all of us assembled here, on Mr. Roosevelt's war-criminals list. I have the honor of occupying first place on that list. We are therefore, so to speak, accomplices in a world-historical sense.

The following story is told by the KdS (Commander of Security Police) in the Lublin district, Johannes Hermann Müller. He had once attended a conference under the chairmanship of the Lublin SS and Police Leader, Odilo Globocnik. The SS and Police Leader was thinking just then about the transport of Polish children from Lublin to Warsaw and the death by freezing of many of these children. Globocnik turned to Sturmbannführer Höfle (one of his trusted assistants) and told him that he had a three-year-old niece. Globocnik could no longer look at the little one without thinking about the others. Höfle did not know what to reply and "looked at Globocnik like an idiot." In the spring of 1943, Höfle's two children, twins who were only a few months old, died of diphtheria. At the cemetery Höfle suddently went wild and shouted: "That is the punishment of heaven for all my misdeeds!" It is perhaps not accidental that the Germans, who were particularly brutal in their treatment of Jewish children, were now most afraid for their own.

CHAPTER SIX

KILLING CENTER OPERATIONS

MAP 5
THE KILLING CENTERS

ORIGINS OF THE KILLING CENTERS

The most secret operations of the destruction process were carried out in six camps located in Poland in an area stretching from the incorporated areas to the Bug. These camps were the collecting points for thousands of transports converging from all directions. In three years the incoming traffic reached a total of close to three million Jews. As the transports turned back empty, their passengers disappeared inside.

The killing centers worked quickly and efficiently. A man would step off a train in the morning, and in the evening his corpse was burned and his clothes were packed away for shipment to Germany. Such an operation was the product of a great deal of planning, for the death camp was an intricate mechanism in which a whole army of specialists played their parts. Viewed superficially, this smoothly functioning apparatus is deceptively simple, but upon closer examination the operations of the killing center resemble in several respects the complex mass-production methods of a modern plant. It will therefore be necessary to explore, step by step, what made possible the final result.

The most striking fact about the killing center operations is that, unlike the earlier phases of the destruction process, they were unprecedented. Never before in history had people been killed on an assembly-line basis. The killing center, as we shall observe it, has no prototype, no administrative ancestor. This is explained by the fact that it was a composite institution that consisted of two parts: the camp proper and the killing installations in the camp. Each of these two parts had its own administrative history. Neither was entirely novel. As separate establishments, both the concentration camp and the gas chamber had been in existence for some time. The great innovation was effected when the two devices were fused. We should therefore begin our examination of the death camp by learning something about its two basic components and how they were put together.

The German concentration camp was born and grew amid violent disputes and struggles between Nazi factions. Even in the earliest days of the Nazi regime, the importance of the concentration camp was fully recognized. Whoever gained possession of this weapon would wield a great deal of power.

In Prussia, Interior Minister (and later Prime Minister) Göring made his bid. He decided to round up the Communists. This was not an incarceration of convicted criminals but an arrest of a potentially dangerous group. "The prisons were not available for this purpose"; hence Göring established concentration camps, which he put under the control of his Gestapo (then, Ministerialrat Diels).

Almost simultaneously, rival camps appeared on the scene. One was set up at Stettin by Gauleiter Karpenstein, another was established at Breslau by SA leader Heines, a third was erected near Berlin by SA leader Ernst. Göring moved with all his might against these "unauthorized camps." Karpenstein lost his post, Ernst lost his life.

But a more powerful competitor emerged. In Munich the police president, Himmler, organized his own Gestapo, and near the town of Dachau he set up a concentration camp which he placed under the command of SS-Oberführer Eicke. Soon Himmler's Gestapo covered the non-Prussian *Länder* (provinces), and in the spring of 1934 Himmler obtained through Hitler's graces the Prussian Gestapo (becoming its "deputy chief"). Along with Göring's Gestapo, Himmler captured the Prussian concentration camps. Henceforth all camps were under his control.

Eicke, the first Dachau commander, now became the Inspector for Concentration Camps. His *Totenkopfverbände* (Death Head Units) became the guards. Thus the camps were severed from the Gestapo, which retained in the administration of each camp only one foothold: the political division, with jurisdiction over executions and releases. After the outbreak of war, Eicke and most of his Totenkopfverbände moved into the field (he was killed in Russia), and his deputy, the later Brigadeführer Glücks, took over the inspectorate.

Eicke's departure marks the midpoint in the development of the concentration camps. Up to the outbreak of war the camps held three types of prisoners:

1. Political prisoners
   a. Communists (systematic roundup)
   b. Active Social Democrats
   c. Jehovah's Witnesses

    d. Clergymen who made undesirable speeches or otherwise man-
       ifested opposition
    e. People who made remarks against the regime and were sent to
       camps as an example to others
    f. Purged Nazis, especially SA men
2. So-called asocials, consisting primarily of habitual criminals and sex
   offenders
3. Jews sent to camps in Einzelaktionen

After 1939 the camps were flooded with millions of people, including
Jewish deportees, Poles, Soviet prisoners of war, members of the
French resistance movements, and so on.

The inspectorate could not keep up with this influx. Therefore,
from 1940 on, the Higher SS and Police Leaders established camps of
their own. We have already noted in previous chapters the transit camps
in the west and the labor camps in Poland. During the last stage of the
destruction process, the Higher SS and Police Leaders also put up
killing centers.

At this point an office stepped in to centralize and unify the concentration camp network: the SS Economic-Administrative Main Office, the organization of Obergruppenführer Oswald Pohl. In a process
that took several years, Pohl finally emerged as the dominant power in
the camp apparatus. His organization incorporated the inspectorate
and enveloped almost completely the camps of the Higher SS and
Police Leaders.

Pohl entered the concentration camp picture from an oblique angle.
He was not a camp commander, nor was he a Higher SS and Police
Leader. In World War I he had been a naval paymaster, and in the early
days of the SS he had served in the *Verwaltungsamt* (Administrative
Office) of the SS-Main Office. (The Verwaltungsamt dealt with financial
and administrative questions for the SS.) On February 1, 1934, Pohl
took over the Verwaltungsamt, and by 1936 he had expanded its activities. It was now concerned also with construction matters, including
the construction of SS installations in concentration camps. The Verwaltungsamt was therefore reorganized to become the *Amt Haushalt
und Bauten* (Budget and Construction Office)—the first major step
toward overall control.

In 1940 Pohl broke loose from the SS-Main Office and established
his own main office, the *Hauptamt Haushalt und Bauten*. At the same
time he set up a chain of SS enterprises in labor and concentration
camps. This business venture could not be placed under the Hauptamt
Haushalt und Bauten, which was nominally a state agency financed
entirely with Reich funds. Therefore, Pohl organized another main
office, the *Hauptamt Verwaltung und Wirtschaft* (VWHA) or Main

Office Administration and Economy. This was Pohl's second step. The double organization was analogous to Heydrich's apparatus before the merger of the *Hauptamt Sicherheitspolizei* (Gestapo and Kripo) and the *Sicherheitshauptamt* (SD) into the RSHA.

On February 1, 1942, Pohl followed Heydrich's example and combined his two main offices into a single organization: the SS Economic-Administrative Main Office or *Wirtschafts-Verwaltungshauptamt* (WVHA).

One month after this consolidation, Pohl took his third major step. To ensure better labor utilization in the camps and to make possible the unhampered growth of his SS enterprises, he swallowed the inspectorate. The WVHA was now fully engaged in the concentration camp business. Hauptamt Haushalt und Bauten (I and II) became *Amtsgruppen A, B,* and *C,* the inspectorate was transformed into *Amtsgruppe D,* and the VWHA (III) emerged as *Amtsgruppe W.*

With the inspectorate's incorporation into the Pohl machine, the administration of the concentration camps acquired an economic accent. The exploitation of the inmate labor supply, which had motivated Pohl to undertake this consolidation, now became the very reason for the existence of concentration camps. This factor brought into the killing center operations the same dilemma that had surfaced in the mobile killing operations and the deportations, namely the need for labor versus the "Final Solution." This time the quandary was entirely an internal SS affair.

The consolidation process did not stop with the incorporation of the inspectorate, for Pohl also bit into the camps of the Higher SS and Police Leaders. He annexed some camps outright, controlled others by installing regional officials responsible to the WVHA (the SS economists), and invaded the killing centers in the Generalgouvernement by acquiring control over the entire camp confiscation machinery in the territory. Concentration camps had become the principal factor in the power structure of Pohl. He in turn had emerged as the dominant figure in the sea of concentration camps.

While Pohl tightened his hold over the camps, the camps absorbed ever larger numbers of inmates. The following figures indicate the growth of the increasingly important army of slaves in concentration camp enclosures:

September 1939: 21,400
April 19, 1943: over 160,000
August 1, 1944: 524,286

The compilations do not include the camps of the Higher SS and Police Leaders, nor do they show the millions of deaths.

To keep up with the influx of victims, the camp network had to be extended. In 1939 there were six relatively small camps. In 1944 Pohl sent Himmler a map that showed 20 full-fledged concentration camps (*Konzentrationslager* or KL) and 165 satellite labor camps grouped in clusters around the big KLs. (Again the camps of the Higher SS and Police Leaders were not included.) Himmler received the report with great satisfaction, remarking that "just such examples show how our business has grown." Pohl's empire was thus characterized by a three-fold growth: the jurisdictional expansion, the increase in the number of camp slaves, and the extension of the camp network.

The six killing centers appeared in 1941–42, at a time of the greatest multiplication and expansion of concentration camp facilities. This is a fact of great importance, for it ensured that the construction and operation of the killing centers could proceed smoothly and unobtrusively.

The death camps operated with gas. There were three types of gassing installations, for the administrative evolution of the gas method had proceeded in three different channels. One development took place in the Technical Referat of the RSHA. This office produced the gas van. In Russia and Serbia the vans were auxiliary devices used for the killing of women and children only. But there was to be one more application. In 1941 Gauleiter Greiser of the Wartheland obtained Himmler's permission to kill 100,000 Jews in his Gau. Three vans were thereupon brought into the woods of Kulmhof (Chelmno), the area was closed off, and the first killing center came into being.

The construction of another type of gassing apparatus was pursued in the Führer Chancellery, Hitler's personal office. For some time, thought had been given in Germany to doctrines about the quality of life, from the simple idea that a dying person may be helped to die to the notion that life not worth living may be unworthy of life. This move from concern for the individual to a preoccupation with society was accomplished by representing retarded or malfunctioning persons, especially those with problems perceived to be congenital, as sick or harmful cells in the healthy corpus of the nation. The title of one monograph, published after the shock of World War I, could in fact be read as suggesting their destruction. It was called *The Release for Annihilation of Life without Value* [*Die Freigabe der Vernichtung lebensunwerten Lebens*]. The last three words of the German phrase were to grace official correspondence during the Nazi years.

Not until after the outbreak of World War II, however, did Hitler sign an order (predated September 1, 1939) empowering the chief of the Führer Chancellery, Reichsleiter Bouhler, and his own personal physician, Dr. Brandt, "to widen the authority of individual doctors with a view to enabling them, after the most critical examination in the realm of human knowledge, to administer to incurably sick persons a mercy death." The intention was to apply this directive only to Germans with mental afflictions, but eventually the program encompassed the following three operations.

1. Throughout the war, the killing, upon determination of physicians' panels, of about 5,000 severely handicapped children in hospital wards.
2. Until the late summer of 1941, the annihilation of about 70,000 adults in euthanasia stations equipped with gas chambers and bottled, chemically pure carbon monoxide gas. The victims, selected from lists screened by psychiatrists, were in the main institutionalized
   a. senile persons, feebleminded persons, epileptics, sufferers from Huntington's chorea and some other neurological disorders,
   b. individuals who had been treated at institutions for at least five years,
   c. criminally insane persons, especially those involved in moral crimes.
   The euthanasia stations, which did not have resident patients, were
   Grafeneck (after it was closed: Hadamar)
   Brandenburg (after it was closed: Bernburg)
   Sonnenstein
   Hartheim
3. From the middle of 1941 to the winter of 1944–45, the pruning of concentration camp inmates too weak or bothersome to be kept alive and the killing of these people, upon superficial psychiatric evaluation, in euthanasia stations under code 14 f 13.

The administrative implementation of this psychiatric holocaust was in the hands of Bouhler's Führer Chancellery. The man actually in charge of the program was a subordinate of Bouhler, Reichsamtsleiter Brack. For the technical aspects of the project, the Reichsamtsleiter obtained the services of Kriminalkommissar Wirth, chief of the Criminal Police office in Stuttgart and an expert in tracking down criminals.

"Euthanasia" was a conceptual as well as technological and administrative prefiguration of the "Final Solution" in the death camps. In the summer of 1941, when the physical destruction of the Jews was in the offing for the whole of the European continent, Himmler consulted with the Chief Physician of the SS, Gruppenführer Dr. Grawitz, on the best way to undertake the mass-killing operation. Grawitz advised the use of gas chambers.

On October 10, 1941, at a "final solution" conference of the RSHA, Heydrich alluded to Hitler's desire to free the Reich of Jews, if at all possible, by the end of the year. In that connection, the RSHA chief discussed the impending deportations to Łódź, and mentioned Riga and Minsk. He even considered the possibility of shipping Jews to concentration camps set up for Communists by Einsatzgruppen B and C in operational areas. The Ostland, emerging as the center of gravity in this scheme, served to crystallize the idea of what was to be done to Reich deportees on their arrival.

By the end of the month the race expert in Bräutigam's office in the East Ministry, Amtsgerichtsrat Wetzel, drafted a letter in which he stated that Brack was prepared to introduce his gassing apparatus in the east. Brack had offered to send his chemical expert, Dr. Kallmeyer, to Riga, and Eichmann had referred to Riga and Minsk in expressing agreement with the idea. "All things considered," wrote Wetzel, "one need have no reservation about doing away with those Jews who are unable to work, with the Brackian devices." There were, however, some second thoughts about directing a continuing flow of transports to the icy regions of the occupied USSR. Dr. Kallmeyer, told to wait in Berlin because of the cold in the east, spent Christmas at home. The scene of the action had already been shifted to the Generalgouvernement.

Under primitive conditions, three camps were built by *Amt Haushalt und Bauten* (after the reorganization of March 1942, the WVHA-C) and its regional machinery at Bełżec, Sobibór, and Treblinka. The sites were chosen with a view to seclusion and access to railroad lines. In the planning there was some improvisation and much economizing; labor and material were procured locally at minimum cost.

Bełżec, in the district of Lublin, was the prototype. Its construction, according to Polish witnesses, was begun as early as November 1941. A locksmith who worked in the camp while it was being built provides the following chronology:

October 1941	SS men approach Polish administration in town of Bełżec with demand for twenty workers. The Germans select the site.
November 1, 1941	Polish workers begin construction of three barracks: a waiting hall leading through a walkway to an ante-room, leading to a third building that had a corridor with three doors to three compartments, each of which had floor piping and an exit door. All six doors (entry and exit) in these three compartments were encased in thick rubber and opened to the outside.
November–December 1941	A contingent of about seventy black-uniformed eastern collaborators (Soviet

	prisoners of war released from captivity) lay narrow-gauge rail, dig pits, and erect a fence.
December 22, 1941	Polish workers are discharged.
January–February 1942	Watchtowers are built.

The Germans at the Bełżec site who had requisitioned the Polish work force were members of an SS construction Kommando. The work was supervised by a "master from Katowice," an unidentified German with some knowledge of Polish who was in possession of building plans. When one of the Poles asked about the purpose of the project, the German only smiled. Some time before Christmas, the construction chief showed the blueprints to an SS noncommissioned officer (Oberhauser) who was stationed in the area and who was going to be a functionary in the administration of the death camps. The drawings were plans of gassing installations. By that time the construction of the buildings was substantially finished, and shortly thereafter the chemist Dr. Kallmeyer arrived from Berlin.

Sobibór, also in the Lublin district, was built, evidently more quickly, in March and April of 1942. Supervision of the construction was in the hands of Hauptsturmführer Thomalla, a master mason regularly assigned to the local construction office in Lublin. Thomalla had some professional help from Baurat Moser, employed by the Kreishauptmann of Chełm (Ansel), in whose territory Sobibór was located. To speed the work, Jewish labor from the surrounding region was employed extensively during the construction phase.

At Treblinka (within the Warsaw district), where euthanasia physician Dr. Eberl was in charge, the Zentralbauleitung of the district, together with two contractors, the firm Schönbrunn of Liegnitz and the Warsaw concern Schmidt und Münstermann (builders of the Warsaw ghetto wall), were readying the camp. Labor for construction was drawn from the Warsaw ghetto. Dr. Eberl also availed himself of the resources of the ghetto for supplies, including switches, nails, cables, and wallpaper. Again, the Jews were to be the unwitting contributors to their own destruction.

Even while the three camps were being erected, transports with Jewish deportees from the Kraków district, the Reich, and the Protektorat were arriving in the Hrubieszów-Zamość area. The director of the Population and Welfare Subdivision of the Interior Division in the Gouverneur's office of Lublin (Türk) was instructed by the General-gouvernement Interior Main Division (Siebert) to assist Globocnik in making room for the Jews pouring into the district. Türk's deputy (Reuter) thereupon had a conversation with Globocnik's expert in Jewish "resettlement" affairs, Hauptsturmführer Höfle. The Hauptsturmführer made a few remarkable statements: A camp was being built at Bełżec, near Generalgouvernement border in subdistrict Zamość. Where on the Dęblin-Trawniki line could 60,000 Jews be unloaded in the meantime? Höfle was ready to receive four or five transports daily at Bełżec. "These Jews would cross the border and would never return to the Generalgouvernement." The discussion, on the afternoon of March 16, 1942, was held a few days before the opening of Bełżec. During the following month Sobibór was finished, and in July, Treblinka.

The terrain of each camp was small—a few hundred yards in length and width. The layout was similar in all three camps. There were barracks for guard personnel, an area where the Jews were unloaded, an undressing station, and an S-shaped walkway, called *Schlauch* (hose), two or three yards wide that was bordered by high barbed-wire fences covered with ivy. The *Schlauch* was traversed by the naked victims on their way to the gassing facilities. The entire arrangement was designed to convince the Jews that they were in a transit camp, where they would be required to clean themselves on the way to the "east." The gas chambers, disguised as showers, were not larger than medium-sized rooms, but during gassings they were filled to capacity. At the beginning, no camp had more than three of these chambers. The gas first used at Bełżec was bottled, either the same preparation of carbon monoxide that had been shipped to the euthanasia stations or possibly hydrogen cyanide. Later, all three camps (Sobibór and Treblinka from the start) were equipped with diesel motors. A German who briefly served at Sobibór recalls a 200-horsepower, eight-cylinder engine of a captured Soviet tank, which released a mixture of carbon monoxide and carbon dioxide into the gas chambers. No crematoria were installed; the bodies were burned in mass graves.

The limited capacity of the camps troubled SS and Police Leader Globocnik; he did not wish to get "stuck." During the summer of 1942 there was congestion of railway traffic in the Generalgouvernement, and the line to Sobibór was under repair. At Bełżec operations were reduced and interrupted, and at Sobibór the stoppage was prolonged. But Treblinka received transports to the point of overflow, and mounds of unburned bodies in various stages of decay confronted new arrivals of deportees.

Between July and September an expansion was undertaken in the three camps. Massive structures, of stone in Bełżec and brick in Treblinka, containing at least six gas chambers in each camp, replaced the old facilities. In the new gas buildings the chambers were aligned on both sides of a corridor, and at Treblinka the engine room was situated at its far end. The front wall of the Treblinka gas house, underneath the gable, was decorated with a Star of David. At the entrance hung a heavy, dark curtain taken from a synagogue and still bearing the Hebrew words "This is the gate through which the righteous pass."

The Generalgouvernement was the location also of a regular concentration camp of the WVHA, where Jewish transports were received from time to time. In German correspondence the camp was referred to as Lublin, whereas its common name after the war was Majdanek. Up to October 1942, the camp had facilities for men only. It had been built to hold prisoners of war (among them Jewish soldiers of the Polish army) under SS jurisdiction. Even during these early days, however, several thousand Jews, including men, women, and children, were brought into the camp from nearby localities. In September–October 1942, three small gas chambers, placed into a U-shaped building, were opened. Two of them were constructed for the interchangeable use of bottled carbon monoxide or hydrogen cyanide gas, the third for cyanide only. The area in front of the building was called *Rosengarten* and *Rosenfeld* (rose garden and rose field). No roses adorned the camp— rather, the SS managers associated the facility with a typical name of Jewish victims. The gassing phase, which resulted in about 500 to 600 deaths per week over a period of a year, came to an end with the decision to wipe out the entire Jewish inmate population in one blow. When the Lublin camp acquired administrative control of the Trawniki and Poniatowa labor camps, mass shootings took place at all three sites in the beginning of November 1943.

While Kulmhof in the Wartheland was being set up with gas vans and a network of gas-chamber camps was established in the Generalgouvernement, a third development came to fruition in the incorporated territory of Upper Silesia. This project was built by a man who had come up in the concentration camp world. He was an early Nazi who had been imprisoned before Hitler came to power, with a top Nazi: Bormann. During the 1930s he had held several posts in Dachau and Sachsenhausen, until (in 1940) he took over a camp of his own. The new camp was located in Upper Silesia.

Originally no great destiny had been intended for this place. The camp was encircled by stagnant fish ponds, which permeated the compound with dampness, mist, and mud. The German army quartered a company of its construction troops there, and the Inspectorate for Concentration Camps, making a survey of the area, decided that, after certain "sanitary and construction" measures were taken, it could use the camp as a quarantine center. A few months later, the new commander approached the German land-acquisition agency in the area, the Bodenamt Schlesien, to confiscate the necessary grounds. Another concentration camp was born. Its commander was Rudolf Höss. Its name was Auschwitz.

In the summer of 1941, Höss was summoned to report (over the head of his chief, Glücks) to Himmler for personal orders. During the interview—which was to leave its mark upon the fate of Jews from all the deportation countries of Europe—Himmler told Höss that the Führer had given the order for the "Final Solution" of the Jewish question. Himmler had chosen Auschwitz because its location near Katowice in Upper Silesia afforded easy access by rail and also because the extensive site offered space for measures ensuring isolation. For details, Himmler directed Höss to talk to Eichmann. Having placed this burden upon the shoulders of Höss, Himmler had only this to add: "We, the SS must carry out this order. If it is not carried out now, then the Jews will later on destroy the German people." During the following weeks, Eichmann came to Auschwitz and discussed with Höss the necessary "details." Höss moved slowly but methodically. Bit by bit, he built his camp into the largest death center the world had ever seen.

To begin with, the camp grounds were expanded. A considerable area in the vicinity was declared to be a "sphere of influence." All people in this area were evicted, so as not to be in the way of the "state-political" tasks of the camp. It was planned to establish a district *owned* by the SS. In line with these plans, which took a long time to materialize, Pohl wrote to the Finance Ministry in November 1942 that the Reichsführer-SS wished to enlarge the area of Auschwitz to 4,640 hectares (17.9 square miles) and that Himmler desired this area to be Reich (SS) property.

On November 3 and December 17–18, two conferences were held under the chairmanship of Oberfinanzpräsident Dr. Casdorf of the Finance Ministry with the participation of the following officials:

Ministerialrtat Dr. Gossel (Finance Ministry)
Regierungsrat Keller (Finance Ministry)
Amtsrat Pape (Finance Ministry)
Ministerialrat Hoffmann (Interior Ministry)
Oberregierungsrat Menke (Interior Ministry)
Brigadeführer Frank (WVHA-A)
Dr. Ast
Dr. Evert (Main Trusteeship Office East)
Schulz (Main Trusteeship Office East)

The reason for the presence of so many officials of various agencies was the complicated nature of the land-transfer process: transfer to Reich ownership of private Polish agricultural and urban property, of land that belonged to the Polish state (then regarded as the former Polish state), of municipal property, of ecclesiastical property, and, last but not least, of property belonging to Germans in the affected area. It was decided that the various agencies would transfer their jurisdictions to the Land Office of the Commissioner for the Strengthening of Germandom (Himmler). But even Himmler must have had a few difficulties, for on May 31, 1943, when the aim of a Reich-owned district *(Gutsbezirk)* had not yet been accomplished, the Oberpräsident of Upper Silesia (Bracht) issued a decree establishing the administrative district *(Amtsbezirk)* of Auschwitz.

In the meantime, Höss went ahead with the construction of killing installations, which were to contain two major improvements. The first of these was compactness. Höss built his installations as combination units, each of which contained an anteroom, a gas chamber, and an oven for body disposal. Second, he decided after visiting Treblinka that the carbon monoxide method was not very "efficient." Accordingly, he introduced in his camp a different type of gas: quick-working hydrogen cyanide (prussic acid—commercial name, Zyklon). Unlike carbon monoxide, however, this gas was *not* produced on the spot. A major administrative effort, stretching out over a period of years, was required to solve some of the complicated problems arising during the erection of the special combination units and the establishment of a dependable gas supply.

The construction program was undertaken by the Zentralbauleitung of Auschwitz under Hauptsturmführer (later Sturmbannführer) Bischoff. At the end of 1941, work was begun to erect a special camp (Auschwitz II) on the moor of Brzeźinka (Birkenau). As in the case of the Generalgouvernement camps, however, gassings with facilities of limited capacity were instituted at Auschwitz before decisions were made to install more elaborate structures designed for mass annihilation. The stages of this development, which involved enlargements, modifications, postponements, and repairs, are summarized in Table 14.

The first gas chamber, in the old camp, was created in the mortuary of the crematorium. In Birkenau, two old peasant houses were remodeled. The windows were filled in, the interior walls were removed, and special, airtight doors were constructed. A barrack nearby served as an undressing room for the deportees entering the chambers. These installations were put to use during 1942. Himmler, Gauleiter Bracht of Upper Silesia, and the local Higher SS and Police Leader (Schmauser) were present at the first test. Himmler had nothing to criticize, but neither did he enter into any conversation.

The bodies of the people killed in the two "bunkers" were buried in mass graves. A survivor reports that in the summer of 1942 the corpses swelled, and a "black, evil-smelling mass oozed out and polluted the

T A B L E 14
GASSING AND CREMATORIUM INSTALLATIONS AT
AUSCHWITZ
(OLD NUMERATION IN PARENTHESES)

Auschwitz Main Camp		
Crematorium (I)		Converted gas chamber, with crematorium, used from early 1942 to the spring of 1943.
Birkenau		
Bunker I		Five small gas chambers, barracks for undressing, adjacent grave, used in 1942.
Bunker II		Larger capacity for gassings, barracks for undressing, adjacent grave, used in 1942 and reconstituted, spring 1944, into Facility V for use on a standby basis during the day; undressing in grove and pits for cremation.
Crematorium (II)	I	Subterranean gas chamber with five furnaces, each with three retorts, March 1943 to November 1944.
Crematorium (III)	II	Subterranean gas chamber with five furnaces, each with three retorts, June 1943 to November 1944.
Crematorium (IV)	III	Surface chamber with two furnaces, each with four retorts. From March 1943. Repeated malfunctions. Destroyed by inmates on October 7, 1944.
Crematorium (V)	IV	Surface chamber with two furnaces, each with four retorts, April 1943 to November 1944.

groundwater in the vicinity." By October the decomposing bodies, covered with maggots, had to be disinterred for burning in pits. The two huts had reached the natural limit of their potential. Now, plans were laid out for the construction of the combination units, each of them complete with a gas chamber, anteroom, and oven. To carry out this project, the Zentralbauleitung in Auschwitz engaged the help of two companies: the SS company Deutsche Ausrüstungswerke (DAW) to make the doors and windows, and the firm Topf and Sons, Erfurt, oven builders. The Topf concern, which specialized in the construction of cremation furnaces, had done such work in concentration camps before.

Originally it had been intended to build crematoria with two furnaces in Birkenau, but following a conference with Oberführer Kammler on February 27, 1942, five-furnace installations were decided upon. Eventually, two such units were constructed, each containing an underground gas chamber called a *Leichenkeller* (corpse cellar), complete with an electric elevator for hauling up the bodies. Two more units were built, as an economy measure, with two furnaces each and a gas chamber called a *Badeanstalt* (bath house) at the surface. The Leichenkeller were very large (250 square yards), and 2,000 persons could be packed into each of them. The Badeanstalten were somewhat smaller. The hydrogen cyanide, solidified in pellets, was shaken into the Leichenkeller through shafts, into the Badeanstalten through side walls. In the gas chamber the material immediately passed into the gaseous state. Thus an altogether more efficient system, guaranteeing much more rapid processing than in the other camps, had been devised in Auschwitz.

However, the construction of these elaborate installations required much more time than the building of the Generalgouvernement killing centers, and it is therefore not surprising that a certain hurry was in evidence. On January 13, 1943, the Zentralbauleitung in Auschwitz complained to the Deutsche Ausrüstungswerke that carpentry work for the crematoria had by no means been completed and that doors for one of the units, "which is urgently needed for the implementation of the special measures," were not yet finished. By way of emphasis, the Zentralbauleitung reminded the DAW that some time ago it had transferred its own workshops to the SS company. On March 31 a note was sent about a door that was to have a peephole, with a reminder that this order was "especially urgent."

In the meantime (January 29, 1943), the Zentralbauleitung reported to Kammler that after the commitment of all available manpower and in spite of "tremendous difficulties," including freezing weather, one of the crematoria was now in place, except for "minor construction details" and the pending delivery by Topf of the ventilation system for the Leichenkeller. The furnace, however, had been tried out in the presence of Engineer Prüfer and functioned perfectly.

While the Auschwitz management was struggling with the completion of the four combination units, the chief of WVHA-D (Glücks) made an inspection tour of concentration camps and noticed that "special buildings" (crematoria) were not situated in particularly favorable locations. He wished that in the future such "special constructions" would be put in a place where it would not be possible for "all kinds of people" to "gaze" at them. Thinking this over, Höss ordered that a "green belt" of trees be planted around Crematoria I and II. The construction was finished.

With the erection of the cremation units, Höss had solved half his task. The procurement of the gas was the other half of the problem. Hydrogen cyanide, or Zyklon, was a powerful lethal agent—a deadly dose was 1 milligram per kilogram of body weight. Packed in containers, the Zyklon was put to use simply by opening the canister and pouring the pellets into the chamber; the solid material would then sublimate. The Zyklon had only one drawback: within three months it deteriorated in the container and thus could not be stockpiled. Since Auschwitz was a receiving station, always on call, it was necessary to have a dependable gas supply.

The SS did not manufacture Zyklon, so the gas had to be procured from private firms. The enterprises that furnished it were part of the chemical industry. They specialized in the "combating of vermin" by means of poison gases. Zyklon was one of eight products manufactured by these firms, which undertook large-scale fumigations of buildings, barracks, and ships; disinfected clothes in specially constructed gas chambers and deloused human beings, protected by gas masks. In short, this industry used very powerful gases to exterminate rodents and insects in enclosed spaces. That it should now have become involved in an operation to kill off Jews by the hundreds of thousands is no mere accident. In German propaganda, Jews had frequently been portrayed as insects. Frank and Himmler had stated repeatedly that the Jews were parasites who had to be exterminated like vermin, and with the introduction of Zyklon into Auschwitz that thought had been translated into reality.

How was the gas supply maintained? To answer this question, we must examine the organization of the extermination industry a little more closely. Basically, we must differentiate here between three structural components: the shareholding channels (ownership), the production and sales organization, and the allocation apparatus. The company that developed the gas method of combating vermin was the Deutsche Gesellschaft für Schädlingsbekämpfung mbH (German Vermin-combating Corporation), abbreviated DEGESCH. The firm was owned by three corporations, and itself controlled two retailers.

The Zyklon was produced by two companies: the Dessauer Werke and the Kaliwerke at Kolín. An I. G. Farben plant (at Uerdingen) produced the stabilizer for the Zyklon. Distribution of the gas was controlled by DEGESCH, which in 1929 divided the world market with an American corporation, Cyanamid. However, DEGESCH did not sell Zyklon directly to users. Two other firms handled the retailing: Heerdt und Lingler (HELI) and Tesch und Stabenow (TESTA). The territory of these two corporations was divided by a line drawn from Cuxhaven through Öbisfelde to Plauen. The area northeast of that line, including Auschwitz, belonged to Tesch und Stabenow. The territorial division between HELI and TESTA gave to HELI mostly private customers and to TESTA mainly the governmental sector, including the Wehrmacht and the SS. On the whole, neither firm sought to invade the territory of the other, but on occasion Dr. Tesch supplied Dachau via Berlin.

The third aspect of the extermination industry was the allocation system. In a war, one cannot simply buy and sell. Each user has to show why he needs the supplies, and upon submission of such evidence, certain quantities are allocated to him. In other words, the territorial monopoly tells him where he has to buy, and the allocation system determines how much he can get.

The central allocation authority was a committee in Speer's Armaments Ministry. The committee divided the supply among export, private firms, and the armed forces. The Armed Forces Main Sanitation Depot fixed the needs of the Wehrmacht and the SS, and the Waffen-SS Central Sanitation Depot was in turn responsible for allocations to SS offices and concentration camps. The working of this apparatus is illustrated in Table 15, which indicates the distributions of Zyklon to various users.

TESTA sold Zyklon in different concentrations. Invoices presented to municipal or industrial clients for fumigations of buildings were printed with columns headed C, D, E, and F, each denoting a category of potency and price. As explained in a letter to the Ostland, strength E was required for the eradication of specially resistant vermin, such as cockroaches, or for gassings in wooden barracks. The "normal" preparation D was used to exterminate lice, mice, or rats in large, well-built structures containing furniture. Human organisms in gas chambers were killed with Zyklon B.

The amounts required by Auschwitz were not large, but they were noticeable. Almost the whole Auschwitz supply was needed for the gassing of people; very little was used for fumigation. The camp administration itself did not buy the gas. The purchaser was Obersturmführer Gerstein, Chief Disinfection Officer in the Office of the Hygienic Chief of the Waffen-SS (Mrugowski). As a rule, all orders passed through the hands of TESTA, DEGESCH, and Dessau. From the Dessau Works, which produced the gas, shipments were sent directly to the Auschwitz Extermination and Fumigation Division.

Notification generally came from Amtsgruppe D, which authorized the Auschwitz administration to dispatch a truck to Dessau "to pick up materials for the Jewish resettlement." Deliveries to SS installations for fumigation purposes were made every six months or so, but Auschwitz required a shipment every six weeks because Zyklon deteriorated easily and a supply had to be on hand at all times. To discerning eyes that frequency was noticeable too.

The delivery system worked dependably until March 1944, when the Dessau Zyklon plant was bombed and heavily damaged. The sudden curtailment of the supply came at a time when the SS was making

T A B L E 15
DISTRIBUTION OF ZYKLON

Reich Ministry for Armaments and War Production
Special Committee Chemical Products
Working Committee Space-Fumigation and Counter-Epidemics
Composition of working committee: Dr. Gerhard Peters (DEGESCH), chairman; Generalarzt Prof. Dr. Rose (Robert Koch Institute); Obermedizinalrat Dr. Christiaensen (Interior Ministry); a representative of Generalarzt Dr. Schreiber (OKW)—generally Dr. Finger or Dr. Wieser

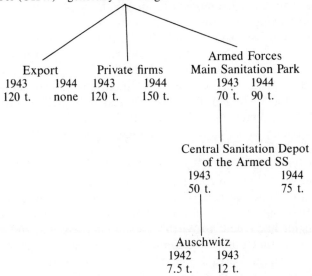

Export		Private firms		Armed Forces Main Sanitation Park	
1943	1944	1943	1944	1943	1944
120 t.	none	120 t.	150 t.	70 t.	90 t.

Central Sanitation Depot
of the Armed SS

1943	1944
50 t.	75 t.

Auschwitz

1942	1943
7.5 t.	12 t.

preparations to send 750,000 Jews to Auschwitz—then the only killing center still in existence. A crisis developed. On April 5, 1944, a Mrugowski representative wrote to DEGESCH requesting immediate shipment of 5 tons of Zyklon B without odor ingredient. The shipment had already been approved by the Armed Forces Main Sanitation Park and was "urgently needed" by the Waffen-SS. A week later, Dr. Evers of Armed Forces Sanitation himself ordered about 2,800 kg and had them shipped to Auschwitz. TESTA hurriedly inquired who was to be billed. A DEGESCH official became worried that the production of Zyklon without odor ingredients would endanger the firm's monopoly. The High Command of the Navy protested that it urgently needed Zyklon for the fumigation of ships.

The SS in the meantime began to be concerned over the possibility that it had received the Zyklon too early. On May 24, the disinfection officer, Obersturmführer Gerstein, wrote a letter to Dr. Peters inquiring how long the shipment would last. When would it deteriorate? So far, it had not been used at all. "On the other hand, under certain circumstances large quantities—that is to say, actually the entire quantity—might have to be used all at once."

The SS did not have to wait too long. By end of May transports were rolling into Auschwitz, and on August 6 the Anti-vermin Office of the SS and Police in Auschwitz asked for more Zyklon. The supply was kept up to the very end. The SS did not run out of gas.

We have seen how the gas-killing method evolved through three separate channels, each more advanced than the previous one: first the carbon monoxide gas vans, then the carbon monoxide gas chambers, and finally the hydrogen cyanide (or Zyklon) combination units. The advantages of Zyklon as a lethal gas became known. Even while Höss was still building his gas chambers in 1942, a distinguished visitor from Lublin, Brigadeführer Globocnik, visited Auschwitz in order to learn of the new method. The Höss discovery posed an immediate threat to his Generalgouvernement rival, Kriminalkommissar Wirth.

This rivalry came to a head one day in August 1942 when Eichmann's deputy, Günther, and the chief disinfection officer, Kurt Gerstein, arrived in Bełżec. They had about 200 pounds of Zyklon with them and were about to convert the carbon monoxide chambers to the hydrogen cyanide method. The unwelcome guests stayed to watch a gassing that took an especially long time (over three hours) because the diesel engine had failed. To Wirth's great embarrassment and mortification, Gerstein timed the operation with a stopwatch. Facing the greatest crisis of his career, Wirth dropped his pride and asked Gerstein "not to propose any other type of gas chamber in Berlin." Gerstein obliged, ordering the Zyklon to be buried on the pretext that it had spoiled.

Höss and Wirth were henceforth enemies. The Auschwitz commander, even after the war, spoke proudly of his "improvements." Conversely, Wirth looked down on Höss as a latecomer and called him his "untalented pupil." Thus there had arisen a class of "founders" and "originators" in mass-death devices, and among these architects of the killing centers there was fierce competition and rivalry.

A recapitulation of the "Final Solution" in the death camps is contained in Table 16.

KILLING OPERATIONS

The success of the killing operations depended, in the first instance, upon the maintenance of secrecy. Unlike any other administrative task confronting the bureaucracy, secrecy was a continuous problem. Pre-

T A B L E 16
THE "FINAL SOLUTION" IN THE DEATH CAMPS

Camp	Main Geographic Origins of Victims	Principal Time Spans of Systematic Killings	Number Killed
Kulmhof	Wartheland Reich, via Łódź	December 1941 to September 1942 and June–July 1944	150,000
Bełżec	Galicia Kraków district Lublin district (including Reich deportees)	March–December 1942	550,000
Sobibór	Lublin district Netherlands Slovakia Reich-Protektorat France Minsk	April–June 1942 and October 1942 to October 1943	200,000
Treblinka	Warsaw district Radom district Białystok district Lublin district Macedonia-Thrace Reich Theresienstadt	July 1942 to October 1943	750,000
Lublin	Lublin district Warsaw district France	September 1942 to September 1943 and November 1943	50,000
Auschwitz	Hungary Poland Incorporated areas Białystok district Wartheland Upper Silesia East Prussia Generalgouvernement Remnant ghettos and labor camps France Netherlands Greece Theresienstadt Slovakia Belgium Reich-Protektorat (direct) Italy Croatia Norway	February 1942 to November 1944	1,000,000

cautionary measures had to be taken before the victims arrived, while they went through the processing, and after they were dead. At no point could any disclosure be permitted; at no time could the camp management afford to be caught off guard. The killers had to conceal their work from every outsider, they had to mislead and fool the victims, and they had to erase all traces of the operation.

CONCEALMENT

We have already noted or at least hinted at a number of concealment measures. Thus the very speed and haste with which the deportation-killing process was carried out was prompted to no small extent by considerations of secrecy. When Viktor Brack of the Führer Chancellery wrote to Himmler about the necessity of speeding up the construction of the Generalgouvernement camps, he pointed out: "You yourself, Reichsführer, said to me some time ago that for reasons of concealment alone we have to work as quickly as possible."

Another concealment measure was verbal camouflage. The most important and possibly the most misleading term used for the killing centers collectively was the "East." This phrase was employed again and again during the deportations. When reference to an individual death camp was necessary, the term used was *Arbeitslager* (labor camp) or *Konzentrationslager* (concentration camp). Birkenau, the Auschwitz killing site, was called *Kriegsgefangenenlager* (PW camp) in accordance with its originally intended purpose, later KL Au II (concentration camp Auschwitz II). Sobibór was appropriately called *Durchgangslager* (transit camp). Since it was located near the Bug, on the border of the occupied eastern territories, the designation fitted the myth of the "eastern migration." When Himmler proposed one day that the camp be designated a *Konzentrationslager*, Pohl opposed the change.

The gas chamber and crematorium units in Auschwitz were known as *Spezialeinrichtungen* (special installations), *Badeanstalten* (bath houses), and *Leichenkeller* (corpse cellars). The diesel engine operated in Bełżec was located in a shack called the "Hackenholt Foundation." (Unterscharführer Hackenholt was the operator of the diesel). The primary term for the killing operation itself was the same that had been employed for the killings in Russia—*Sonderbehandlung* (special treatment). In addition, there was some terminology more appropriate to the killing center operations, such as *durchgeschleusst* (dragged through) or *gesondert untergebracht* (separately quartered).

Next to verbal camouflage it was most important to close the mouths of the inner circle; hence all camp personnel, especially top personnel, were sworn to silence. Höss made such a promise to Himmler before he started his task. He observed complete secrecy, not speaking to any outsider about his work. Only once did he break his word: "At the end of 1942," relates Höss, "my wife's curiosity was aroused by remarks made by the Gauleiter of Upper Silesia, Bracht, regarding happenings in the camp. She asked me whether this was the truth, and I admitted that it was. That was the only breach of the promise I had given to the Reichsführer."

A Treblinka guard, Unterscharführer Hirtreiter, once spent a furlough with his girl friend, Frieda Jörg, in Germany. The girl knew of Hirtreiter's past experiences with "euthanasia" operations at the insane asylum of Hadamar. Full of curiosity, she asked him, "What are you doing in Poland now? Bumping people off, eh?" Hirtreiter did not reply.

However, not all the participants could keep the burden of their knowledge to themselves. In 1943 the Auschwitz administration asked the Security and Order Police in the west not to confront Jews with "disturbing remarks about the place and nature of their future utilization" or "resistance-provoking indications or speculations about their intended quarters." Instances are also recorded indicating that guards sometimes trumpeted out the news to newly arrived victims even in the killing centers. When Obersturmführer Gerstein, the gas expert, completed his tour of the Generalgouvernement camps in the late summer of 1942, he spilled the whole secret on the Warsaw-Berlin express to a fellow passenger, Swedish diplomat Baron von Otter. The baron reported the existence of the killing centers to Stockholm, but the Swedish government did not disseminate the information to the world.

Closely related to the oath of silence was another precautionary measure, the control of visitors. Visitors were high officials of the Reich or of the party who arrived for "inspections." The concentration camp administration was especially touchy about such inspections. On November 3, 1943, Glücks ordered that visitors were not to be shown the brothels and the crematoria; neither was there to be any talk about these installations. In case anyone did happen to notice the smoking chimneys, he was given the standard explanation that the crematorium was burning corpses that resulted from epidemics.

There were welcome visitors and unwelcome visitors. Following a visit by Justice Minister Thierack to Auschwitz on January 8, 1943, Höss sent him an album of photographs with a little note in which he expressed the hope that the Reichsminister would "enjoy them." Unwelcome visitors were primarily unannounced visitors. Frank, the Generalgouverneur of Poland, was extremely anxious to get details about killing centers. Once, he got a report "that there was something going on near Bełżec"; he went there the next day. Globocnik showed him how Jews were working on an enormous ditch. When Frank asked what would happen to the Jews, he got the standard answer: they would be sent farther east. Frank made another attempt. He expressed to Himmler the wish to pay a visit to Lublin, and Himmler urged him not to go there. Finally, Frank tried to spring a surprise visit to Auschwitz. His car was stopped and diverted with the explanation that there was an epidemic in the camp. Later Frank complained to Hitler about his frustrated visit. Hitler is said to have replied: "You can very well imagine that there are executions going on—of insurgents. Apart from that I do not know anything. Why don't you speak to Heinrich Himmler about it?" And so, Frank was back where he started.

Although the entrances to the camps could be watched, the back door was frequently open, even in the secluded killing centers of the Generalgouvernement. A German noncommissioned officer heard a great deal about Bełżec in the Deutsches Haus of Rawa Ruska and in the Ratskeller of neighboring Chełm. On his way to Chełm one day, at the Rawa Ruska railway station, he saw a deportation train. He asked a railway policeman where the Jews had come from. They were probably the last ones from Lwów, the policeman explained. And how far were they going? To Bełżec. And then? Poison. When his own train came, he shared a compartment with the wife of a railway policeman. Her husband, on duty on the train, joined them. The woman was going to point out Bełżec on the way. "Now it comes." A strong sweetish smell greeted them. "They are stinking already," said the woman. "Oh, nonsense, that is the gas," her husband explained.

Auschwitz, with its great industrial activity, had a constant stream of incoming and outgoing corporate officials, engineers, construction men, and other personnel, all excellent carriers of gossip to the farthest corners of the Reich. There was also a large number of Germans living in the Auschwitz area who were perpetually aware of the killing center. One railroad man, observing the fences and guard posts of Auschwitz I on one side of the tracks and of Auschwitz II on the other, concluded that he was in the midst of it all. Another railroad functionary noticed that his apartment was filled with a sweetish odor, and the windows were covered with a bluish film. Even those at more distant points could see physical indications of killing operations. From the Katowice direction the fires of Auschwitz were visible from a distance of twelve miles. Inevitably, these German residents talked about annihilation and cremation, and some of them became regular sources of news for colleagues in the Reich.

The powerful rumor network did not reach German listeners alone. The news of the killing centers was carried to the populations of several countries in the form of a story that out of the fat of corpses the Germans were making soap. To this day the origin of the soap-making rumor has not been traced, but one clue is probably the postwar testimony of the SS investigator Dr. Konrad Morgen, who at one time was quite active in Poland. One of Morgen's subjects of special interest was Brigadeführer Dirlewanger. It must be stressed that Dirlewanger had nothing to do with the killing centers. He was the commander of a notorious unit of SS unreliables, which in 1941 was stationed in the Generalgouvernement. What did this man do? According to Morgen,

> Dirlewanger had arrested people illegally and arbitrarily, and as for his female prisoners—young Jewesses—he did the following against them: He called together a small circle of friends consisting of members of a Wehrmacht supply unit. Then he made so-called scientific experiments, which involved stripping the victims of their clothes. Then they [the victims] were given an injection of strychnine. Dirlewanger looked on, smoking a cigarette, as did his friends, and they saw how these girls were dying. Immediately after that the corpses were cut into small pieces, mixed with horsemeat, and boiled into soap.
>
> I would like to state here, emphatically, that here we were only concerned with a suspicion, although a very urgent one. We had witnesses' testimony concerning these incidents, and the Security Police in Lublin had made certain investigations.

On July 29, 1942, the chief of the ethnic Germans in Slovakia, Karmasin, had written a letter to Himmler in which he described the "resettlement" of 700 "asocial" ethnic Germans. One of the difficulties, wrote Karmasin, was the spreading of the rumor (furthered by the clergy) that the "resettlers" would be "boiled into soap." In October 1942 the Propaganda Division in the Lublin district reported the rumor circulating in the city that now it was the turn of the Poles to be used, like the Jews, for "soap production." In the *Generaldirektion der Ostbahn,* railroad officials talking about gassings would say jokingly that another distribution of soap was in the offing.

The SS and Police could not arrest the spread of rumors—they persisted long after the war. Still less could German agencies deal with reasoned deductions and predictions. Killing centers could be hidden, but the disappearance of major communities was noticed in Brussels and Vienna, Warsaw and Budapest. How, then, did the few thousand guards in the death camps handle the millions of arrivals? How did the Germans kill their victims?

THE "CONVEYER BELT"

The killing operation was a combination of physical layout and psychological technique. Camp officials covered every step from the train platform to the gas chambers with a series of precise orders. A show of force impressed upon the victims the seriousness of unruliness or recalcitrance, even as misleading explanations reassured them in their new, ominous surroundings. Although there were breakdowns and mishaps in this system, it was perfected to a degree that justified its characterization by an SS doctor as a conveyer belt.

The initial action in the predetermined sequence was notification of the camp that a transport was arriving. Notice was followed by a mobilization of guards and inmates who were going to be involved in the processing. Everyone knew what would happen and what he had to do. From the moment the doors of a train were opened, all but a few of the deportees had only two hours to live.

The arriving Jews, on the other hand, were unprepared for a death camp. Rumors and intimations that had reached them were simply not absorbed. These forewarnings were rejected because they were not sufficiently complete, or precise, or convincing. When, in May 1942, a group of deportees was being marched from Zolkiewka to the Krasnystaw station (where a train was to take them to Sobibór), Polish inhabitants called out to the column: "Hey, Jews, you are going to burn!" A survivor of that transport recalls: "The meaning of these words escaped us. We had heard of the death camp of Bełżec, but we didn't believe it." A sophisticated Viennese physician who was in a cattle car remembers that another deportee noticed a sign in a railway station and called out "Auschwitz!" The physician saw the outlines of an "immense camp" stretched out in the dawn and he heard the shouts and whistles of command. "We did not know their meaning," he says. In the evening, he inquired where a friend had been sent and was told by one of the old prisoners that he could see him "there." A hand pointed to the chimney, but the new inmate could not understand the gesture until the truth was explained to him in "plain words." Another physician, from Holland, reports:

> I refused to . . . leave any room for the thought of the gassing of the Jews, of which I could surely not have pretended ignorance. As early as 1942 I had heard rumors about the gassing of the Polish Jews. . . . Nobody had ever heard, however, when these gassings took place, and it was definitely not known that people were gassed immediately upon arrival.

The great majority of the deportees could not grasp the situation so long as they did not know the details of the killing operation, the when and the how. Those who came with premonitions and forebodings were usually unable to think of a way out. On a Warsaw transport to Treblinka in August 1942, a young deportee heard the words, "Jews, we're done for!" The old men in the car began to say the prayer for the dead. Another young man, stepping off a train in Treblinka, saw mounds of clothing and said to his wife that this was the end. Cognition was thus converted to fatalism more readily than to escape or resistance.

The German administrators, however, were determined not to take chances, lest some impetuous resister in the crowd create a dangerous confrontation. They were going to move swiftly while reinforcing Jewish illusions to the last possible moment. To this end they set a pattern of procedures that was virtually the same in every camp, save only for those variations that stemmed from the different layouts and installations in each enclosure.

The ramps at Bełżec, Sobibór, and Treblinka were too short to accommodate lengthy trains. At each of these camps, transports were backed into the compound to be unloaded a few cars at a time. On the Bełżec ramp the arriving Jews were received with the music and singing of a ten-man inmate orchestra.

Kulmhof was reachable only by road or narrow-gauge railway. Initially, deportees were brought from the immediate vicinity on trucks. Trains from the Łódź ghetto halted at Warthbrücken (Koło), where the victims were sometimes kept overnight in the local synagogue and from where they were taken by truck to Kulmhof. Later a more complicated logistic procedure was instituted to avoid public display of the deported Jews in Warthbrücken. The victims were loaded on a narrow-gauge train and kept overnight in a mill at Zawacki. They were then driven to Kulmhof in trucks.

At Auschwitz the ramp was first located between the old camp and Birkenau. Those who were directed to the Auschwitz I gas chamber "streamed" through the gate. When Birkenau was opened, long columns ran through a gauntlet several hundred yards long to one of the crematoria. Not until the spring of 1944 was the spur built in Birkenau. On the new ramp, trains were unloaded a short distance from the gas chambers. The cars, emptied of the living and the dead, were moved to a fumigation installation. One hot day, a loadmaster opened up a car and was jolted when a blackened corpse tumbled out. The car was filled with bodies that camp personnel had neglected to remove.

Following the unloading of the trains, there was a twofold selection procedure. The old, infirm, and sometimes small children were separated on the platform. At Bełżec sick people were placed face down near a pit to be shot. At Sobibór, where trucks picked up the aged and the infants, guards would occasionally try to toss the babies from a considerable distance into the vehicle. At Treblinka those unable to walk were taken to a pit near the infirmary for shooting. From the first Auschwitz ramp, trucks would remove the old and the infirm to the gas chambers.

The camps also selected strong persons for labor. In the General-gouvernement camps or Kulmhof, very few individuals were needed as work crews, and women among those chosen were but a handful. Asked about the children, a former member of the SS establishment in Treblinka declared at his trial that "saving children in Treblinka was impossible." Labor requirements at Auschwitz were greater, and at the Birkenau platform SS doctors (Mengele, König, Thilo, or Klein) would choose employable Jews for the industrial machine. Selections were not very thorough, however. The victims were paraded in front of the physician, who would then make spot decisions by pointing to the right for work or to the left for the gas chamber.

Men and women were separated for undressing in barracks. An impression was being created that clothes were to be reclaimed after showers. At Sobibór, one of the SS men, dressed in a white coat, would issue elaborate instructions about folding the garments, sometimes adding remarks about a Jewish state that the deportees were going to build in the Ukraine. At Kulmhof the victims were told that they would be sent for labor to Germany, and in Bełżec a specially chosen SS man made similar quieting speeches. In all three of the Generalgouverne-ment camps, there were special counters for the deposit of valuables. The hair of the women was shorn, and the procession was formed, men first. In Sobibór, groups of fifty to one hundred were marched through the "hose" by an SS man walking in front and four or five Ukrainians following at the rear of the column. At Bełżec, screaming women were prodded with whips and bayonets. The Jews arriving in Treblinka, states Höss, almost always knew that they were going to die. Some-times they could see mountains of corpses, partially decomposed. Some suffered nervous shock, laughing and crying alternately. To rush the procedure, the women at Treblinka were told that the water in the showers was cooling down. The victims would then be forced to walk or run naked through the "hose" with their hands raised. During the winter of 1942–43, however, the undressed people might have had to stand outdoors for hours to wait their turn. There they could hear the cries of those who had preceded them into the gas chambers.

The Auschwitz procedure evolved in stages. In April 1942, Slovak Jews were gassed in Crematorium I, apparently with their clothes on. Later, deportees from nearby Sosnowiec were told to undress in the yard. The victims, faced by the peremptory order to remove their clothes, men in front of women and women in front of men, became apprehensive. The SS men, shouting at them, then drove the naked men, women, and children into the gas chamber. During the third stage, in 1942, the abuse was replaced by politeness, and the speech making by Aumeier, Grabner, and Hössler began. The victims were now told to undress for their showers, before the soup that would be served afterwards became cold. For added security, gassings would be scheduled for a time before daybreak, when the camp inmates were still sleeping, or for the night hours, after the curfew had gone into effect.

At Birkenau, illusion was the rule. It was not always simple or possible, inasmuch as at least some of the deportees had observed the sign *Auschwitz* as the train passed through the railway yards, or had seen flames belching from the chimneys, or had smelled the strange, sickening odor of crematoria. Most of them, however, like a group from Salonika, were funneled through the undressing rooms, were told to hang their clothes on hooks and remember the number, and promised food after the shower and work after the food. The unsuspecting Greek Jews, clutching soap and towels, rushed into the gas chambers. Nothing was allowed to disturb this precarious synchronization. When a Jewish inmate revealed to newly arrived people what was in store for them, he was cremated alive. Only in the case of victims who were brought in from nearby ghettos in Upper Silesia (Sosnowiec and Będzin) and who had intimations of Auschwitz was speed alone essential. These people were told to undress quickly in their "own best interest."

Once there was a major incident in front of an Auschwitz gas chamber. A transport that had come in from Belsen revolted. The incident occurred when two thirds of the arrivals had already been shoved into the gas chamber. The remainder of the transport, still in the dressing room, had become suspicious. When three or four SS men entered to hasten the undressing, fighting broke out. The light cables were torn down, the SS men were overpowered, one of them was stabbed, and all of them were deprived of their weapons. As the room was plunged into complete darkness, wild shooting started between the guard at the exit door and the prisoners inside. When Höss arrived at the scene, he ordered the doors to be shut. Half an hour passed. Then, accompanied by a guard, Höss stepped into the dressing room, carrying a flashlight and pushing the prisoners into one corner. From there they were taken out singly into another room and shot.

Selections were carried out only on the platform, in order to pick out deportees who would be able to work, but also within the camp, to eliminate inmates too sick or too weak to work any longer. The usual occasion for the choosing of victims was the roll call, where everybody was present; another place was the hospital; and sometimes selections were carried out block by block. One former inmate, recalling such targeting, says: "I tried to make myself as inconspicuous as possible, not too erect, yet not slouching; not too smart, yet not sloppy; not too proud, yet not too servile, for I knew that those who were different died in Auschwitz, while the anonymous, the faceless ones, survived." A young intellectual from Italy, who was in an Auschwitz hospital because of a swollen foot, was told by a gentile Polish inmate: "You Jew, finished. You soon ready for crematorium." In Treblinka, to have been bruised in the face was considered a calamity. The wounded man, "stamped," was a candidate for selection at the next roll call.

In Auschwitz the victims would try every subterfuge to escape. They tried to hide. Occasionally they tried to argue. A nineteen-year-old girl asked the Auschwitz women's camp commander, Hössler, to excuse her. He replied, "You have lived long enough. Come, my child, come." Driven with whips between cordons of Kapos and guards, the naked people who had been picked out were loaded on trucks and driven to the gas chamber or to a condemned block. Before Christmas in 1944, 2,000 Jewish women were packed into Block 25, which had room for 500. They were kept there for ten days. Soup cauldrons were pushed through a gap in the door by the fire guard. At the end of ten days, 700 were dead. The rest were gassed.

Gassing would begin with a command. At Treblinka a German would shout to a Ukrainian guard: "Ivan, water!" This was a signal to start the motor. The procedure was not necessarily fast. With no room to move in the small chambers, the victims stood for thirty or forty minutes before they died. According to one Treblinka survivor, people were sometimes kept in the chambers all night without the motor being turned on. At Bełżec, where Oberscharführer Hackenholt was in charge of the motor, a German visitor, Professor Pfannenstiel, wanted to know what was going on inside. He is said to have put his ear to the wall and, listening, to have remarked: "Just like in a synagogue." At Kulmhof, the doors to the van were closed by Polish workers. One was inadvertently locked in with the Jews and raged in despair to get out. The Germans decided that it would not be prudent to open the door for him.

When the Auschwitz victims filed into the gas chamber, they discovered that the imitation showers did not work. Outside, a central switch was pulled to turn off the lights, and a Red Cross car drove up with the Zyklon. An SS man, wearing a gas mask fitted with a special filter, lifted the glass shutter over the lattice and emptied one can after another into the gas chamber. Although the lethal dose was one miligram per kilogram of body weight and the effect was supposed to be rapid, dampness could retard the speed with which the gas was spreading. Untersturmführer Grabner, political officer of the camp, stood ready with stopwatch in hand. As the first pellets sublimated on the floor of the chamber, the victims began to scream. To escape from the rising gas, the stronger knocked down the weaker, stepping on prostrate victims in order to prolong their own lives by reaching gas-free layers of air. The agony lasted for about two minutes, and as the shrieking subsided, the dying people slumped over. Within fifteen minutes (sometimes five), everyone in the gas chamber was dead.

The gas was now allowed to escape and after about half an hour, the door was opened. The bodies were found in tower-like heaps, some in sitting or half-sitting positions, children and older people at the bottom. Where the gas had been introduced, there was an empty area from which the victims had backed away, and pressed against the door where the bodies of men who in terror had tried to break out. The corpses were pink in color, with green spots. Some had foam on the lips, others bled through the nose. Excrement and urine covered some of the bodies, and in some pregnant women the birth process had started. The Jewish work parties *(Sonderkommandos),* wearing gas masks, dragged out the bodies near the door to clear a path and hosed down the dead, at the same time soaking the pockets of poison gas remaining between the bodies. Then the Sonderkommandos had to pry the corpses part.

In all the camps bodily cavities were searched for hidden valuables, and gold teeth were extracted from the mouths of the dead. In Crematorium II (new number) at Birkenau, the fillings and gold teeth, sometimes attached to jaws, were cleaned in hydrochloric acid, to be melted into bars in the main camp. At Auschwitz the hair of the women was cut off after they were dead. It was washed in ammonium chloride before being packed. The bodies could then be cremated.

ERASURE

There were three methods of body disposal: burial, cremation in ovens, and burning in the open. In 1942 corpses were buried in mass graves in Kulmhof, the Generalgouvernement camps, and Birkenau. Before long this mode of dealing with the dead gave rise to second thoughts. In Birkenau, near the huts that constituted the first gas chambers on the site, the summer sun took its effect. A survivor recalls that corpses began to swell, the earth's crust broke open, and a "black evil-smelling mass oozed out and polluted the groundwater in the vicinity." At Sobibór during the same summer, the graves heaved in the heat, the fluid from the corpses attracted insects, and foul odors filled the camp. Moreover, the many hundreds of thousands already buried posed a psychological problem. Ministerialrat Dr. Linden, sterilization expert in the Interior Ministry, on a visit to the Lublin district, is quoted by an SS man to have remarked that a future generation might not understand these matters. The same consideration had prompted the Gestapo chief Müller to order Standartenführer Blobel, commander of Einsatzkommando 4a, to destroy the mass graves in the eastern occupied territories. Blobel and his "Kommando 1005" also moved into Kulmhof to investigate what could be done with the graves there. He constructed funeral pyres and primitive ovens, and even tried explosives.

In addition to these devices, Kulmhof had something special—a bone-crushing machine. On July 16, 1942, the deputy chief of the Gettoverwaltung, Ribbe, sent a letter to "Eldest of the Jews" Rumkowski requesting a canvass of the Łódź ghetto for a bone crusher, "whether manually operated or motor driven." He added openly, "The Sonderkommando Kulmhof is interested in this crusher." The ghetto apparently had no such machine, for a few months later Biebow sent to the Łódź Gestapo the papers concerning the purchase of a mill from the firm Schriever and Company in Hamburg. Biebow asked the Gestapo to keep the sales record. "For certain reasons" he himself did not wish to keep it. When Höss visited Kulmhof, Blobel promised the Auschwitz commander that he would send him a mill "for solid substances." However, Höss preferred to destroy his bone material with hammers.

By 1942–43 exhumations were in progress at all of the killing centers. In Kulmhof Jewish work parties opened the mass graves and dragged the corpses into newly dug pits and into a primitive oven. In Bełżec the process was begun in the fall of 1942 within a firing area of the camp capable of destroying 2,000 bodies per day. A second, somewhat smaller firing position was started a month later, and the two were used concurrently, day and night, until March 1943. Excavators appeared in Sobibór and Treblinka, where the corpses (moved by narrow-gauge railway in Sobibór, and dragged in Treblinka) were stacked and burned on firing grids built with old railway tracks.

Kulmhof, the Warthegau camp, stopped gassings after the deportations of 1942, though it reopened briefly in 1944. Bełżec, with 550,000 dead, shut down its chambers at the end of 1942. Treblinka, overflowing with bodies, went on through the summer of 1943, and Sobibór continued with interruptions until the fall of 1943. Thereafter, the full burden of the "Final Solution" was assumed by Birkenau and its crematoria. Until the arrival of the transports from Hungary, beginning in mid-May 1944, the task was not a special problem. The prospective inflow, however, brought major changes. As of May 11, 1944, the crematoria crews (Sonderkommandos) numbered 217. On August 30, 1944, 878 men were employed in two shifts, labeled simply "day" and "night." The theoretical daily capacity of the four Birkenau crematoria was somewhat over 4,400, but, with breakdowns and slowdowns, the practical limit was almost always lower. During May and June the Hungarian Jews alone were being gassed at a rate of almost 10,000 a day, and higher numbers may have been reached when the Łódź transports arrived in the second half of August. Anticipating these developments, the Auschwitz specialist in charge of body disposal, Hauptscharführer Moll—a man described as a sadist with indefatigable energy—directed the digging of eight or nine pits more than forty yards in length, eight yards wide, and six feet deep. On the bottom of the pits the human fat was collected and poured back into the fire with buckets to hasten the cremations. Survivors report that children were sometimes tossed alive into the inferno. The rotten remains were cleaned up once in a while with flame throwers. Although the corpses burned slowly during rain or misty weather, the pits were found to be the cheapest and most efficient method of body disposal. In August 1944, when 20,000 corpses had to be burned on some days, the open pits broke the bottleneck.

Thus the capacity for destruction was approaching the point of being unlimited. Simple as this system was, it took years to work out in constant application of administrative techniques. It took millennia in the development of Western culture.

LIQUIDATION OF THE KILLING CENTERS AND THE END OF THE DESTRUCTION PROCESS

Although the killing centers were employed almost constantly, their existence was comparatively short. The first camp to be liquidated was Kulmhof. The Sonderkommando of Higher SS and Police Leader Koppe (Kommando Hauptsturmführer Bothmann) ceased its work there at the end of March 1943 and went to Croatia. In February 1944, Greiser proposed Bothmann's recall in order to "reduce" the Łódź ghetto, but Kulmhof had only a brief revival during June–July of that year. The camp was finally liquidated on January 17–18, 1945. The Jewish burial Kommando was shot, and the buildings were set afire.

In the Generalgouvernement the Bug camps (Treblinka, Sobibór, and Bełżec) were evacuated in the fall of 1943. The Wirth Kommando, which had constructed these camps, was ordered to destroy them without leaving a trace. At Treblinka a farm was built, and a Ukrainian was invited to run it for income. Pine trees were planted at Bełżec, but a Polish postwar investigator found the terrain dug up, with hands, bones, and flesh exposed where the local population had been searching for valuables. Wirth and his men were transferred as a unit to the

Istrian peninsula in Italy to defend roads against partisans. There Wirth met his death in the spring of 1944 from a bullet in his back, and Reichleitner (of Sobibór) was killed on patrol.

Lublin was evacuated more hurriedly. At the end of July 1944, a Red Army salient overtook the camp, and with it huge stores of clothes. The discoveries made by the Soviets in Lublin were immediately publicized in the world press, to the great consternation of Generalgouverneur Frank. The frightened Frank immediately accused Koppe, the former Higher SS and Police Leader in the Wartheland, who had replaced Krüger in the Generalgouvernement. "Now we know," Frank said, "you cannot deny that." Koppe replied that he knew absolutely nothing about these things and that apparently it was a matter between Heinrich Himmler and the camp authorities. "But already in 1941," said Frank, "I heard of such plans, and I spoke about them." Well, then, the Higher SS and Police Leader replied, that was Frank's business, and he, Koppe, could not be expected to worry about it.

During the latter part of 1944, only one camp was still operating at full capacity—Auschwitz. From May through October the reduction of most of the remaining Jewish population clusters was in progress. During this period about 600,000 Jews were brought into the killing center. With Romania and Bulgaria already out of reach, transport breaking down, Jewish laborers desperately needed in war industry, and the Jews in mixed marriages exempt, the destruction process was nearing its conclusion. In November 1944, Himmler decided that for practical purposes the Jewish question had been solved. On the twenty-fifth of that month he ordered the dismantling of the killing installations. That day, Auschwitz I and II were merged into the concentration camp Auschwitz, and Auschwitz III, which housed plants of the I. G. Farben Company and other enterprises, became the concentration camp Monowitz.

I. G. Farben had already made preparations for a departure. From April 4, 1944, the industrial area was repeatedly photographed by the Allied Mediterranean Air Force, and on August 20, September 13, December 18, and again on December 26, Monowitz was systematically bombed. During the summer the front was stabilized at the Vistula. However, the Red Army was across the river at two points, Opatów and Baranów, and this was enough ground for Dr. Dürrfeld, the I. G. Auschwitz chief, to make his evacuation plans.

Among the inmates there was restlessness. A resistance organization had finally been set up in Auschwitz. It had links with the resistance movement outside the camp, including the London-oriented Poles and Communists. Once, in March 1944, the idea of burning down the crematoria had surfaced among the Jewish crews assigned to the removal and burning of bodies. The occasion was the imminent gassing of a large number of Czech Jews from Theresienstadt, who had been kept for six months in the so-called family camp inside Birkenau. The Jewish Sonderkommando wanted the Jews in the family camp to set fire to their barracks, while a revolt would take place in the crematoria, but the families could not be convinced that their lives were about to be extinguished until they were in the changing room, confronted by armed SS men and dogs. There, dropping all pretense, an Oberschar-führer told them to step into the gas chamber. The Sonderkommando, which watched it all happen, renewed its plans several months later, but now the resistance organization in the camp urged a postponement. Finally, by October there was no doubt in the minds of the cremation workers that they themselves were going to be killed, but the resistance organization insisted that rebellion be avoided at all costs. At this point, it became clear that the needs of the Jewish inmates diverged sharply from the interests of the non-Jews. The Jewish victims saw little chance for survival in continued acquiescence, whereas the gentiles, fearing the effect of German reprisals and looking toward deliverance through the Red Army, had too much to lose in an uprising. On the afternoon of October 7, 1944, a desperate Sonderkommando, armed with explosives and three stolen hand grenades as well as insulated pliers for cutting the barbed wires, made their attempt alone. Four hundred and fifty inmates and three SS men died in the battle, and Crematorium III was set on fire. The SS quickly discovered that four women in the "Union" plant had furnished the Sonderkommando with explosives to do the job. The women were publicly hanged by Camp Commander Hössler.

What the Jews could not accomplish with their meager resources the camp administration was to undertake itself. The remaining crematoria were cleaned out by Jewish work details. A young woman recalled that while cleaning the ovens, she got bones and ashes in her hair, her mouth, and her nostrils. Another party had to clean out eighteen inch deposits of fat in the chimneys.

But Auschwitz still existed, still held on to tens of thousands of inmates, and for two months the camp awaited the Soviet offensive. During November, Soviet reinforcements were observed moving into the Baranów bridgehead. On January 12, 1945, Soviet armored columns moved out of Baranów. The general offensive had begun. By January 16 the Soviets had reached the I. G. Farben calcium mines at Kressendorf, and on the evening of the same day Soviet planes attacked the camp. During the next day, German officials scurried out of the city of Katowice. That same night the rumble of artillery fire was heard in Auschwitz itself.

On the evening of January 17, the last roll call was taken. The count was 31,894 in Auschwitz (including Birkenau) and 35,118 in Monowitz, including outlying satellite camps. That day the evacuation of the inmates was decided upon. As orders, changed every few hours, were received, those capable of walking thirty miles were separated from those who could walk only to the Auschwitz railroad station and those who could not walk at all. Hospitalized inmates tried to decide whether to leave as ordered or to remain, taking the chance of being killed by the SS at the last moment. For the next two days, 58,000 prisoners were moved out, all but a few on foot, in freezing weather. On January 20, Obergruppenführer Schmauser issued instructions to liquidate the inmates that were left behind. An SS detachment shot 200 Jewish women and then blew up the buildings that had housed crematoria I and II.

The Germans themselves now prepared to leave. As records were destroyed in the SS medical block on January 17, Dr. Mengele seized his research notes on twins to carry them personally to Berlin. Two days later, the German self-defense units melted away, and Soviet planes appeared again, this time starting large fires. By the 20th, I. G. Farben destroyed its records. The next day, as Soviet artillery was shelling Auschwitz, the camp officials were on their way. Two Soviet divisions, the 100th and the 107th, of the 60th Army of the First Ukrainian Front were advancing on Auschwitz. The killing center was now on the front line. From the Wehrmacht it had originally been acquired, and to the Wehrmacht it was now returned. A cordon of German troops still ringed the camp, and Security Police detachments roamed in the compound, still killing prisoners. On January 23 the SS set fire to barracks full of clothing in the "Canada" section. At 1 A.M. of the 27th, the SS blew up the last crematorium (new number IV), which had been kept for the disposal of bodies until the last moment. In midafternoon of that day, in the course of half an hour, Soviet troops took Auschwitz and Birkenau.

When the Soviets moved in, twenty-nine of thirty-five storerooms had been burned down. In six of the remaining ones, the liberators found part of the camp's legacy: 368,820 men's suits, 836,255 women's coats and dresses, 5,525 pairs of women's shoes, 13,964 carpets, large quantities of children's clothes, toothbrushes, false teeth, pots and pans. In abandoned railway cars hundreds of thousands of additional items of apparel were discovered, and in the tannery the Soviet investigation commission found seven tons of hair. More than 7,000 inmates, still alive, greeted their liberators, while hundreds lay dead where they had dropped.

With the killing centers gone, ex-Auschwitz inmates, Hungarian deportees, and prisoners from disbanded labor camps were dumped into concentration camps in the Reich. In Gleiwitz about 14,000 inmates from Auschwitz and outlying satellite camps (four of them at

Gleiwitz itself) were loaded on trains and transported to Buchenwald, Sachsenhausen, Gross Rosen, and Mauthausen. From the latter two camps, already filled, they were rerouted to Dachau, Dora (Mittelbau) and Ravensbrück. The trips lasted from about three days to as long as a week. On some of the trains the prisoners were jammed into roofless, low-sided railroad cars, in which they ate snow and from which they threw out corpses. Buchenwald had been a major receiving point for some time: between May 1944 and March 1945, over 20,000 Jews poured into the camp. The influx resulted in a new labor supply for war industry.

As Soviet forces pushed through western Hungary, the commander of Mauthausen, near Linz (Austria), received orders to take in thousands of Jews who had been building the *Süd-Ostwall* (Southeast Defense Line). These laborers, guarded by the Volkssturm, were moved on foot from the Hungarian border through the Alps, where Gendarmerie took over for the remaining segment to Mauthausen. A survivor recalls that in the Alpine town of Eisenerz a crowd emerging from a movie threw stones at the marchers and that deportees were shot in the town. Others, moving over the Präbichl, a nearby mountain, on April 7 and 8, were commanded by guards to run downhill. As they ran, fire was opened on them from behind bushes and trees. Many finally arrived at Mauthausen without shoes, clad in rags, and full of lice.

From the remnant ghettos and camps in the Baltic area, evacuated in 1944, Jews arrived at the Stutthof concentration camp, a mile from the Baltic coast east of the Vistula river. Like Auschwitz, Stutthof was divided into men's and women's compounds. Most of the inmates were women, and most of the women were Jewish. When the Soviet offensive of January 1945 came to a halt a few miles south of Stutthof, the majority of the prisoners were moved to the interior. About 3,000 women were shot on the shore or thrown from ice into the water. Not until the resumption of the Soviet advance in April did the remaining inmates face evacuation. On April 27, three barges were loaded at Hela under Soviet bombers. One, with sick inmates, was directed to Kiel, and two arrived in the early morning hours of May 3 at Neustadt, twenty miles north of Lübeck. As the victims waded ashore during the day, they were shot at by SS men and naval personnel, while German officers photographed the scene from gardens in their homes.

The old, established camps did not have enough room for the influx of new inmates, and hence one camp was greatly expanded to take in the overflow. This was Bergen-Belsen, at Celle, near Hannover in the northwestern part of Germany. Bergen-Belsen was originally a Wehrmacht camp for wounded prisoners of war. In the fall of 1943, Pohl acquired half the grounds in order to set up an internment camp there.

He needed a place from which foreign nationals could be repatriated—in the words of a Foreign Office official, a camp that would not give rise to "atrocity propaganda." While Bergen-Belsen thus started out as a model camp, it could not afford an inspection by a foreign government even in its early days. Instead of calling the camp an *Internierungslager,* a legal brain had therefore designated it as an *Aufenthaltslager,* which means a camp where people stay.

Toward the end of 1944, Pohl took over the second half of the camp. This transfer was simple, because the Wehrmacht prisoner-of-war chief by that time was Obergruppenführer Berger of the SS Main Office. Some of the old Auschwitz officials now moved into Bergen-Belsen. Hauptsturmführer Kramer, former Birkenau (Auschwitz II) commander, got the top post. Dr. Fritz Klein, an Auschwitz camp doctor, became chief camp doctor of Bergen-Belsen. Kramer immediately introduced the Auschwitz routine, including the lengthy roll calls.

In Theresienstadt, Obersturmführer Rahm was involved in a last attempt to resume the destruction process. At the end of February 1945, several inmate engineers and eighty working inmates were sent to a nearby eighteenth-century fortress with instructions to seal off apertures and tear down cells for the purpose of making up a hermetically sealed "vegetable warehouse." As rumors and unrest spread through the camp, Rahm, shouting at the Jewish technical department to keep everyone quiet, suddenly broke off the project.

By February and March the front lines began to disintegrate. More and more soldiers surrendered, major cities were given up, labor camps and concentration camps had to be evacuated. From east and west, transports with forced laborers and camp inmates were rolling inward. Some of the railway cars were shunted to side rails and abandoned to Allied bombers.

In Bergen-Belsen the camp administration broke down. As tens of thousands of new inmates were dumped into the camp (in the single week of April 4–13, 1945, the number was 28,000), the food supply was shut off, roll calls were stopped, and the starving inmates were left to their own devices. Typhus and diarrhea raged unchecked, corpses rotted in barracks and on dung heaps. Rats attacked living inmates, and bodies of the dead were eaten by starving prisoners.

In the meantime Himmler, who had long despaired of victory, made some of the biggest concessions of his life. He permitted several thousand inmates to go to Switzerland and Sweden. He allowed Red Cross trucks to distribute food to some of the camps. Finally, he ordered that the evacuation of threatened concentration camps be stopped and that they be handed over to the Allies intact. The last order was overruled by Hitler, who was incensed by reports that liberated Buchenwald inmates were plundering Weimar. On April 24, 1945, the General Secretary of the International Red Cross, Dr. Hans Bachmann, visited Kaltenbrunner in Innsbruck. The chief of the RSHA invited him to send foodstuffs to Jews and offered to liberate a few Jews who were Allied nationals. After the conference, at dinner, Kaltenbrunner directed the conversation to politics and attempted to give a lengthy explanation of the character of National Socialist *Weltanschauung.*

By the end of April the front was dissolving. Prospective war criminals looked east and west and saw Allied armies coming from both directions. The end was staring them in the face. Some committed suicide. Some gave up. Some went into hiding. In Munich on April 30, 1945, as American troops were moving into the city, the former chief of Amtsgruppe A of the WVHA, August Frank, walked into the office of the police president and obtained a false identification card. He was caught anyway. In Austria, Globocnik was arrested and he killed himself.

From Oranienburg, the WVHA headquarters, a motorcade of SS officials and their families set out for Ravensbrück and from there to Flensburg. Obersturmbannführer Höss was among them. In Flensburg he sought out Himmler, who advised him to cross into Denmark as a Wehrmacht officer. Höss managed to get false papers from Kapitän zur See Luth—he was now Franz Lang, *Bootsmaat* (Sailor). But not for long. He too was caught.

Himmler himself wandered about Germany, a lone, hunted figure. He was recognized and arrested, whereupon he swallowed poison.

Even as the armies were fighting their final battle, Eichmann called his men together to tell them that the end was near. While one of them was "whimpering like a child," Eichmann said that the feeling of having killed five million enemies of the state had given him so much satisfaction that he would jump laughingly into the grave. But Eichmann did not jump, and after spending months in American captivity, unrecognized, he fled and disappeared without a trace. He was seized fifteen years later by Israeli agents in Argentina.

On the Italian-Swiss frontier, just before the collapse, the German Ambassador to Italy, Rudolf Rahn, was unable to get into Switzerland. As he stood in the snow, he thought about the Jews: "Are we now going to share the fate of this unfortunate nation? Will we be dispersed in all directions, to give of our tenacity and ability to the welfare of other nations—only to provoke their resistance? Shall Germans too be fated to be at home in every place and welcome in none?"

In the Protektorat, still held by German troops, the last commander of Theresienstadt, Rahm, received the last report from the chief of the Jewish "Self-administration" *(Selbstverwaltung),* Rabbi Murmelstein, on May 5, 1945. In his memorandum on that report, which dealt with a variety of topics including statistics of typhus, Murmelstein noted that the Obersturmführer had promised him 300 kilograms of Zyklon. On the same day, the rabbi, drawing the "right political consequences at the right moment," tendered his resignation to a representative of the International Red Cross. Rahm himself quit that evening.

Meanwhile, as Soviet spearheads closed in on Berlin, the director of the Generalbetriebsleitung Ost (Präsident Ernst Emrich) called his staff together in a bunker on April 23 to advise everyone to go home. When the offices of the Generalbetriebsleitung were overrun by the Soviets, Reichsbahnoberinspektor Bruno Klemm, who had presided over many a conference on Jewish transports, was captured. Last seen by a colleague interned with him in Poznań, he has since been missing.

In his own bunker, the supreme architect of the destruction of the Jews, Adolf Hitler, dictated a political testament during the early morning hours of April 29, 1945. In this legacy he said:

> It is untrue that I or anyone else in Germany wanted the war in 1939. It was desired and instigated exclusively by those international statesmen who were either of Jewish descent or worked for Jewish interests. I have made too many offers for the control and limitation of armaments—which posterity will not for all time be able to disregard—for the responsibility for the outbreak of this war to be laid on me. I have, further, never wished that after the first fatal world war a second against England, or even America, should break out. Centuries will pass away, but out of the ruins of our towns and monuments the hatred against those finally responsible, whom we have to thank for everything, international Jewry and its helpers, will grow. . . .
>
> I also made it quite plain that if the nations of Europe were once more to be regarded as mere chattel to be bought and sold by these international conspirators in money and finance, then that race, Jewry, which is the real criminal of this murderous struggle, will be saddled with the responsibility. Furthermore, I left no one in doubt that this time not only would millions of children of Europe's Aryan peoples die of hunger, not only would millions of grown men suffer death, and not only would hundreds of thousands of women and children be burned and bombed to death in the cities—but also the real criminal would have to atone for his guilt, even if by more humane means.
>
> After six years of war, which in spite of all setbacks will go down one day in history as the most glorious and valiant demonstration of a nation's life purpose, I cannot forsake the city which is the capital of this Reich. As the forces are too small to make any further stand against the enemy attack at this place and our resistance is gradually being weakened by men who are as deluded as they are lacking in initiative, I should like, by remaining in this town, to share my fate with those, the millions of others, who have also taken it upon themselves to do so. Moreover, I do not wish to fall into

the hands of an enemy who requires a new spectacle organized by the Jews for the amusement of their hysterical masses.

I have decided therefore to remain in Berlin and there of my own free will to choose death at the moment when I believe the position of the Führer and Chancellor itself can no longer be held.

CHAPTER SEVEN

THE
NATURE
OF THE
PROCESS

THE PERPETRATORS

The Germans killed five million Jews. The onslaught did not come from the void; it was brought into being because it had meaning to its perpetrators. It was not a narrow strategy for the attainment of some ulterior goal, but an undertaking for its own sake, an event experienced as *Erlebnis*—lived and lived through by its participants.

The German bureaucrats who contributed their skills to the destruction of the Jews all shared in this experience, some in the technical work of drafting a decree or dispatching a train, others starkly at the door of a gas chamber. They could sense the enormity of the operation from its smallest fragments. At every stage they displayed a striking pathfinding ability in the absence of directives, a congruity of activities without jurisdictional guidelines, a fundamental comprehension of the task even when there were no explicit communications. One has the feeling that when Reinhard Heydrich and the ministerial *Staatssekretäre* met on the morning of January 20, 1942, to discuss the "Final Solution of the Jewish Question in Europe," they understood each other.

In retrospect it may be possible to view the entire design as a mosaic of small pieces, each commonplace and lusterless by itself. Yet this progression of everyday activities, these file notes, memoranda, and telegrams, embedded in habit, routine, and tradition, were fashioned into a massive destruction process. Ordinary men were to perform extraordinary tasks. A phalanx of functionaries in public offices and private enterprises was reaching for the ultimate.

With every escalation there were also barriers. Economic problems exacted their cost. Contemplative thought troubled the mind. Yet the destruction of the Jews was not disrupted. Continuity is one of its crucial characteristics. At the threshold of the killing phase, the flow of administrative measures was unchecked. Technological and moral obstacles were overcome. The unprecedented march of men, women, and children into the gas chambers was begun. How was the deed accomplished?

THE DESTRUCTIVE EXPANSION

The German destructive effort evolved on several planes. On one we may see an alignment of agencies in a destructive machine. Upon another we may discern an evolution of procedures for the accomplishment of destructive tasks. On a third we may note the substantive development, step by step, of the destruction process. Finally, we may observe an attempt to set up multiple processes aimed at new victims and pointing to an annihilation of group after group in the German power sphere.

Basic was the immersion in destructive activity of the bureaucratic apparatus as such. We know that as the process unfolded, its requirements became more complex and its fulfillment involved an ever larger number of agencies, party offices, business enterprises, and military commands. The destruction of the Jews was a total process, comparable in its diversity to a modern war, a mobilization, or a national reconstruction.

An administrative process of such range cannot be carried out by a single agency, even if it is a trained and specialized body like the Gestapo or a commissariat for Jewish affairs, for when a process cuts into every phase of human life, it must ultimately feed upon the resources of the entire organized community. That is why we find among the perpetrators the highly differentiated technicians of the armament inspectorates, the remote officials of the Postal Ministry, and—in the all-important operation of furnishing records for determination of descent—the membership of an aloof and withdrawn Christian clergy. The machinery of destruction, then, was structurally no different from organized German society as a whole; the difference was only one of function. The machinery of destruction *was* the organized community in one of its special roles.

Established agencies rely on existing procedures. In his daily work the bureaucrat made use of tried techniques and tested formulas with which he was familiar and which he knew to be acceptable to his superiors, colleagues, and subordinates. The usual practices were applied also in unusual situations. The Finance Ministry went through condemnation proceedings to set up the Auschwitz complex, and the German railroads billed the Security Police for the transport of the Jews, calculating the one-way fare for each deportee by the track kilometer. Swift operations precipitated greater complications and necessitated more elaborate adjustments. In the course of the roundup of the Warsaw Jews during the summer of 1942, the ghetto inhabitants left behind their unpaid gas and electricity bills, and as a consequence the German offices responsible for public utilities and finance in the city had to marshal all their expertise to restore an administrative equilibrium.

Although the apparatus strove to maintain the customary mode of operation to deal with a variety of problems, there was a tendency within the bureaucratic structure to erase old established boundaries of administrative freedom when they inhibited an acceptance of new challenges or an exploitation of new opportunities. The process of destruction was in its very nature limitless. That is why power became more open-ended, why latitudes were widened and capabilities increased. Over time it became easier to write an ordinance regulating the conduct of victims or to take action against them directly.

In the realm of public regulation, fewer basic laws were being promulgated, and "implementary decrees" were less and less germane to the laws to which they referred. An ordinance did not even have to appear in a legal gazette. In December 1938, Heinrich Himmler, omitting the customary submission of rules to an official register, "provisionally" placed directly in the newspapers a regulation withdrawing driver's licenses from Jews. When the legality of Himmler's action was challenged in court, the highest court upheld his method on the ground that a proclamation issued "under the eyes of the Highest Reich Authorities" without generating their protest was law.

The rise of government by announcement was accompanied by a greater permissiveness in the making of internal decisions. Orders were specific commands, but at the same time they could contain broad authorizations. What was mandatory was also a mandate. When Göring permitted Heydrich to inaugurate the "Final Solution," the "charge" was a vast delegation of power. Not surprisingly, written directives would give way to oral ones. Hitler himself may never have signed an order to kill the Jews. On the other hand, there are records of his utterances in the form of comments, questions, or "wishes." What he actually meant, or whether he really meant it, might have been a matter of tone as well as of language. When he spoke "coldly" and in a "low voice" about "horrifying" decisions "also at the dinner table," then his audience knew that he was "serious."

Oral orders were given at every level. Höss was told to build his death camp at Auschwitz in a conversation with Himmler. Stangl received instructions about Sobibór from Globocnik on a park bench in Lublin. A railroad man in Kraków, responsible for scheduling death trains, recalls that he was told by his immediate superior to run the transports whenever they were requested by the SS.

In essence, then, there was an atrophy of laws and a corresponding multiplication of measures for which the sources of authority were more and more ethereal. Valves were being opened for a decision flow.

The experienced functionary was coming into his own. A middle-ranking bureaucrat, no less than his highest superior, was aware of currents and possibilities. In small ways as well as large, he recognized what was ripe for the time. Most often it was he who initiated action.

Thousands of proposals were introduced in memoranda, presented at conferences, and discussed in letters. The subject matter ranged from dissolution of mixed marriages to the deportation of the Jews of Liechtenstein or the construction of some "quick-working" device for the annihilation of Jewish women and children at Łódź and the surrounding towns of the Warthegau. At times it was assumed that the moment had come, even if there was no definite word from above. Hans Globke wrote anti-Jewish provisions in a decree on personal names in December 1932, before there was a Nazi regime or Führer. The Trusteeship Office in Warsaw began to seize Jewish real property "in expectation" of a "lawful regulation," meanwhile performing the "indispensable" preparatory work. Not always, however, was such spontaneity welcome at central offices in Berlin. When the Security Police in the Netherlands sought to induce sterilizations by holding out the prospect of immunity from deportation to couples in mixed marriage who could prove their inability to have children, Eichmann's deputy, Günther, expressed his disapproval because no such scheme had been worked out for the Jews in Germany itself. The Reich, said Günther, had to be a model in such matters. Eichmann himself once exceeded a guideline, seizing Hungarian Jews in the Reich by mistake. Commenting about his act in an Israel court, he said: "Humanly, this is possible and understandable."

In the final analysis, laws or decrees were not regarded as ultimate sources of power but only as an expression of will. In this view a particular decree might not have provided for all that had to be done; on occasion it might even have interfered with the task at hand. If an ordinance was regarded as not limiting, if it was thought to be only an example of the kind of actions that might be taken, an official might proceed outside its boundaries, legislating on a parallel plane. The Law for the Restoration of the Professional Civil Service provided that Jewish civil servants were to be dismissed. Analogously, or "sinngemäss," Jewish fellowship holders at the University of Freiburg were deprived of their stipends. If instructions frustrated action, they could even be disregarded altogether. An example is a directive, issued in the Generalgouvernement, to pay Jewish workers in the "free" market 80 percent of the wages received by Poles. The problem in several localities was that Jewish laborers had not been paid by their employers in the first place, inasmuch as the Jewish councils were expected to provide compensation out of their own funds. In the Puławy district the German army, not wishing to start payments, promptly dismissed its Jews, but in Częstochowa the German City Kommissar wrote the following in his offical report: "I assume that also these instructions may be lost locally and I have acted accordingly."

The machinery of destruction, moving on a track of self-assertion, engaged in its multipronged operation in an ever more complicated network of interlocking decisions. One might well ask: What determined the basic order of this process? What accounted for the sequence of involvement? What explains the succession of steps? We know that the bureaucracy had no master plan, no fundamental blueprint, no clear-cut view of its actions. How then was the process steered? How did it take on *Gestalt?*

A destruction process has an inherent pattern. There is only one way in which a scattered group can effectively be destroyed. Three steps are organic in the operation:

Definition

|

Concentration (or seizure)

|

Annihilation

This is the invariant structure of the basic process, for no group can be killed without a concentration or seizure of the victims, and no victims can be segregated before the perpetrator knows who belongs to the group.

There are additional steps in a modern destructive undertaking. These measures are required not for the annihilation of the victim but for the preservation of the economy. Basically, they are all expropriations. In the destruction of the Jews, expropriatory decrees were introduced after every organic step. Dismissals and Aryanizations came after the definition; exploitation and starvation measures followed concentration; and the confiscation of personal belongings was incidental to the killing operation. In its completed form a destruction process in a modern society will thus be structured as shown in this chart:

Definition

|

Dismissals of employees and expropriations of business firms

|

Concentration

|

Exploitation of labor and starvation measures

|

Annihilation

|

Confiscation of personal effects

The sequence of steps in a destruction process is thus determined. If there is an attempt to inflict maximum injury upon a group of people, it is therefore inevitable that a bureaucracy—no matter how decentralized its apparatus or how unplanned its activities—should push its victims through these stages.

The expansion of destruction did not stop at this point. As the machine was thrown into high gear and as the process accelerated toward its goal, German hostility became more generalized. The Jewish target became too narrow; other targets were added. This development is of the utmost importance, for it casts a revealing light upon the perpetrators' fundamental aim.

If a group seeks merely the destruction of hostile institutions, the limit of its most drastic action would be drawn with the complete destruction of the bearers of the institutions. The Germans, however, did not draw the line with the destruction of Jewry. They attacked still other victims, some of whom were thought to be like Jews, some of whom were quite unlike Jews, and some of whom were Germans. The Nazi destruction process was, in short, not aimed at institutions; it was targeted at people. The Jews were only the first victims of the German bureaucracy; they were only the first caught in its path. That they should have been chosen first is not accidental. Historical precedents, both administrative and conceptual, determined the selection of the people that for centuries had been the standby victim of recurring destructions. No other group could fill this role so well. None was so vulnerable. But the choice was not confined to the Jews. The following are three illustrations.

Example I The destruction process engulfed a group classified as a parasitic people leading a parasitic life: the Gypsies. There were 34,000 to 40,0000 Gypsies in the Reich. In accordance with a Himmler directive, the Criminal Police was empowered to seize all persons who looked like Gypsies or who wandered around in "Gypsy like" manner. Those who were seized were classified as follows:

Z   Full Gypsy (*Zigeuner*)
ZM+   Gypsy Mischling, predominantly Gypsy
ZM   Gypsy Mischling with equal Gypsy and German "bloodshares" (*Blutsanteile*)
ZM−   Gypsy Mischling, predominantly German
NZ   Free of Gypsy blood (*Nicht Zigeuner*)

The victims in the first three categories were subjected to special wage regulations, taxes, and movement restrictions. Special provisions were made for "privileged Gypsy mixed marriages," and so on. In the 1940s the Germans went one step further. Mobile units of the Security Police in Russia killed roving Gypsies, the military commander in Serbia concentrated Gypsies and shot them, and the SS and Police rounded up Gypsies inside and outside the Reich for deportation to ghettos, concentration camps, and killing centers.

Example II The Poles in the territories incorporated by the Reich were in a rather precarious position. It had been planned to shove them into the Generalgouvernement, while the incorporated provinces to the west were to have become purely German. But that program, like the forced emigration of the Jews from Europe, collapsed. In the back of some people's minds, a "territorial solution" now loomed for these Poles. On May 27, 1941 an interministerial conference took place under the chairmanship of Staatssekretär Conti of the Interior Ministry. The subject of discussion was the reduction of the Polish population in the incorporated territories. The following proposals were entertained: (1) no Pole to be allowed to marry before the age of twenty-five; (2) no permission to be granted unless the marriage was economically sound; (3) a tax on illegitimate births; (4) sterilization following illegitimate birth; (5) no tax exemptions for dependents; (6) permission to submit to abortion to be granted upon application of the expectant mother.

One year later, on May 1, 1942, Gauleiter Greiser of the incorporated Wartheland reported to Himmler that the "special treatment" of 100,000 Jews in his Gau would be completed in another two or three months. Greiser then proceeded in the same paragraph to request Himmler's permission for the use of the experienced Sonderkommando at Kulmhof in order to liberate the Gau from still another danger that threatened "with each passing week to assume catastrophic proportions." Greiser had in his province 35,000 tubercular Poles. He wanted to kill them. The suggestion was passed on to health expert Blome (Conti's deputy), who wanted to refer the matter to Hitler. Months passed without a decision. Finally, Greiser expressed his disappointment to Himmler in words that recall the analogy principle: "I for my person do not believe that the Führer has to be bothered with this question again, especially since he told me only during our last conversation, with reference to the Jews, that I may deal with them in any way I pleased."

Example III In consequence of an agreement between Himmler and Justice Minister Thierack, so-called asocials were transferred from prisons to concentration camps. On November 16, 1944, after the transfer of the "asocials" had largely been completed, the judiciary met to discuss a weird subject: ugliness. The phrase on the agenda was "gallery of outwardly asocial prisoners." The summary of that conference states:

> During various visits to the penitentiaries, prisoners have always been observed who—because of their bodily characteristics—hardly deserve

the designation human: they look like miscarriages of hell. Such prisoners should be photographed. It is planned that they too shall be eliminated. Crime and sentence are irrelevant. Only such photographs should be submitted which clearly show the deformity.

THE OBSTACLES

A destructive development unparalleled in history had surfaced in Nazi Germany. The bureaucratic network of an entire nation was involved in these operations, and its capabilities were being expanded by an atmosphere facilitating initiatives in offices at every level. Destruction was brought to its logical, final conclusion, and even as this fate overtook the Jews, a veritable target series was established to engulf yet other groups.

The German bureaucracy, however, did not always move with unencumbered ease. From time to time barriers appeared on the horizon and caused momentary pauses. Most of these stoppages were occasioned by those ordinary difficulties encountered by every bureaucracy in every administrative operation: procurement difficulties, shortages, mixups, misunderstandings, and all the other annoyances of the daily bureaucratic process. We shall not be concerned with these occurrences here. But some of the hesitations and interruptions were the products of extraordinary administrative and psychological obstacles. These blocks were peculiar to the destruction process alone, and they must therefore claim our special attention.

Administrative Problems

The destruction of the Jews was not a gainful operation. It imposed a strain upon the administrative machine and its facilities. In a wider sense, it became a burden that rested upon Germany as a whole.

One of the most striking facts about the German apparatus was the sparseness of its personnel, particularly in those regions outside the Reich where most of the victims had to be destroyed. Moreover, that limited manpower was preoccupied with a bewildering variety of administrative undertakings. Upon close examination, the machinery of destruction turns out to have been a loose organization of part-timers. There were at most a handful of bureaucrats who could devote all their time to anti-Jewish activities. There were the "experts" on Jewish affairs in the ministries, the mobile killing units of the Reich Security Main Office, the commanders of the killing centers. But even an expert like Eichmann had two jobs: the deportation of Jews and the resettlement of ethnic Germans. The mobile killing units had to shoot Jews,

Gypsies, commissars, and partisans alike, while a camp commander like Höss was host to an industrial complex next to his gas chambers.

In the totality of the administrative process, the destruction of the Jews presented itself as an additional task to a bureaucratic machine that was already straining to fulfill the requirements of the battlefronts. One need think only of the railroads, which served as the principal means for transporting troops, munitions, supplies, and raw materials. Every day, available rolling stock had to be allocated, and congested routes assigned for trains urgently requested by military and industrial users. Notwithstanding these priorities, no Jew was left alive for lack of transport to a killing center. The German bureaucracy was not deterred by problems, never resorting to pretense, like the Italians, or token measures, like the Hungarians, or procrastinations, like the Bulgarians. German administrators were driven to accomplishment. Unlike their collaborators, German decision makers never contented themselves with the minimum. They always did the maximum.

Indeed there were moments when an agency's eagerness to participate in the decision making led to bureaucratic competition and rivalry. Such a contest was in the offing when Unterstaatssekretär Luther concluded an agreement with the Reich Security Main Office to preserve the Foreign Office's power to negotiate with Axis satellites on Jewish matters. Again, within the SS itself, a jealous struggle was waged between two technocrats of destruction, Obersturmbannführer Höss and Kriminalkommissar Wirth, over the replacement of carbon monoxide with Zyklon B in the death camps. This bureaucratic warfare was also reflected in the attempt of the judiciary to conserve its jurisdiction in Jewish affairs. When that attempt was finally given up, Justice Minister Thierack wrote to his friend Bormann: "I intend to turn over criminal justice jurisdiction against Poles, Russians, Jews, and Gypsies to the Reichsführer-SS. In doing so, I base myself on the principle that the administration of justice can make only a small contribution to the extermination of these peoples." This letter reveals an almost melancholy tone. The judiciary had done its utmost; it was no longer needed.

The bureaucrats did not spare themselves, nor could they spare the economy. Just how expensive was the destruction of the Jews? What were the effects of this cost? Table 17 reveals the economic aspects of the operations. An analysis of the table reveals two important trends: with the progress of the destruction process, gains declined and expenditures tended to increase. Looking at the table horizontally, we discover that in the preliminary phase financial gains, public or private, far outweighed expenses but that in the killing phase receipts no longer balanced losses. let us examine the net cost of the killing phase a little more closely.

German confiscations during the second half of the process were

---

T A B L E 17
THE ECONOMIC BALANCE SHEET

Receipts, Gains, Savings	Expenditures and Losses
Preliminary Phase	
Net profits to industry from purchase and liquidations of Jewish enterprises: ca. one-fourth to one-half of value of Jewish business property in Reich-Protektorat area. These profits probably amounted to billions of Reichsmark.	Loss of markets abroad in consequence of buyers' resistance and boycott
	Loss of scientific manpower because of emigration
Tax on profits made in acquisitions of Jewish firms (during fiscal years 1942, 1943, 1944): 49,000,000 reichsmark)	
Reich Flight Tax: 900,000,000 reichsmark	
Reich Property Tax (fine): 1,127,000,000 reichsmark	
Wage differentials and other industry savings as result of employment of Jewish labor: probably in tens of millions	
Wage differentials, special income tax, and other wage savings accruing to Reich: probably in tens of millions	
Exactions from ghettos for German administration and walls	Direct expenditures for personnel and overhead (prior to killing phase)
Confiscation under the 11th Ordinance (securities and bonds): 186,000,000 reichsmark	Direct expenditures for: Personnel and overhead (in killing operations) Transport Camp installations (in hundreds of millions)

largely confined to personal belongings. Within Germany itself most of the assets had already been taken. In occupied Polish and Soviet territories, the victims had few possessions from the start, while in the satellite countries, Jewish property abandoned by the deportees was claimed by collaborating governments. Costs, on the other hand, were more extensive. Only the visible outlays, particularly for deportations and killings, were comparatively small. Freight cars were used for

T A B L E   17 *(continued)*
THE ECONOMIC BALANCE SHEET

Receipts, Gains, Savings	*Expenditures and Losses*
Killing Phase	
Confiscation under the 11th Ordinance (not including securities and bonds): 592,000,000 reichsmark	Extraordinary bill for razing of Warsaw ghetto: 150,000,000
Confiscations in German occupied territories	Loss of unpaid rents and other Jewish debts
Exactions from Jewish communities in Reich by Gestapo for transports	Loss of Jewish labor
Gain of apartment space for rent	

transport. German personnel were employed sparingly, both in killing units and killing centers. The camps as a whole were constructed and maintained with thrift, notwithstanding a complaint by Speer that Himmler was using scarce building materials too extravagantly. The installations were erected with camp labor, and the inmates were housed in large barracks with no light and no modern toilet facilities. The investment in gas chambers and ovens was almost modest. All of this economizing was possible because it did not jeopardize the process, either in scale or speed.

Sheer savings, however, were not the decisive consideration. The paramount aim was the completion, in the fullest sense of the word, of the destruction process. A case in point was the razing of the Warsaw ghetto ruins after the battle of April–May 1943. For this Himmler project the Finance Ministry received a bill in the amount of RM 150,000,000. Himmler felt that a park should obliterate the site of the ghetto, lest Warsaw's Poles fill the empty space and the city grow back to its prewar size.

A more important assertion of total destruction was the forfeiture of the Jewish labor potential. Himmler never made any pretense that for him the destruction of the Jews had priority even over armaments. When procurement officials objected to removals of Jewish workers, Himmler had only this reply: "The argument of war production, which nowadays in Germany is the favorite reason for opposing anything at all, I do not recognize in the first place." In the measured language of the Ministry for Eastern Occupied Territories, the priority of the destruction process was phrased as follows: "Economic questions should not be considered in the solution of the Jewish question."

The loss of Jewish labor was brought about by successive restrictions, dislocations, and deportations. From the beginning, Jews were dismissed from jobs. In the east the Jewish population in its entirety was crowded into ghettos. There the incarcerated communities were engaged in production, but the ghetto was not an ideal place for major manufacturing. Its industry was undercapitalized, its residents underemployed, its laborers undernourished. Once the killings were under way, the SS itself attempted to husband Jewish workers in its camps, but eventually that remnant was to disappear as well.

Germany was at war. The economies of the occupied countries were harnessed to German needs. Foreign goods were demanded for the German market even as foreign workers were transported to German factories and farms. In the wake of these expanding requirements for output and in the face of the growing shortage of labor, a reservoir of Jewish manpower was sacrificed to the "Final Solution." Of all the costs that were generated by the destruction process, this relinquishment of an increasingly irreplaceable pool of labor was the greatest single expenditure.

Psychological Problems

The most important problems of the destruction process were not administrative but psychological. The very conception of the drastic Final Solution was dependent on the ability of the perpetrators to cope with weighty psychological obstacles and impediments. The psychological blocks differed from the administrative difficulties in one important respect. An administrative problem could be solved and eliminated, but the psychological difficulties had to be dealt with continuously. They were held in check but never removed. Commanders in the field were ever watchful for symptoms of psychological disintegration. In the fall of 1941 Higher SS and Police Leader Russia Center von dem Bach shook Himmler with the remark: "Look at the eyes of the men of this Kommando, how deeply shaken they are. These men are finished for the rest of their lives. What kind of followers are we training here? Either neurotics or savages!" Von dem Bach was not only an important participant in killing operations. He was also an acute observer. With this remark he pointed to the basic psychological problem of the German bureaucracy, namely that the German administration had to make determined efforts to prevent the breakdown of its men into either "savages" or "neurotics." This was essentially a dual task—one part disciplinary, the other moral.

The disciplinary problem was understood clearly. The bureaucrats were fully aware of the dangers of plundering, torture, orgies, and atrocities. Such behavior was first of all wasteful from an administrative point of view, for the destruction process was an organized undertaking which had room only for organized tasks. Moreover, "excesses" attracted attention to aspects of the destruction process that had to remain secret. Such were the activities of Brigadeführer Dirlewanger, whose rumored attempts to make human soap drew the attention of the public to the killing centers. Indeed, atrocities could bring the entire "noble" work into disrepute.

What was wasteful administratively was dangerous psychologically. Loose behavior was an abuse of the machine, and a debauched administration could disintegrate. That was why the German administration had a certain preference for quick, blow-type action. Maximum destructive effect was to be achieved with minimum destructive effort. The personnel of the machinery of destruction were not supposed to look to the right or to the left. They were not allowed to have either personal motives or personal gains. An elaborate discipline was introduced into the machine of destruction.

The first and most important rule of conduct of this discipline was the principle that all Jewish property belonged to the Reich. So far as Himmler was concerned, the enforcement of this rule was a success. In 1943 he told his Gruppenführer:

> The riches which they [the Jews] owned we have taken from them. I have given strict orders, which Obergruppenführer Pohl has carried out, that this wealth should naturally be delivered to the Reich. We have taken nothing. Individuals who have transgressed are being punished in accordance with an order which I gave in the beginning and which threatened that anyone who takes just one mark is a condemned man. A number of SS men—not many—have transgressed against that order, and they will be condemned to death mercilessly. We had the moral right vis-à-vis *our* people to annihilate *this* people which wanted to annihilate us. But we have no right to take a single fur, a single watch, a single mark, a single cigarette, or anything whatever. We don't want in the end, just because we have exterminated a germ, to be infected by that germ and die from it. I will not stand by while a slight infection forms. Whenever such an infected spot appears, we will burn it out. But on the whole we can say that we have fulfilled this heavy task with love for our people, and we have not been damaged in the innermost of our being, our soul, our character.

There is, of course, considerable evidence that more than a few individuals "transgressed" against the discipline of the destruction process. No estimate can be formed of the extent to which transport Kommandos, killing units, the ghetto and killing center personnel, and even Kommando 1005—the grave-destruction Kommando—filled their pockets with the belongings of the dead. Moreover, we should note that Himmler's rule dealt only with *unauthorized* takings by participating personnel in the field. It did not deal with *authorized* distributions to the participants.

The essence of corruption is to reward people on the basis of their proximity to the loot—in a corrupt system the tax collectors become rich. In the course of the destruction process, many distributions were made to the closest participants. Examples are the Finance Ministry's appropriation of fine furniture during the deportations of Jews from Germany; the distribution of better apartments to civil servants; the cuts taken by the railways, SS and Police, and postal service in the allocation of the furniture of the Dutch, Belgian, and French Jews; the "gifts" of watches and "Christmas presents" to SS men and their families. The destruction process had its own built-in corruption. Only unauthorized corruption was forbidden.

The second way in which the Germans sought to avoid damage to "the soul" was in the prohibition of unauthorized killings. A sharp line was drawn between killings pursuant to order and killings induced by desire. In the former case a man was thought to have overcome the "weaknesses" of "Christian morality"; in the latter case he was overcome by his own baseness. That was why in the occupied USSR both the army and the civil administration sought to restrain their personnel from joining the shooting parties at the killing sites.

Perhaps the best illustration of the official attitude is to be found in an advisory opinion by a judge on Himmler's Personal Staff, Obersturmbannführer Bender. Bender dealt with procedure to be followed in the case of unauthorized killings of Jews by SS personnel. He concluded that if purely political motives prompted the killing, if the act was an expression of idealism, no punishment was necessary unless the maintenance of order required disciplinary action or prosecution. However, if selfish, sadistic, or sexual motives were found, punishment was to be imposed for murder or for manslaughter, in accordance with the facts.

The German disciplinary system is most discernible in the mode of the killing operation. At the conclusion of the destruction process, Hitler remarked in his testament that the Jewish "criminals" had "atoned" for their "guilt" by "humane means." The "humaneness" of the destruction process was an important factor in its success. It must be emphasized, of course, that this "humaneness" was evolved not for the benefit of the victims but for the welfare of the perpetrators. Time and again, attempts were made to reduce opportunities for "excesses" and *Schweinereien* of all sorts. Much research was expended for the development of devices and methods that arrested propensities for uncontrolled behavior and at the same time lightened the crushing psychological burden on the killers. The construction of gas vans and gas chambers, the employment of Ukrainian, Lithuanian, and Latvian auxiliaries to kill Jewish women and children, the use of Jews for the burial and burning of bodies—all these were efforts in the same direction. Efficiency was the real aim of all that "humaneness."

So far as Himmler was concerned, his SS and Police had weathered the destruction process. In October 1943, when he addressed his top commanders, he said to them:

> Most of you know what it means when 100 corpses lie there, or 500 lie there, or 1,000 lie there. To have gone through this and—apart from the exceptions caused by human weakness—to have remained decent, that has hardened us. That is a page of glory in our history never written and never to be written.

However, the descent into savagery was not nearly so important a factor in the destruction process as the feeling of growing uneasiness that pervaded the bureaucracy from the lowest strata to the highest. That uneasiness was the product of moral scruples—the lingering effect of two thousand years of Western morality and ethics. A Western bureaucracy had never before faced such a chasm between moral precepts and administrative action; an administrative machine had never been burdened with such a drastic task. In a sense the task of destroying the Jews put the German bureaucracy to a supreme test. The German technocrats solved also that problem and passed also this test.

To grasp the full significance of what these men did we have to understand that we are not dealing with individuals who had their own separate moral standards. The bureaucrats who were drawn into the destruction process were not different in their moral makeup from the rest of the population. The German perpetrator was not a special kind of German. What we have to say here about his morality applies not to him specially but to Germany as a whole. How do we know this?

We know that the very nature of administrative planning, of the jurisdictional structure, and of the budgetary system precluded the special selection and special training of personnel. Any member of the Order Police could be a guard at a ghetto or on a train. Every lawyer in the Reich Security Main Office was presumed to be suitable for leadership in the mobile killing units; every finance expert to the Economic-Administrative Main Office was considered a natural choice for service in a death camp. In other words, all necessary operations were accomplished with whatever personnel were at hand. However one may wish to draw the line of active participation, the machinery of destruction was a remarkable cross section of the German population. Every profession, every skill, and every social status was represented in it. We know that in a totalitarian state the formation of an opposition movement outside the bureaucracy is next to impossible. However, if there is very serious opposition in the population, if there are insurmountable psychological obstacles to a course of action, such impediments reveal themselves *within* the bureaucratic apparatus. We know what such barriers will do, for they emerged clearly in the Italian Fascist state. Again and again the Italian generals and consuls, prefects and police inspectors, refused to cooperate in the deportations. The destruction process in Italy and the Italian-controlled areas was carried out against unremitting Italian opposition. No such opposition is to be found in the German area. No obstruction stopped the German machine of destruction. No moral problem proved insurmountable. When all participating personnel were put to the test, there were very few lingerers and almost no deserters. The old moral order did not break through anywhere along the line. This is a phenomenon of the greatest magnitude.

How did the German bureaucrat cope with his moral inhibitions? He did so in an inner struggle, recognizing the basic truth that he had a choice. He knew that at crucial junctures every individual makes decisions, and that every decision is individual. He knew this fact as he faced his own involvement and while he went on and on. At the same time he was not psychically unarmed. When he wrestled with himself, he had at his disposal the most complex psychological tools fashioned during centuries of German cultural development. Fundamentally, this arsenal of defenses consisted of two parts: a mechanism of repressions and a system of rationalizations.

First of all, the bureaucracy wanted to hide its deeds. It wanted to conceal the destructive process not only from all outsiders but also from the censuring gaze of its own conscience. The repression proceeded through five stages.

As we might expect, every effort was made to hide the ultimate aim of the destruction process from Axis partners and from the Jews. Inquiries such as Hungarian Prime Minister Kállay put to the Foreign Office about the disappearance of European Jewry or questions that foreign journalists in Kiev asked army authorities about mass shootings could obviously not be answered. Rumors, which could spread like wildfire, had to be smothered. "Plastic" evidence, such as "souvenir" photographs of killings, mass graves, and the wounded Jews who had risen from their graves, had to be destroyed.

Despite such attempts, the annihilation of the Jews was becoming an open secret. As early as October 1941, a Viennese enterprise referred to deportation as causing "more or less quick and certain doom." In 1942 a Berlin firm refused to assign to the Finance Ministry the pensions of Jewish employees who had been "shoved off." The remittances were not a Jewish property right that the Reich could claim for itself;

they were assistance payments intended for beneficiaries, and in one case at issue there was no indication that the pensioner was "still alive." Much later a Viennese court, tied to legal presumptions and procedures, could not manage to be so insightful. In May 1944 the RSHA complained to the Justice Ministry that the *Landgericht* in Vienna was making too many inquiries to elicit the whereabouts of deported Jews for the purpose of rendering decisions in proceedings involving proof of descent. The Landgericht had been told repeatedly, said the complaint, that no information could be given about deportees, but the court had persisted in making inquiries. Quite apart from the fact that the "Jews" (that is, the persons seeking clarification of their status) had been given plenty of time to clear questions about their descent, these people were only trying to hide their ancestry in order to remove themselves from the effect of "Security Police measures." For these reasons, and because of more pressing war work, the Security Police could not furnish replies.

Thus, the first stage in the repression was to shut off the supply of information from all those who did not have to know it. Whoever did not participate was not supposed to know. The second stage was to make sure that whoever knew would participate.

There was nothing so irksome as the realization that someone was watching over one's shoulder, that someone would be free to talk and accuse because he was not himself involved. This fear was the origin of what Leo Alexander has called the "blood kit," the irresistible force that drew every official "observer" into the destruction process. The "blood kit" explains why so many office chiefs of the Reich Security Main Office were assigned to mobile killing units and why staff officers with killing units were ordered to participate in the killing operations. The "blood kit" also explains why Unterstaatssekretär Luther of the Foreign Office's Abteilung Deutschland insisted that the Political Division countersign all instructions to embassies and legations for the deportation of Jews. Finally, the "blood kit" explains the significant words spoken by Generalgouverneur Frank at the conclusion of a police conference in Kraków: "We want to remember that we are, all of us assembled here, on Mr. Roosevelt's war-criminals list. I have the honor of occupying first place on that list. We are therefore, so to speak, accomplices in a world-historical sense."

The third stage in the process of repression was the prohibition of criticism. Public protests by outsiders were extremely rare. The criticisms were expressed, if at all, in mutterings on the rumor circuit. It is sometimes hard even to distinguish between expressions of sensationalism and real criticism, for often the two were mixed. One example of such mixed reactions is to be found in the circulation of rumors in

Germany about the mobile killing operations in Russia. The Party Chancellery, in confidential instructions to its regional machinery, attempted to combat these rumors. Most of the reports, the chancellery stated, were "distorted" and "exaggerated." "It is conceivable," the circular continued, "that not all of our people—especially people who have no conception of the Bolshevik terror—can understand sufficiently the necessity for these measures." In their very nature, "these problems," which were sometimes "very difficult," could be solved "in the interest of the security of our people" only with "ruthless severity."

In the German documents we found a singular example of a genuine public protest. A Catholic priest named Lichtenberg prayed for the Jews in open services at St. Hedwig's Cathedral in Berlin. He prayed not only for baptized Jews but for all the Jewish victims. Placed in custody, he pronounced himself a foe of National Socialism and declared that he wanted to share the fate of the Jews in the East in order to pray for them there. Released from prison, Lichtenberg died on the way to a concentration camp.

Within the bureaucracy we find a few more examples of criticism, though again it was very seldom outspoken protest. Of course, it was permissible to criticize measures from the viewpoint of German welfare. There was an unbelievable amount of discussion about the Mischlinge and Jews in mixed marriages—that is, persons against whom action could not be taken without hurting Germans. One may note the voluminous correspondence dealing with the adverse effects of anti-Jewish measures on the war effort. Once in a while it was permissible to mention the harmful psychological effects of killings on the perpetrators, but a sharp line was drawn between such criticisms and the implication that the destruction process itself was intrinsically wrong.

A director of the Reichsbank, Wilhelm, overstepped the line when he cautioned his chief, Puhl, not to visit concentration camps and when he announced his refusal to participate in the distribution of Jewish belongings with the words: "The Reichsbank is not a dealer in secondhand goods." Generalkommissar Kube of White Russia violated the injunction against moral condemnations by making accusations against the Commander of Security Police in White Russia, Strauch. Kube implied that Jews—at least those who had come from Germany ("from our own cultural level")—were human beings and that Straunch and his killers were maniacs and sadists who had satisfied their sexual lust during shootings. Strauch did not take kindly to such criticism. In a complaint against Kube he wrote that "it was regrettable that we, in addition to having to perform this nasty job, were also made the target of mudslinging." In the Interior Ministry the expert on Jewish affairs, Ministerialrat Lösener, was disturbed by reports of killings that had occurred in Riga. He began to put questions to his chief, Staatssekretär Stuckart, and requested a transfer. After a while, a colleague asked Lösener to stop pestering the Staatssekretär, for Stuckart's position was difficult enough.

On the highest level the following story was told by Gauleiter Schirach's secretary. While Schirach's wife was staying in a hotel in Amsterdam, she watched a roundup of Jews at night. The Jewish women "screamed terribly." Mrs. Schirach's nerves were so much on edge that she decided to tell her husband about it. The Gauleiter advised her to tell the story to Hitler himself, since the Führer would not tolerate such "abuses." During their next visit to Hitler, Mrs. Schirach told the story. Hitler listened "ungraciously," interrupting several times and telling her not to be so sentimental. Everyone present found the exchange between Hitler and Mrs. Schirach "very embarrassing." The conversation broke down, no one spoke, and Mr. and Mrs. Schirach left the room. The Schirachs departed the next day without saying good-bye.

In its fourth stage the repressive mechanism eliminated the destruction process as a subject of social conversation. Among the closest participants, it was considered bad form to talk about the killings. This is what Himmler had to say on the subject in his speech of October 4, 1943:

> I want to mention here very candidly a particularly difficult chapter. Among us it should be mentioned once, quite openly, but in public we will never talk about it. Just as little as we hesitated on June 30, 1934, to do our duty and to put comrades who had transgressed [the brownshirts] to the wall, so little have we talked about it and will ever talk about it. It was with us, thank God, an inborn gift of tactfulness, that we have never conversed about this matter, never spoken about it. Every one of us was horrified, and yet every one of us knew that we would do it again if it were ordered and if it were necessary. I am referring to the evacuation of the Jews, to the extermination of the Jewish people.

This then was the reason why that particular "page of glory" was never to be written. There are some things that can be done only so long as they are not discussed, for once they are discussed they can no longer be done.

We know, of course, that among those who were not quite so close to the killing operations the sensations of the destructive process were irresistible. The rumor network was spread all over Axis Europe. One Foreign Office official stationed in Rome mentions that he discussed details of the killings with at least thirty of his colleagues. But the urge to talk was not so deep in men who were heavily involved in the destructive process. Höss, the Auschwitz commander, says that he never spoke about his job even to his wife. She found out about what he was doing because of an inadvertent remark by a family friend, Gauleiter Bracht. The Treblinka guard Hirtreiter never spoke of his task at all.

The fifth and final stage in the process of repression was to omit mention of "killings" or "killing installations" even in the secret correspondence in which such operations had to be reported. The reader of these reports is immediately struck by their camouflaged vocabulary: "Final Solution of the Jewish question", "solution possibilities" "special treatment" "evacuation" "special installations" "dragged through," and many others.

There is one report that contains a crude cover story. In 1943 the Foreign Office inquired whether it would be possible to exchange 30,000 Baltic and White Russian Jews for Reich Germans in Allied countries. The Foreign Office representative in Riga replied that he had discussed the matter with the Security Police commander in charge. The Commander of Security Police had felt that the "interned" Jews could not be sent away for "weighty Security Police reasons." As was known, a large number of Jews had been "done away with" in "spontaneous actions." In some places these actions had resulted in "almost total extermination." A removal of the remaining Jews would therefore give rise to "anti-German atrocity propaganda."

A particularly revealing example of disassociation may be found in a private letter written by a sergeant of the Rural Police to a police general. The sergeant, at the head of twenty-three German gendarmes and five hundred Ukrainian auxiliary policemen, had killed masses of Jews in the Kamenets-Podolsky area. These are excerpts from his letter.

> Naturally we are cleaning up considerably, especially among the Jews. . . .
>
> I have a cozy apartment in a former children's asylum. One bedroom and a living room with all of the accessories. Practically nothing is missing. Naturally, the wife and the children. You will understand me. My Dieter and the little Liese write often, after their fashion. One could weep sometimes. It is not good to be a friend of children as I was. I hope that the war, and with it the time of service in the East, soon ends.

The process of repression was continuous, but it was never completed. The killing of the Jews could not be hidden completely, either from the outside world or from the inner self. Therefore the bureaucracy was not spared an open encounter with its conscience. It had to pit argument against argument and philosophy against philosophy. Laboriously, and with great effort, the bureaucracy had to justify its activities.

Psychological justification is called rationalization. The Germans employed two kinds of rationalizations. The first was an attempt to justify the destruction process as a whole. It was designed to explain why the Jews had to be destroyed. It was focused on the Jew. The other explanations served only to justify individual participation in the destruction process—a signature on a piece of paper or the squeeze of a trigger. They were focused entirely on the perpetrator. Let us consider first the broad rationalizations that encompassed the whole destruction process. In the formation of these justifications, old conceptions about the Jew, reinforced and expanded by new propaganda, played an important role. Precisely how did German propaganda function in this process?

The Germans had two kinds of propaganda. One was designed to produce action. It exhorted people to come to a mass meeting, to boycott Jewish goods, or to kill Jews. This type of propaganda does not concern us here since it was confined, on the whole, to the incitement of demonstrations and pogroms, the so-called *Einzelaktionen*. But the Germans also engaged in a campaign that consisted of a series of statements implying that the Jew was evil. This propaganda had a very important place in the arsenal of psychological defense mechanisms.

Repeated propagandistic allegations may be stored and drawn upon according to need. The statement "The Jew is evil" is taken from the storehouse and is converted in the perpetrator's mind into a complete rationalization: "I kill the Jew because the Jew is evil." To understand the function of such formulations is to realize why they were being constructed until the very end of the war. Propaganda was needed to combat doubts and guilt feelings wherever they arose, whether inside or outside the bureaucracy, and whenever they surfaced, before or after the perpetration of the acts.

In fact, we find that in April 1943, after the deportations of the Jews from the Reich had largely been completed, the press was ordered to deal with the Jewish question continuously and without letup. In order to build up a storehouse, the propaganda had to be turned out on a huge scale. "Research institutes" were formed, doctoral dissertations were written, and volumes of propaganda literature were printed by every conceivable agency. Sometimes a scholarly investigation was conducted too assiduously. One economic study, rich in the common jargon but uncommonly balanced in content, appeared in Vienna with the notation "Not in the book trade"—the author had discovered that the zenith of Jewish financial power had been reached in 1913. On the other hand, the publication of more suitable literature could even lead to bureaucratic competition. Thus Unterstaatssekretär Luther of the

Foreign Office had to assure Obergruppenführer Berger of the SS Main Office that the Foreign Office's pamphlet *Das russische Tor ist aufgestossen (The Russian Gate Is Thrown Open)* in no way competed with Berger's masterpiece *Der Untermensch (The Subhuman)*.

What did all this propaganda accomplish? How was the Jew portrayed in this unending flow of leaflets and pamphlets, books, and speeches? How did the propaganda image of the Jew serve to justify the destruction process?

First of all, the Germans drew a picture of an international Jewry ruling the world and plotting the destruction of Germany and German life. "If international-finance Jewry," said Adolf Hitler in 1939, "inside and outside of Europe should succeed in plunging the nations into another world war, then the result will not be the Bolshevization of the earth and with it the victory of the Jews, but the annihilation of the Jewish race in Europe." In 1944 Himmler said to his commanders: "This was the most frightening order which an organization could receive—the order to solve the Jewish question," but if the Jews had still been in the rear, the front line could not have been held, and if any of the commanders were moved to pity, they had only to think of the bombing terror, "which after all is organized in the last analysis by the Jews."

The theory of world Jewish rule and of the incessant Jewish plot against the German people penetrated into all offices. It became interwoven with foreign policy and sometimes led to preposterous results. Thus the conviction grew that foreign statesmen who were not very friendly toward Germany were Jews, part-Jews, married to Jews, or somehow dominated by Jews. Streicher did not hesitate to state publicly that he had it on good Italian authority that the Pope had Jewish blood. Similarly, Staatssekretär Weizsäcker of the Foreign Office once questioned the British chargé d'affaires about the percentage of "Aryan" blood in Mr. Rublee, and American on a mission in behalf of refugees.

This type of reasoning was also applied in reverse. If a power was friendly, it was believed to be free of Jewish rule. In March 1940, after Ribbentrop had succeeded in establishing friendly relations with Russia, he assured Mussolini and Ciano that Stalin had given up the idea of world revolution. The Soviet administration had been purged of Jews. Even Kaganovich (the Jewish Politburo member) looked rather like a Georgian.

The claim of Jewish world rule was to be established irrefutably in a show trial. Toward the end of 1941 the Propaganda Ministry, the Foreign Office, and the Justice Ministry laid plans for the trial of Herschel Grynzpan, a man who had assassinated a German embassy official (vom Rath) in Paris in 1938. The trial was to prove that Grynzpan's deed was part of a "fundamental plan by international Jewry to drive the world into a war with National Socialist Germany," but it was never held because the Justice Ministry in its eagerness had made the fatal mistake of adding homosexuality to the indictment. At the last moment it was feared that Grynzpan might reveal "the alleged homosexual relations of Gesandtschaftsrat vom Rath." And so the whole scheme was dropped.

When Germany began to lose the war in Stalingrad, the propaganda machine sought to make up in sheer volume of endless repetition for the "proof" it had failed to obtain in the ill-fated Grynzpan trial. The Jew was now the principal foe, the creator of capitalism and communism, the sinister force behind the entire Allied war effort, the organizer of the "terror raids," and, finally, the all-powerful enemy capable of wiping Germany off the map. By February 5, 1943, the press had to be cautioned not to "over-estimate the power of the Jews." On the same day, however, the following instructions were issued:

> Stress: If we lose this war, we do not fall into the hands of some other states but will all be annihilated by world Jewry. Jewry firmly decided to exterminate all Germans. International law and international custom will be no protection against the Jewish will for total annihilation.

How was this theory applied to justify specific operations? The "Jewish conspiracy" was used over and over again. We find the theory in the correspondence of the German Foreign Office, which pressed for deportations in Axis countries on the ground that the Jews were a security risk. The Jews were the spies, the enemy agents. They could not be permitted to stay in coastal areas because, in the event of Allied landings, they would attack the defending garrisons from the rear. The Jews were inciters of revolt; that was why they had to be deported from Slovakia in 1944. The Jews were the organizers of the partisan war, the "middlemen" between the Red Army and the partisan field command; that was why they could not be permitted to remain alive in partisan-threatened areas. The Jews were the saboteurs and assassins; that was why the army chose them as hostages in Russia, Serbia, and France. The Jews were plotting the destruction of Germany; and that was why they had to be destroyed. In Himmler's words: "We had the moral right vis-à-vis our people to annihilate this people which wanted to annihilate us." In the minds of the perpetrators, therefore, this theory turned the destruction process into a kind of preventive war.

However, the Jews were portrayed not only as a world conspiracy but also as a criminal people. This is the definition of the Jews as furnished in instructions to the German press:

> Stress: In the case of the Jews there are not merely a few criminals (as in every other people), but all of Jewry rose from criminal roots, and in its very nature it is criminal. The Jews are no people like other people, but a pseudo-people welded together by hereditary criminality. . . . The annihilation of Jewry is no loss to humanity, but just as useful as capital punishment or protective custody against other criminals.

And this is what Streicher had to say: "Look at the path which the Jewish people has traversed for millennia: Everywhere murder; everywhere mass murder!"

A Nazi researcher, Helmut Schramm, collected all the legends of Jewish ritual murder. The book was an immediate success with Himmler. "Of the book *The Jewish Ritual Murders,*" he wrote to Kaltenbrunner, "I have ordered a large number. I am distributing it down to Standartenführer [SS colonel]. I am sending you several hundred copies so that you can distribute them to your Einsatzkommandos, and above all to the men who are busy with the Jewish question. *The Ritual Murders* was a collection of stories about alleged tortures of Christian children. Actually, hundreds of thousands of Jewish children were being killed in the destruction process. Perhaps that is why *The Ritual Murders* became so important. In fact, Himmler was so enthusiastic about the book that he ordered Kaltenbrunner to start investigations of "ritual murders" in Romania, Hungary, and Bulgaria. He also suggested that Security Police people be put to work tracing British court records and police descriptions of missing children, "so that we can report in our radio broadcasts to England that in the town of XY a child is missing and that it is probably another case of Jewish ritual murder."

How the theory of Jewish criminality was applied in practice may be seen in the choice of some of the expressions in the reports of killing operations, such as the term *execution* (in German, *hingerichtet, exekutiert, Vollzugstätigkeit*). In correspondence dealing with the administration of the personal belongings taken from dead Jews, the SS used the cover designation "utilization of the property of the Jewish thieves."

A striking example of how the theory invaded German thinking is furnished in the format of portions of two reports by the army's Secret Field Police in occupied Russia:

Punishable offenses by members of the population

Espionage	1
Theft of ammunition	1
Suspected Jews *(Judenverdacht)*	3

Punishable offenses by members of the population

Moving about with arms *(Freischärlerei)*	11

Theft	2
Jews	2

In the culmination of this theory, to be a Jew was a punishable offense. Thus it was the function of the rationalization of criminality to turn the destruction process into a kind of judicial proceeding.

A third rationalization that focused on the Jew was the conception of Jewry as a lower form of life. Generalgouverneur Frank was given to the use of such phrases as "Jews and lice." In a speech delivered on December 19, 1940, he pointed out that relatives of military personnel surely were sympathizing with men stationed in Poland, a country "which is so full of lice and Jews." But the situation was not so bad, he continued, though of course he could not rid the country of lice and Jews in a year. On July 19, 1943, the chief of the Generalgouvernement Health Division reported during a meeting that the typhus epidemic was subsiding. Frank remarked in this connection that the "removal" of the "Jewish element" had undoubtedly contributed to better health in Europe. He meant this not only in the literal sense but also politically: the reestablishment of sound living conditions on the European continent. In a similar vein, Foreign Office Press Chief Schmidt once declared during a visit to Slovakia, "The Jewish question is no question of humanity, and it is no question of religion; it is solely a question of political hygiene."

In the terminology of the killing operations, the conception of Jews as vermin is again quite noticeable. Dr. Stahlecker, the commander of Einsatzgruppe A, called the pogroms conducted by the Lithuanians "self-cleansing actions." In another report we find the phrase "cleansing-of-Jews actions." Himmler spoke of "extermination." Many times the bureaucracy used the word *Entjudung*. This expression, which was used not only in connection with killings but also with reference to Aryanization of property, means to *rid something of Jews*. Again, we discover the term *judenrein*, which in exact translation means *clean of Jews*. Finally, in the most drastic application of this theory, a German fumigation company, the Deutsche Gesellschaft für Schädlingsbekämpfung, was drawn into the killing operations by furnishing one of its lethal products for the gassings of a million Jews. Thus the destruction process was also turned into a "cleansing operation."

In addition to the formulations that were used to justify the whole undertaking as a war against "international Jewry," as a judicial proceeding against "Jewish criminality," or simply as a "hygienic" process against "Jewish vermin," there were also rationalizations fashioned in order to enable the individual bureaucrat to justify his individual task in the destruction process. It must be kept in mind that most of the participants did not fire rifles at Jewish children or pour gas into gas chambers. A good many, of course, also had to perform these very "hard" tasks, but most of the administrators and most of the clerks did not see the final, drastic link in these measures of destruction.

Most bureaucrats composed memoranda, drew up blueprints, signed correspondence, talked on the telephone, and participated in conferences. They could destroy a whole people by sitting at their desks. Except for inspection tours, which were not obligatory, they never had to see "100 bodies lie there, or 500, or 1,000." However, these men were not naive. They realized the connection between their paperwork and the heaps of corpses in the East, and they also realized the shortcomings of arguments that placed all evil on the Jew and all good on the German. That was why they were compelled to justify their individual activities. Their justifications contain the implicit admission that the paperwork was to go on regardless of the actual plans of world Jewry and regardless of the actual behavior of the Jews who were about to be killed. We can divide the rationalizations focused on the perpetrators into five categories.

The oldest, the simplest, and therefore the most effective rationalization was the doctrine of superior orders. First and foremost there was discipline. First and foremost there was duty. No matter what objections there might be, orders were given to be obeyed. A clear order was like absolution. Armed with such an order, a perpetrator felt that he could pass his responsibility and his conscience upward. When Himmler addressed a killing party in Minsk, he told his men that they need not worry. Their conscience was in no way impaired, for they were soldiers who had to carry out every order unconditionally.

Every bureaucrat knows, of course, that open defiance of orders is serious business, but he also knows that there are many ingenious ways of evading orders. In fact, the opportunities for evading them increase as one ascends in the hierarchy. Even in Nazi Germany orders were disobeyed, and they were disobeyed even in Jewish matters. We have mentioned the statement of Reichsbankdirektor Wilhelm, who would not participate in the distribution of "secondhand goods." Nothing happened to him. A member of the Reich Security Main Office, Sturmbannführer Hartl, simply refused to take over an Einsatzkommando in Russia. Nothing happened to this man either. Even Generalkommissar Kube, who had actually frustrated a killing operation in Minsk and who had otherwise expressed himself in strong language, was only warned.

The bureaucrat clung to his orders not so much because he feared his superior (with whom he was often on good terms) but because he feared his own conscience. The many requests for "authorization," whether for permission to mark Jews with a star or to kill them, demonstrate the true nature of these orders. When they did not exist the bureaucrats had to invent them.

The second rationalization was the administrator's insistence that he did not act out of personal vindictiveness. In the mind of the bureaucrat, duty was an assigned path; it was his "fate." The German bureaucrat made a sharp distinction between duty and personal feelings. He insisted that he did not "hate" Jews, and sometimes he even went out of his way to perform "good deeds" for Jewish friends and acquaintances. When the trials of war criminals started, there was hardly a defendant who could not produce evidence that he had helped some half-Jewish physics professor, or that he had used his influence to permit a Jewish symphony conductor to conduct a little while longer, or that he had intervened on behalf of some couple in mixed marriage in connection with an apartment. While these courtesies were petty in comparison with the destructive conceptions that these men were implementing concurrently, the "good deeds" performed an important psychological function. They separated "duty" from personal feelings. They preserved a sense of "decency." The destroyer of the Jews was no "anti-Semite."

Staatssekretär Keppler of the Office of the Four-Year Plan was interrogated after the war as follows:

Question [by Dr. Kempner of the prosecuting staff]: Tell me, Mr. Keppler, why were you so terribly against the Jews? Did you know the Jews?

Answer: I had nothing against the Jews.

Question: I am asking for the reason. You were no friend of the Jews?

Answer: Jews came to me. Warburg invited me. Later Jews looked me up in the Reich Chancellery and asked me to join the board of directors of the Deutsche Bank.

Question: When were you supposed to join the board of directors?

Answer: I didn't want to; it was in 1934, they wanted to give me a written assurance that I would be a director in half a year. If I had been such a hater of Jews, they would not have approached me.

Question: But you transferred capital from Jews into Aryan hands.

Answer: Not often. I know the one case of Simson-Suhl. Also the Skoda-Wetzler Works in Vienna. But it turned out that was no Jewish enterprise.

Keppler was then asked whether he had not favored the "disappearance" of the Jews from Germany. The Staatssekretär fell back on Warburg, with whom he had once had an "interesting discussion." The interrogator broke in with the remark that "now we do not want to talk about anti-Semitism but about the Final Solution of the Jewish question." In that connection, Keppler was asked whether he had heard of Lublin. The Staatssekretär admitted hesitantly that he had heard of Lublin and offered the explanation that he was "deeply touched by this matter." What did Keppler do when he was touched like this? "It was very unpleassnt for me, but after all it was not even in my sphere of jurisdiction."

Another defendant in a war crimes trial, the former commander in Norway, Generaloberst von Falkenhorst, offered the following explanations for his order to remove Jews from Soviet prisoner-of-war battalions in his area. Falkenhorst pointed out that, to begin with, there were no Jews among these prisoners, for the selection had already taken place in Germany (i.e., the Jewish prisoners had already been shot as they were shuttled through the Reich). The order was consequently "entirely superfluous and might just as well not have been included. It was thoughtlessly included by the officer of my staff who was working on it, from the instructions sent to us, and I overlooked it." The general then continued:

> For the rest it may be inferred from this that the Jewish question played as infamous a part in Norway as elsewhere, and that I and the Army were supposed to have been particularly anti-Semitic.
>
> Against this suspicion I can only adduce the following: First, that in Scandinavian countries there are only very few Jews. These few are hardly ever in evidence. The sum total in Norway was only about 350. [Actual figure, 2,000.] A negligible number among two or three million Norwegians. These [Jews] were collected by [Reichskommissar] Terboven and according to orders despatched to Germany by steamship. In this manner the Jewish problem in Norway was practically solved [i.e., by deportation to Auschwitz].
>
> As regards myself, I made at this time an application to Terboven at the request of the Swedish Consul, General Westring, in Oslo, who did not much like visiting Terboven, for the release of a Jew of Swedish nationality and of his family with permission to leave the country, gladly and, as a matter of course, fulfilling the Consul's wish to facilitate the return of these people to Stockholm.
>
> If I had been a rabid anti-Semite I could, without further ado, have refused this request, for the matter did not concern me in the slightest.
>
> On the one hand, however, I wanted to help the Swedish Consul, and, on the other hand, I have nothing against the Jews. I have read and heard their writings and compositions with interest, and their achievements in the field of science are worthy of the highest respect. I have met many fine and honorable people among them.

How widespread the practice of "good deeds" must have been may be gauged from the following remark by Heinrich Himmler: "And then they come, our 80,000,000 good Germans, and each one has his decent Jew. It is clear, the others are swine, but this one is a first-class Jew. Of all those who speak thus, no one has seen it, no one has gone through it." But even if Himmler regarded these interventions as expressions of misplaced humanity, they were necessary tools in the attempt to crystallize one of the important justifications for bureaucratic action—duty. Only after a man had done "everything humanly possible" could he devote himself to his destructive activity in peace.

The third justification was the rationalization that one's own activity was not criminal, that the next fellow's action was the criminal act. The Ministerialrat who was signing papers could console himself with the thought that he did not do the shooting. But that was not enough. He had to be sure that *if* he were ordered to shoot, he would not follow orders but would draw the line right then and there.

The following exchange took place during a war crimes trial. A Foreign Office official, Albrecht von Kessel, was asked by defense counsel (Dr. Becker) to explain the meaning of "Final Solution."

> *Answer:* This expression "final solution" was used with various meanings. In 1936 "final solution" meant merely that all Jews should leave Germany. And, of course, it was true that they were to be robbed; that wasn't very nice, but it wasn't criminal.
>
> *Judge Maguire:* Was that an accurate translation?
>
> *Dr. Becker:* I did not check on the translation. Please repeat the sentence.
>
> *Answer:* I said it was not criminal; it was not nice, but it was not criminal. That is what I said. One didn't want to take their life; one merely wanted to take money away from them. That was all.

The most important characteristic of this dividing line was that it could be *shifted* when the need arose. To illustrate: Once there was a Protestant pastor by the name of Ernst Biberstein. After several years of ministering to his congregation, he moved into the Church Ministry. From that agency he came to another office which was also interested in church matters—the Reich Security Main Office. That agency assigned him to head a local Gestapo office. Finally he became the chief of Einsatzkommando 6 in southern Russia. As commander of the Kommando, Biberstein killed two or three thousand people. These people, in his opinion, had forfeited the right to live under the rules of war. Asked if there were Jews among the victims, he replied: "It is very difficult to determine that. Also, I was told at that time that wherever there were Armenians, there were not so many Jews." To Biberstein the moral dividing line was like the receding horizon. He walked toward it, but he could never reach it.

Among the participants in the destruction process there were very few who did not shift the line when they had to cross the threshold. One reason why the person of Generalkommissar Kube is so important is that he had a firm line beyond which he could not pass. The line was arbitrary, and very advanced. He sacrificed Russian Jews and fought desperately only for the German Jews in his area. But the line was fixed. It was not movable, it was not imaginary, it was not self-deceptive. We have indicated that the destruction process was autonomous, that it could not be stopped internally. The adjustable moral standard was one of the principal tools in the maintenance of this autonomy.

There was a fourth rationalization that implicitly took cognizance of the fact that all shifting lines are unreal. It was a rationalization that was built on a simple premise: No man alone can build a bridge and no man alone can destroy the Jews. The participant in the destruction process was always in company. Among his superiors he could always find those who were doing more than he; among his subordinates he could always find those who were ready to take his place. No matter where he looked, he was one among thousands. His own importance was diminished, and he felt that he was replaceable, perhaps even dispensable.

In such reflective moments the perpetrator quieted his conscience with the thought that he was part of a tide and that there was very little a drop of water could do in such a wave. Ernst Göx, who served in the Order Police and who rode the trains to Auschwitz, was one of those who felt helpless. "I was always a socialist," he said, "and my father belonged to the Socialist Party for fifty years. When we talked with each other—which was often—I always said that if there was still justice, things could not go on like that much longer." When Werner von Tippelskirch, a Foreign Office official, was interrogated after the war, he pointed out that he had never protested against the killing of Jews in Russia because he had been "powerless." His superiors, Erdmanns-dorff, Wörmann, and Weizsäcker, had also been "powerless." All of them had waited for a "change of regime." Asked by Prosecutor Kemp-ner whether it was right to wait for a change of regime "and in the meantime send thousands of people to their death," von Tippelskirch replied, "A difficult question." For Staatssekretär von Weizsäcker him-self the question of what he could have done was circular. If he had had influence he would have stopped measures altogether. But the "if" presupposed a fairyland. In such a land he would not have had to use his influence.

The fifth rationalization was the most sophisticated of all. It was also a last-ditch psychological defense, suited particularly to those who saw through the self-deception of superior orders, impersonal duty, the shifting moral standard, and the argument of powerlessness. It was a rationalization also for those whose drastic activity or high position placed them out of reach of orders, duty, moral dividing lines, and helplessness. It was the jungle theory.

Oswald Spengler once explained this theory in the following words: "War is the primeval policy of all living things, and this to the extent that in the deepest sense combat and life are identical, for when the will to fight is extinguished, so is life itself." Himmler remembered this theory when he addressed the mobile killing personnel at Minsk. He told them to look at nature. Wherever they would look, they would find combat. They would find it among animals and among plants. Whoever tired of the fight went under.

From this philosophy Hitler himself drew strength in moments of meditation. Once, at the dinner table, when he thought about the destruction of the Jews, he remarked with stark simplicity: "One must not have mercy with people who are determined by fate to perish."

T H E V I C T I M S

So far we have pointed out how the Germans overcame their administrative and psychological obstacles. We have dealt with the problems of the bureaucratic machine. But the internal technocratic and moral conflicts do not fully explain what happened. In a destruction process the perpetrators do not play the only role; the process is shaped by the victims too. It is the *interaction* of perpetrators and victims that is "fate." We must therefore discuss the reactions of the Jewish community and analyze the role of the Jews in their own destruction.

When confronted by a force, a group can react in five ways: by resistance, by an attempt to alleviate or nullify the threat (the undoing reaction), by evasion, by paralysis, or by compliance. Let us consider each in turn.

The reaction pattern of the Jews is characterized by almost complete lack of resistance. In marked contrast to German propaganda, the documentary evidence of Jewish resistance, overt or submerged, is very slight. On a European-wide scale the Jews had no resistance organization, no blueprint for armed action, no plan even for psychological warfare. They were completely unprepared. In the words of Anti-Partisan Chief and Higher SS and Police Leader Russia Center von dem Bach, who observed Jews and killed them from 1941 to the end:

Thus the misfortunate came about . . . . I am the only living witness but I must say the truth. Contrary to the opinion of the National Socialists that the Jews were a highly organized group, the appalling fact was that they had no organization whatsoever. The mass of the Jewish people were taken completely by surprise. They did not know at all what to do; they had no directives or slogans as to how they should act. That is the greatest lie of anti-Semitism because it gives the lie to the slogan that the Jews are conspiring to dominate the world and that they are so highly organized. In reality they had no organization of their own at all, not even an information service. If they had had some sort of organization, these people could have been saved by the millions; but instead they were taken completely by surprise. Never before has a people gone as unsuspectingly to its disaster. Nothing was prepared. Absolutely nothing. It was not so, as the anti-Semites say, that they were friendly to the Soviets. That is the most appalling misconception of all. The Jews in the old Poland, who were never communistic in their sympathies, were, throughout the area of the Bug eastward, more afraid of Bolshevism than of the Nazis. This was insanity. They could have been saved. There were people among them who had much to lose, business people; they didn't want to leave. In addition there was love of home and their experience with pogroms in Russia. After the first anti-Jewish actions of the Germans, they thought now the wave was over and so they walked back to their undoing.

The Jews were not oriented toward resistance. Even those who contemplated a resort to arms were given pause by the thought that for a limited success of a handful, the multitude would suffer the consequences. Outbreaks of resistance were consequently infrequent, and almost always they were local occurrences that transpired at the last moment. Measured in German casualties, Jewish armed opposition shrinks into insignificance. The most important engagement was fought in the Warsaw ghetto (sixteen dead and eighty-five wounded on the German side, including collaborators). Following the breakout from the Sobibór camp, there was a count of nine SS men killed, one missing, one wounded, and two collaborators killed. In Galicia sporadic resistance resulted in losses also to SS and Police Leader Katzmann (eight dead, twelve wounded). In addition, there were clashes between Jewish partisans and German forces in other parts of the east, and occasional acts of resistance by small groups and individuals in ghettos and killing centers. It is doubtful that the Germans and their collaborators lost more than a few hundred men, dead and wounded, in the course of the destruction process. The number of men who dropped out because of disease, nervous breakdowns, or court martial proceedings was probably greater. The Jewish resistance effort could not seriously impede or retard the progress of destructive operations. The Germans brushed that resistance aside as a minor obstacle, and in the totality of the destruction process it was of no consequence.

The second reaction was an attempt to avert the full force of German measures. The most common means of pursuing this aim were written and oral appeals. By pleading with the oppressor, the Jews sought to transfer the struggle from a physical to an intellectual and moral plane. If only the fate of the Jews could be resolved with arguments rather than with physical resources and physical combat—so Jewry reasoned—there would be nothing to fear. A petition by Rabbi Kaplan to French Commissioner Xavier Vallat reflects this Jewish mentality. Among other things, the rabbi pointed out that a pagan or an atheist had the right to defame Judaism, but in the case of a Christian, did not such an attitude appear "spiritually illogical as well as ungrateful?" To prove his point, Kaplan supplied many learned quotations. The letter is as though it were not written in the twentieth century. It is reminiscent of the time toward the close of the Middle Ages when Jewish rabbis used to dispute with representatives of the Church over the relative merits of the two religions.

Yet, in various forms, some more eloquent than others, the Jews appealed and petitioned wherever and whenever the threat of concentration and deportation struck them: in the Reich, in Poland, in Russia, in France, in the Balkan countries, and in Hungary. Everywhere the Jews pitted words against rifles, dialectics against force, and almost everywhere they lost.

Petitioning was an established tradition, familiar to every Jewish household, and in times of great upheaval many a common man composed his own appeal. Ghettoization curtailed this independent activity, as individual Jews no longer had regular access to "supervisory authorities." Families exposed to particular privations were now dependent on Jewish councils or other Jewish institutions for immediate relief. The councils in turn became the representatives of the community vis-à-vis the perpetrator. They carefully formulated statements and addressed them to appropriate offices.

In satellite countries, such as Romania and Bulgaria, the Jewish leadership would probe for weaknesses or sympathy at the highest levels of government; at that, the eventual outcomes of Jewish representations to these unstable rulers hinged on the evolving fortunes of war. In German-occupied Salonika, Rabbi Koretz "tearfully" asked Greek puppet officials to intercede with the German overlords, lest the 2,000-year-old community of that city be totally "liquidated." His was a lost cause. In the ghettos of Poland, the Jewish councils had few opportunities to approach any ranking administrator. The chairman of the

Warsaw Jewish Council, Adam Czerniaków, would make weekly rounds to see various German functionaries. He would outline his problems to them and occasionally he would ask them to transmit his requests to their superiors. At night he poured his frustrations into a diary.

The ghetto councils in particular had to plead for what they needed, whether it was food, coal, or the right to levy taxes. At the same time they would also try to ward off a danger (an arrest of hostages) or seek a reduction of hardship (an early curfew). When Czerniaków was required to finance the ghetto wall, he argued in effect that a prisoner does not pay for his prison.

In a flow of petitions the fewest were ever approved, but a very small success had a significant effect on the petitioners. With the grant of some concession, the German supervisor would instantaneously become a patron. He might only allow some soap to be shipped into a ghetto for hygienic reasons, or he might permit the reopening of schools for a temporary normalization, or he might authorize the transfer of municipal fees, in the amount contributed by ghetto tenants, to Jewish organizations for welfare. Any manifestation of such solicitude would encourage the pleaders and fetter them even more to their course of action.

The largest setbacks, on the other hand, would not put an end to the entreaties. Failure of efforts on behalf of an entire group would lead to maneuvers to save it in part. Internal struggles could then ensue over the contents and timing of an appeal. The preparation of a list could become a matter of life and death—not to be included was to be abandoned. An example is the conflict within the Vienna Jewish community over the petitioning for exemptions from deportations. At the end of 1941, when the community organization made an "agreement" with the Gestapo about "exempt" categories, the head of the Jewish war invalids, who had been left out of the "negotiations," accused the deportation expert of the Community (Kultusgemeinde) of "sacrificing" the disabled veterans. Later on, when the war invalids were pressed to the wall, the leaders of the veterans' organization discussed the advisability of presenting an independent petition. One of the war-invalid chiefs remarked: "Fundamentally, I am of the opinion that we cannot afford a war with the Kultusgemeinde." Another commented: "The Hauptsturmführer will say to himself 'These are Jews, and those are Jews. Let them fight among themselves. Why should I worry about that?' He [the SS-Hauptsturmführer] will eventually drop us in this matter." Thereupon the head of the war veterans said: "My answer is that in such an eventuality it will be time to disband our organization."

In many situations the Jews would also use bribes. Money was more effective than verbal submissions, but the objects attained by such payments were limited and the benefits short-lived. Typical were offers for the release of forced laborers or a ransom of Jews about to be shot. Sometimes the aim was more diffuse. If key officials could profit personally from the continued existence of the community, they might help to keep it alive. Not surprisingly, the bribery worried Heinrich Himmler. It did not, however, affect the progress of his operations.

There was yet another way in which the Jews tried to avoid disaster. They anticipated German wishes, or divined German orders, or attempted to be useful in serving German needs. A Jewish council in Kislovodsk (Caucasus), acting with full awareness of the German threat, confiscated all Jewish valuables, including gold, silver, carpets, and clothing, and handed the property to the German Commander. The council in Šiauliai (Lithuania) had been asked three times whether any births had occurred in the ghetto and, each time it had replied in the negative. At one point, however, the council was confronted with twenty pregnancies. It decided to use persuasion and, if need be, threats on the women to submit to abortions. One woman was in her eighth month. The council decided that in this case a doctor would induce premature birth and that a nurse would kill the child. The nurse would be told to proceed in such a way that she would not know the nature of her act.

The most important mode of anticipatory action was the widespread effort, particularly in Eastern Europe, to seek salvation through labor. Indeed, the records of several ghettos reveal an upward curve of employment and output. The zeal with which the Jews applied themselves to the German war effort accentuated the differences of interests that paired industry and armament inspectorates against the SS and Police, but the Germans were resolving their conflicts to the detriment of the Jews. Generally, Jewish production did not rise fast enough or high enough to support the entire community. In the balance of payments of many an East European ghetto, the gap between income and subsistence living could not be bridged with limited outside relief or finite sales of personal belongings. Starvation was increasing, and the death rate began to rise. The clock was winding down even as German deportation experts were appearing at the ghetto gates. Ultimately, "productivization" did not save the ghettos. The Germans deported the unemployed, the sick, the old, the children. Then they made distinctions between less essential and more essential labor. In the final reckoning, all of Jewish labor was still Jewish.

The Jewish dedication to work was based on a calculation that liberation might come in time. To hold on was the essential consideration also of appeals and the many forms of Jewish "self-help," from the elaborate social services in the ghetto communities to the primitive "organization" in the killing centers. The Jews could not hold on; they could not survive by appealing.

The basic reactions to force are fundamentally different from each other. Resistance is opposition to the perpetrator. Nullification or alleviation is opposition to the administrative enactment. In the third reaction, evasion, the victim tries to remove himself from the effects of force by fleeing or hiding. The phenomenon of flight is more difficult to analyze. We know that the emigration of approximately 350,000 Jews from Germany and German-occupied Czechoslovakia before the war was forced. In many cases the emigrating Jews had been deprived of their livelihood, and they reacted to the consequences of anti-Jewish measures rather than in anticipation of disaster. The flight of the Belgian and Parisian Jews in 1940 and the evacuation of Soviet Jews a year later was compounded with mass migrations of non-Jews. Here again, the flight was not a pure reaction to the threat of the destruction process but also a reaction to the war. We know that only a few thousand Jews escaped from the ghettos of Poland and Russia; that only a few hundred Jews hid out in the large cities of Berlin, Vienna, and Warsaw; that only a handful of Jews escaped from camps. Von dem Bach mentions that in Russia there was an unguarded escape route to the Pripet Marshes, but few Jews availed themselves of the opportunity. In the main, the Jews looked upon flight with a sense of futility. The great majority of those who did not escape early did not escape at all.

There were instances when in the mind of the victim the difficulties of resistance, undoing, or evasion were just as great as the problem of automatic compliance. In such instances the futility of all alternatives became utterly clear, and the victim was paralyzed. Paralysis occurred only in moments of crisis. During ghetto-clearing operations, many Jewish families were unable to fight, unable to petition, unable to flee, and also unable to move to the concentration point to get it over with. They waited for the raiding parties in their homes, frozen and helpless. Sometimes the same paralytic reaction struck Jews who walked up to a killing site and for the first time gazed into a mass grave half-filled with the bodies of those who had preceded them.

The fifth reaction was automatic compliance. To assess the administrative significance of that cooperation, one must view the destruction process as a composite of two kinds of German measures: those that perpetrated something upon the Jews and involved only action by Germans, such as the drafting of decrees, the running of deportation trains, shooting, or gassing, and those that required the Jews to do something, for instance, the decrees or orders requiring them to register their property, obtain identification papers, report at a designated place for labor or deportation or shooting, submit lists of persons, pay fines, deliver up property, publish German instructions, dig their own graves, and so on. A large component of the entire process depended on Jewish participation—the simple acts of individuals as well as organized activity in councils.

Often the Jews were marshaled by the Germans directly. Word would come through ordinances, placards, or loudspeakers. In answer to summonses, lines would form or processions would march, almost without end. To some close observers of these scenes, the assembled crowds appeared to have lost all capacity for independent thought. Jewish resistance organizations attempting to reverse the mass inertia spoke the words: "Do not be led like sheep to slaughter." Franz Stangl, who had commanded two death camps, was asked in a West German prison about his reaction to the Jewish victims. He said that only recently he had read a book about lemmings. It reminded him of Treblinka.

Not all Jewish cooperation was purely reflexive observance of German instructions, nor was all of it the last act of emaciated, forsaken people. There was also an institutional compliance by Jewish councils employing assistants and clerks, experts and specialists. During the concentration stage the councils conveyed German demands to the Jewish population and placed Jewish resources into German hands, thereby increasing the leverage of the perpetrator in significant ways. The German administration did not have a special budget for destruction, and in the occupied countries it was not abundantly staffed. By and large, it did not finance ghetto walls, did not keep order in ghetto streets, and did not make up deportation lists. German supervisors turned to Jewish councils for information, money, labor, or police, and the councils provided them with these means every day of the week. The importance of this Jewish role was not overlooked by German control organs. On one occasion a German official emphatically urged that "the authority of the Jewish council be upheld and strengthened under all circumstances."

Members of the Jewish councils were genuine if not always representative Jewish leaders who strove to protect the Jewish community from the most severe exactions and impositions and who tried to normalize Jewish life under the most adverse conditions. Paradoxically, these very attributes were being exploited by the Germans against the Jewish victims.

The fact that so many of the council members had roots in the Jewish community or had been identified from prewar days with its concerns gave them a dual status. They were officiating with the authority conferred upon them by the Germans but also with the authenticity they derived from Jewry. Day by day they were reliable agents in the eyes of the German perpetrators while still retaining the trust of Jews. The contradiction became sharper and sharper even as they kept on appealing, to the Germans for relief, to the Jews for acquiescence.

Similarly, when the councils endeavored to obtain concessions, they made a subtle payment. Placing themselves into a situation of having to wait for German decisions, they increased not only their own subservience but also that of the entire community, which perforce was waiting as well.

The councils could not subvert the continuing process of constriction and annihilation. The ghetto as a whole was a German creation. Everything that was designed to maintain its viability was simultaneously promoting a German goal. The Germans were consequently aided not only by Jewish enforcement agencies but also by the community's factories, dispensaries, and soup kitchens. Jewish efficiency in allocating space or in distributing rations was an extension of German effectiveness, Jewish rigor in taxation or labor utilization was a reinforcement of German stringency, even Jewish incorruptibility could be a tool of German administration. In short, the Jewish councils were assisting the Germans with their good qualities as well as their bad, and the very best accomplishments of a Jewish bureaucracy were ultimately appropriated by the Germans for the all-consuming destruction process.

If we should now review the Jewish reaction pattern, we would see its two salient features as a posture of appeals alternating with compliance. What accounts for this combination? What factors gave rise to it? The Jews attempted to tame the Germans as one would attempt to tame a wild beast. They avoided "provocations" and complied instantly with decrees and orders. They hoped that somehow the German drive would spend itself. This hope was founded in a 2,000-year-old experience. In exile the Jews had always been a minority, always in danger, but they had learned that they could avert or survive destruction by placating and appeasing their enemies. Even in ancient Persia an appeal by Queen Esther was more effective than the mobilization of an army. Armed resistance in the face of overwhelming force could end only in disaster.

Thus over a period of centuries the Jews had learned that in order to survive they had to refrain from resistance. Time and again they were attacked. They endured the Crusades, the Cossack uprisings, and the czarist persecution. There were many casualties in these times of stress, but always the Jewish community emerged once again like a rock from a receding tidal wave. The Jews had never really been annihilated. After surveying the damage, the survivors had always proclaimed in affirmation of their strategy the triumphant slogan, "The Jewish people lives [*Am Israel Chai*]." This experience was so ingrained in the Jewish consciousness as to achieve the force of law. The Jewish people could not be annihilated.

Only in 1942, 1943, and 1944 did the Jewish leadership realize that, unlike the pogroms of past centuries, the modern machinelike destruction process would engulf European Jewry. But the realization came too late. A 2,000-year-old lesson could not be unlearned; the Jews could not make the switch. They were helpless.

Let us not suppose, however, that compliance was easy. If it was difficult for the Germans to kill, it was harder still for the Jews to die. Compliance is a course of action that becomes increasingly drastic in a destruction process. It is one thing to comply with an order to register property but quite another to obey orders in front of a grave. The two actions *are* part of the same habit. The Jews who registered their property were also the ones who lined up to be killed. The Jews who lined up on a killing site were the ones who had registered their property. Yet these two activities are very different in their effects. Submission is altogether more burdensome in its last stages than in its beginning, for as one goes on, more and more is lost. Finally, in the supreme moment of crisis the primeval tendency to resist aggression breaks to the surface. Resistance then becomes an obstacle to compliance, just as compliance is an obstacle to resistance. In the Jewish case the cooperation reaction was the stronger one until the end.

European Jewry consequently made every effort to reinforce its traditional behavior, much as the German bureaucrats were buttressing their thrust into destruction. The Jews, like the Germans, developed psychic mechanisms for suppressing unbearable truths and for rationalizing extreme decisions. One is struck by the fact that the Germans repeatedly employed very crude deceptions and ruses. The Jews were bluffed with "registrations" and "resettlements," with "baths" and "inhalations." At each stage of the destruction process the victims thought that they were going through the last stage. And so it appears that one of the most gigantic hoaxes in world history was perpetrated on five million people noted for their intellect. But were these people really fooled? Or did they deliberately fool themselves?

The Jews did not always have to be deceived, they were capable of deceiving themselves. Not everyone discovered everything at once—that would hardly have been possible. But neither could the discovery of the "Final Solution" be avoided indefinitely by all. Even those who were sealed in their ghettos had to become conscious of a growing silence outside. The killings might have been secluded and shrouded in secrecy, but the disappearance of people could not be concealed. In the

Warsaw ghetto, the isolated Adam Czerniaków wrote down statistics of Jews deported from Lublin and other cities, and, as he did so, he could not ward off thoughts about the ominous implications of those occurrences. Yet rumors and reports seeping through ghetto walls did not reverse the momentum of Jewish actions. The Jewish leadership clung to the tenet that German orders could not be refused in the absence of clear evidence that the victims were facing an imminent death. Seldom did the councils ask themselves if they should go on without reliable indications that everyone would be safe. Sometimes, notably in Belgium and Slovakia, facts were gathered systematically and passed on to England or Switzerland. More often the news was not placed on the table, and inevitable conclusions were not drawn. Between growing doubts and unwanted revelations, the councils persevered in their course. In two instances council chairmen approached the *Germans* for information. In July 1942, Czerniaków repeatedly asked German Security Police officers if the deportations were going to start. He was assured that the rumors were untrue. The Viennese Elder, Löwenherz, walked into the Vienna Gestapo office to inquire whether the deportees were actually dead. He was told they were alive.

In the Łódź ghetto, where mass deportations began as early as January 1942 and from which more than a fourth of the residents were removed by April of that year, an SS officer explained that the deportees were staying in a well-equipped camp, repairing roads and working in agriculture. The very next month, truckloads of clothing were unloaded in ghetto warehouses. Letters and identity cards fell out of the garments. No more had to be found out. After the subsequent deportation waves, the Jewish ghetto chroniclers would chart the mood of the remaining people by noting the fluctuating prices of a consumers' product. The commodity was saccharin.

In Lithuania the Jewish population was inundated by shootings from the very beginning. We know from a detailed report of Einsatzkommando 3 how in seventy-one localities the Jews were being decimated. Fourteen of these communities were struck more than once at intervals averaging a week. A residual fraction of Lithuanian Jewry clung to what was left. One survivor of the Kaunas ghetto recalls that in its closing days the slogan of the victims was "life for an hour is also life."

Throughout Europe the Jewish communities strove for continuity. They treated the sick who would not have time to recover, they fed the unemployed who would not work again, they educated the children who would not be allowed to grow up. For a middle-aged leadership there was no alternative. Younger people also were caught in the psychological web. The children, however, were least prone to fall into illusion.

When in the Theresienstadt ghetto a transport of children was funneled to ordinary showers, they cried out: "No gas!"

The Jewish repressive mechanism was largely self-administered, and it could operate automatically, without any misleading statements or promises by German functionaries or their non-German auxiliaries. In the minutes of meetings held by the Vienna Jewish war invalids, we discover the same significant absence of direct references to death and killing centers that we have already noted in German correspondence. The Jewish documents abound with such roundabout expressions as "favored transport" (meaning Theresienstadt transport), "I see black," "to tempt fate," "final act of the drama," etc. The direct word is lacking.

The attempt to repress unbearable thoughts was characteristic not only of the ghetto community but of the killing center itself. In Auschwitz the inmates employed a special terminology of their own for killing operations. A crematorium was called a "bakery," a man who could no longer work—and who was therefore destined for a gas chamber—was designated a "Moslem," and the depot holding the belongings of the gassed was named "Canada." These, it must be emphasized, are not Nazi terms; they are expressions by the victims. They are the counterparts of the Nazi vocabulary and, like the German euphemisms, they were designed to blot out visions of death.

There were junctures, of course, when the issue could not be evaded, when forgetting was no longer effective. In such moments of crisis the victims, like the perpetrators, resorted to rationalizations. The Jews, too, had to justify their actions. It is interesting to note how the two principal rationalizations emerged directly from the repressive pattern.

The Germans were notably successful in deporting Jews by stages, because those who remained behind would reason that it was necessary to sacrifice the few in order to save the many. The operation of this psychology may be observed in the Vienna Jewish community, which concluded a deportation "agreement" with the Gestapo, with the "understanding" that six categories of Jews would not be deported. Again, the Warsaw ghetto Jews argued in favor of cooperation and against resistance on the grounds that the Germans would deport sixty thousand Jews but not hundreds of thousands. The bisection phenomenon occurred also in Salonika, where the Jewish leadership cooperated with the German deportation agencies upon the assurance that only "Communist" elements from the poor sections would be deported, while the "middle-class" would be left alone. This fatal arithmetic was also applied in Vilna, where Judenrat chief Gens declared: "With a hundred victims I save a thousand people. With a thousand I save ten thousand."

In situations where compliance with death orders could no longer be rationalized as a life-saving measure, there was still one more justification: the argument that with rigid, instantaneous compliance, unnecessary suffering was eliminated, unnecessary pain avoided, and necessary torture reduced. The entire Jewish community, and particularly the leadership, now concentrated all its efforts in one direction—to make the ordeal bearable, to make death easy.

This effort is reflected in the letter the Jewish Council in Budapest sent to the Hungarian Interior Minister on the eve of the deportations: "We emphatically declare that we do not seek this audience in order to lodge complaints about the merit of the measures adopted, but merely ask that they be carried out with a humane spirit."

Moritz Henschel, chief of the Berlin Jewish community from 1940 to 1943, defended the assistance rendered by his administration to the Germans during the roundups in the following words:

> It could be asked: "How could you permit yourself to take part in this work in any manner whatsoever?" We cannot really decide whether we acted for the best, but the idea which guided us was the following: if we do these things, then this will always be carried out in a better and gentler way than if others take it upon themselves—and this was correct. Direct transports by the Nazis were always done roughly—with terrible roughness.

And this was Rabbi Leo Baeck, chief of the Reich Association of Jews in Germany:

> I made it a principle to accept no appointments from the Nazis and to do nothing which might help them. But later, when the question arose whether Jewish orderlies should help pick up Jews for deportation, I took the position that it would be better for them to do it, because they could at least be more gentle and helpful than the Gestapo and make the ordeal easier. It was scarcely in our power to oppose the order effectively.

When Baeck was in Theresienstadt, an engineer who had escaped from Auschwitz informed him about the gassings. Baeck decided not to pass on this information to anyone in the ghetto city because "living in the expectation of death by gassing would only be harder."

The supreme test of the compliance reaction came in front of the grave. Yet here, too, the Jews managed to console themselves. From one of the numerous German eyewitness reports comes the following typical passage:

> The father was holding the hand of a boy about ten years old and was speaking to him softly; the boy was fighting his tears. The father pointed to the sky, stroked his head, and seemed to explain something to him. . . . I remember a girl, slim and with black hair, who passed close to me, pointed to herself, and said, "Twenty-three." . . . The people, completely naked,

went down some steps which were cut in the clay wall of the pit and clambered over the heads of the people lying there, to the place where the SS man directed them. Then they lay down in front of the dead or injured people; some caressed those who were still alive and spoke to them in a low voice. Then I heard a series of shots.

The German annihilation of the European Jews was the world's first completed destruction process. For the first time in the history of Western civilization the perpetrators had overcome all administrative and moral obstacles to a killing operation. For the first time, also, the Jewish victims, caught in the straightjacket of their history, plunged themselves physically and psychologically into catastrophe. The destruction of the Jews was thus no accident. When in the early days of 1933 the first civil servant wrote the first definition of "non-Aryan" into a civil service ordinance, the fate of European Jewry was sealed.

CHAPTER EIGHT

RESCUE

The most effective rescue is that which is undertaken before the danger point has been reached. In the Jewish case this meant emigration before the outbreak of war. However, the prewar migration was limited by two decisive factors. The first was the inability of the European Jews to foresee the future. The second was the limitation of reception facilities for prospective emigrants. Most of the world's surface offered no economic base for a new, productive life, and the two countries that historically had been the most feasible goals of Jewish emigration, the United States and Palestine, were saddled with entry restrictions.

In the United States the maximum number of immigrants to be admitted in one year was fixed in accordance with the following formula:

$$\frac{\text{Yearly quota of admissible persons born in a given country}}{150,000} = \frac{\text{Population of U.S. in 1920 whose "national origin" was traced to such country}}{\text{Total population of European descent in U.S. in 1920}}$$

On April 28, 1938, the "national origin immigration quotas" were consequently distributed as follows:

Great Britain	65,721
Germany (including Austria)	27,370
Eire	17,853
Poland	6,524
Italy	5,802
Sweden	3,314
Netherlands	3,153
France	3,086
Czechoslovakia	2,874
USSR	2,712
Norway	2,377
Switzerland	1,707
Belgium	1,304
Denmark	1,181
Hungary	869

Yugoslavia	845
Finland	569
Portugal	440
Lithuania	386
Romania	377
All other states under the quota system	fewer than 300

Until 1939 the United States provided a ready haven for German- and Austrian-born Jews who wanted to emigrate and who had the money for train and ship fare. That year the German quota was over-subscribed, and many of the Polish-born Jews in the Reich-Protektorat area, assigned to the much smaller quota of Poland, faced a long waiting list.

The Jews were therefore dependent upon Palestine as well. Here, however, they encountered all the difficulties created by British Middle Eastern policy. The British were thinking not only about the Jews but also about the Arabs. In the event of war, the support of the world Jewish community was assured in any case. The Jews could not choose sides; the Arabs could. That consideration was decisive.

The mandate that the British government had received from the League of Nations provided in Article 6 that "the Administration of Palestine, while ensuring that the rights and position of other sections of the population are not prejudiced, shall facilitate Jewish immigration under suitable conditions." These words allowed for considerable inter-pretation. In 1922 the Colonial Secretary (Winston Churchill) inter-preted the provision to hold that "this immigration cannot be so great in volume as to exceed whatever may be the economic capacity of the country at the time to absorb new arrivals. It is essential to ensure that the immigrants should not be a burden upon the people of Palestine as a whole, and that they should not deprive any section of the present population of their employment."

In pursuance of this policy the British allowed unrestricted entry of so-called capitalists, that is, Jews who had a certain amount of money in pounds sterling. Workers, on the other hand, were no longer free to immigrate in unlimited numbers. In May 1939 the Colonial Office moved to bring the Jewish Palestine-bound refugee migration to a conclusion. In a statement of policy that has become known as the "White Paper," the British declared that "His Majesty's government do not read [their previous statements] as implying that the mandate requires them, for all time and in all circumstances, to facilitate the immigration of Jews into Palestine subject only to consideration of the country's economic cap-city." The time had come to take account also of the political situation. The Arab population was exhibiting "widespread . . . fear of indefinite Jewish immigration." Accordingly, Jewish immigration was to be permitted only for another five years, at the rate of 10,000 per year. In addition, "as a contribution to the solution of the Jewish refugee problem," 25,000 refugees were to be admitted as soon as the High Commissioner was satisfied that adequate provision for their maintenance was ensured.

The year 1939 was thus a year of crisis. The number of Jews who were clamoring to get out was greater than the number that the world was willing to receive. In the year before the war the Jews of the Reich-Protektorat area were seeking places of refuge in areas that offered little hope for work and subsistence. Fifty thousand found a haven, at least for an interim period, in Britain. Thousands of families booked passage for Cuba to wait there for quota entry into the United States. Many thousands clogged ships on the way to Japanese-occupied Shanghai. Tens of thousands went only as far as France, Belgium, and Holland, where most of them were overtaken by German armies in 1940. The total picture can no longer be reconstructed with accuracy, for the Jews went from one country to the next, but the following table is an approximate listing, by initial area of departure and ultimate place of destination.

From	
Old Reich and Sudeten	320,000
Austria	130,000
Bohemia-Moravia	25,000

To	
United States	155,000
Palestine	70,000
Other countries out of German reach	up to 150,000
Countries overtaken by Germans	over 100,000

With the onset of the war and the beginning of the "Final Solution of the Jewish question" in Europe, the problem of migration was fundamentally altered. Before the war the Jews made every attempt to hold on, and the Germans applied every pressure to effect a Jewish mass departure. By 1941 all the Jews of German-dominated Europe wanted to leave, but now the German machinery of destruction held them captive.

On the outside the issue between the world Jewish community and the Allied governments had sharpened. Before the war the Jews could argue only that emigration was necessary for the relief of misery, and the Allied position was correspondingly based on "absorptive capacities" and "political considerations." Now rescue had become for the Jews a matter of life and death. If the Nazi ring could not be sprung open and the Jews brought to a safe destination, they would die in mounting numbers as the catastrophe quickened. The British government and its helpers were not moved to drastic action by this situation. The old reasons for barring the Jews from Palestine were even stronger now, and the old arguments with respect to the political situation were reinforced with the war. Significantly, however, the dichotomy between the Jewish and Allied positions was not from the outset clearly visible. The Jews were slow to react to the challenge. When the apparatus of Jewish organizations was finally activated on behalf of the victims in Europe, the Jewish leadership, already confronted with millions of dead, was prepared to do little more than save those who were already safe.

We have pointed out repeatedly that the Jews did not anticipate the "Final Solution." When they woke up to the facts, the disaster was already upon them. By the summer of 1942, however, the volume of deportations and killings had far surpassed the limits within which such an operation could be kept secret from the outside world. Hints, rumors, and reports began to accumulate in information-gathering agencies at widely scattered points.

Yet even then these signals were not fully exploited. Insofar as any messages reached a Jewish organization in Palestine, Britain, or the United States, they rested in uncertain hands. The Jews had not created a central intelligence apparatus of their own. As passive recipients of data they did not build upon knowledge or study documents for clues to larger facts. Hence each new communication came to them as a surprise, even as late as 1944. Allied intelligence agencies were in a better position to assemble and assess information, but they in turn lacked the frame of mind and sense of urgency that would have been required to address the Jewish fate. Consequently, they were either slow to evaluate and disseminate material in their possession or they did not do anything at all.

Without an effective *a priori* intelligence effort aimed at acquisition of precise evidence of critically important German actions against the Jews, a coherent account of the disaster could not emerge in time. Analytical connections were not made, and implications were not seen. The process of destruction was observed mainly in segments: shootings, deportations, and camps. At the beginning, at least, the shooting operations were perceived as incidents of slaying and massacres. Deportations were disappearances, and camps were a virulent form of labor utilization. Not until the end did the true nature of these phenomena become self-evident.

The following are some of the significant reports received by the press, Jewish organizations, and Allied governments, together with the reactions to which these accounts gave rise. It may be noted that throughout the process of discovery, the findings, when published, were seldom front-page news.

During the summer of 1941 and intermittently thereafter, the British Government's Code and Cypher School intercepted and deciphered wireless Order Police reports of shootings in the occupied USSR. These messages, which frequently mentioned Jews, included among others the following:

An SS-Cavalry Brigade report on August 17, 1941, of 7,819 "executions" in the Minsk area

A summary report on the same day by von dem Bach, noting 30,000 shootings

Seventeen reports between August 23 and 31, 1941, on shootings of Jews in groups ranging from 61 to 4,200 in the southern sector

A report on September 12, 1941, by Police Regiment South on the shooting of 1,255 Jews at Ovruch

Intercepts of the German police communications were regularly sent to the Military Intelligence section concerned with Germany (MI 14), and weekly summaries were presented to the Prime Minister.

On March 1, 1942, Dr. Henry Shoskes (Chaim Szoszkies), a Jewish leader who had left Warsaw at the beginning of the German occupation, presented detailed figures of dead in the ghettos of Poland. The monthly average, he said, was 10,000.

From Lisbon, the Office of Strategic Services received a report, dated June 20, 1942, that began with the words "Germany is no longer persecuting the Jews. It is systematically exterminating them." The information came from a British officer who had escaped from captivity by hiding in the Warsaw ghetto at the beginning of June. The officer spoke of filth and malnutrition. "Children die atrophied." He mentioned a "Jewish militia of human vermin." He then said that Himmler had visited Frank in April to tell him that Jews were not disappearing fast enough to please the Führer, and that the orders were the "virtual extermination" of all Jews by a specified date. A trial speeding up had been ordered at Lublin, "where for a time trainloads were taken daily to the Sobibór station in the suburbs, thence to an isolated area where they were machinegunned." Peasants left nearby farms because of the stench of thinly covered corpses.

Following the highly public roundups of Jews in Paris and Warsaw during July, news of the greatest import was received in Switzerland. As summarized in a message, dated August 8, 1942, by the chief of the Geneva office of the World Jewish Congress, Dr. Gerhard Riegner, the report referred to a plan discussed and under consideration in the

Führer headquarters according to which the Jews of Europe were to be deported to the east and "exterminated at one blow" to resolve once and for all the Jewish question in Europe. Among methods "under discussion" for planned action in the autumn was prussic acid. Riegner added that he was transmitting this information "with all necessary reservation as exactitude cannot be confirmed," but that his informant had close connections with highest German authorities and that his reports were generally speaking reliable. His cable was sent via the American and British consulates to Rabbi Stephen Wise in the United States and M. P. Sidney Silverman in England. Silverman got the information, Wise did not. Silverman then transmitted the message to Rabbi Wise. The rabbi, who was American Jewry's most prominent leader, decided to carry the report to Undersecretary of State Sumner Welles. The Undersecretary asked him not to release the story until an attempt could be made to confirm it.

While the State Department was attempting to verify the contents of the Riegner telegram, reports of the Jewish catastrophe were multiplying in the press. *Newsweek* noted on August 10, 1942, that trainloads of Warsaw Jews were vanishing into "black Limbo." On August 20, *The New York Times* quoted the French newspaper *Paris Soir* of the previous day to the effect that Jews from France were being deported to "Polish Silesia." On October 5, 1942, the Jewish Telegraphic Agency reported systematic deportations of Jews from Łódź who, said the agency, "are poisoned by gas." The November 1942 issue of the *Jewish Frontier*, published in New York, contained an exceptionally detailed description of the processing of Jews in Chełmno (Kulmhof), complete with data about gas vans. On November 23, Hebrew newspapers in Palestine, reacting to cumulative reports, appeared with black borders.

It is at this time that Wise, no longer restrained by the Department of State, made his disclosures, and during the next few days, news items appeared in *The New York Times,* albeit in its inside pages. On November 25, the paper carried a report, based on information from the Polish Government in Exile, that mentioned Bełżec, Sobibór, and Treblinka. Added to this article was an item from Jerusalem with details about concrete buildings on the former Russian frontier used as gas chambers and about crematoria at Oświęcim (Auschwitz). The same page contained also a figure, supplied by Dr. Wise, of two million Jewish dead. On the next day, *The New York Times* quoted Dr. Ignacy Szwarcbart, a Jewish member of the Polish National Council in London, to the effect that Jews were being gassed and that in Bełżec they were being subjected to death by electric current. The same issue of the paper cited Dr. Wise with "before" and "after" figures by country. Prussic acid was mentioned by Wise as having been abandoned in favor of air bubbles, and bodies, he said, were being exploited for fat, soap, and lubricants.

Clearly, the transmission and publication of the facts had taken several months. One million Jews had been gassed or shot during this period alone. In the end, accurate statements about these events had been mixed with the rumors of electrocutions and soap making. Incomplete and sketchy as this picture was, it constituted an outline of annihilation. The underpowered Jewish organizations, however, could see no way of dealing with this situation directly. Any independent action against the Germans was altogether inconceivable. Thus, in the United States, the Jewish leadership confined itself to mobilizing support in its own community, the churches, and the government. Within this domestic horizon, much energy was expended on an arousal campaign, complete with plans for demonstrations, processions, broadcasts, and advertisements. The peak of the effort was to be a meeting with Roosevelt, and after a month of lobbying, on December 8, 1942, a five-man delegation was admitted to the White House. The Jewish leaders came with two memoranda, one a twenty-page descriptive summary similar to the contents of newspapers reports then being published, the other a short appeal calling on the President to warn the Nazis and to establish a commission that could receive evidence for submission to "the bar of public opinion." Roosevelt was "cordial" and assured the delegates that their memoranda would be given "full consideration."

Having taken this half-step, the Jewish leaders received a part of what they had asked for. On December 17, 1942, the Allied governments issued a declaration entitled "German Policy of Extermination of the Jewish Race," which stated that the responsible perpetrators "shall not escape retribution."

When the U.S. chargé d'affaires at the Vatican, Harold H. Tittmann, asked Cardinal Secretary of State Maglione whether there was not something the Holy See could do "along similar lines," the cardinal replied that the papacy was "unable to denounce publicly particular atrocities." It could only condemn atrocities in general. For the rest, "everything possible was being done privately to relieve the distress of the Jews." The Pope did utter some public words in his lengthy Christmas message at the end of 1942. As he talked about the war dead, their widows and orphans, the victims of air raids, and refugees, he included a sentence about the "hundreds of thousands" who, without fault and "sometimes only because of their nationality or race," were "consigned to death or to a slow decline." The generality of this language became the subject of a specific discussion between the Pontiff and Tittmann.

On that occasion, Pius XII said that he had spoken "clearly enough," and he was surprised when the American told him that there were some who did not share his belief. The Pope, reiterating his policy, then said to Tittmann that, when talking about atrocities, he could not name the Nazis without at the same time mentioning the Bolsheviks.

Gestures having for the moment been exhausted, no further action was in the offing. For the Jewish leadership, however, an issue had arisen that was not going to disappear. What did these leaders propose to do in this situation? On January 6, 1943, Henry Monsky, president of B'nai Brith, called a preliminary meeting of the American Jewish Conference. In his letter of invitation, which was sent to thirty-four Jewish organizations, he wrote:

> American Jewry, which will be required in large measure to assume the responsibility of representing the interests of our people at the Victory Peace Conference, must be ready to voice the judgment of American Jews along with that of other Jewish communities of the free countries with respect to the post-war status of Jews and the upbuilding of a Jewish Palestine.

In this letter no warning to the Germans is proposed, no scheme to put an end to the destruction process is suggested; the destruction of the European Jews is not even mentioned. The European Jews are already given up, and all thoughts turn to postwar salvage. Clearly the world-wide Jewish action machinery—the network of Jewish pressure groups—was at a standstill. Budgets were at a low point. The Holocaust was unopposed. The paralysis was complete.

On January 21, 1943, Undersecretary of State Welles received Cable 482 from the Legation in Berne. The cable contained a message from Riegner, who reported that Jews were being killed in Poland at the rate of 6,000 a day, and that Jews in Germany and Romania were starving to death. Welles passed on the cable to Wise and instructed Minister Harrison to keep sending full reports from Switzerland. The Jewish organizations now seemed to be jolted. A mass meeting was held in Madison Square Garden, relief agencies doubled their efforts, and rescue schemes poured into Washington.

The Jewish restlessness apparently disquieted the State Department, and the department took the position that the question had to be "explored." Some of its political experts then decided to suppress the flow of information. A cable (numbered 354) was dispatched under the signature of Undersecretary Welles to Harrison in Berne. It referred to "Your cable 482, January 21." The text then proceeded as follows:

> In the future we would suggest that you do not accept reports submitted to you to be transmitted to private persons in the United States unless

such action is advisable because of extraordinary circumstances. Such private messages circumvent neutral countries' censorship and it is felt that by sending them we risk the possibility that steps would necessarily be taken by the neutral countries to curtail or forbid our means of communication for confidential official matter.

The cable was initialed by four officers of the Foreign Service. The message was handled only by the European Division and the political adviser of the State Department; the undersecretary is believed to have signed the document without full awareness of its contents. It appears, then, that the career men were attempting to withhold the information not only from the Jewish community but also from the men who directed the affairs of the United States government.

On March 15, the principal Jewish organizations in the United States formed a Joint Emergency Committee on European Jewish Affairs, and before long, the Jewish leaders were given another opportunity to be heard. British Foreign Secretary Eden had arrived in Washington for conferences with U.S. officials, and on March 27, at noon, Stephen Wise of the American Jewish Congress and Judge Joseph Proskauer of the American Jewish Committee met with Eden at the British Embassy. Invoking an ancient Jewish formula, they suggested that the Allies "issue a public declaration to Hitler asking him to give Jews permission to leave occupied Europe." In reply, Eden characterized the scheme as "fantastically impossible." The Jewish representatives then requested England's help to get the Jews out of Bulgaria. Eden's response to this plea was that "Turkey does not want any more of your people." Wise and Proskauer thereupon went to the State Department to talk with Undersecretary Welles, who promised to press their ideas in a conference with Eden that afternoon.

During that meeting, the American Secretary of State Hull brought up the problem of rescuing the Jews in the presence of President Roosevelt, Harry Hopkins, Undersecretary Welles, British Ambassador Halifax, and the Assistant Undersecretary of State in the British Foreign Office, William Strang. Hopkins summarized the exchange as follows:

> Hull raised the question of the 60 or 70 thousand Jews that are in Bulgaria and are threatened with extermination unless we could get them out and, very urgently, pressed Eden for an answer to the problem. Eden replied that the whole problem of the Jews in Europe is very difficult and that we should move very cautiously about offering to take all Jews out of a country like Bulgaria. If we do that, then the Jews of the world will be wanting us to make similar offers in Poland and Germany. Hitler might well take us up on any such offer and there simply are not enough ships and means of transportation in the world to handle them.

Eden said that the British were ready to take about 60 thousand more Jews to Palestine but the problem of transportation, even from Bulgaria to Palestine is extremely difficult. Furthermore, any such mass movement as that would be very dangerous to security because the Germans would be sure to attempt to put a number of their agents in the group. They have been pretty successful with this technique both in getting their agents into North and South America.

Eden said that the forthcoming conferences in Bermuda on the whole refugee problem must come to grips with this difficult situation.

Eden said he hoped that on our side we would not make too extravagant promises which could not be delivered because of lack of shipping.

The U.S.–British Bermuda conference to which Eden had referred was a forum for futile discussions. When Jewish groups in the United States attempted to elicit some commitments from the Allied governments, a senior American official, Assistant Secretary of State for Special Problems Breckenridge Long, expressed a secret anxiety in his private diary. One danger in such activities, he wrote, was that they might "lend color to the charges of Hitler that we are fighting this war on account of and at the instigation and direction of our Jewish citizens." Given such reasoning, a decision not to help the Jews could be a psychological guarantee of the purity of the Allied cause.

During the following months two abortive rescue schemes were considered in London and Washington. The British government, through the Swiss legation in Berlin, offered to admit to Palestine 5,000 Jewish children from the Generalgouvernement and the occupied eastern territories. The German Foreign Office agreed to deliver the children to Britain in exchange for interned Germans. The British refused to release any Germans on the ground that the children were not nationals of the British Empire. That was where the matter rested.

The second rescue scheme evolved when Undersecretary of State Welles cabled to Berne for more information about the destruction of the European Jews. In reply he received what appears to be a plan by Romanian dictator Antonescu for the release of some 60,000 Jews in exchange for money. The State Department experts were not enthusiastic about a ransoming attempt. They had to be worn down by the department's economic adviser Dr. Herbert Feis, the weighty intervention of the Treasury Department's Foreign Funds Control Division under John Pehle, and an appeal by Rabbi Wise to President Roosevelt himself. After eight months the State Department issued a license enabling Jewish organizations to deposit money to the credit of Axis officials in blocked accounts in Switzerland. The license was issued over the opposition of the British Foreign Office, which—in the words of a note delivered to the American Embassy in London by the British

Ministry of Economic Warfare—was concerned with the "difficulties of disposing of any considerable number of Jews" in the event of their release from Axis Europe.

The rescue effort was failing. Within the State Department there was disinclination to undertake large-scale action, within the Foreign Office there was fear of large-scale success, and within Axis Europe fewer and fewer Jews remained. The frustrations inherent in this situation finally resulted in an establishment of special rescue machinery in the American Jewish community and in the United States government itself.

From August 29 to September 2, 1943, the first session of the American Jewish Conference, which had been called seven months before, met in deliberation. The destruction of the European Jews was still not on its agenda. In the preliminary meeting only two substantive points had been drawn up for discussion: "rights and status of Jews in the post-war world" and "rights of the Jewish people with respect to Palestine." In the words of the B'nai Brith delegate David Blumberg, the purpose of the conference was the formulation of a program to be heeded "by the proper authorities after the war is over." Rabbi Stephen Wise, as delegate of the American Jewish Congress, then declared that the Conference would have to deal immediately with the problem of rescuing European Jewry.

An observer, the chairman of the British section of the World Jewish Congress, Dr. Maurice L. Perlzweig, proposed that the Conference urge the Allied nations to demand from the Axis the release of its Jewish victims and to proclaim the right of asylum for any Jews who should succeed in escaping. The conference thereupon adopted a resolution calling for a "solemn warning" to the Axis and the establishment of a "temporary asylum" for the Jews. The delegates then adjourned and left the business of the conference in the hands of an interim committee which on October 24, 1943, established a rescue commission.

It was late now. More than a year had passed since the receipt of Riegner's momentous telegram, and much that the Jewish leaders had done since then, including their various pressure and publicity oriented activities, was a process of going through motions. Once, the executive vice president of the American Jewish Committee, Morris Waldman, writing to the committee's president Proskauer, said outright that "Nothing will stop the Nazis except their destruction. The Jews of Europe are doomed whether we do or we don't." Moreover, even when the Jewish organizations did something in concert for a perceived emergency, they remained divided over the long-range future. On October 27, 1943, four days after the establishment of the rescue commission by the American Jewish Conference, the adamantly non-Zionist American Jewish Committee withdrew from the Conference. A summary of the position taken by the American Jewish Committee, dated November 8, 1943, contains such points as these: "There is a sharp division among American Jews on the Zionist issue. . . . We should concentrate on winning the war. . . . We have opposed present demands for Jewish control of immigration to Palestine." Proskauer communicated this text to Secretary of State Hull, and the reply, in a two-page letter over Hull's signature, referred directly to the fissure in the Jewish community: "As you indicate," wrote Hull, "there is considerable difference of opinion among the Jewish people as to the policies which should be pursued in rescuing and assisting these unfortunate people, and no one course of action would be agreeable to all persons interested in this problem."

The rescue commission, still functioning, planned its actions in the old groove. One of its efforts was directed toward the creation of a parallel agency in the government. Outside the American Jewish Conference, a newly formed Emergency Committee to Save the Jewish People of Europe, led by a young man, Peter Bergson, exerted pressure as well. Bergson's group short-circuited the uncooperative Assistant Secretary Long, and appealed directly to newly appointed Undersecretary of State Stettinius and to Congress for action. A decisive step was taken when Morgenthau made a "personal report" to Roosevelt on the State Department's conduct in the refugee question. Reacting to this intervention, Roosevelt established a War Refugee Board by executive order, dated January 22, 1944, and named the secretaries of State, Treasury, and War (Hull, Morgenthau, and Stimson) as its members. The executive director was John Pehle of the Treasury Department. The board maintained its own network of special representatives abroad.

The rescue program had thus been centralized. A specific agency had been created for the task. The agency had centers for the receipt of information, means of communication, and powers of negotiation. Moreover, it could call upon private Jewish organizations for detailed knowledge, age-old experience, and—in the event of ransom possibilities—"quickly available funds." The challenge came soon, for in the spring of 1944 Hungarian Jewry was threatened with destruction.

On March 19, 1944, the Hungarian government, which had refused to deport its Jews, was overthrown, and the line to Auschwitz was cleared. For the Germans there was no further barrier; for Hungarian Jewry there was no more protection. Between the Jews and the gas chambers there remained only a series of predetermined bureaucratic steps. However, the activation of these steps required a certain amount of preparation, and the Germans did not have very much time. They were losing the war. Every day the German position was becoming more difficult. The steady buildup of this destructive operation was the work of an administrative machine in which the bolts were already beginning to loosen. Everything therefore depended on the ability of outside forces to recognize these weaknesses and to immobilize the machine before it could deliver its blow, but time was of the essence.

There was now a great deal of information in the hands of the U.S. government. Reports had been obtained with descriptions of Warsaw, Rawa Ruska, Majdanek, and Treblinka. The most remarkable document, however, was about Auschwitz. The two-part report, prepared by a Polish source, was written on August 10 and 12, 1943, and received in London by the Office of Strategic Services (OSS). In the Washington headquarters of the OSS, it was passed by F. L. Belin to Dr. William Langer (Chief of the Research and Analysis Branch) with a note stating that the Polish source had asked that the subject be given publicity. Belin's cover letter was dated April 10, 1944, and was marked "secret." The report contained the following information. The number of prisoners at the moment of writing was 137,000. Up to September 1942, 468,000 nonregistered Jews had been gassed. Between September 1942 and the beginning of June 1943, the camp received approximately 60,000 Jews from Greece; 50,000 from Slovakia and the Protectorate; 60,000 from Holland, Belgium, and France; and 16,000 from Polish towns. At the beginning of August, 15,000 Jews arrived from Sosnowiec and Będzin. Two percent of all of these people were still alive. On arrival, men were separated from women and taken by lorry to the gas chamber in Birkenau. The report added that before entering the gas chamber the condemned were bathed. There were three crematoria in Birkenau that could burn 10,000 people daily. Jewish girls were experimented on with artificial insemination and sterilization. In winter, prisoners worked in wooden shoes. Of more than 14,000 Gypsies, 90 percent had been gassed. Poles were arriving in large numbers; professionals among them had been executed, and women were subjected to sadism. "History," said the report, "knows no parallel of such destruction of human life." As many as 30,000 people had been gassed in a single day. The report went on to list names. The commanding officer was Obersturmbannführer Höss. Hauptsturmführer Schwartz was "one of the most deadly enemies of Poland." Hauptsturmführer Aumeier was stated to be in charge of hangings and shootings. A woman warden, Mandel, was named as a personification of evil. The Political Department was under Untersturmführer Grabner. Oberscharführer Boger and several others were listed as torturers. Although the facts in the report had manifestly been gathered by the Polish underground in the camp itself, the OSS official, Belin, who transmitted the account to

Langer, noted that he had been given no indication as to the reliability of the source. "This report," he said, "is for your information and retention."

Even as the OSS was filing away the most detailed portrayal of Auschwitz that had been brought to its attention, two young Slovak Jews, Rudolf Vrba (then Walter Rosenberg) and Alfred Wetzler, escaped from the camp and made long statements about their observations to the Jewish Council of Slovakia in Žilina. After translation from the Slovak into other languages, the material was sent on to Hungary, Palestine, and Switzerland. Neither the clandestine dissemination of the information nor its subsequent routing was a rapid procedure. In Switzerland, OSS station chief Allen Dulles addressed the document to War Refuge Board representative Roswell McClelland with a note saying "it seems to be more in your line." McClelland immediately dispatched the report to Executive Director Pehle, but by then it was June 16, 1944.

Yet another, inconspicuous, event occured on April 4, 1944: an Allied reconnaissance aircraft appeared over Auschwitz. The flight was the first of several photographic intelligence missions launched for the specific purpose of acquiring information about "Activity at I. G. Farbenindustrie/Synthetic Oil and Synthetic Rubber Works at Oswiecim." From Allied air bases in Italy, Auschwitz had come within range, and as German industrialists were building plants in the eastern portions of the Greater Reich, American bombers of the 15th Air Force were going to strike at these new targets. The Auschwitz industries, according to interpretations of photographs, were partially still under construction, and the output of oil there had not yet risen to significant levels. Hence the building activity was being watched to determine the optimum time for a raid. All the photographs were accordingly centered on Auschwitz III (Monowitz). No one analyzed these pictures at the time to discover what was revealed in their corners: the gas chambers. The bombing of Auschwitz III, with 500-pound bombs, commenced in August and was repeated three times in September and December:

Date	Number of Bombers	Bombs Dropped
August 20, 1944	127 B-17's	1,336
September 13, 1944	96 B-24's	943
December 18, 1944	2 B-17's and 47 B-24's	436
December 26, 1944	95 B-24's	679

The four raids over Monowitz were all aimed at an oil refinery in an estimated area of 1,100 by 1,200 yards and at a rubber plant occupying an area of 1,800 by 1,200 yards. Several facilities were knocked out, but the Germans were able to repair roofs of buildings, and track damage was insufficient to choke traffic. Bombings conducted in formation at fairly high altitudes could not be expected to be highly accurate, and repeated attempts to destroy a target were not an uncommon occurrence. That was the setting in which any proposal to disrupt the killing operations from the air was going to be weighed by Allied governments.

Spurred by the German invasion of Hungary and the Vrba-Wetzler reports of gassings in Auschwitz, several Jewish groups in Bratislava and Budapest requested bombings of the gas chambers in Auschwitz and of the railway lines leading to the death camp. The messages, transmitted to Jerusalem and Switzerland, reached the British and American governments during the second half of June. In Britain the suggestion to bomb Auschwitz was made by Chaim Weizmann (President of the World Zionist Organization) and Moshe Shertok (head of the Political Department of the Jewish Agency in Palestine) in a meeting on June 30 with the Parliamentary Undersecretary for Foreign Affairs, G. H. Hall. They made the point without much emphasis. A week later, on July 6, the two Jewish representatives met with British Foreign Secretary Eden and, at the end of a long list of proposals, added a request for the bombing of the railway lines. Eden replied that he had already referred the gas-chamber bombing suggestion to the Air Ministry and that he would now supplement it by including the railways. An explanatory Jewish note of July 11 stated that bombing the death installations was "hardly likely to achieve the salvation of the victims to any appreciable extent," but that it would constitute a message to the Germans. On August 13, Air Commodore Grant could not find Birkenau. Before anything could be undertaken, he wrote to V. Cavendish-Bentinck of the Joint Intelligence Committee, he would need some aerial photographs of the place. Finally, on September 1, 1944, Richard Law, minister of state in the Foreign Office, sent an official reply to Weizmann. As promised, said Law, Eden had immediately put the proposal to the Secretary of State for Air. The matter had received the most careful consideration of the Air Staff, but because of "the very great technical difficulties involved," the Foreign Office had "no option but to refrain from pursuing the proposal in present circumstances." Law said he realized that the decision was going to prove a "disappointment" to Weizmann, but, he added, "you may feel fully assured that the matter was most thoroughly investigated."

In the meantime, parallel requests had been received by the War Refugee Board in Washington. At the suggestion of Executive Director Pehle, the chairman, Morgenthau, sent a paraphrase of a cable, calling for the bombardment of railway junctions at Kashau *(sic)* and Pressov to the War Department, where Assistant Secretary McCloy passed it on to the Civil Affairs Division, which in turn handed the proposal to the

Operations Division for action. The Operations Division felt that, inasmuch as McCloy had directed the request to the Civil Affairs Division, the reply should come from there. Operations considered that appropriate action on its part could consist of drafting the answer that the Civil Affairs Division might send to Secretary Morgenthau. The suggested phrasing, signed by Major General J. E. Hull (the Operations Division's group chief for theaters of war) on June 26, was that air strikes were "impracticable" for the reason that they would require "diversion of considerable air support essential for the success of our forces now engaged in decisive operations." Pehle then received a cable from his representative in Switzerland (McClelland) containing another proposal for bombings of railway lines, and he promptly renewed his requests on June 29. On July 3, 1944, McCloy's assistant, Colonel Harrison Gerhardt, wrote the following memorandum to McCloy: "I know you told me to 'kill' this but since those instructions, we have received the attached letter from Mr. Pehle. I suggest that the attached reply be sent." The suggested answer contained, almost word for word, the Operations Division's formulation.

Half a million Jews were killed in Auschwitz between May and November 1944. The decision not to bomb the gas chambers during that time was a product, in the first instance, of perceptual insufficiencies: the Jews lacked knowledge; the Allies, motivation. The Jewish proposals, presented in an uncoordinated manner at the last moment, were either incomplete or they failed to provide specifics about the targets. The Allied replies, couched in the ready-made language of diplomatic or bureaucratic usage, were drafted without serious reflection or prolonged preoccupation in matters pertaining to the Jewish disaster. More fundamentally, bombing was an idea whose time had not come. Neither Jewish traditions nor Allied doctrines could make it an imperative. The Jewish leaders were not accustomed to thinking about rescue in terms of physical force, and Allied strategists could not conceive of force for the purpose of rescue.

If any major part of the remaining Jewish community was to be saved, such action would have to be taken with nonphysical means. To this end some preparations had been made. The War Refugee Board and Jewish organizations had posted their representatives at the perimeter of the destruction arena. There the rescuers waited for openings, opportunities, and offers. Incredibly enough, an offer was to come.

On April 6 and 7, at a time when the German momentum in Hungary was approaching its climax, the Armaments Ministry secured from Hitler himself an authorization to remove 100,000 of the expected Jewish deportees from Auschwitz to construction projects that were then being planned by the Pursuit Planes Staff. Two and a half weeks after this diversion had been authorized, Obersturmbannführer Eichmann called to his office in the Budapest Hotel Majestic a leader of the Jewish rescue committee in Hungary, Joel Brand. Eichmann received Brand with words in the following vein:

> Do you know who I am? I have carried out the Aktionen in the Reich—in Poland—in Czechoslovakia. Now it is Hungary's turn. I let you come here to talk business with you. Before that I investigated you—and your people. Those from the Joint and those from the Agency. And I have come to the conclusion that you still have resources. So I am ready to sell you—a million Jews. All of them I wouldn't sell you. That much money and goods you don't have. But a million—that will go. Goods for blood—blood for goods. You can gather up this million in countries which still have Jews. You can take it from Hungary. From Poland. From Austria. From Theresienstadt. From Auschwitz. From wherever you want. What do you want to save? Virile men? Grown women? Old people? Children? Sit down—and talk.

Brand was a careful negotiator. How was he to get goods, he asked, that the Germans could not confiscate on their own? Eichmann had the answer. Brand was to go abroad. He was to negotiate directly with the Allies and bring back a concrete offer. With these words Eichmann dismissed Brand, warning him in parting that the discussion was a Reich secret that no Hungarian was allowed to suspect.

Sometime in the beginning of May, following a railway conference in Vienna that determined the routing of the transports, Eichmann called Brand again. "Do you want a million Jews?" If so, Brand was to leave immediately for Istanbul. He was to bring back an offer to deliver trucks. "You deliver one truck for every hundred Jews. That is not much." The total would be 10,000 vehicles. The trucks had to be new and suitable for winter driving. "You can assure the Allies that these trucks will never be used in the West. They will be employed exclusively on the eastern front." In addition, the Germans would be pleased if the Allies would throw in a few thousand tons of tea, coffee, soap, and other useful items.

Cautiously Brand replied: "Mr. Obersturmbannführer, I personally can believe that you will keep your word, but I do not possess ten thousand trucks. The people with whom I must negotiate in Istanbul will demand guarantees. Nobody is going to deliver ten thousand trucks in advance. What assurance can you offer that these million Jews will actually be freed?"

Eichmann thereupon gave a decisive answer. "You think we are all crooks. You hold *us* for what *you* are. Now I am going to prove to you that I trust you more than you trust me. When you come back from Istanbul and tell me that the offer has been accepted, I will dissolve

Auschwitz and move 10 percent of the promised million to the border. You take over the 100,000 Jews and deliver for them afterwards one thousand trucks. After then the deal will proceed step by step. For every hundred thousand Jews, a thousand trucks. You are getting away cheap."

Brand had to conceal his excitement. For the first time he saw a way out. If the verbal assurance could be given in time, the Jews could score a major breakthrough without delivering a single vehicle. To be sure, the Germans could change their conditions. So far they had made no concessions. But if Brand could return with a promise, the Germans could not kill so long as they wanted the trucks. Without blood, no merchandise.

Eichmann's initiative, according to his testimony in Jerusalem, had been influenced largely by the propensity of rival SS factions to negotiate with the Jews. He was going to confine the offer to freeing 100,000 Jews, but then thought that only a major gesture, involving a million, was going to have any impact. When Himmler approved the scheme, Eichmann was actually surprised. Himmler, believing that the Jews might make deliveries, was thinking about motorizing the 8th SS-Cavalry Division *Florian Geyer* and the 22d SS-Volunteer Cavalry Division *Maria Theresia,* both assigned to Hungary.

The rescue committee now telegraphed to Istanbul that Brand would be arriving there. The answer came quickly: "Joel should come, Chaim will be there." To the committee this could mean only that Chaim Weizmann himself would be on hand.

On May 15 Brand saw Eichmann for the last time. It was the day on which the deportations began. Eichmann warned Brand to return quickly. If the offer came in time, Auschwitz would be "blown up," and the deportees now leaving Hungary would be the first to be sent to the border.

On the following day, Brand secured "full powers" from the Central Council of the Hungarian Jews; he also received a companion: a Jew who had served the Abwehr, Bandi Grosz. The two went to Vienna and, paying for their fare in dollars, left by special plane to Istanbul.

When Brand landed at the Istanbul airport, he made a disturbing discovery. The Jewish Agency had not processed an entry visa for him, and "Chaim" was not there. The man to whom Jerusalem had referred was not the agency's chief executive, Chaim Weizmann, but the chief of its Istanbul office, Chaim Barlasz, and that man was riding around in the city at the very moment of the plane's arrival to obtain a visa for Brand. Fortunately, Brand's counterintelligence companion, Grosz, had many connections in Istanbul. After a few telephone calls by Grosz, the two men were allowed to move into a hotel. There the Jewish Agency representatives were waiting for the emissaries.

Brand was angry and excited. "Comrades, do you realize what is involved? . . . We have to negotiate. . . . With whom can I negotiate? Do you have the power to make agreements? Twelve thousand people are hauled away every day . . . that is five hundred an hour. . . . Do they have to die because nobody from the Executive is here? . . . I want to telegraph tomorrow that I have secured agreement. . . . Do you know what is involved, comrades? The Germans want to negotiate. The ground is burning under their feet. They feel the coming of the catastrophe. Eichmann has promised us an advance of a hundred thousand Jews. Do you know what this means? . . . I insist, comrades, that a man come here whom all the world knows. The Germans are observing us. They will know at once that Weizmann is here or Shertok. Even if you cannot accomplish anything concrete with the Allies while I am here, I can go back and tell Eichmann that the Agency has accepted. Then Auschwitz can be blown up."

To the representatives of the Jewish Agency the matter was not so simple. They could not be sure, they said, that a telegram sent to Jerusalem would arrive there without mutilation. No one had enough influence to obtain a plane. No representative of the War Refugee Board was on the scene. Brand wanted to reach Steinhardt, the American Ambassador in Ankara. "Steinhardt," he said, "is supposed to be a good Jew. And besides that, a good man." But no plane seat could be bought for a trip to Ankara. The hours began to pass, then the days. Brand, still waiting for someone to arrive in Istanbul, gave the Jewish Agency representatives some important data. "I gave the comrades an accurate plan of the Auschwitz concentration camp. I demanded the bombing of the gas chambers and crematories insofar as this was technically possible. I demanded diversions and air strikes against the junctions on the railway lines which led to Auschwitz. I gave our comrades accurate information about places where parachute troops could land, and I gave them a list of documents and other things that the parachutists absolutely had to have to get through. I named a number of addresses of reliable helpers on the roads to Budapest."

Brand had exhausted his mission, and it was exhausting him in turn. In repeated discussions with the Jewish Agency representatives he gained the distinct impression that they did not quite realize what was at stake. "They did not, as we did in Budapest, look daily at death."

As Brand waited for a reply, a number of unexpected things began to happen. For a few days he was in danger of deportation. The Turkish authorities had ordered his apprehension, together with Bandi Grosz, although the latter was a "director" of a Hungarian transport corporation engaged in discussion with the director of a Turkish state transport company. Why the deportation of Grosz? Already Brand suspected that the British were controlling the "main switch," but he dismissed the thought. "I could not believe," he states, "that England—this land which alone fought on while all other countries of Europe surrendered to despotism—that this England which we had admired as the inflexible fighter for freedom wanted simply to sacrifice us, the poorest and weakest of all the oppressed."

Soon, however, another curious situation arose. Moshe Shertok was unable to obtain a visa to Turkey. The agency decided to bring Brand to Aleppo in British-occupied Syria; there Shertok was to meet him. On June 5, 1944, after fifteen fruitless days in Istanbul, Brand, with a British visa in his German passport, boarded the Taurus express train. When the train passed through Ankara, a representative of the Jewish Revisionists (Irgun), accompanied by an Orthodox party man, got on to warn him that he was moving into a "trap." Shertok had not obtained a visa because the British wanted to lure Brand into British-controlled territory, where they could arrest him. Britain was in this matter no "ally." They did not want his mission to succeed. If he continued on his journey, he would never be able to return; he would be arrested.

Brand was confused. The train was about to pull out, and he decided to stay on it. On June 7, 1944, he arrived in Aleppo. A porter entered the compartment and took off Brand's luggage. Brand wanted to follow the porter, when an Englishman in civilian clothes blocked his way.

"Mister Brand?"

"Oh, yes."

"This way, please."

Before Brand knew what was happening, two plainclothesmen had pushed him into a waiting jeep whose motor was already running. He tried to resist, but it was too late.

Brand's reports in Istanbul had been passed on to London and Washington. In the British capital, the Cabinet Committee on Refugees, which included Foreign Secretary Eden and Colonial Secretary Oliver Stanley, met on May 31 and adopted a negative stance. Six days later, as Brand was boarding his train for Aleppo, the British Embassy in Washington sent a detailed aide-mémoire to the Department of State. If the suggestion had come from the Gestapo, said the British note, it was a clear case of blackmail. Ten thousand lorries would strengthen the enemy. To leave selections of persons for exchange in Hitler's hands, without providing for Allied internees and prisoners, would lay governments open to serious protest. Weizmann had been told of the proposal, but no comment had been made to him beyond a statement that the United States had been informed. Weizmann had merely observed that it looked like one more attempt to embarrass the Allies, but that he wanted to reflect on the affair. On June 6 Weizmann wrote to Eden, saying that the story had given him a "shock" and requesting a meeting with the Foreign Secretary.

Not until June 11 was Shertok permitted to interview Brand in Aleppo. Brand, answering questions for six hours in two sessions, said at one point that six million Jews were dead. In his notes Shertok wrote: "I must have looked a little incredulous, for he said: 'Please believe me: they have killed six million Jews; there are only two million left alive.'" When the session was over, Shertok went into a huddle with the British representatives. Then he turned to Brand. "Dear Joel, I have to tell you something bitter now. You have to go south. The British demand it. I have done everything to change this decision, but it is a decision of the highest authorities. I could not alter it."

For a second Brand did not understand what had been said to him. When he finally caught on, he screamed: "Do you know what you are doing? That is simply murder! That is mass murder. If I don't return our best people will be slaughtered! My wife! My mother! My children will be first! You have to let me go! I have come here under a flag of truce. I have brought you a message. You can accept or reject, but you have no right to hold the messenger. . . . I am here as the messenger of a million people condemned to death. . . . What do you want from us? What do you want from me?"

Brand was brought to Cairo for exhaustive intelligence interrogations. Henceforth he was a prisoner. Shertok returned to Jerusalem, where he reported to the Jewish Agency on June 14 and, with David Ben Gurion, to the British High Commissioner on the 15th. He wanted to fly to London, but needed air priority. On the 21st, the American Consul General in Jerusalem told him that War Refugee Board representative Ira Hirschmann, who had missed meeting with Brand in Turkey, was going to Cairo and wanted to see Shertok there also. Shertok now flew to Cairo, where Hirschman had caught up with Brand. On the 23rd, Shertok received his air priority, but delayed the trip for two days to settle some matters in Jerusalem. He arrived in London on the 27th and, with Weizmann, went to see Undersecretary Hall on the 30th and Foreign Minister Eden on July 6. At the July 6 meeting the two Jewish leaders reiterated their desire that "an intimation should be given to Germany that some appropriate body is ready to meet for discussing the rescue of the Jews." Eden expressed his "profound sympathy," but he had to act in unison with America and had to have the agreement of the Soviet Government. The Foreign Secretary "doubted" that ransom was a possible course. There could not be "anything that looked like negotiating with the enemy."

There were to be no negotiations, just as there was to be no bombing. Only parachutists were dropped, but these Jewish volunteers from Palestine were released over military targets, where most of them could die for England.

By the beginning of July most of the Hungarian Jews were dead. The Jews of Budapest were waiting for their turn. They were saved at the last moment, when the Regent Horthy and the Sztójay government, wearied by the protests of neutral states and the Church and frightened by intercepted Anglo-American teletype messages containing among other things the Jewish requests for target bombings of Hungarian government offices as well as the names of seventy prominent officials, decided to stop the operation in its tracks. Two days after the deportations had come to a halt outside the Hungarian capital, Prime Minister Churchill wrote the following letter to Eden:

> There is no doubt that this is probably the greatest and most horrible crime ever committed in the whole history of the world, and it has been done by scientific machinery by nominally civilised men in the name of a great state and one of the leading races of Europe. It is quite clear that all concerned in this crime who may fall into our hands, including the people who only obeyed orders by carrying out the butcheries, should be put to death after their association with the murders Has been proved. . . . There should therefore, in my opinion, be no negotiations of any kind on this subject. Declarations should be made in public, so that everyone connected with it will be hunted down and put to death.

This letter reveals a great deal about the British Prime Minister's thoughts. In these instructions Churchill was not particularly concerned with the safety of the Jews; he was worried about the reputation of the German nation. The culprits had disgraced their race.

The Jews continued to be gassed. Outside Hungary the operation was not over. The Jews were being deported from Italy, they were shipped out from the islands of Greece, they were hauled out of the ghetto of Łódź, they were thinned out in Theresienstadt, they were moved out of Polish labor camps. In the fall came the turn of the remaining Slovakian Jews.

Once more, ransom negotiators were sent out from Germany. This time the associate president of the Zionist Organization in Hungary, Kastner, accompanied by Standartenführer Becher, arrived in Switzerland. They too were conferring with the wrong party. On the opposite side stood the president of the Jewish community in Switzerland, Saly Mayer. He disliked the negotiations and refused to promise the Germans anything. If Saly Mayer reflected upon his tactics after the war, his only consolation must have been the circumstance that the SS and Police were determined to destroy the Slovak Jews in any case. The negotiators on the German side had not been the right party either.

In Cairo, Joel Brand remained in custody. His mission had failed, and his wife and children in Budapest had almost paid the penalty for the failure. He was constantly afraid that they might still have to pay. But the British would not let him go. He was now invited to clubs and hotels, more as an object of curiosity than a source of intelligence information. One day at the British-Egyptian Club, Brand was engaged in conversation by a man who did not introduce himself. The Englishman asked once more about the Eichmann offer and how many Jews were involved. Brand replied that the offer encompassed a million people. "But Mr. Brand," the British host exclaimed, "what shall I do with those million Jews? Where shall I put them?" There were no longer a million. The entire network of standby organizations had become a vast organization of bystanders.

By the beginning of 1945, five million Jews were dead. There were no more gassings. Auschwitz had been abandoned. But tens of thousands of Jews were still to die. On October 15, 1944, Judge Proskauer of the American Jewish Committee telegraphed McCloy, urging that internees in concentration camps be recognized by the U.S. Government as prisoners of war, but the assistant secretary of war expressed doubt that such a step was "legally justified" or that it would "really help" the people it was designed to assist. During the shadow months of the Nazi regime, Roswell McClelland of the War Refugee Board negotiated in Berne with Standartenführer Becher of the SS and Police for the amelioration of conditions in the camps. In the final weeks the International Red Cross also made itself felt. The Germans began to release thousands of Jews. The Allied armies found the remainder alive, dying, or dead in the camps. Many of the survivors had lost enough body weight to look like living corpses.

APPENDIX A

GERMAN RANKS

T A B L E A-1
CIVIL SERVICE RANKS

Rank	*Administrative Unit*
Reichsminister	Reichsministerium
Staatssekretär—StS.	
Unterstaatssekretär—UStS.	Abteilung
Ministerialdirektor—MinDir.	
Ministerialdirigent—MinDirig.	Unterabteilung or Amt or or Amtsgruppe
Ministerialrat—MinRat.	Referat
Oberregierungsrat—ORR.	
Regierungsrat—RR.	
Botschaftsrat (Foreign Office)—BR.	
Gesandtschaftsrat (Foreign Office)—GR.	
Legationsrat (Foreign Office)—LR.	
Amtsrat—AR.	

T A B L E A-2
SS AND ARMY RANKS

SS	German Army	U.S. Army
Reichsführer—RF-SS	Generalfeldmarschall—Gfm.	General of the army
Oberst-Gruppen-führer—Obstgruf.	Generaloberst—Gen-obst.	General
Obergruppenführer—OGruf.	General der Infanterie, Artillerie, etc.—Gen. d. Inf.	Lieutenant general
Gruppenführer—Gruf.	Generalleutnant—Glt.	Major general
Brigadeführer—Bgf. or Brif.	Generalmajor—Gen-maj.	Brigadier general
Oberführer—Obf.		
Standartenführer—Staf.	Oberst—Obst.	Colonel
Obersturmbannführer—OStubaf.	Oberstleutnant—Obstlt.	Lieutenant colonel
Sturmbannführer—Stubaf.	Major—Maj.	Major
Hauptsturmführer—HStuf.	Hauptmann—Hptm.	Captain
Obersturmführer—OStuf.	Oberleutnant—Olt.	First lieutenant
Untersturmführer—UStuf.	Leutnant—Lt.	Second lieutenant

APPENDIX B

STATISTICAL
RECAPITULATON

T A B L E B-1
DEATHS BY CAUSE

Ghettoization and general privation		over 800,000
Ghettos in German-occupied Eastern Europe	over 600,000	
Theresienstadt and privation outside of ghettos	100,000	
Transnistria colonies (Romanian and Soviet Jews)	100,000	
Open-air shootings		over 1,300,000
Einsatzgruppen, Higher SS and Police Leaders, Romanian and German armies in mobile operations; shootings in Galicia during deportations; killings of prisoners of war and shootings in Serbia and elsewhere		
Camps		up to 3,000,000
German		

Death camps	up to 2,700,000	
Auschwitz	1,000,000	
Treblinka	up to 750,000	
Bełżec	550,000	
Sobibór	up to 200,000	
Kulmhof	150,000	
Lublin	50,000	

Camps with tolls in the low tens of tousands or below	150,000	
Concentration camps (Bergen-Belsen, Buchenwald, Mauthausen, Dachau, Stutthof, and others)		
Camps with killing operations (Poniatowa, Trawniki, Semlin)		
Labor camps and transit camps		
Romanian		
Golta complex and Bessarabian transit camps	100,000	
Croatian and other	under 50,000	
Total		5,100,000

NOTE: Ghettos in German-occupied Eastern Europe, open-air shootings, and Auschwitz figures are rounded to the nearest hundred thousand, other categories to the nearest fifty thousand.

T A B L E B-2
DEATHS BY COUNTRY

Poland	up to	3,000,000
USSR	over	700,000
Romania		270,000
Czechoslovakia		260,000
Hungary	over	180,000
Lithuania	up to	130,000
Germany	over	120,000
Netherlands	over	100,000
France		75,000
Latvia		70,000
Yugoslavia		60,000
Greece		60,000
Austria	over	50,000
Belgium		24,000
Italy (including Rhodes)		9,000
Estonia		2,000
Norway	under	1,000
Luxembourg	under	1,000
Danzig	under	1,000
	Total	5,100,000

NOTE: Borders refer to 1937. Converts to Christianity are included, and refugees are counted with the countries from which they were deported.

T A B L E B-3
DEATHS BY YEAR

1933–1940	under	100,000
1941		1,100,000
1942		2,700,000
1943		500,000
1944		600,000
1945		100,000
	Total	5,100,000

NOTE: Rounded to the nearest 100,000.

SELECT BIBLIOGRAPHY

Most of the sources used in this abbreviated version of *The Destruction of the European Jews* are documents. Some are diaries, testimony, memoirs, monographs, and newspapers. All may be found in the unabridged three-volume edition, where they are entered in footnotes at the bottom of the pages. Inasmuch as the student edition consists of excerpts from the longer work, arranged in the same sequential order, the reader's search for the appropriate citation should not be extraordinarily difficult.

The select bibliography does not contain all the works that have been utilized for these chapters. It is a brief guide for readers interested in a range of specific topics within a broad framework of Holocaust historiography.

B A C K G R O U N D

Dubnow, Simon. *History of the Jews in Russia and Poland*. 3 vols. Philadelphia: Jewish Publication Society, 1916–1920. The author was killed in the Riga ghetto in December 1941. He had written a ten-volume world history of the Jewish people which has not been translated into English.

———. *Nationalism and History*. Philadelphia: Jewish Publication Society, 1958. Essays on Jewish emancipation, cultural autonomy, and Zionism.

Eckhardt, A. Roy. *Elder and Younger Brothers*. New York: Scribners, 1967. Christian-Jewish relations from the perspective of a Protestant theologian.

Eidelberg, Shlomo, ed. and trans. *The Jews and the Crusaders—The Hebrew Chronicles of the First and Second Crusades.* Madison, Wisc.: University of Wisconsin Press, 1977. Rare contemporary accounts of Jewish reactions to medieval persecutions.

Fein, Helen. *Accounting for Genocide.* New York: Free Press, 1979. An attempt to explain vulnerability to destruction in numbers.

Friedlander, Henry, and Milton, Sybil, eds. *The Holocaust—Ideology, Bureaucracy and Genocide* (The San Jose Papers). Millwood, NY: Kraus International, 1980. Essays, with emphasis on elites.

Gregorius, Ferdinand. *The Ghetto and the Jews of Rome.* New York: Schocken, 1948. Eyewitness description by a historian of the last medieval ghetto (mid-1800s).

Kisch, Guido. *The Jews in Medieval Germany.* Chicago: Chicago University Press, 1949. Definitive exploration of their legal status.

Kochan, Lionel, ed. *The Jews in Soviet Russia Since 1917.* 2nd ed. London: Oxford University Press, 1970. Essays on selected topics.

Kren, George, and Rappaport, Leon. *The Holocaust and the Crisis of Human Behavior.* New York: Holmes and Meier, 1980. Analytical.

Liptzin, Solomon. *Germany's Stepchildren.* Philadelphia: Jewish Publication Society, 1944. Essays on prominent Jews in Germany, with emphasis on literary figures of the 19th and 20th centuries.

Marcus, Jacob R. *The Jew in the Medieval World.* 1938. Reprint. Westport, Conn.: Greenwood Press, 1975. Documents from A.D. 315 to 1728.

Marcus, Joseph. *Social and Political History of the Jews in Poland, 1919–1939.* Berlin: Mouton Publishers, 1983. Delves into such topics as Jewish political parties, housing, schools, and employment. Contains some valuable demographic and economic data.

Mosse, George L. *The Crisis of German Ideology.* New York: Grosset & Dunlap, 1964. The first of several books, comprised mainly of essays, in which the author explores intellectual and pseudointellectual antecedents of Nazism.

Mosse, Werner E., ed. *Entscheidungsjahr 1932.* Tübingen: J.C.B. Mohr, 1966. Long essays on political movements and Jewish reactions on the eve of the Nazi takeover.

Parkes, James. *A History of the Jewish People.* Chicago: Quadrangle Books, 1962. Best short history.

Poliakov, Léon. *The History of Anti-Semitism.* 3 vols. New York: Vanguard Press, 1965–1975. Fairly extensive treatment of the subject from antiquity to the 19th century.

Ruppin, Arthur. *The Jews in the Modern World.* 1934. Reprint. New York: Arno Press, 1973. Ruppin was the foremost expert on Jewish population in his day.

Schwartz, Solomon. *The Jews in the Soviet Union*. Syracuse: Syracuse University Press, 1951. Dated, but still valuable. Makes extensive use of Soviet press and other Russian materials.

Sombart, Werner. *The Jews and Modern Capitalism*. 1913. Reprint. New York: Burt Franklin, 1969. Pre-World War I view of a German writer with wide influence.

Trachtenberg, Joshua. *The Devil and the Jews*. New Haven: Yale University Press, 1943. The classic book on medieval conceptions of Jewry.

Vago, Bela, and Mosse, George L., eds. *Jews and Non-Jews in Eastern Europe, 1918–1945*. New York: Wiley, 1974. Essays concentrating on the Jewish situation in Hungary, Romania, and the USSR by specialists.

PERPETRATORS AND VICTIMS

Adam, Uwe Dietrich. *Judenpolitik im Dritten Reich*. Düsseldorf: Droste Verlag, 1972. Highly sophisticated study of the evolution of anti-Jewish laws, procedures, and decisions in Nazi Germany.

Aly, Götz, and Roth, Karl Heinz. *Die restlose Erfassung*. Berlin: Rotbuch Verlag, 1984. The significance of census taking, registrations, and list making.

Bauer, Yehuda, and Rotenstreich, Nathan. *The Holocaust as Historical Experience*. New York: Holmes and Meier, 1981. Papers focused on Jewish responses, with discussions.

Beyerchen, Alan D. *Scientists under Hitler*. New Haven: Yale University Press, 1977. German physicists and the ouster of their Jewish colleagues.

Blatter, Janet, and Milton, Sybil. *Art of the Holocaust*. New York: Rutledge Press, 1981. Paintings and drawings by ghetto and camp victims.

Browning, Christopher R. *The Final Solution and the German Foreign Office*. New York: Holmes & Meier, 1978. A careful study based on original documents.

———. *Fateful Months: Essays on the Emergence of the Final Solution*. New York: Holmes & Meier, 1985. Four insightful essays, with much documentary evidence, on the emergence of the Final Solution during the pivotal period 1942–1943.

Deschner, Günther. *Reinhard Heydrich*. New York: Stein and Day, 1981. A biography of the commander of the German Security Police.

SELECT BIBLIOGRAPHY

Dimsdale, Joel, ed. *Survivors, Victims, and Perpetrators.* Washington: Hemisphere Publishing Corp., 1980. Essays by political scientists, historians, sociologists, psychologists, and psychiatrists.

Gilbert, Martin. *The Macmillan Atlas of the Holocaust.* New York: Macmillan, 1982. Outline maps filled with statistical information.

Gutman, Ysrael, and Rotkirchen, Livia, eds. *The Catastrophe of European Jews—Antecedents, History, and Reflections.* New York: KTAV [1977–1978]. An anthology of essays.

Heston, Leonard L., and Heston, Renate. *The Medical Casebook of Adolf Hitler.* New York: Stein and Day, 1980. Hitler's medical history, based on available records. Analysis of diagnoses and treatments.

Höhne, Heinz. *The Order of the Death's Head.* New York: Coward-McCann, 1970. Political history of the SS.

International Military Tribunal. *Trial of the Major War Criminals* 42 vols. Nuremberg, 1947–1949. Transcript of the trial in English, documents in German.

Jewish Black Book Committee. *The Black Book.* New York: Duell, Sloane, 1946. An early compilation of evidence, with heavy reliance on decrees and ordinances, newspaper reports, and eyewitness accounts.

Jones, J. Sydney. *Hitler in Vienna 1907–1913.* New York: Stein and Day, 1983. A reconstruction of Hitler's years in the capital of Austria-Hungary.

Kenrick, Donald, and Gratton, Paxton. *The Destiny of Europe's Gypsies.* New York: Basic Books, 1972. The most complete account of the destruction of the Gypsies in the English language.

Kotze, Hildegard von, ed. *Heeresadjutant bei Hitler.* Stuttgart: Deutsche Verlags-Anstalt, 1974. The diary of Gerhard Engel, army adjutant who observed Hitler at close range from 1938 to 1943. Illuminates Hilter's attitudes and actions in Jewish matters.

Krausnick, Helmut et al. *Anatomy of the SS State.* New York: Walker, 1965. Sophisticated analysis of the SS as an instrument of government.

Lang, Jochen von, ed. *Eichmann Interrogated.* New York: Farrar, Straus & Giroux, 1983. Revealing excerpts of pre-trial interrogation by Israeli police.

Mendelsohn, John, ed. *The Holocaust.* New York: Garland Publishing, 1982. Eighteen volumes of documents drawn from National Archives. Most were used in Nuremberg trials, some are U.S. documents. No index.

Milgram, Stanley. *Obedience to Authority.* New York: Harper and Row, 1974. The famous simulation at Yale of drastic orders and their implementation.

Neumann, Franz. *Behemoth.* 2nd ed. New York: Oxford University Press, 1944. The classic work on the structure of Nazi Germany.

Nuremberg Military Tribunals. *Trial of War Criminals.* 15 vols. Washington, D.C., 1947–1949. Excerpts from testimony and selections of documents. In English. The twelve cases deal with high-level bureaucracy, generals, industry (Krupp, I. G. Farben, Flick, Dresdner Bank), SS and Police (particularly mobile killings in Russia and camps).

Office of United States Counsel for Prosecution of Axis Criminality. *Nazi Conspiracy and Aggression.* 8 vols. and 2 supp. Washington, D.C. 1946–58. Documents in English translation.

Orlow, Dietrich. *The History of the Nazi Party.* 2 vols., 1969 and 1972. Pittsburgh: University of Pittsburgh Press. Covers 1919–1945. Thorough and carefully written study on the basis of documents.

Poliakov, Léon. *Harvest of Hate.* Syracuse: Syracuse University Press, 1954. First general history concentrating on the perpetrators, published 1951 in French on the basis of documents then available. Short, solid account.

Rosenbaum, Irving J. *The Holocaust and Halakha.* New York: KTAV, 1976. Rabbinical responses given to observant Jews for conduct in situations of extreme duress.

Smith, Bradley F. *Adolf Hitler.* Stanford, Calif.: Hoover Institution, 1967. His background and upbringing in a clear, convincing book. Destroys a great deal of psychoanalytic hypothesizing.

———. *Heinrich Himmler.* Stanford, Calif.: Hoover Institution, 1971. Childhood and youth of the commander of the SS and Police, based on Himmler's diary and other sources. Conclusive proof that for Himmler Nazism was an occupational choice.

Speer, Albert. *Infiltration.* New York: Macmillan, 1981. A retrospective view by the former Reich minister for war production on his relations with the SS and Police.

THE DESTRUCTION PROCESS IN REGIONS

Adler, H. G. *Theresienstadt 1941–45.* Tübingen: J. C. B. Mohr, 1955. Detailed account of conditions in the Theresienstadt ghetto. Many statistics.

———. *Der verwaltete Mensch.* Tübingen: J. C. B. Mohr, 1974. The deportations from Germany. A large book with many long excerpts from documents.

Arad, Yitzhak. *Ghetto in Flames.* Jerusalem: Yad Vashem, 1980. The fate of the Jews in Vilna, 1941–1943. Some emphasis on the aborted Jewish resistance.

Braham, Randolph. *The Politics of Genocide.* 2 vols. New York: Columbia University Press, 1981. Definitive, detailed description of the destruction of the Jews of Hungary. Much material also on rescue attempts.

Chary, Frederick B. *The Bulgarian Jews and the Final Solution.* Pittsburgh: University of Pittsburgh Press, 1972. Well documented.

Dickinson, John K. *German and Jew.* Chicago: Quadrangle Books, 1967. The life and death of an obscure victim.

Dobroszycki, Lucjan, ed. *The Chronicle of the Lodz Ghetto 1941–1944.* New Haven: Yale University Press, 1984. Substantial excerpts from the log of official Jewish chroniclers who recorded daily events in the ghetto. An unduplicated record of ghetto life.

Ehrenburg, Ilya, and Grossman, Vasily, eds. *The Black Book.* New York: Holocaust Library, 1981. Survivors' accounts compiled in the USSR during and shortly after the war.

Flender, Harold. *Rescue in Denmark.* New York: Simon and Schuster, 1963. The escape of Danish Jewry to Sweden.

Fraenkel, Josef, ed. *The Jews of Austria.* London: Valentine Mitchell, 1967. Substantial essays. Last part deals with destruction.

Friedman, Philip. *Martyrs and Fighters.* New York: Frederick Praeger, 1954. Selections from memoirs and other sources on the Warsaw Ghetto.

———. *Roads to Extinction.* New York and Philadelphia: Conference on Jewish Social Studies and Jewish Publication Society, 1980. Collected essays. Focus on Poland.

Gutman, Ysrael. *The Jews of Warsaw 1939–1945.* Bloomington: Indiana University Press, 1982. Carefully written history of the largest ghetto in Europe, with emphasis on battle of 1943.

Haft, Cynthia. *The Bargain and the Bridle.* Chicago: Dialog press, 1983. Jewish leadership in France. A history of the *Union Générale des Israélites en France.* Informative.

Hilberg, Raul; Staron, Stanislaw; and Kermisz, Josef, eds. *The Warsaw Diary of Adam Czerniakow.* New York: Stein and Day, 1979. Daily entries by the chairman of the Jewish Council in the ghetto.

Katz, Robert. *Black Sabbath.* New York: Macmillan, 1969. The deportation of the Rome Jews in vivid detail.

Krausnick, Helmut, and Wilhelm, Hans-Heinrich. *Die Truppe des Weltanschauungskrieges.* Stuttgart: Deutsche Verlags-Anstalt, 1981. Massive study of the *Einsatzgruppen* in the occupied USSR. Emphasizes *Einsatzgruppe* A in the north.

Levai, Eugene. *Black Book on the Martyrdom of Hungarian Jewry.*
Zurich and Vienna: Central European Times Publishing Co. and
Panorama Publishing Co., 1948. Valuable account based on scarce
Hungarian archival material. Covers also events in Romania.

Levy, Claude, and Tillard, Paul. *Betrayal at the Vel D'Hiv.* New York:
Hill and Wang, 1969. Deportation from Paris. Though based on documents, no footnotes. Style is journalistic.

Marrus, Michael R., and Paxton, Robert O. *Vichy France and the Jews.*
New York: Basic Books, 1981. The French role.

Mechanicus, Philip. *Year of Fear.* New York: Hawthorne Books, 1968.
The diary of a Jewish journalist awaiting deportation in the transit
camp Westerbork, Holland.

Michaelis, Meir. *Mussolini and the Jews.* London: Oxford University
Press, 1978. A fully researched diplomatic history spanning the years
from 1922 to 1945.

Presser, Jacob. *The Destruction of the Dutch Jews.* New York: Dutton,
1969. A large book, exhaustive treatment.

Ringelblum, Emmanuel. *Notes from the Warsaw Ghetto.* New York:
McGraw-Hill, 1959. The diary of a Jewish historian in the ghetto.
Some entries not included.

Rybakov, Anatoli. *Heavy Sand.* New York: Viking, 1981. Holocaust
novel by a Soviet author depicting the destruction of a Jewish community in the occupied USSR.

Trunk, Isaiah. *Judenrat.* New York: Macmillan, 1972. Comprehensive
study of the ghettos in Poland.

Tushnet, Leonard. *Pavement of Hell.* New York: St. Martin's Press,
1972. Three substantial essays on the chairmen of the Jewish councils
of Lodz, Warsaw, and Vilna.

————. *The Uses of Adversity.* New York: Thomas Yoseloff, 1966.
Starvation and death in the Warsaw ghetto. The author, a physician,
discusses medical studies conducted in the ghetto.

C A M P S

Améry, Jean. *At the Mind's Limits.* Bloomington: Indiana University
Press, 1980. Reflections of an intellectual survivor of Auschwitz.
Thoughts about homelessness, torture, and resentment.

Cohen, Elie A. *Human Behavior in the Concentration Camp.* New
York: Norton, 1953. The author, an Auschwitz survivor, is a physician. Deals with medical aspects in a clinical way, describes psychological dimensions psychoanalytically.

Des Pres, Terrence. *The Survivor*. New York: Oxford University Press, 1976. The theory of survival as a function of living one's life for others even under extreme conditions.

Donat, Alexander, ed. *The Death Camp Treblinka*. New York: Holocaust Library, 1979. Accounts by survivors.

Feig, Konnilyn G. *Hitler's Death Camps*. New York: Holmes and Meier, 1981. A lucid account, camp by camp, based on a large collection of published works.

Frankl, Viktor E. *From Death Camp to Existentialism*. Boston: Beacon Press, 1949. A Viennese physician's recollection of Auschwitz. Focus on his mental reactions.

Höss, Rudolf. *Commandant in Auschwitz*. Cleveland: World Publishing Co., 1959. Memoir.

Müller, Filip. *Eyewitness Auschwitz*. New York: Stein and Day, 1979. The unique memoir of a survivor who worked for three years in gas chambers and crematoria.

Novitch, Miriam, ed. *Sobibor*. New York: Holocaust Library, 1980. Short survivors' accounts.

Phillips, Raymond, ed. *Trial of Josef Kramer* (The Belsen Trial). London: William Hodge & Co., 1949. Transcript of trial of concentration camp personnel of Auschwitz and Belsen.

Wiesel, Elie. *Night*. New York: Hill and Wang, 1960. The insightful memoir of the most famous Auschwitz survivor.

C O N S E Q U E N C E S   A N D R E A C T I O N S

Balabkins, Nicholas. *West German Reparations to Israel*. New Brunswick, N.J.: Rutgers University Press, 1971. Detailed history of the 1953 agreement and its implementation.

Bauer, Yehuda. *American Jewry and the Holocaust*. Detroit: Wayne State University Press, 1981. Rescue and relief activities of the American Jewish Joint Distribution Committee.

———. *The Holocaust in Historical Perspective*. Seattle: University of Washington Press, 1978. Four essays focused on the bystanders.

Bower, Tom. *The Pledge Betrayed*. Garden City: Doubleday, 1982. The fate of war criminals in the postwar years.

Fackenheim, Emil. *The Jewish Return into History*. New York: Schocken Books, 1978. Philosophical essays about Auschwitz and Israel.

Feingold, Henry L. *The Politics of Rescue*. New Brunswick, N.J.: Rutgers University Press, 1971. Scholarly treatment of U.S. policy under the Roosevelt administration.

Ferencz, Benjamin. *Less Than Slaves*. Cambridge: Harvard University Press, 1979. History of claims against private German employers of forced labor.

Friedlander, Saul. *Pius XII and the Third Reich*. New York: Knopf, 1966. Vatican policy toward Nazi Germany with emphasis on the Holocaust.

Friedman, Philip. *Their Brothers' Keepers*. New York: Crown, 1957. Humanitarian efforts by governments and individuals.

Gilbert, Martin. *Auschwitz and the Allies*. New York: Holt, Rinehart and Winston, 1981. U.S. and British reactions to the Jewish catastrophe.

Häsler, Alfred A. *The Lifeboat is Full*. New York: Funk and Wagnalls, 1967. Switzerland as a haven.

Laqueur, Walter. *The Terrible Secret*. Boston: Little, Brown, 1980. A reconstruction of the way in which the news of the killings of the European Jews was transmitted and received outside Axis Europe. Speculative.

Lewy, Guenther. *The Catholic Church and Nazi Germany*. New York: McGraw-Hill, 1964. Highly documented. Primarily the church *in* Germany.

Morley, John F. *Vatican Diplomacy and the Jews during the Holocaust 1939–1945*. New York: KTAV, 1980. Diplomatic history based on Vatican documents.

Morse, Arthur D. *While Six Million Died*. New York: Random House, 1967. Critical study of U.S. policy.

Penkower, Monty. *The Jews Were Expendable*. Urbana: University of Illinois Press, 1983. On omissions and failures.

Ross, Robert W. *So It Was True*. Minneapolis: The University of Minnesota Press, 1980. The contemporaneous coverage of Nazi actions against Jews in the Protestant press of America.

Ryan, Allan. *Quiet Neighbors: Prosecuting Nazi War Criminals in America*. San Diego: Harcourt Brace Jovanovich, 1984. The denaturalization and deportation cases of the 1970s and 1980s, by an attorney who headed the Office of Special Investigations in the Department of Justice.

Snoek, Johan M. *The Grey Book*. New York: Humanities Press, 1970. Reactions of the Protestant and Orthodox churches in several countries.

Vogel, Rolf. *The German Path to Israel*. Chester Springs, PA: Dufour Editions, 1969. Postwar German-Israel relations.

Wasserstein, Bernard. *Britain and the Jews of Europe, 1935–1945*. London: Oxford University Press, 1979. Diplomatic history of British policy.

Weissberg, Alex. *Desperate Mission*. New York: Criterion, 1958. Story of Joel Brand's ransom mission in 1944.

Wyman, David. *Paper Walls*. Amherst, Mass.: University of Massachusetts Press, 1968. The role of the State Department in the failure to exploit rescue possibilities.

———. *The Abandonment of the Jews*. New York: Pantheon, 1984. A history of paper plans and non-rescue. Detailed account of the non-bombing of Auschwitz gas chambers.

INDEX

Achamer-Pifrader, Humbert, 138
Acmecetca (Akmechet), 142
Ahlwardt, Herman, 15–18, 157
Akmechet. See Acmecetca
Albert, Wilhelm, 85
Alexianu, Gheorghe, 141
Alytus, 108
Ananiev, 135
Anielewicz, Mordechai, 205, 208, 209
Ansel, Werner, 228
Armyansk, 114
Artemovsk, 141
Aumeier, Hans, 246, 321
Auerswald, Heinz, 85, 86, 89, 93, 94, 201
Auschwitz
  bombing proposals, 322–7
  construction, 231–4, 265
  as destination of transports, 181, 185,
    189–90, 191, 197, 213, 239
  estimated dead, 239, 338
  gas supply, 234–8
  killing operations, 240–2, 244–50, 303
  liquidation of camp, 251–6, 331
  reports about camp, 304, 314, 321–2
Austria, 41, 62, 158, 176, 185, 255, 257,
  309, 311, 339. See also Vienna

Babtai, 108
Bach-Zelewski, Erich von dem, 110, 133,
  136, 137, 140, 148, 151, 274, 293, 298,
  313
Bachmann, Hans, 257
Baden, 59
Baeck, Leo, 59–61, 63, 179, 304
Balti, 116, 117, 131, 134
Bamberg, 173, 182
Bang, Paul, 56
Baranów, 252

Baranowicze, 146
Barlasz, Chaim, 326
Bavaria, 53, 59
Bebenroth, Erich, 171
Becher, Kurt, 330–1
Becker, Henryk, 201
Becker, Herbert 72, 291
Będzin, 247, 321
Belgium, 239, 302, 309, 311, 321, 339
Belin, Ferdinand Lammot, 321
Bełżec, 185, 189, 194, 195, 198, 227–9, 238–
  42, 245–6, 248, 250, 251, 314, 338
Ben Gurion, David, 329
Bender, Horst, 276
Berdichev, 111
Berezovka, 141, 142
Bergen-Belsen, 255, 256, 338
Berger, 256, 284
Bergson, Peter, 320
Berlin, 41, 53, 59, 61, 179–82, 186, 222,
  258, 280, 298
Bermuda conference, 318
Bernburg, 226
Bessarabia, 107, 108, 142, 338
Best, Werner, 55, 159
Biała-Podlaska, 200
Białystok (city), 110, 190, 211
Białystok (district), 108, 147, 153, 189, 191,
  239
Biberstein, Ernst, 105, 123, 291
Biebow, Hans, 85, 94, 212, 213, 250
Bierkamp, Walter, 72
Binger, Ludwig, 191
Birk, Louis, 186
Birkenau. See Auschwitz
Bischof, Max, 85, 86, 91
Bischoff, 232
Blaskowitz, Johannes, 70

INDEX

Blobel, Paul, 126, 152, 153, 249, 250
Blome, Kurt, 29, 269
Blumberg, David, 319
B'nai B'rith, 319
Bock, Wilhelm, 179
Boehm, Johannes, 202
Boepple, Ernst, 216
Bogdanovca (Bogdanovka), 142
Boger, Wilhelm, 321
Böhme, Horst, 138
Bohemia-Moravia. See Protektorat
Bonnet, Georges, 159
Borisov, 128
Bormann, Martin, 10, 161, 163, 230, 171
Bosshammer, Friedrich, 169
Bothmann, Hans, 251
Böttcher, Herbert, 73, 199
Bouhler, Philip, 225
Bovensiepen, Otto, 179
Bracht, Fritz, 67, 232, 241, 282
Brack, Viktor, 226, 227, 239
Bracken, (police), 81
Brand, Joel, 325–31
Brandenburg, 226
Brandt, Dr. Karl, 225
Brandt, Karl-Georg, 202
Bratislava, 323
Breslau (Lower Silesia), 59, 67, 222
Brest-Litovsk, 110, 147
Brizgys, Vincent, 118
Brno, 183
Brunner, Alois, 177, 181
Brunner, Anton, 177
Brussels, 243
Bryansk, 140
Brzezinka (Birkenau). See Auschwitz
Buber, Martin, 61
Buchenwald, 255, 256, 338
Bucher, Rudolf, 129
Budapest, 182, 243, 304, 323, 327, 331
Bug (river), 135, 141, 193, 215, 221, 240, 294
Bühler, Josef, 165, 167, 187, 189, 193, 201
Bukovina, 107, 117, 142
Bulgaria, 252, 271, 286, 295, 317, 318
Bundists, 206
Bürckel, Josef, 160

Cairo, 329, 331
Caligula, Emperor, 21
Canaris, Wilhelm, 143

Carl, Heinrich, 143
Casdorf (Finance Ministry), 231
Caucasus, 138
Cavendish-Bentinck, Victor, 323
Celle, 255
Cernăuţi, 117
Charvat (Police President), 53
Chełm, 200, 228, 242
Chelmno (Kulmhof), 314
Chernigov, 109
Christiaensen (Interior Ministry), 237
Churchill, Winston, 310, 330
Ciano, Galeazzo, 284
Cologne, 59, 184
Communists, 206, 222
Conti, Leonardo, 216
Crimea, 114, 115, 127, 128, 135, 138, 139, 141
Croatia, 239, 251, 338
Cuba, 311
Czechoslovakia, 45, 298, 309, 325, 339. See also Prague; Protektorat; Slovakia; and under individual cities
Czerniaków, Adam, 66, 76, 82, 85, 89, 95, 200–3, 296, 302
Czestochowa, 79, 86, 92, 93, 183, 213, 266
Czortków, 121

Dachau, 186, 222, 230, 236, 255, 338
Dalnik, 117, 118, 153
Daluege, Kurt, 101
Danzig, 65–7, 71, 339
Daugavpils, 108
DAW (Deutsche Ausrüstungswerke), 234
DEGESCH (Deutsche Geselschaft für Schädlingsbekämpfung), 235–7
Denmark, 166, 256, 309
Dessauer Werke, 235, 236
Diehm (SS and Police leader), 73
Diels, Rudolf, 222
Dilli, Gustav, 171
Dirlewanger, Oskar, 243, 275
Dnepropetrovsk, 109, 111, 141
Dniester (river), 116, 135, 141
Doberke, Walter, 180, 181
Domanevka. See Dumanovca
Dora (Mittelbau), 255
Drechsel, Hans, 74
Düben, 104, 106
Dulles, Allen, 322
Dumanovca (Domanevka), 142

Dürrfeld, Walter, 252
Düsseldorf, 171
Dvinsk. *See* Daugavpils
Dzhankoy, 115

East Prussia, 67, 71, 110, 189, 191, 239
Eberl, Irmfried, 171, 228
Ebner, Karl, 177
Edelman, Marek, 208
Eden, Anthony, 318, 323, 328–30
Eggert, Albert, 171
Eichmann, Adolf, 162–6, 169, 170, 174,
    176, 231, 238, 257, 266, 270, 324, 325
Eicke, Theodor, 222
Einsatzgruppen and Einsatzkommandos,
    65, 66, 133
Eisenerz, 255
Emmerich, Walter, 90, 91
Emrich, Ernst, 171, 258
Emrich, Wilhelm, 171
Engert, Georg, 46
England. *See* Great Britain
Eppstein, Paul, 179, 181, 184
Erdmannsdorff, Otto von, 292
Ernst, Karl, 222
Erren, Gerhard, 147
Essen, 171
Estonia, 105, 122, 150, 153, 339
Evers (Armed Forces Sanitation), 237
Evert (Main Trusteeship Office East), 231

Fähnrich (Railways), 173
Falkenhorst, Nikolaus von, 290
Fatgen, Rudolf, 191
Feis, Herbert, 318
Ferber, Karl Josef, 46
Finger (High Command of the Armed
    Forces), 237
Finland, 310
First, Izrael, 206
Fischer, Ludwig, 82, 85, 86, 90, 95
Fischmann, Josef, 182
Forster, Albert, 67
France, 161–3, 171, 239, 285, 295, 309, 311,
    321, 339
Frank, August, 257
Frank, Hans
    death camps, 241–2, 252
    "Final Solution," 162, 165, 187–8, 313
    position, personality, and pronounce-
        ments, 69–70, 73, 77–9, 216–17, 235,
        279, 287
    star identification, 75
    Warsaw Ghetto, 82–90
Frankfurt am Main, 12, 15, 23, 41, 173,
    176, 182
Frauendorfer, Max, 187
Frederic, Dr. (pseud.), 214
Freisler, Roland, 165
Frenkel, Paul, 208
Freter (colonel), 207
Frick, Wilhelm, 29, 52, 62
Friedel, Fritz, 211
Fröhlich, Wilhelm, 171
Fromm, Friedrich, 129
Fuchs, Gunter, 138

Gaecks, Walter, 191
Galicia, 22, 73, 108, 121, 189, 190, 192, 197,
    199, 210, 214, 239, 294, 338
Ganzenmüller, Albert, 170, 171, 194
Garfinkiel, Mieczyslaw, 196
Gate, Dr. (Economist, Generalgouverne-
    ment), 91
Geibel, Paul Otto, 73
Geler, Eliezer, 208
Genicke, 130
Gens, Jacob, 149, 303
Gercke, Rudolf, 171
Gerhardt, Harrison, 324
Gerlach, Hellmut von, 27
Gestein, Kurt, 236–8, 241
Gerteis, Adolf, 70, 191
Gestapo, 71, 81, 104, 106, 175–81. *See also*
    RSHA
Gienanth, Kurt Freiherr von, 70
Girzick, Ernst, 177, 178
Gleiwitz, 254, 255
Globke, Hans, 56, 266
Globocnik, Odilo, 73, 167, 211, 217, 228,
    229, 238, 257, 265
Glogojanu (General), 117
Glücks, Richard, 222, 234, 241
Goebbels, Josef, 48, 49, 159, 167, 181
Golta prefecture, 141, 142, 153, 338
Göring, Hermann, 10, 11, 48–52, 60, 101,
    143, 160, 163, 167, 222, 265
Gorlovka, 141
Gossel, Karl, 231
Gottberg, Curt von, 148, 149
Göttingen, 104

Gottong, Heinrich, 75
Göx, Ernst, 292
Grabner, Maximilian, 246, 248, 321
Grafeneck, 226
Grant (Air Commodore), 323
Grassler, Franz, 86
Grawitz, Ernst, 133, 227
Great Britain, 161, 286, 302, 209–12, 323, 328, 330
Greece, 239, 321, 330, 339
Greiser, Arthur 67, 75, 85, 90, 162, 215, 225, 251, 269
Grochów, 82
Gross, Walter, 28, 29
Gross Rosen, 255
Grosz, Bandi, 326–8
Grünwald, Hans-Dietrich, 72
Grynzpan, Herschel, 284, 285
Günther, Rolf, 169, 170, 238, 266
Gürtner, Franz, 52, 56
Gutwasser (RSHA), 169, 184
Gypsies, 74, 268, 269, 321

Hackenholt, Loren, 240, 248
Hadamar, 226, 241
Haenicke, Siegfried, 70
Haensch, Walter, 126
Hagen, Wilhelm, 83, 215, 216
Halder, Franz, 103
Halifax, Edward, 317
Hall, George Henry, 223, 329
Hamburg, 174, 250
Hammann, Joachim, 142
Hanke, Karl, 67
Hannover, 255
Harrison, Leland, 316
Hartheim, 226
Hartl, Albert, 152, 169, 288
Hartmann, Richard, 169
Harttmann (Railways), 171
Heess, Walter, 137, 138
Heines, Edmund, 222
Hela, 255
HELI (Heerdt und Lingler GmbH), 235
Hellwig, Otto, 211
Hennicke, Karl, 133
Henschel, Moritz, 179–81, 304
Hess, Rudolf, 29, 52, 62
Heydrich, Reinhardt
    Canaris Agreement, 140
    Einsatzgruppen, 103–6, 128

emigration and expulsions, 65–6, 160
"Final Solution," 163–6, 226–7, 263, 265
ghettos, 11, 50, 65, 73, 74
movement restrictions, 53–4
position, 101, 169
race pollution cases, 43, 48
resorts, 49
star identification, 57
Hildebrandt, Richard, 71
Himmler, Heinrich
    background and upbringing, 70–1
    concentration camps and death camps, 222, 225, 226, 232, 240, 242, 252, 269
    concessions in 1945, 256
    drivers' licenses, 53, 265
    Einsatzgruppen and other killing units, 102–3, 106, 139, 140
    German names, 56
    ghettos, 147, 151, 207, 210
    mass graves, 152
    personal philosophy, 18, 99, 133, 136–7, 273–5, 277, 281, 284, 286
    Poles, 215–16
    position, 70–74, 101, 110, 161, 222
    soap rumor, 243
    suicide, 257
    transport, 170, 194
Hirsch, Otto, 59–61
Hirschland, Georg, 61
Hirschmann, Ira A., 329
Hirtreiter, Josef, 241, 282
Hitler, Adolf
    annihilation decisions, 102–3, 157–8, 161, 163–4, 166, 168, 265, 293
    appeal to by Jewish leadership, 60
    complaints to, 143, 215–16, 281
    concentration camps, 242, 256
    eviction decree, 52
    euthannasia order, 225
    German names, 56
    Mischlinge, 37, 44
    Nuremberg laws, 29
    partisan war, 129
    Poles, 259
    race pollution problems, 18, 29, 43, 44, 47
    reports to Hitler, 153
    star identification decree, 57
    testament, 258–9
Hoepner, Erich, 114
Hofmann, Otto, 166

Hoffmann, Heinz Hugo, 46
Hoffmann, Kurt, 231
Höfle, Hermann (Lublin), 190, 202, 217, 228, 229
Höhmann, Gottlieb, or Gottlob, 202
Holland. *See* Netherlands
Hopkins, Harry, 317
Höppner, Rolf-Heinz, 162
Höring, Emil, 72
Horthy, Miklós, 330
Höss, Rudolf, 231–2, 234, 238, 241, 246, 247, 250, 257, 265, 271, 281, 321
Hössler, Franz, 246, 248, 253
Hotin, 108, 116
Huber, Franz Josef, 177, 178
Hull, Cordell, 317, 320
Hull, John Edwin, 324
Hummel, Herbert, 187, 188
Hungary, 70, 239, 250, 271, 286, 310, 322–6, 330, 339
Hunsche, Otto, 169

Isopescu, Modest, 142
Istanbul, 325–8
Italy, 239, 252, 271, 309, 322, 330, 339

Jacobi, Karl, 171, 173
Jäger, Karl, 106, 122, 142
Janów, 147
Jarke, Alfred, 83
Jeckeln, Friedrich, 110, 111, 148
Jelgava, 107
Jerusalem, 14, 323, 326, 327, 329
Jodl, Alfred, 102
Jonava, 108
Jorg, Frieda, 241
Josephus, 23
Jost, Heinz, 138, 145

Kaganovich, Lazar, 284
Kallenbach, Richard, 185
Kállay, Miklós, 278
Kallmeyer, Helmut, 227, 228
Kaltenbrunner, Ernst, 151, 257, 286
Kamenets-Poodolsky, 111, 145, 282
Kamenka, 123, 124
Kammler, Hans, 210, 233, 234
Kanał, Izrael, 206, 208
Kaplan, Jacob, 295
Karmasin, Franz, 243
Karpenstein, Wilhelm, 222

Kaschau, 323
Kassel, 129
Kastner, Rudolf, 330
Katowice (Upper Silesia), 231, 253
Katzenberger, Lehmann, 45–7
Katzmann, Fritz, 73, 192, 211, 294
Kaunas, 107–8, 120–2, 149, 152, 185, 302
Kedainiai, 108
Keitel, Wilhelm, 207
Keller (Finance Ministry), 231
Kempner, Robert M. W., 289, 292
Keppler, Wilhelm, 289, 290
Kessel, Albrecht von, 291
Kharkov, 115
Khemelnik, 127
Kiel, 104,. 255
Kielce, 79, 102, 183
Kiev, 108, 110, 125, 129, 134, 152, 278
Killy, Leo, 37
Kislovodsk (Caucasus), 297
Kleemann, Wilhelm, 60
Klein, Fritz, 246, 256
Kleinmann, Wilhelm, 170
Klemm, Bruno, 173, 258
Klimaitis, Algis or Jonas, 120, 121
Klingelhöfer, Waldemar, 105
Klopfer, Gerhard, 165
Kobryń, 147
Koch, Erich, 67
Koch, Hans, 129
Koch (Railways), 191
Kodyma, 114
Köhle (Ostbahm), 191
Koło, 82, 245
Kołomyja, 198
König, Hans Wilhelm, 246
Königsberg, 11, 191
Königshaus, Franz, 191
Koppe, Wilhelm, 71, 251, 242
Korczak, Janusz, 203
Koretz, Zvi (Sewy), 295
Korherr, Richard, 185
Kowel, 147
Kovno. *See* Kaunas
Kozower, Phillipp, 179–81
Kraków (city), 76, 79, 162
Kraków (district), 73, 189, 228, 239
Kramer, Josef, 256
Kremenchug, 114
Kressendorf, 253
Kripo, 71, 81

Kritzinger, Friedrich Wilhelm, 165
Krohn, Johannes, 52
Krosigk, Lutz Schwerin von, 210
Kryschak (RSHA), 169
Krzemieniec (Kremenets), 121
Krüger, Fredrich Wilhelm, 73, 75, 193, 194, 252
Kube, Wilhelm, 143, 144, 148–51, 120, 288, 292
Kulmhof, 162, 185, 189, 195, 225, 230, 239, 245, 246, 248–51, 314, 338
Kundt, Ernst, 187
Kutschera, Franz, 73

Lambrecht (Warsaw district), 83
Lammers, Hans Heinrich, 37, 56, 163–5
Länderbank, Vienna, 85
Lange, Rudolf Erwin, 166
Langer, William, 321, 322
Latvia, 108, 121, 143, 148, 150, 153, 339
Latvians, 105, 120, 122, 139, 151, 190
Law, Richard, 323
Leibbrand, Max, 171
Leibbrandt, Georg, 143, 148, 165
Leipzig, 104
Leist, Ludwig, 82
Lejkin, Jakub, 20, 206
Leningrad, 108, 109, 119
Ley, Robert, 161
Lichtenbaum, Marek, 86, 202, 206
Lichtenberg, Bernard, 186, 280
Lida, 152
Liepája, 104, 143
Lilienthal, Arthur, 184
Linden, Herbert, 249
Lipski, Jozef, 159
Lithuania, 108, 110, 118, 135, 136, 142, 148, 151, 153, 302, 309, 339
Lithuanians, 105, 120–2, 139, 143, 144
Litzmannstadt. See Łódz (ghetto)
Łódz (ghetto)
    administration, 84–8, 170, 190
    conditions, 84, 95–6
    deportations from, 196, 197, 211–13, 245, 266, 302
    deportations to, 164, 179, 226
    formation, 79–81, 83–4, 90
    rumors and reports about, 314
Lohse, Hinrich, 143, 144
Long, Breckenridge, 318, 320
Lösener, Bernard, 29–32, 36, 37, 62, 281

Lower Silesia, 67
Lubartów, 215
Lübeck, 255
Lublin (city), 76
Lublin (death camp), 150, 185, 189, 210, 230, 239, 242, 252, 290, 338
Lublin (district), 73, 78, 82, 162, 190, 196, 199, 215–17, 228–9, 239, 243
Lublin (ghetto), 74, 79, 193, 195, 201, 302, 313
Luth (Navy), 257
Łuck, 147
Luther, Martin (church leader), 13–15, 18, 23, 157
Luther, Martin (Foreign Office), 165, 166, 271, 279, 283
Luxembourg, 339
Łwów, 110, 121, 201, 211, 214, 216, 242

McClelland, Roswell, 322, 331
McCloy, John J., 331
Macedonia-Thrace, 239
Madagascar, 7, 74, 82, 159–62, 321
Maedel, Walter, 184, 185
Magdeburg, 14
Maglione, Luigi Cardinal, 315
Majdanek. See Lublin (camp)
Makeyevka, 141
Mandel, Maria, 321
Mangold, Philipp, 171
Manstein, Ernst von, 129
Marder, Karl, 85
Marijampole, 108
Markl, Hermann, 46
Martin, Friedrich, 169
Massute, Erwin, 191
Mauthausen, 255
Mayer, Saly, 330
McClelland, Roswell, 324
McCloy, John J., 323
Medicus, Franz Albrecht, 29
Melitopol, 109
Mengele, Josef, 246, 254
Menke (Interior Ministry), 231
Merin, Moses (Moszek), 196, 197
Meyer, Alfred, 151, 165, 167
Meyer, Eugen, 191
Mielec, 201
Minsk
    deportations from, 152, 239
    deportations to, 164, 175, 183–4, 226

Himmler visit, 136–7, 288, 293
Jewish labor, 149–50
killings in, 108, 110, 134, 185, 313
roundups, 114, 151
Moder, Paul, 73
Moes, Ernst, 169
Mogilev, 110
Mohns, Otto, 93
Moll, Otto, 251
Monsky, Henry, 316
Moravska Ostrava, 160
Morowski (Berlin Food Office), 180
Morgen, Georg Konrad, 243
Morgenthau, Henry Jr., 320, 323, 324
Moscow, 109, 151
Moser (Baurat), 80, 85, 228
Mosse, Martha, 179, 181
Mostovoye, 135
Mrugowski, Joachim, 236, 237
Müller, Heinrich, 103, 160, 164, 166, 169,
178
Müller, Johannes Hermann, 217
Munich, 171, 174, 222, 257
Murmelstein, Benjamin, 177, 178, 257, 258
Mussolini, Benito, 284

Nebe, Artur, 104, 136, 137
Netherlands, 20, 239, 266, 309, 311, 321,
339
Neumann, Erich, 165
Neustadt, 255
Nevel, 135
Norway, 166, 239, 290, 309, 339
Novak, Franz, 169, 160, 162, 163
Novomoskovsk, 141
Novoukrainka, 134
Nuremberg, 12, 21, 29, 45, 51, 75, 182

Oberg, Carl-Albrecht, 73
Oberhauser, Josef, 228
Odessa, 108, 117, 118, 142, 153
Ohlendorf, Otto, 104–6, 126, 127
OKH (Army High Command), 123, 144
OKW (Armed Forces High Command),
237
Olshanka, 114
Opatów, 252
Oppeln, 105, 191
Oslo, 290
Ostland, 139, 142–7, 152, 153

Oswiecim. See Auschwitz
Otter, von (Swedish legation, Berlin), 241

Paersch, Fritz, 90
Palestine, 161, 304, 310, 314, 316, 318–20,
322, 323, 330
Palfinger, Alexander, 85
Panevežys, 108
Panzinger, Friedrich, 138
Pape (finance Ministry), 231
Paris, 313
Pavlograd, 141
Pehle, John, 318, 320, 322–4
Peicher (Railways), 191
Perlzweig, Maurice L., 319
Persai, 122
Persterer, Alois, 127
Peters, Gerhard Friedrich, 237
Pfannenstiel, Wilhelm, 248
Pfundtner, Hans, 29, 56
Philo, 23
Pińsk, 134, 147
Piotrkow Trybunalski (Petrikau), 74
Pius XII, 316
Pohl, Oswald, 152, 210, 223–5, 231, 240,
255, 256, 275
Poland, 64–96, 158–9, 187–217, 239, 309,
339. See also under cities and dis-
tricts
Poles, 83, 192, 195–6, 199, 208, 210, 214–16
Poniatowa, 230, 338
Portugal, 310
Poznán, 65, 258
Präbichl (mountain), 255
Prague, 53, 63, 160, 184, 185
Prešov, 323
Pretzsch, 104, 106
Prienai, 122
Proskauer, Joseph, 317, 320, 331
Protektorat (Bohemia-Moravia), 57, 62,
185, 239, 311. See also Prague
Prüfer, Franz Wilhelm, 179–81, 234
Prussia, 53, 59, 65, 221
Prützmann, Hans Adolf, 110
Puhl, Emile Johann, 280
Puławay, 266

Radom (city), 79
Radom (district), 73, 79, 94, 162, 189, 216,
239
Radomyshl, 135

Rahm, Karl, 256, 257
Rahn, Rudolf, 256, 257
Rasch, Otto, 133, 138
Rašeiniai, 108, 122
Rath, Ernst vom, 285
Rathje, Hans Ulrich, 86
Rau, Werner, 171
Rawa Ruska (Galicia), 190, 192, 198, 320
Ravensbrück, 255, 257
Rediess, Wilhelm, 71
Regensburg, 12, 14
Reich Security Main Office. See RSHA
Reichenau, Walter von, 110, 128, 129
Reichleitner, Franz, 252
Reinhardt, Hans, 114
Reuter, Fritz, 228
Rhodes, 339
Ribbe, Friedrich Wilhelm, 85, 250
Ribbentrop, Joachim, 159, 284
Richter, Erich, 191
Rickert (Reichstag deputy), 16
Riecke, Hans Joachim, 56
Riege, Paul, 72
Riegner, Gerhard, 313, 314, 316
Riga, 107, 110, 121, 149, 164, 185, 190, 226, 280, 282
Ringelblum, Emmanuel, 200, 201, 204
Rödiger, Conrad von, 55
Rokiškis, 108, 122
Romania, 131, 141, 252, 286, 295, 310, 316, 339
Rome (ancient), 5, 9
Roosevelt, Franklin Delano, 315, 317, 318, 320
Rose, Gerhard, 237
Rosenberg, Alfred, 10, 151, 322
Rösler, Karl, 129
Rothaug, Oswald, 46, 47
Rothmund, Heinrich, 55
Rothschild, Sigmund, 176
Rovno, 111
RSHA (Reich Security Main Office), 63, 65, 71, 72, 100–4, 171–2, 182–4, 225, 227
Rublee, George, 284
Rumkowski, Chaim, 77, 80, 85, 212, 250
Rundstedt, Karl von, 129
Russia. See USSR
Rust, Bernard, 62

Saar, 53
Sachsenhausen, 230, 255

Salonika, 295, 303
Sambol, Wolf, 198
Sambor, 121
Sammern-Frankenegg, Ferdinand von, 73, 207, 209
Sarasai, 122
Sarter, Adolf, 171
Saxony, 59
Sayn und Wittgenstein, Friedrich Theodor, Prince zu, 123
Schacht, Hjalmar, 158
Schäfer, Johannes, 80, 85
Scharrer, Franz, 191
Schedler (SS and Police leader), 73
Schellenberg, Walter, 103, 106, 163
Schelp, Fritz, 171
Scherner, Julian, 73
Schiedermair, Rolf, 62
Schindler, Max, 70
Schirach, Baldur von, 281
Schmauser, Ernst Heinrich, 71, 232, 254
Schmid, Theodor, 191
Schmidt, Paul Karl, 287
Schmidt-Klevenow, Kurt, 35
Schmidt und Münstermann, 228
Schnell, Paul, 171, 173
Schniewindt, Otto, 129
Schön, Waldemar, 82, 85, 91
Schönbrunn construction firm, 228
Schöngrath, Karl Eberhard, 72, 110, 166, 187
Schramm, Helmut, 286
Schreiber, Walter, 237
Schrenk (Railways), 182
Schubert, Heinz Hermann, 127
Schultz, Johannes, 171
Schulz (Main Trusteeship Office East), 231
Schwartz (SS, Auschwitz area), 321
Schwarz, Franz Xaver, 69
Seel, Hanns, 29
Seetzen, Heinz, 116
Seiler, Irene, 45–7
Semlin, 338
Seraphim, Peter-Heinz, 144
Serbia, 137, 225, 268, 285, 338
Shanghai, 311
Shertok, Moshe, 323, 327–9
Shoskes, Henry, 313
Šiauliai (Lithuania), 142, 297
Siebert, Friedrich Wilhelm, 228
Siemens concern, 213
Silesia. See Upper Silesia

Sillich, Kurt, 191
Silverman, Sidney, 314
Simferopol, 115, 127, 128, 141
Simon, Alfred, 171
Slonim, 146, 147
Slovakia, 161, 239, 243, 285–7, 302, 321
Slutsk, 142
Smolensk, 109, 140
Sobibór, 183, 185, 189, 193, 200, 227–9, 239, 240, 244–6, 249–52, 265, 294, 313, 314, 338
Sommer, Walter, 29
Sonnenstein, 224
Sosnowiec, 190, 247, 321
Speer, Albert, 170
Spengler, Oswald, 293
Spindler, Alfred, 90
Sporrenberg, Jakob, 71, 73, 211
SS, 70–4, 99, 100, 106, 139, 145, 235
Stahl, Heinrich, 60, 63
Stahlecker, Franz Walter, 114, 120, 138, 287
Stalin, Josef, 284
Stalino, 141
Stange, Otto, 171, 173
Stangl, Franz, 183, 265, 299
Stanisławów, 198
Starokonstantinov, 111, 134
Steinhardt, Lawrence, 327
Stephanus, (Major), 141
Stettin, 160, 222
Stettinius, Edward R., 320
Stier, Walther, 191, 192
Stock, Walter, 179
Strauch, Eduard, 150, 151, 280
Streckenbach, Bruno, 72, 77, 78, 106
Streicher, Julius, 17, 284, 285
Stroop, Jürgen, 73, 207, 209
Stübbs, Gerhard, 179, 181
Stuckart, Wilhelm, 29, 30, 56, 165, 281
Stutthof, 150, 255, 338
Sudeten, 53, 185, 311
Switzerland, 54–5, 309, 313, 316, 318, 322, 323, 330, 331
Syria, 328
Szepticki, Andreas, 214
Szerynski, Jozef, 89, 202, 203
Sztójay, Döme, 330
Szwarcbart, Ignacy, 314

Tallinn, 108, 164
Tarnopol, 111, 121

Tartu, 108
Terboven, Josef, 290
Tesch, Bruno, 236
TESTA (Tesch und Stabenow Extermination Co.), 235–6
Theresienstadt
    administration and population, 256, 257, 304, 325, 338
    deportations from, 185, 191, 330
    deportations to, 166, 178, 182, 183, 186, 253, 303
Thier, Teobald, 73
Thierack, Otto, 18, 241, 269, 271
Thilo, Heinz, 246
Thomalla, Richard, 228
Thomas, Georg, 138, 144, 153
Tippelskirch, Werner von, 292
Tittmann, Harold H., 315, 316
Tomaszów, 195
Trampedach, Friedrich, 143, 145
Transnistria, 141, 142, 338
Trawniki, 209, 230, 338
Treblinka
    construction, 227–30
    as destination of transports, 185, 189, 193–4, 239
    estimated dead, 239, 338
    killing operations, 232, 244–6, 248, 282, 299
    liquidation of camp, 250, 251
    reports about camp, 195, 203, 241, 314, 321
Treibe, Paul, 171
Trestioreanu, Constantin, 117
Türk, Richard, 228
Turkey, 317, 328

Uebelhoer, Friedrich, 80, 81, 85, 94
Ukmerge, 108
Ukraine, 107, 109, 110, 119, 123, 139, 144, 145, 147, 153
Ukrainians, 105, 121, 139, 190, 199, 209, 214, 246
United States, 309, 310, 311, 314–18, 319, 323–4
Upper Silesia, 65, 67, 71, 189, 190, 191, 232, 239, 241, 247
USSR, 99, 100, 102, 107, 225, 309, 339. See also Caucasus, Crimea, Ostland, Ukraine, White Russia, and under names of individual cities
Utena, 108

Vallat, Xavier, 295
Vandžiogala, 108
Ventzki, Werner, 85
Verbeck, Franz Heinrich, 191
Vershovsky, Senitsa, 118
Vienna, 12, 24, 41, 53, 63, 160, 177, 181, 183–5, 191, 326. See also Austria
Vilna. See Vilnius
Vilnius, 108, 122, 149, 150, 152, 303
Vinnitsa, 125
Vistula (river), 82, 252, 255
Vitebsk, 135
Vitenberg. See Witenberg, Yitzhak
Volhynia-Podolia, 147
Vrba, Rudolf, 322

Wächter, Otto, 78
Wagner, Gerhard, 29
Wagner, Eduard, 65, 103–4, 106
Wagner, Robert, 160
Waisenegger (Radom district), 94
Walbaum, Jost, 187
Waldman, Morris, 319
Warburg, 289
Warlimont, Walter, 102
Warsaw (city), 22, 66, 298
Warsaw (district), 198, 239, 266
Warsaw (ghetto)
    battle, 199–210, 213–4, 294
    formation and administration, 74, 82–6, 89–96, 228, 294, 313
    deportations from, 109, 194, 197, 199–210, 213–14
Warthbrücken, 211, 245
Warthegau See Wartheland
Wartheland, 67, 71, 75, 94, 162, 189, 190, 191, 197, 225, 239, 269
Weimar, 257
Weinmann, Erwin, 105
Weirauch, Lothar, 216
Weizmann, Chaim, 323, 326–9
Weizsäcker, Ernst von, 159, 284, 292
Welles, Sumner, 314, 316–18
West Prussia, 65, 66, 71

Westring, 290
White Russia, 107, 128, 148, 153, 280
Widmann, Albert, 137, 138
Wieser (OKW), 237
Wilhelm, Karl Friedrich, 280, 288
Wigand, Arpad, 73
Willstätter, Richard, 61
Winkler, Gerhard, 72
Wirth, Christian, 226, 238, 251, 252, 271
Wise, Stephen, 314–19
Witenberg, Yitzhak, 149, 150
Wöhler, Otto, 130
Wohlthat, Helmut, 158, 160
Wöhrn, Fritz, 169
Wolff, Karl, 137, 193–4
Wołkowysk, 184
Wolstayn (Bełzec escapee), 195
Wörmann, Ernst, 158, 159, 292
Worthoff, Hermann, 202
Württemberg, 59
Würzburg, 183
WVHA (Economic-Administrative Main Office), 223–4

Yampol, 116
Yanovichi, 135
Yugoslavia, 310, 339. See also Croatia; Macedonia; Serbia.

Zabel, Martin, 191
Zahn, Albrecht, 191
Zamość, 195, 196, 229
Zawacki, 245
Zbonszyn, 158
Zech, Karl, 73
Zhitomir, 108, 114, 116, 130
Zilina, 322
Zimmermann (Security Police, Białystok), 211
Zionists, 206
Zoepf, Wilhelm, 257
Zolkiewka, 244
Zörner, 78, 199
Zyklon, 232, 234–8, 248, 258, 271

ABOUT THE AUTHOR

Raul Hilberg is the John G. McCullough Professor of Political Science at the University of Vermont, where he has taught since 1956. As a youth in Vienna before the war, he saw the ascent of the Third Reich; as a soldier in the U.S. Army he witnessed its collapse; and as a member of the War Documentation Project he examined masses of German records in their original folders. He began his work on *The Destruction of the European Jews* in 1948. Later he published a number of studies about the fate of European Jewry, including, of course, the first edition of this landmark work. He frequently testifies for the Department of Justice in cases against individuals implicated in the killings, and he serves as a member of the U.S. Holocaust Memorial Council.